Books and Beyond

Books and Beyond

The Greenwood Encyclopedia of New American Reading

VOLUME 4: T–Z

Edited by

KENNETH WOMACK

GREENWOOD PRESS
Westport, Connecticut • London

Library of Congress Cataloging-in-Publication Data

Books and beyond : the Greenwood encyclopedia of new American reading / edited by Kenneth Womack.
    p. cm.
  Includes bibliographical references and index.
  ISBN: 978-0-313-33738-3 (set : alk. paper) — ISBN: 978-0-313-33737-6 (v. 1 : alk. paper) — ISBN: 978-0-313-33740-6 (v. 2 : alk. paper) — ISBN: 978-0-313-33741-3 (v. 3 : alk. paper) — ISBN: 978-0-313-33742-0 (v. 4 : alk. paper)
  1. Books and reading—United States—Encyclopedias. 2. Reading interests—United States—Encyclopedias. 3. Popular literature—United States—Encyclopedias. 4. Fiction genres—Encyclopedias. 5. American literature—History and criticism. 6. English literature—History and criticism. I. Womack, Kenneth.
  Z1003.2B64   2008
  028'.9097303—dc22   2008018703

British Library Cataloguing in Publication Data is available.

Library of Congress Catalog Card Number: 2008018703
ISBN: 978–0–313–33738–3 (set)
        978–0–313–33737–6 (vol. 1)
        978–0–313–33740–6 (vol. 2)
        978–0–313–33741–3 (vol. 3)
        978–0–313–33742–0 (vol. 4)

First published in 2008

Greenwood Press, 88 Post Road West, Westport, CT 06881
An imprint of Greenwood Publishing Group, Inc.
www.greenwood.com

Printed in the United States of America

The paper used in this book complies with the
Permanent Paper Standard issued by the National
Information Standards Organization (Z39.48–1984).

10 9 8 7 6 5 4 3 2 1

Contents

T

TERRORISM FICTION

Definition. The initial complexity in defining "terrorism fiction" is the necessity of defining "terrorism." Despite the ubiquity of the term in contemporary discourse, it is surprisingly difficult to arrive at unambiguous agreement about what acts, precisely, can be gathered together under the label of "terrorist actions," let alone what groups or individuals can be called "terrorists." To a certain degree this is a matter of differing political stances: as the familiar expression reminds us, one man's terrorist is another man's freedom fighter. Alex Houen points out, for example, that "organizations such as the African National Congress (ANC) in South Africa, and the Palestine Liberation Organization (PLO) that were once widely declared to be 'terrorist' have over recent years been accepted internationally as legitimate political parties" (Houen 2002, 7). Even fixing the use of the term historically can be challenging. Although Andrew Sinclair's history of terrorism (2003) encompasses events from Greek antiquity onward, there is general agreement that the actual term "terrorism" first came into use with the French Revolution, and that because of the contemporaneous development of the mass media "the insurgent terrorism that evolved in the second half of the nineteenth century was something new and not merely a repetition of the violent conspiracies that marked political history long before Brutus stabbed Caesar" (Scanlan 2001, 5).

One good working definition of terrorism is given by Cindy C. Combs and Martin Slann in their *Encyclopedia of Terrorism*, where they define the essential term "as a synthesis of war and theatre, a dramatization of the most proscribed kind of violence—that which is perpetrated on innocent victims—played before an audience in the hope of creating a mood of fear for political purposes" (Combs and Slann 2003, 209). Certain aspects of this definition might be more or less applicable in given situations, but the presence of the audience is fundamental; a terrorist act "is, essentially, theatre, an act played before an audience, designed to call the attention of millions, even hundreds of millions, to an often unrelated situation through shock" (Combs and Slann 2003, 209). The actual violence inherent to terrorism, then, is secondary. The terrorist act is intended primarily as an act of communication, a message delivered to most observers through the mass media that appropriates and reports on such events. Through this message the terrorist hopes to dictate, or at least alter, the public discourse on a given issue, making it possible to discuss terrorism as "primarily a matter of discursive and figurative practices" (Houen 2002, 4). Terrorism is essentially performative.

In Nicholson Baker's *Checkpoint*, one character recognizes this feature of terrorist actions by telling a potential presidential assassin that he is "talking about leaping onto the world stage. You don't have any idea what you might set in motion, what kind of uproar" (Baker 2004, 26). It is precisely these aspects of terrorism—the attempt to "leap onto the world stage" and the various kinds of "uproar" that follow—that have constituted the core of American literature's engagement with terrorism in recent decades. In his 2005 essay "Dangerous Characters" Benjamin Kunkel, in a quick aside, defines the American terrorist novel as "the novel proposing terrorists among its main characters, and meant as literature rather than disposable suspense fiction" (Kunkel 2005, 14). This definition is serviceable (although it assumes a clear line can be drawn between "literature" and "disposable suspense fiction") but fails to recognize another characteristic almost universal among American fictional works concerning terrorism: the central interest in the terrorist's attempt and/or ability to alter world discourse and, particularly in the wake of the attacks of September 11, 2001, the ways in which world discourse responds. Although this thematic concern may be too abstract or diffuse to describe a genre as clearly delineated as, say, cyberpunk, it does provide a shared foundation and allows these texts to be considered as a group.

History. Novels of the late 1800s and early 1900s with terrorism themes—even *The Princess Casamassima* by the American-born James—were set in Europe and concerned European political struggles and stereotyped figures, primarily the bomb-throwing anarchist. Although such bombings were not unknown in America, they did not find any significant or lasting place in American literature. Terrorism itself virtually disappeared from the Western worldview for much of the twentieth century, displaced by the two World Wars and the advent of the Cold War, and only reasserted itself with the anticolonial and countercultural movements of the late 1960s and, still more significantly, the growing symbiosis between television and political violence. In this scheme, the definitive event for the reemergence of terrorism as a major force in Western life was the "first global terrorist broadcast," the abduction and eventual murder of Israeli athletes at the 1972 Munich Olympics by the group Black September (Scanlan 2001, 12).

Despite isolated acts of terrorism within the United States in the last third of the twentieth century (e.g., occasional, usually minor, bombings by radical political groups; the letter bombs sent by the Unabomber; the 1993 bombing of the World Trade Center; the 1995 Oklahoma City explosion), "terrorism" in the American imagination, and thus in American fiction, continued to be conceived of primarily as a phenomenon associated with foreign actors and foreign settings, primarily the Middle East. This changed, of course, on September 11, 2001 (hereafter "9/11"), when four American airliners hijacked by operatives of the Islamic extremist group al-Qaeda crashed into the Pentagon, a Pennsylvania field, and the World Trade Center, which subsequently collapsed on live television. We are still only beginning to see how American novelists will ultimately respond to 9/11 and to a new age in which terrorism is central to American political discourse. As Kunkel notes, fiction

---

TERRORISM IN THE NINETEENTH CENTURY?

Until recent years, terrorism played a relatively minor role in American literature, largely because it occupied a relatively minor place within the American imagination. In *Plotting Terror,* her seminal 2001 study of the relationship between novelists and terrorists in contemporary fiction, Margaret Scanlan argues that the first significant fictional texts about terrorism were produced in the late nineteenth and early twentieth century by authors such as Henry James, Fyodor Dostoevsky, and Joseph Conrad.

"registers historical change profoundly but not swiftly, for the simple reason that it usually takes several years to conceive, write, revise and publish a book" (Kunkel 2005, 14). At this writing major American works that address 9/11 and its aftermath have begun to appear, but it is possible to see them as still functioning in a primarily reactive mode, not yet breaking new ground in suggesting ways we can conceive of and come to terms with our shared new reality. It is clear, at any rate, that American terrorist fiction will continue to be shaped and changed by 9/11 for many years to come, in ways that we can, for the moment, only begin to guess.

Trends and Themes

Landmarks of American Terrorist Fiction Prior to 9/11

Thomas Harris, Black Sunday *(1975).* As noted previously, Kunkel, in defining American terrorist fiction, is at pains to distinguish it from works that can be easily labeled as "disposable suspense fiction." Scanlan, in *Plotting Terror,* is similarly dismissive of "a popular fiction" that directly emulates "the quick sound bites, glossy images, scandals, and explosions of television programming" and that "does not make too many demands on its readers" (Scanlan 2001, 161). Terrorists have, over the past few decades, played an increasingly prominent role as the villains of such texts, and although they do not properly fall within the bounds of this study, it is worth looking at one of the most visible and widely imitated of these narratives in order to consider the boundaries between "serious" and "disposable" fiction.

Highly successful when published, and as filmed two years later by the director John Frankenheimer, *Black Sunday* concerns an attempt by operatives of the real-life terrorist group Black September to detonate a bomb in a blimp flying over the Super Bowl, thus killing thousands of spectators, including the President of the United States. Although Black September orchestrates and backs the scheme, its main operative is an American, Michael Lander, who has become mentally unbalanced due to years as a prisoner of war in Vietnam and his subsequent failure to return to mainstream American life or to maintain his marriage. The terrorist plot is opposed by agents of the American FBI and Israeli Mossad, and the suspense of the novel and the engagement of the reader depend entirely on the question of whether they will succeed in preventing the detonation.

Black Sunday is undeniably gripping, but the terrorists within it are almost entirely divorced from any sense of historical or geographic reality; they exist only to be opposed and defeated by the story's heroes. Given the focus on and characterization of Lander, even much of this function is displaced onto the traumatic American experience in Vietnam, making the treatment of terrorism still more incidental to the story. There is no sustained effort in the book to understand the terrorists themselves, or terrorism as a strategy; there is no serious consideration of what the aftermath of their plot would be, beyond the straightforward calculation of the physical harm done. These absences mark the distinction between the kind of sensationalist narratives dismissed by Kunkel and Scanlan and the more serious, literary texts we are classifying as "terrorism fiction" for the purposes of this essay.

That said, *Black Sunday* has been very influential and can be seen as the vanguard of a range of narratives in which "terrorist" serves as the unexamined label applied to villains to be overcome in binary confrontations between good and evil. The use of terrorists in such roles became particularly popular with the collapse of the Soviet Union and the end of the Cold War, which effectively eliminated Russians as the bad guys of choice. The novels of Tom Clancy, for example, which exist primarily to fetishize the martial technology of the United States, move from confrontations with the Soviet military to showdowns with figures described on book jackets with terms like "Middle Eastern madmen." At this writing probably the most culturally visible example of this use of terrorism is the television series *24*. Depending upon exactly what form they take, narratives of this kind might be considered **adventure fiction, true crime fiction, military literature, mystery fiction, spy fiction,** or techno-thrillers.

Don DeLillo, Mao II (1991). When the journal *Studies in the Novel* published a special issue on "Terrorism and the Postmodern Novel" in 2004, seven of the ten essays included mentioned Don DeLillo, with five focusing extensively on his work. Similarly, in Margaret Scanlan's *Plotting Terror,* the first chapter is dedicated to DeLillo, and specifically *Mao II.* Put simply, Don DeLillo is the key figure in American literature's recent engagement with terrorism, and *Mao II* is the key text for understanding his conception of terrorism, a conception that has proved highly influential.

By the time he came to *Mao II,* his eleventh novel, DeLillo had already indicated a significant interest in terrorism in his earlier novels. In *Players* (1977), the central character, Lyle Wynant, witnesses a murder on the floor of the New York Stock Exchange and is drawn into the conspiracy of the group of terrorists who committed it and who plan further attacks against Wall Street. In *The Names* (1982), a group of Americans in Greece are intrigued and eventually endangered by a terrorist cult that kills people based simply on the spelling of their names. In both these early works, the "terrorist" groups lack readily accessible political motivation and are detached from any meaningful sense of history or ideology. They are essentially conspiracies that exist for the sheer baroque pleasure of conspiracy, illuminating the hidden connections and ineffable forces that disrupt any stable sense of how life operates but illustrating still more strongly DeLillo's debt to his postmodernist predecessors, particularly Thomas Pynchon. For most critics these early works are eclipsed by later, more ambitious and assured DeLillo texts, such as the 1988 *Libra,* which is a speculative biography of Lee Harvey Oswald from his childhood through the Kennedy assassination and his death. Whether *Libra* itself can properly be considered terrorism fiction may well depend on whether the Kennedy assassination can be treated as a terrorist act; it has never been clearly linked to any particular political demand, and there is no compelling evidence that Oswald committed the act with an audience in mind, therefore such an identification seems tentative at best.

In *Mao II,* however, terrorism, and specifically the relationship between writing and terrorism, takes center stage. The central figure of the book is the novelist Bill Gray, a cult figure who has become more famous for his reclusive habits than his two published novels. Gray is reminiscent of J.D. Salinger or Pynchon but has most frequently been seen by critics as a stand-in for DeLillo himself. In the first section of the book Brita Nilsson, a photojournalist who has worked in war zones but is now compiling a collection of portraits of famous authors, travels to Gray's secluded home, becoming the first outsider to meet or speak with him in many years. As they talk while she is photographing him, she mentions a fear of terrorists that leads her to take elaborate precautions when she travels. This prompts Bill to begin discussing terrorists and how they have robbed him of his sense of power as a novelist:

> There's a curious knot that binds novelists and terrorists. In the West we become famous effigies as our books lose the power to shape and influence. . . . Years ago I used to think it was possible for a novelist to alter the inner life of the culture. Now bomb-makers and gunmen have taken that territory. They make raids on human consciousness. What writers used to do before we were all incorporated. (DeLillo 1991, 41)

Nilsson seems to regard this essentially as meandering chat, but the remainder of the book charts Gray's attempt to reclaim some of the power he feels he has lost to terrorism. Abandoning the third novel he has completed but feels unable to publish, Gray begins a solitary journey to the Middle East in a quixotic attempt to trade himself for a poet who has been taken hostage by a terrorist group in Lebanon, thus making use of the fame that, given the powerlessness of art, has become his only tool for attempting to promote change. Along the way he becomes acquainted with George Haddad, a character with ambiguous connections to both the literary and the terrorist worlds, and in conversations with him he expands upon the points he has made to Nilsson:

> novelists and terrorists are playing a zero-sum game. . . . What terrorists gain, novelists lose. The degree to which they influence mass consciousness is the extent of our decline as shapers of sensibility and thought. . . . Beckett is the last writer to shape the way we think and see. After him, the major work involves midair explosions and crumbled buildings. (DeLillo 1991, 156–157)

Haddad extrapolates from this premise, suggesting that terrorists must then be "the only possible heroes for our time," and that "in societies reduced to blur and glut . . . only the terrorist stands outside." Gray rejects such idealization as "pure myth," (DeLillo 1991, 158), but this idea—that terrorists have displaced novelists as the only possible source of meaningful resistance—permeates *Mao II* and has become the haunting possibility that must be confronted in any consideration of the relationship between artistic creation and terrorist violence. It is an idea that Scanlan echoes in *Plotting Terror* when she postulates "both writers and terrorists . . . as remnants of a romantic belief in the power of marginalized persons to transform history" (Scanlan 2001, 2).

Gray rejects Haddad's claims, but the remainder of *Mao II* presents little reason to be optimistic about the power of writers. Struck by a car in Cyprus, Gray dies in the hold of a tanker taking him to Lebanon, whereupon the very identity that has become his only resource is stolen from his body and sold to "some militia in Beirut" (DeLillo 1991, 217). Since nobody knows of his self-appointed mission, even the fame that is the remnant of his artistic ability proves useless. Indeed, the very idea of being a writer seems suffused with nostalgia in *Mao II,* as though the novelist has already faded completely into obsolescence. What makes the novel a touchstone of recent American treatments of terrorism is the connection Gray explicitly makes, and which subsequent authors of terrorism fiction freely draw upon: the competition between writers and terrorists for the right and the ability to play a role on the world stage, to possess a voice that can be raised in resistance.

Paul Auster, Leviathan *(1992).* Something similar to Gray's fate befalls another novelist who abandons writing in search of some more effective means of action: Bejamin Sachs, the central character of *Leviathan* (a novel dedicated to Don DeLillo). Sachs, however, goes beyond Gray, not merely seeking interaction with terrorists but abandoning writing to become one himself.

In *Leviathan* the author's obvious, thinly fictionalized counterpart is not Sachs but rather his best friend and fellow novelist, Peter Aaron, who shares with Auster not only a set of initials but also the broad outlines of a biography. *Leviathan* takes the form of a memoir written by Aaron, immediately after he learns Sachs has died, in an effort to justify—or at least make comprehensible—Sachs's actions to the authorities who have been pursuing him. A left-leaning writer who defines his occupation largely in terms of political opposition and resistance, Sachs finds himself in "the era of Ronald Reagan" becoming "increasingly marginalized . . . in the present climate of selfishness and intolerance, of moronic, chest-pounding Americanism, his opinions sounded curiously harsh and moralistic" (Auster 1992, 116). A series of accidents and violent encounters further convince Sachs not only that writing is useless as a means of promoting change but also that restricting his actions to writing is cowardly: "'for all my self-righteous opinions and embattled stances, I'd never put myself on the line'" (Auster 1992, 253). He changes tactics, deciding that "'there was a moral justification for certain forms of political violence. Terrorism had its place in the struggle . . . for enlightening the public about the nature of institutional power'" (Auster 1992, 252). Sachs reinvents himself, rather melodramatically, as "the Phantom of Liberty," and begins traveling around the United States blowing up replicas of the Statue of Liberty. He takes care that nobody is injured by his actions and accompanies his explosions with brief, idealistic messages urging a renewed dedication to democracy and a charitable attitude toward others.

Sachs keeps this routine up for more than two years before apparently being killed in a mishap with one of his bombs, but despite his sense that he is making "a much greater mark than he had ever thought possible" (Auster 1992, 263), *Leviathan* cannot quite bring itself to endorse his notion that he has arrived at an effective means of political articulation. Considering Sachs's frequently mentioned brilliance as a writer, for example, the messages that accompany his explosions are stunningly banal. An example: "'Neglect the children, and we destroy ourselves. We exist in the present only to the degree that we put our faith in the future'" (Auster 1992, 243–244). This resembles a Whitney Houston ballad rather more than serious political discourse. The evidence that the Phantom is "making a mark" is similarly thin: "Phantom of Liberty T-shirts and buttons were on sale in novelty shops, jokes had begun to circulate, and just last month two strippers in Chicago had presented an act in which the Statue of Liberty was gradually disrobed and then seduced by the Phantom" (Auster 1992, 263). Far from providing the inescapable narrative that is the aim of terrorist action, Sachs has only generated fodder for the grinding wheels of popular consumption. Surrendering his status as a writer has only made Sachs more complicit in the system he opposes. That said, this does not necessarily mean that he would have been better off as a writer. His friend Aaron remains a novelist, but the text he produces—*Leviathan*—is written strictly for official consumption, to be given to the FBI only when and if they figure out that Sachs had been the Phantom. In fact, Aaron hopes that this will not happen, feeling that "the best possible outcome" would be "a perfect standstill, not one word spoken by either side" (Auster 1992, 3). Aaron, then, is a writer reduced to the hope that he will never be read, whose text can at best serve no purpose beyond furthering the knowledge of the state; he is the writer rendered utterly compliant, incapable of resistance. *Leviathan* essentially echoes *Mao II*'s doubts about the relevance of the writer in an age of terrorism, only adding the additional thought that the terrorist, too, is ultimately just as powerless.

  Philip Roth, Operation Shylock *(1993) and* American Pastoral *(1997).* Whereas DeLillo and Auster encourage, or at least allow, an identification of themselves with their characters, such an entanglement of fact and fiction is never more explicit than in *Operation Shylock,* a text that is packaged as a novel but that for much of its length seems more accurately described by its subtitle: *A Confession. Shylock* is narrated by "Philip Roth," a Jewish American author whose most famous book is *Portnoy's Complaint* and whose biography matches precisely with the "real" Roth's. The preface to the book claims that it is "as accurate an account as I am able to give of actual occurrences that I lived through during my middle fifties and that culminated, early in 1988, in my agreeing to undertake an intelligence-gathering operation for Israel's foreign intelligence service" (Roth 1993, 13). Space does not permit here a full exploration of *Shylock*'s labyrinthine narrative shape and its narrator's frequently baffling encounters with doubles, spies, and terrorists. For our immediate purposes, what is most significant is the narrator's attempt to write about his experiences and how that attempt is frustrated. Having produced a manuscript that details his adventures, "Roth" shows it to Louis Smilesburger, the Mossad operative who has played a significant role in the narrative, eventually recruiting "Roth" and dispatching him on his "intelligence-gathering operation" to Athens. Smilesburger, a genial if vaguely ominous figure, generally approves of "Roth's" decision to write the book (which is, of course, *Operation Shylock* itself) but asks for one change: the omission of Chapter 11, "twelve thousand words describing the people I convened with in Athens, the circumstances that brought us together, and the subsequent expedition, to a second European capital" (Roth 1993, 357). Smilesburger claims not only that revealing the details of the operation will endanger ongoing Israeli interests but also that the account "Roth" has written is in fact laughably inaccurate: "'you haven't the slightest idea of what happened. You grasp almost nothing of the objective reality. Its meaning evades you completely'" (Roth 1993, 390). He suggests, in fact, that "'It might be altogether accurate to call the *entire* five hundred and forty-seven pages hypothetical formulation,'" that to label the narrative "'a subjectivist fable . . . solves everything'" (Roth 1993, 390–91). An implication of this "solution," of course, is that fiction is safe because it can have no significant force or meaning in the "real" world. Though "Roth" reacts angrily to this suggestion and claims to be in no way "obliged to him, his agency, or the state of Israel to suppress those forty-odd pages" (Roth 1993, 357), Smilesburger presses his argument, offering "Roth" money and even implying that the Mossad might feel obliged to destroy his reputation—again figured here as the novelist's most important attribute—if he publishes Chapter 11. Smilesburger, in fact, is given the final line of the novel proper: "'Let your Jewish conscience be your guide'" (Roth 1993, 398).

The page immediately following contains a brief "Note to the Reader" that employs almost exactly a wording "Roth" had considered and rejected earlier in the novel: "This book is a work of fiction . . . This confession is false" (Roth 1993, 399). Chapter 11, of course, does not appear. The note to the reader perfectly book-ends and perfectly contradicts the preface, and we are left with a narrative that folds in upon itself, simultaneously claiming the status of both fiction and fact. Whatever the factual nature of *Operation Shylock,* it goes even further than *Mao II* in illustrating the fundamental irrelevance of the writer in a setting contested by the competing narratives of terrorism and the state. "Roth" himself acknowledges that allowing Smilesburger to inspect his manuscript—a step, significantly, that he takes although it could be easily avoided—"ran counter to all the inclinations of one whose independence as a writer, whose *counter-suggestiveness* as a writer, was simply second nature" (Roth 1993, 377). In effect, however, "Roth" has already surrendered the status of writer. His meaningful actions in the novel are taken not as a novelist, but as an operative of the state, and they are precisely the actions that he ultimately chooses to be silent about—precisely the actions that are inaccessible to him as a writer. It is the state that has become the writer, casting "Roth" as a character in a narrative that he confesses he is incapable of even understanding. Indeed, he does not even understand why he allows himself to be taken up in it: "I could not name for myself what it was that drew me in or understand whether what was impinging on this decision was absolutely everything or absolutely nothing" (Roth 1993, 358). Scanlan reads *Operation Shylock* as implying that "art and terrorism are equally illusory and politically ineffective," as marking the last gasp of a dying belief "that marginalized people can change the world" (Scanlan 2001, 123). Indeed, by the end of the novel "Roth" has been reduced from an author to nothing more than a character, easily manipulated by forces beyond his knowledge or control. That he shares the name and biography of his literal creator in itself efficiently indicates where Roth might rank the power and influence of the writer at this stage in history.

Four years later Roth returned to the theme of terrorism and the writer's power in *American Pastoral,* albeit here in a domestic context and through a more conventional fictional frame. *Pastoral* is narrated by Nathan Zuckerman, who has been Roth's alter ego in many books and who is here concerned with the life and fate of Seymour "the Swede" Levov, a childhood acquaintance he learns has recently died. In the early 1940s, the Swede, a high school student a few years older than Zuckerman, had been a hero to the Jewish population of Newark because of his tremendous athletic feats, coupled with his blue-eyed, blond good looks and dignified, mature behavior. In years of war and stress, the Swede seemed to represent success and hope, hope above all for assimilation and acceptance into the American mainstream; the Swede was "a boy as close to a goy as we were going to get" (Roth 1998, 10).

When Zuckerman encounters the Swede again decades later, as both men have entered their declining years, it seems that the Swede has completely fulfilled this early promise, becoming a successful and admired businessman and the head of his own family of accomplished sons. Indeed, his talk of himself—and his endless bragging about his sons—reflect a life and a personality so completely identified with the American ideal that Zuckerman comes to think that he lacks any interior life, any sense of irony or imperfection at all, that "there's nothing here but what you're looking at. . . . He is not faking all this virginity. You're craving depths that don't exist" (Roth 1998, 39).

A few months later, however, Zuckerman learns at his high school reunion that the Swede has died and learns moreover the central tragedy of his life, which he had kept hidden from Zuckerman during their meeting: in his first marriage the Swede had a daughter, Merry, who in 1968 detonated a bomb in a rural post office to protest the Vietnam War, killing a doctor and earning herself the media nickname "the Rimrock Bomber." For the Swede's brother, who tells Zuckerman this, the bombing was more a matter of family than national politics: "There was no way back for my brother from that bomb. That bomb detonated his life. His perfect life was over. Just what she had in mind" (Roth 1998, 69). Shortly afterward, in the midst of a dance with an old sweetheart, Zuckerman himself disappears as the novel transforms into his "realistic chronicle," his attempt to imagine the Swede's life and reconcile the banal portrait of the American dream he met with his new knowledge of the "daughter who transports him out of the longed-for American pastoral and into everything that is its antithesis and its enemy, into the fury, the violence, and the desperation of the counterpastoral—into the indigenous American berserk" (Roth 1998, 86).

Zuckerman can conjure any number of possible explanations for Merry's act—anger over a childhood stutter, unresolved sexual tension with her father, the conflicts inherent to the mixed marriage between the Swede and Merry's Christian mother—but both he and the reader remain aware throughout that, however convincingly he imagines his way into the Swede's head, it remains a dream, a reverie conjured on the dance floor. No real answer is possible; the terrorist act here is beyond understanding or explanation, a sign only of the impossibility of understanding. Alex Houen writes that terrorism blows "a hole in the very fabric of everydayness," that it "is not just a rupture *in* history, then, but a rupture *of* history," a denial of the very possibility of crafting a meaningful narrative (Houen 2002, 14). *American Pastoral* is a demonstration of this function, moving beyond DeLillo's fear that terrorism has become the only means of inscribing resistance to the still more troubling possibility that terrorism cannot be read at all.

Kinky Friedman, The Mile High Club *(2000)*. Although it is part of a humorous mystery series that clearly belongs within the popular tradition elided by Kunkel and Scanlan, *The Mile High Club* by country singer turned detective novelist Kinky Friedman is an indication that by the end of the twentieth century some trace of the ambiguities and anxieties the terrorist had come to represent for "serious" authors could be found even in the most apparently ephemeral of genres. Like most of Friedman's books, *The Mile High Club* concerns the adventures of a thinly fictionalized version of himself (here, for the sake of clarity, referred to as "Kinky") who operates as a private detective in New York City. The books are known primarily for their humorous tone and witty use of language but occasionally address very dark subjects with an undertone of bleak fatalism. *Mile High* takes this tendency to extremes in detailing how Kinky becomes involved with, and ultimately enables, a terrorist plot.

The central plot revolves around the contents of a pink suitcase, which comes into Kinky's possession when Khadija, a beautiful woman he meets on a flight to New York, asks him to watch it while she goes to the restroom. When the plane lands Kinky finds that Khadija has vanished, and he feels that he has little choice but to take the case home with him. There he finds that he has become an object of interest to the State Department, which is clearly seeking both Khadija and her case. Kinky could, of course, turn the case over to them; his decision not to do so appears to arise partly out of a sense of chivalric duty to Khadija and partly out of a fear that he will be in trouble himself if he does so, but it also derives largely, of course, from the private detective's traditional reliance on his own abilities and distrust of authority. Neither prevents him from opening the locked case to discover "a large plastic Baggie full of enough passports to make a customs agent put in for overtime." The passports are from various countries and in various names, though many of the women pictured resemble Khadija and many of the men pictured appear related to her. Kinky's friend Rambam, a "real" detective, offers an opinion troubling enough when *Mile High* was published and even more so now: "'I think you're looking at how the next bunch of World Trade Center bombers are planning to get away'" (Friedman 2000, 65). This line of dialogue introduces the theme of terrorism into the novel, but *Mile High* never really gets more specific than this concerning exactly who its "terrorists" are; they are never identified or understood beyond simplistic representations of Middle Eastern Muslims opposed, for unspecified reasons, to Israel and the United States. To a large degree, in other words, the novel participates in the populist understanding of terrorism, which emphasizes hostility and otherness over nuance and specific political aims.

Kinky hides the passports in the bottom of his cat's litter box and continues to withhold them both from the State Department and from Khadija, who does eventually reappear. His hope that she is merely a dupe of the actual terrorists is greatly enhanced by their two sexual encounters, though neither, significantly, involves actual intercourse. Israeli agents also become involved in the hunt for the passports, as does Khadija's brother Ahkmed, who late in the novel invades Kinky's loft and nearly kills him in a brawl. Shortly after this fight, Khadija calls and begs Kinky to come to her hotel room, but the call is a ruse—when Kinky returns from the unkept rendezvous, he finds that the passports have, at last, been discovered and taken. Significantly, it is not Kinky but, again, Rambam who puts together the pieces of the puzzle, deducing that the terrorists could only have realized the passports were in the litter box by combining knowledge from Ahkmed's invasion (when the cat, in protest, has scattered her waste throughout the apartment) with knowledge from Khadija's earlier visit (before this occurred)—and that, in fact, there is no Khadija and never has been a Khadija, but only Ahkmed in disguise.

The immediate inclination is to treat this as a joke, played largely at the expense of traditional mysteries and the conventional image of the private eye as masculine hero. Friedman has not only managed to craft a mystery that hinges upon the placement of feline feces but also has maneuvered his decidedly heterosexual hero into not one but two homosexual encounters. That the hero is, to a large degree, himself might be taken simply as adding to the joke, though there is clearly a subversion of normative genre expectations. What truly renders *The Mile High Club* disturbing, however, and expels it from the realm of the merely popular and transient, is its conclusion. In the very brief final chapter of the novel, Kinky is again on a plane when a beautiful woman asks him to watch her bag. This leads directly into the novel's final paragraph: "After she'd gone, a flight attendant came by with a batch of newspapers and I took one at random and unfolded it. As long as I live I'll never forget the headline. It read: TWA FLIGHT 800 BLOWN FROM THE SKIES. TERRORISM SUSPECTED" (Friedman 2000, 223). The implication that the passports Kinky failed to adequately preserve played a role in the tragedy is clear and, particularly given the invocation of an actual airline disaster, provides a stunning end to the novel, one that could not be suffered to stand in the context of any normative detective story. The novels we have examined by DeLillo, Auster, and Roth propose that the writer is silenced in the age of terrorism, but surely *The Mile High Club* is just as troubling in its suggestion that the autonomous individual, the hero who can act outside the control of the dominant system, is just as powerless, just as impotent, just as incapable of true understanding, as the writer. Although 9/11 had not yet occurred, Freidman's text provides a fitting end to a decade in which American fiction had become increasingly troubled by the possibilities of terror.

Contexts and Issues

American Terrorist Fiction after 9/11. The attacks of 2001 clearly called for a new kind of terrorism fiction; from the perspective of the smoldering remains of the World Trade Center, the activities of the Phantom of Liberty or the Rimrock Bomber barely seem to qualify as terrorism at all. Only a little more than three months after 9/11, DeLillo himself, in an essay entitled "In the Ruins of the Future," sought to instigate a consideration of how the American writer could meaningfully respond to an event of such magnitude. Significantly, he begins by seeking an understanding of the terrorists themselves, seeing them as reacting against "the power of American culture to penetrate every wall, home, life and mind. Terror's response is a narrative that has been developing over years, only now becoming inescapable." The polyvalent, continual babble of American narrativizing is answered, shockingly, by the singular plot of terror, which seeks to deaden and silence multiplicity: "Plots reduce the world." In this reading of the terrorist attacks DeLillo echoes Murray Jay Siskind, the eccentric intellectual of his 1985 *White Noise,* who tells his friend Jack to deal with impending death by becoming a killer rather than a dier, by plotting a murder: "We start our lives in chaos. . . . To plot is to affirm life, to seek shape and control" (DeLillo 1998, 291–292).

He follows Siskind in interpreting the formation of narrative through violence as one means of affirming the coherent self, but DeLillo does not go on to advocate that we ourselves become killers. Rather, his purposefully fragmented and digressive essay argues forcibly that we respond to plot with *plots*, that we continue to insist upon our own investment in a ceaseless variety of narrative. The very stories we tell of the disaster become the crucial basis of our survival and recovery: "There are 100,000 stories crisscrossing New York, Washington, and the world. . . . There are the doctors' appointments that saved lives, the cell phones that were used to report the hijackings" (2001). Tellingly, even the stories of those who invent their involvement in the attacks become significant: "This is also the counternarrative, a shadow history of false memories and imagined loss" (2001). The centerpiece of DeLillo's essay is the story of how his nephew Marc and Marc's wife and children, who live a few blocks from the towers, react to the unfolding events of the day, at several points believing they are going to die but eventually reaching the safety of a shelter and resuming something like normalcy. Despite DeLillo's acknowledgement of his relationship to the characters, the story is valuable precisely because it is not remarkable, because it could be anyone's story or even an invention. What is valuable is the act of narrating itself, the refusal to be silenced in the face of the terror narrative that threatens to overwhelm all.

For DeLillo the job of the writer is thus not to create another all-encompassing narrative opposed to that of terror, but rather to insist upon a return to narrative as personal, partial, and incomplete, to contribute to the limitless mosaic of plots that do not insist upon domination: "the event asserts its singularity. . . . The writer tries to give memory, tenderness and meaning to all that howling space" (2001). Nor does the opposition to terror mean that DeLillo is prepared to position the writer as abandoning his own stance of resistance; the writer is still seeking, like the terrorist, to subvert the transient dominant culture of pure spectacle and consumption, "the global momentum that seemed to be driving unmindfully toward a landscape of consumer-robots" (2001). DeLillo makes clear, however, that the strategy of the terrorist is a dead-end ("there is no logic in apocalypse" [2001]); he would, perhaps, align himself instead with "the protesters in Genoa, Prague, Seattle" whose opposition to the Americanization of the globe is not fanatically one-dimensional but "a moderating influence, trying to slow things down, even things out, hold off the white-hot future" (2001). The writer, similarly, must resist the universalizing strategies of both American hegemony and terrorist absolutism, seeking instead a middle ground of possibility, openness, and alternatives.

The DeLillo of "In the Ruins of the Future" seems optimistic that such a writer's strategy will ultimately be more successful than the terrorist's; his essay concludes on a note of faith that New York City will again become a place that "will accommodate every language, ritual, belief and opinion" (2001). This optimism is surprising not only because it followed so closely upon 9/11 but also because it is at odds with the darker implications of much recent fiction that addresses terrorism and the writer's relationship to it, including DeLillo's own.

It remains to be seen how closely DeLillo's own fiction will correspond with the optimism of his essay; his *Falling Man,* a novel said to directly address the events of 9/11, is scheduled to be published in June 2008. By and large American fiction is still functioning in a responsive state, reacting against the attacks rather than seeking to present new alternatives or viewpoints. Terrorism fiction since 9/11 has been dominated by three impulses: the attempt to come to terms with the shock of the attacks themselves; a quest, usually failed, to understand and represent terrorism in a coherent and comprehensible way; and a satiric dismay with the way the national discourse, and particularly political discourse, has increasingly treated the attacks and terrorism in general in a reductive, jingoistic way, particularly in the service of military adventures abroad.

The cartoonist Art Spiegelman's *In the Shadow of No Towers* (2004) provides an instructive example of how these impulses play out. Spiegelman previously won acclaim for *Maus* (1986), an autobiographical graphic novel in which he presented his struggle to come to terms with his father, a concentration camp survivor (see **holocaust literature**). The first part of *No Towers* consists of a series of oversized comic strips Spiegelman published, mostly in European periodicals, beginning in 2002. Employing a collagelike variety of graphic styles and page layouts, Spiegelman begins by trying to represent his own experiences on the fateful day; much like DeLillo's nephew, Spiegelman lived only a few blocks from the towers and spent 9/11 in a frantic effort to unite his family and reach safety, all the while witnessing the actual collapse of the buildings. The early strips very much have the feel of a man revisiting a trauma over and over again in an attempt to frame it in a meaningful way, with certain images—most notably the north tower's structure seeming to glow with heat just before it collapses—recurring on almost every page.

As the strips progress, however, they become increasingly preoccupied not with 9/11 itself but with the response of the Bush administration and the rush to war in Afghanistan and, later, Iraq. Spiegelman's self-images increasingly express despair: "I thought I'd lose my life on 9/11—I lost my mind soon after, and lost my last speck of faith in the U.S.A. when this cabal took over" (Spiegelman 2004, 8). The opportunities he saw for renewal and deeper understanding in the original event are lost: "The towers have come to loom far larger than life . . . but they seem to get smaller every day" (Spiegelman 2004, 10). Ultimately, it seems, Spiegelman abandons the effort to say anything meaningful himself about either the attacks or their aftermath; the second part of *No Towers* is given over to a series of reproductions of colorful, oversized comic strips from the first decades of the twentieth century. Although many of these strips contain images that resonate with the disaster—a giant pushing his way through the buildings of New York City, a firecracker set off during a reading of the Declaration of Independence—Spiegelman readily confesses that their central appeal is essentially escapist. They are "vital, unpretentious ephemera from the optimistic dawn of the 20th century . . . they were just right for an end-of-the-world moment" (Spiegelman 2004, 11). Taken as a whole, *No Towers* is the work of a mind struggling to come to terms with its historical moment and ultimately unable to express much beyond pain, confusion, and an urgent desire for solace and sense. In different ways and in different keys, these are the notes American terrorism fiction is still striking.

Lorraine Adams, Harbor *(2004).* Although it appeared three years after 9/11, *Harbor* is conspicuously set in the years before the attacks and clearly shows the influence of Adams's work as an investigative reporter for *The Washington Post,* particularly her work on FBI counterterrorism squads. The central figure of the book is Aziz Arkoun, an Algerian who stows away on a cargo ship and arrives in Boston in the mid-1990s. Through flashbacks spaced throughout the book, we come to understand that Aziz has fled his native country because of the horrific civil war there driven largely by fundamentalist Islamic militias. Aziz knows Americans do not understand or care about his country: "'The CIA has no one in Algeria. If they did, how would they tell who is who? I am Algerian, and *I* could not tell'" (Adams 2004, 278). Aziz himself had mistakenly been taken into one of the militias and forced to do horrible things to preserve his own life; now his only goal is to find "a place where you could talk, truly talk, and say whatever it was that haunted you at night alone" (Adams 2004, 115).

In America Aziz becomes associated with a loose network of fellow refugees, many of whom he had known in his home village of Arzew, and most of whom, like him, are in the United States illegally. Like Aziz, most of them are only seeking to find a comfortable life for themselves away from the dangers of their home, and most of them are not religious and feel only disdain for those motivated by religious extremism: "If people wanted to believe this jihad shit, so be it" (Adams 2004, 269). A number of them are, however, involved in illegal activities, at least in part because they are unable to obtain well-paying jobs. Aziz's cousin Rafik, the first to take him in when he arrives, is at the center of these activities, smuggling cigarettes and hash and running ambitious shoplifting schemes. Through these activities he becomes associated with a few characters who do appear to be Islamic fundamentalists preparing for a terrorist attack within the United States. These characters, however, are kept almost entirely offstage; Aziz and most of his friends are entirely innocent of such plans or motivations. Even when one of his closest friends, Ghazi, contemplates going to Afghanistan to join the jihad, it is only because he can think of no other method of suicide that will "show your father . . . you were a man" (Adams 2004, 262).

Aziz and his friends, then, are represented in an almost entirely sympathetic way as essentially innocents seeking to find their way in a strange and often hostile culture after having suffered greatly in their previous lives. If they do not understand American culture, however, still less does it understand them, and this is where *Harbor* discovers its real tragedy. In the second half of the book the story of Aziz and his fellow Algerians is interlaced with scenes of FBI agents, and eventually an entire interagency task force, investigating them as potential terrorists. The FBI agents themselves are also represented sympathetically—they obviously mean well and are interested in arriving at the truth, not simply persecuting people—but from the beginning they are handicapped by a near-total misunderstanding of the Algerians. Only one of the agents speaks Arabic, and then only well enough to know he cannot really grasp regional variations; the head of the task force has to be told, very late in the book, that there is in fact a war happening in Algeria. Adams is careful to make the agents aware of their shortcomings: "'we don't have to *know* them. We can't, ever. We can just piece something here with something there and draw logical conclusions. It's flawed, of course it's flawed. But it's better than the alternative'" (Adams 2004, 282). Whether it is actually better is debatable. In the closing scenes of the book the FBI arrests almost all the Algerian characters, resulting in a publicity coup, but we learn that the guiltiest easily get away whereas the most innocent receive harsh and excessive sentences. Aziz himself is deported back to Algeria, where he disappears, almost certainly killed. *Harbor,* ultimately, is less about terrorism than it is about the American inability to understand or reliably identify the terrorist, and the harm that is done by that misunderstanding.

Nicholson Baker, Checkpoint *(2004).* Like *Harbor,* Nicholson Baker's slim novel *Checkpoint* is not concerned primarily with terrorism itself but rather with the official response to terrorism and the ways in which a discourse shaped by terror leads to tragedy. Whereas Adams is willing to assign the failings of her FBI characters to well-intentioned ignorance, Baker's text is shaped by an angry conviction that the Bush administration's wars in Afghanistan and Iraq are due to willfully selfish, shortsighted disinterest in doing the right thing. In *No Towers,* Spiegelman had begun to document the anger he felt over the transmutation of 9/11 into jingoistic war frenzy; *Checkpoint* represents this anger taken to its extreme.

In form, the book deliberately recalls Baker's 1992 *Vox,* which consisted in its entirety of a phone conversation between a man and a woman culminating in an episode of phone sex. *Checkpoint* similarly takes the form of a single long conversation, this one between two men in a Washington, D.C., hotel room. The conversation is recorded, and the novel takes the form of a transcript of the recording, with each speaker identified as he would be in a play. Jay, the first speaker, has summoned his old friend Ben to the hotel room where, at the beginning of the book, he tells him that he is going to assassinate President Bush.

At the time of its publication *Checkpoint* was denounced by some conservative commentators as being virtually an act of treason, but although it expresses some genuine anger toward Bush, it is important to note that the book does not endorse Jay's plan. Jay, in fact, is represented as being clearly unbalanced; he speaks of a history of troubled relationships and transient jobs, and among the weapons he plans to use in his assault are "radio-controlled flying saws" (Baker 2004, 14) and "these homing bullets, and all you had to do was put the bullets in a box along with a photograph of the person you wanted to shoot and they were able to seek that person out" (Baker 2004, 63). Ben, although acknowledging his own distaste for Bush, never agrees to Jay's plan or even indicates that he thinks it would be the right thing to do, and at the end of the book he succeeds in disarming Jay and persuading him to leave the room peacefully.

The identification of *Checkpoint* as terrorism fiction is somewhat tentative. Jay's proposed action itself cannot be described as clearly terrorist, since its primary intention is not to make a political point to a watching audience but simply to punish someone through the use of violence. Nor does Jay and Ben's wandering conversation touch explicitly upon terrorism, except when Jay describes part of the American campaign in Iraq as "so obviously terror bombing" (Baker 2004, 19); indeed, their neglect of the topic of 9/11 is so complete that it must be deliberate on Baker's part. What qualifies the book as terrorism fiction is less its content than its context, the understanding on the part of the reader that the actions Bush has taken that have upset Jay to this degree have been licensed, in the national discourse, by the continual invocations of 9/11 and the specter of terrorism in general. *Checkpoint* is a conversation that makes sense only as a critique of the larger conversation provoked by 9/11. The basic point is the same as the one Adams makes in *Harbor*: we have failed to understand or account for our true enemy, instead turning against the innocent. Where Adams's response to this is sadness, however, Baker's is rage.

John Updike, Terrorist *(2006).* To date, John Updike is the most visible and prominent American author to undertake the daunting task of directly representing the mind of a terrorist in the wake of 9/11. The central figure of *Terrorist* is Ahmad Mulloy, born in impoverished New Prospect, New Jersey, to an Irish-American mother and an Egyptian father and about to graduate high school as the book opens. Ahmad's father was not particularly religious and abandoned the family when Ahmad was an infant; despite this, Ahmad has, since the age of eleven, sought his identity in Islam, driven by his constant sense that "God is another person close beside him, a Siamese twin attached in every part, inside and out, and to whom he can turn in every moment in prayer. God is his happiness" (Updike 2006, 40). Ahmad is angered and confused by what he perceives as the Godlessness of American society. His desire to be complete in his devotion to God leaves him open to fairly transparent manipulation by his imam, who steers him away from preparation for college and into a job driving a truck for a furniture business owned by Lebanese immigrants. Charlie Chebab, the son of the business's owner, rides along with Ahmad on his deliveries, testing him through various conversations about history, religion, and politics. At one point the two men look across the water to the place where the towers had been, and Charlie lectures Ahmad on the necessity of opposing "the enemies around us, the children and fat people in shorts giving us their dirty looks" (Updike 2006, 187), eventually eliciting Ahmad's willingness to die in this cause. Gradually the plan becomes clear: Ahmad is to drive a truck full of explosives into the Lincoln Tunnel and detonate it, flooding the tunnel and causing untold deaths. Having grown increasingly disgusted with the society that surrounds him, Ahmad anticipates his mission with "high, selfless joy" (Updike 2006, 274).

The book's second major character is Jack Levy, a guidance counselor caught in an unhappy marriage and nearing retirement at Ahmad's school. Jack takes an interest in Ahmad, although this interest is rapidly displaced by his interest in Ahmad's mother, with whom he has an affair. A nonpracticing Jew, Jack can only confirm Ahmad's sense of American life as lacking a sense of the divine: "'I was born fallen away. My father hated Judaism, and his father before him. They blamed religion for the world's misery—it reconciled people to their problems'" (Updike 2006, 295). Despite his lack of faith, however, Jack finds the courage—when a chain of rather unlikely coincidences lead to him learning of Ahmad's plan—to climb into the cab of the truck with him, in an attempt to talk him out of pushing the button on his bomb.

Nothing about their subsequent conversation indicates that he succeeds; Ahmad easily disposes of Jack's arguments and seems unwavering in his commitment to his mission. Jack himself comes to accept the apparently inevitable, refusing to leave the truck when he has the opportunity and even urging Ahmad to go through with it: "'Why should I care? A woman I was crazy about has ditched me, my job is a drag, I wake up every morning at four and can't get back to sleep'" (Updike 2006, 303). It is not Jack who keeps Ahmad's hand from the button but rather his own sudden epiphany, a vision of God as motivated by creation rather than destruction: "He does not want us to desecrate His creation by willing death. He wills life" (Updike 2006, 306). Released from the conviction of his mission, a numbed Ahmad follows a jubilant Jack's instructions to turn back towards New Jersey and certain arrest. Although the bomb does not go off, the book hardly ends on a note of triumph or even relief: Ahmad simply surveys the scuttling crowds of New Yorkers around him, "each one of them impaled live upon the pin of consciousness, fixed upon self-advancement and self preservation. That, and only that. 'These devils', Ahmad thinks, 'have taken away my God'" (310).

For all its ambition and the skill with which it is written, *Terrorist* ultimately fails to imagine or represent the mind that could have pushed the button Ahmad fails to—or, by extrapolation, the mind that could have steered an airliner into a building full of workers. Ahmad's epiphany has no direct cause in the book; it is essentially an instance of wishful thinking, a mark of the gap between ourselves and a meaningful grasp of the reality of terrorism. Nor does the book convincingly repudiate Ahmad's criticisms of America; DeLillo's essay wishes to oppose terrorism with a vision of America as able to "accommodate every language, ritual, belief and opinion" (DeLillo 2001), but the America of *Terrorist* is, indeed, Godless and basically hollow, empty of true meaning or affect. As readers we are glad that Ahmad does not set off his bomb, but we also feel the tragedy of his loss of the God he has felt near him—"the concrete living God who stands beside Ahmad as close as the sunshine warming the skin of his neck" (Updike 2006, 188)—since the beginning of the book. If Adams responds to our failure to comprehend terrorism with sadness and Baker with anger, Updike responds with resignation.

Clifford Chase, Winkie *(2006), and Ken Kalfus,* A Disorder Peculiar to the Country *(2006).* In the wake of the anger and sorrow that have understandably dominated the first wave of American terrorism fiction after 9/11, it is perhaps unavoidable that writers would next turn to satire and farce, unlikely as such a strategy might have seemed in the immediate wake of the attacks. In these works, again, the authors are concerned not so much with the attacks themselves as with their aftermath, the ways in which "terrorism" is incorporated into the national discourse, becoming a signifier that can be attached to almost anything for rhetorical effect.

The title character of Clifford Chase's *Winkie,* for example, is a sentient teddy bear who is mistaken by the authorities for a serial bomber based on Theodore Kaczynski, the Unabomber. At his trial, Winkie is charged with crimes that begin with terrorism and eventually include such historically resonant offenses as "corrupting the youth of Athens," "holding the false doctrine that the sun is the center of the world and the earth moves," "witchcraft," and "acts of gross indecency with certain young men of London" (Chase 2006, 85). The trial, in other words, is an enactment of every show trial of a societal scapegoat in Western history, and Chase's addition of "terrorism" to the list suggests that he, no less than Baker, has severe reservations concerning the uses the term has been put to in recent discourse. This is not to say that terrorism does not exist, of course; there is an actual bomber in the book, though he does his greatest harm not to society but to Winkie, by destroying Winkie's offspring before dying himself. The damage done by the bomber, however, is completely out of proportion with the absurdly excessive official response, which lays all the sins of humanity at the feet of an innocent toy, choosing persecution over understanding.

Marginally more serious—or at least marginally more realistic—is Ken Kalfus's *A Disorder Peculiar to the Country,* which focuses on Joyce and Marshall Harriman, a Manhattan couple going through a bitter divorce. The primary issue to be settled between them is who will retain their apartment, which each seems to value more than their two small children. On the morning of 9/11, Joyce, who was supposed to be aboard one of the hijacked planes, and Marshall, who works in the World Trade Center, each believe the other to have died; each is openly disappointed to learn this is not the case. Although both afterward suffer from the anxiety and fear common to all in the wake of the attacks, most of their feelings are funneled into ever more vitriolic and heated attacks on each other, which themselves increasingly take on the forms and jargon of terrorism. Marshall in particular begins to identify with the impulses felt by the terrorists: "their crappy disordered existences, these shameful skirmishes, this soiled money, the debasement, this cruelty, this insensitivity, this impiety had become intolerable to God" (Kalfus 2006, 185). In the novel's peak scene of black humor Marshall builds a suicide bomb—from plans he finds on the Internet—and attempts to detonate it in the presence of his family, first announcing "God is great" (Kalfus 2006, 189)—not because he particularly believes this, but because that is what terrorists say. When the bomb fails to go off Joyce irritably demands to look at it and tries (unsuccessfully) to fix the problem, as the children look idly on. The scene is simultaneously terrifying and hilarious, a demonstration of how "terrorism" is detached from its real roots in history and social conflict to become available for any purpose.

The political significance of Kalfus's themes is made most visible in a closing scene in which Joyce and Marshall reconcile as part of a crowd that has gathered at Ground Zero to celebrate the end of the War on Terror, which, in a sudden lurch into alternative history, has turned out just as we were told it would: our servicemen greeted as heroes, Iraq a healthy and burgeoning democracy that no longer requires their presence, and Osama bin Laden captured. In such a world, it seems, everything is perfect, and even the most hated enemy can once again become the beloved. It is the ultimate fantasy of farcical triumph for contemporary terrorism literature, a world in which terrorism need not be understood because it has ceased to exist.

Bibliography

Adams, Lorraine. *Harbor.* New York: Vintage, 2004.

Auster, Paul. *Leviathan.* New York: Penguin, 1992.

Baker, Nicholson. *Checkpoint.* New York: Vintage, 2004.

Chase, Clifford. *Winkie.* New York: Grove, 2006.

Combs, Cindy C., and Martin Slann. *Encyclopedia of Terrorism.* New York: Checkmark Books, 2003.

DeLillo, Don. "In The Ruins Of The Future." *Guardian,* 22 Dec. 2001. http://www.guardian.co.uk/Archive/Article/0,4273,4324579,00.html

———. *White Noise: Text and Criticism.* Ed. Mark Osteen. New York: Penguin, 1998.

———. *Mao II.* New York: Penguin, 1991.

———. *Libra.* New York: Penguin, 1988.

———. *The Names.* New York: Knopf, 1982.

———. *Players.* New York: Knopf, 1977.

Friedman, Kinky. *The Mile High Club.* New York: Simon & Schuster, 2000.

Harris, Thomas. *Black Sunday.* New York: Signet, 1975.

Houen, Alex. *Terrorism and Modern Literature: From Joseph Conrad to Ciaran Carson.* Oxford: Oxford University Press, 2002.

Kalfus, Ken. *A Disorder Peculiar to the Country.* New York: Harper, 2006.

Kunkel, Benjamin. "Dangerous Characters." *The New York Times Book Review,* 11 Sept. 2005.

Roth, Philip. *American Pastoral.* New York: Vintage, 1998.

———. *Operation Shylock: A Confession.* New York: Vintage, 1993.

Scanlan, Margaret. *Plotting Terror: Novelists and Terrorists in Contemporary Fiction.* Charlottesville: University Press of Virginia, 2001.

Sinclair, Andrew. *An Anatomy of Terror: A History of Terrorism.* London: Pan Books, 2003.

Spiegelman, Art. *In the Shadow of No Towers.* New York: Pantheon, 2004.

Updike, John. *Terrorist.* New York: Knopf, 2006.

Further Reading

DeLillo, Don. "In The Ruins of the Future." *Guardian,* 22 Dec. 2001; Foertsch, Jacqueline, ed. "Special Issue: Terrorism and the Postmodern Novel." *Studies in the Novel* 36 (2004): 3; Houen, Alex. *Terrorism and Modern Literature: From Joseph Conrad to Ciaran Carson.* Oxford: Oxford University Press, 2002; Kunkel, Benjamin. "Dangerous Characters." *The New York Times Book Review,* 11 Sept. 2005; Scanlan, Margaret. *Plotting Terror: Novelists and Terrorists in Contemporary Fiction.* Charlottesville: University Press of Virginia, 2001; Sinclair, Andrew. *An Anatomy of Terror: A History of Terrorism.* London: Pan Books, 2003; Wesley, Marilyn C. *Violent Adventure: Contemporary Fiction by American Men.* Charlottesville: University Press of Virginia, 2003.

JOSEPH S. WALKER

TIME TRAVEL FICTION

Definition. The concept of time travel is used in literature as a device that relies upon the conceit of characters visiting their past or their future. It is employed in **science fiction** with some frequency, often in order to explore ideas about the nature of history, causality, experience, or narrative. In **historical fantasy**, particularly **adventure fiction** for young adults, time travel is often an enabling device, the mechanism through which a viewpoint character is transported to the main setting of the story. Superhero **comic books** are rife with time-traveling characters, particularly master villains whose access to the "time stream" is the source of their being a menace. Time travel has also been used in mainstream fiction (i.e., by authors who are not self-consciously writing in genre), typically in the service of meditations on love and memory (e.g., Jack Finney's 1970 *Time and Again*).

It is thus not quite correct to refer to time travel *solely* as a thematic subgenre of science fiction, because the device of having a character travel to the past or future clearly fulfills some of the same narrative functions as any protagonistic journey does: the portal through time is another version of mythologist Joseph Campbell's threshold to the underworld, through which the genre hero must pass in order to begin his or her adventures in earnest. In generic fantasy, for example, characters from the contemporary world may find themselves transported to a quasi-historical setting by unspecified magical forces, but the transported hero may as well be in Edgar Rice Burroughs' Barsoom (i.e., a fantasy Mars in the far distant past) as in medieval Europe, which shows that historical or causal connection of past to future is merely color rather than a central element driving the plot or the characters' concerns. Similarly, the device of time travel enables entry to an otherwise inaccessible Shangri-la of the future so that the tourist-protagonist of a utopian fiction can show us what is to be seen there (e.g., Heinlein 2004).

Time travel is closely related to the science fiction subgenre of *alternate history*, which includes a parallel universe or para-time story. In alternate history an author both posits a chronology that branches off at some recognizable nexus from historical events, and tells a story set within that chronology (Hellekson 2001). However, it is possible for a story set in a different era to be either, both, or neither. For example, a story about a man who visits the Jurassic period to hunt dinosaurs, returning to the present to dine out on the tale, is time travel but not alternate history (De Camp 1956); a story about a woman who lives in a world where the Axis won World War II is alternate history but not time travel (Dick 1962); and a story where the South wins the Civil War because Afrikaners from the future arm Robert E. Lee and his men with AK-47s (Turtledove 1992)—or *loses* it because a historian from the future interferes with a Confederate victory at Gettysburg (Moore 1953)—is both. But a story about a British adventurer who is present at the Charge of the Light Brigade at Balaclava and observes what *really* happens when the six hundred rode forth into the valley of death is neither, falling instead into the category of **historical fiction**—or possibly even secret history, depending upon how seriously the author intends us to take his speculations (Fraser 1973).

History. The seminal science-fictional time travel novel is widely regarded to be *The Time Machine* (1895), by H.G. Wells (1866–1946). But Mark Twain (1835–1910) pioneered the device of time travel a few years earlier with *A Connecticut Yankee in King Arthur's Court* (1889). Foote (1991) argues that the emergence of time travel in popular literature—though prefigured by stories of sleepers and the fey-touched, such as "Rip van Winkle" and "Thomas the Rhymer"—can be traced to a particularly American vision of time and space that equates the Old World with the past and the New World with the future. This, combined with Twain's efforts to make sense of two contradictory (and again particularly American) impulses—a naïve nostalgia for the past versus an ethnocentric valorization of the technological progress and cultural sophistication of the "modern" present—makes *Connecticut Yankee* a confrontation between nostalgic and progressive visions of history that both technological progress and cultural sophistication come up wanting.

The science fiction grandmaster Robert Heinlein (1907–1988), himself a noted contributor to the subgenre, observed that while it was Twain who *invented* the time travel story, it was Wells who pointed out its contradictions—that is, the extent to which conundrums of cause-and-effect and paradoxes of free will emerge once the device is employed (Nahin 1999, 54). Much of the subsequent history of time travel stories can be seen as a working out of these contradictions, as authors imagined the consequences of changing the past or gaining knowledge of the future under different fictional parameters.

With the emergence of a robust, commercial genre of science fiction magazines and paperbacks in the mid-twentieth century, the device of time travel became a staple science-fictional trope (Ash 1977). The pioneering pulp magazine publisher Hugo Gernsback (1884–1967) even serialized *The Time Machine* in the pages of one of his early "scientifiction" magazines. Time travel subsequently became a recognizable popular culture motif as well, as is suggested by its prevalence in comic books, television, movies, and elsewhere. But because it has served as the science-fictional device within which literary speculation about physical theories of space and time can be indulged, time travel stories in science fiction *per se* have been responsive to developments in physics (Nahin 1999). For example, Larry Niven's short story "Rotating Cylinders and the Possibility of Global Causality Violation" (Niven 1977) takes its title from the scholarly article of the same name by physicist Frank J. Tipler, which suggests that a sufficiently massive, infinitely long rotating cylinder can produce conditions allowing a traveler to move back in time by following a path around the cylinder (Tipler 1974). In Niven's story, the attempt to construct such a device activates a "defense mechanism" whereby the universe arranges its elements to hamper the attempt by causing the sun to go nova (i.e., to blow up) before the work is finished.

Trends and Themes. There are three basic types of time travel protagonists, each of whom implies a particular kind of time travel story: (1) the Connecticut Yankee (who visits the historical past), (2) the Chronic Argonaut (who visits the "historical" future), and (3) the Bootstrapper (who acts recursively and usually paradoxically upon his or her own biography). Each of these basic types has its variations, and it is possible for a particular time-traveling character to be of a "mixed" rather than a "pure" type—for example, Jud Eliot in Robert Silverberg's *Up the Line* (Silverberg 1969) is a Time Courier (whose job is to escort tourists into the historical past) who uses his access to the past to find and sleep with a distant ancestor (Connecticut Yankee), but his dalliances result in a paradoxical self-duplication that brings him to the baleful attention of the Time Patrol (Bootstrapper).

It is useful, however, to regard each kind of protagonist as representing a type of time travel story, embodying a particular view of the operation of history or nature of time, and characterized by particular themes, motifs, and ideas. Both the Connecticut Yankee and the Chronic Argonaut stories are concerned with grand theories of history: the former, as it connects to notions of progress and motifs of nostalgia; the latter, in terms of evolution and cosmology (in other words, the ultimate fates of humanity and the universe). In contrast, the Bootstrapper story is oriented toward questions of causality and individual free will, and its protagonists often find themselves dealing with unforeseen results that seem to bring them into being.

The Connecticut Yankee. The *Connecticut Yankee* is a time traveler who arrives in the historical past for an indefinite period, perhaps even permanently, very much like a latter-day Robinson Crusoe. The knowledge this traveler has of either the future or modern science and technology gives him or her an edge, allowing the character to take action against the dangers and discomforts of the past. Mark Twain's Yankee,

Hank Morgan, gives this category its cognomen, but L. Sprague de Camp (1907–2000) established the ground rules for telling this kind of story as science fiction, in which the deployment of modern knowledge in historical times is the central conceit (De Camp 1941). In *Lest Darkness Fall,* de Camp's Yankee, Martin Padway, is mysteriously transported from the twentieth century to sixth-century Rome. There he uses his extensive technical know-how to create virtually single-handedly entire industries and thereby produce a sort of industrial revolution that enables Rome to avoid both barbarian incursions and Byzantine meddling, all in the hopes of staving off the Dark Ages in Europe. Whereas Twain glosses over the industrialization of Camelot, de Camp describes in great detail the processes through which Padway develops his anachronistic innovations, success building on success: the invention of the printing press leading to the newspaper leading to a telegraph-like semaphore system, and so on. More recently, Leo Frankowski's novels about Conrad Stargard do de Camp one better, embellishing with much greater detail a similar storyline about overcoming social and intellectual inertia in order to introduce both cultural and technical anachronisms. This time, the hero is an American-trained Polish engineer cast back in time to medieval Poland who takes it upon himself to stop the Mongol incursions by bringing about an industrial revolution over the space of four thick novels (Frankowski 1986 and its sequels).

In what may be called the *Yankee Reversed,* the character's special knowledge is either nugatory or actually dangerous. For example, in Poul Anderson's "The Man Who Came Early" (1956), a U.S. soldier transported to medieval Iceland is undone, despite his sidearm and his technical knowledge, because of his unfamiliarity with local norms and customs. In Larry Niven's stories of Svetz the Time Traveler (Niven 1973), Svetz is the operator of a time cage sent back from the highly polluted thirtieth century to procure exotic specimens for the hereditary (and feeble-minded) secretary-general of the U.N. But because time travel is a fantasy, he winds up collecting more exotic creatures than he realizes: sent for a horse, he finds Pegasus; sent for a whale, he finds Moby Dick—and so forth.

In contrast, the *Eternal Yankee* is a traveler charged with either the enforcement or exploration of a particular historical chronology, and possessed of the tools and know-how to fulfill a mission. In these stories, the limits of the time traveler's knowledge is often a central motif. Asimov's Eternals are semimonastic temporal technocrats who specialize in altering history to maximize what is, according to their calculations, human happiness; they are confounded by "silent centuries" down the time stream that have been sealed off to them by mysterious forces

(Asimov 1955). Connie Willis's (1985; 1992; 1998) Balliol historians are academic specialists whose fieldwork takes them to the actual past; the extent to which their training has or has not prepared them for their encounter with the past is often at issue in Willis's stories. Kage Baker's Company novels center on the cyborg recruits of Dr. Zeus, Incorporated (the company that invented the time machine), who are able to act on its behalf and change the past despite the immutability of the *recorded* past by virtue of the gaps in that record.

The Chronic Argonaut. The *Chronic Argonaut* differs from the closely related *Sleeper* (a much more common type of character, often used to visit a utopian setting and listen to the natives explain how their society operates) who arrives in the future without a time machine per se: after a Rip-van-Winkle-like period of sleep or suspended animation (e.g., McMullen 1998), having undergone time dilation as a result of traveling at relativistic velocities (i.e., the compression of local time compared to that of slower-moving observers as a result of speeds close to that of light; e.g., Niven 1976), or via some other mysterious, magical, or undisclosed mechanism (e.g., Heinlein 2004). In any case, the Sleeper's journey through time is one-way and forward, just like ours. In contrast, the Chronic Argonaut may return to his or her own time, or travel across different eras; in either case, the journey is instructive for what it lets the reader see of the great changes wrought by time.

The progenitor of this category is the unnamed protagonist of H.G. Wells's *The Time Machine*. He is a "modern" man who goes forward in time expecting future society to have found scientific answers to the questions and problems that perplexed late Victorian England—that is, he is a chronic argonaut on a voyage of discovery. He visits a future in which society is divided into the beautiful and child-like Eloi and the troglodytic but intelligent Morlocks; the Morlocks run the technical apparatuses of this far-future world, and in return they are permitted to literally prey on the Eloi. The stratification of the society he visits is frequently noted to be a comment on the class divisions of Wells's own time.

The hard science fiction writer Stephen Baxter (1957–) picks up the story where Wells ended it, that is when the Time Traveler activates his time machine and vanishes, never to be seen again (Baxter 1995). In Baxter's vision, the Time Traveler cannot return to his original future, encountering instead time-traveling Morlocks who are rational, scientific, and nowhere near as bloodthirsty as the ones in the original novel. Baxter's Time Traveler, accompanied by a Morlock, ranges up and down the time stream, visiting alternate universes as well as the dawn of time and the end of the universe, all in the service of explicating a scientific cosmology of extraordinary complexity and great beauty that paradoxically both dwarfs human efforts and gives them significance (a persistent theme of Baxter's work is the particular responsibility of consciousness in an unconscious universe).

In contrast to the active efforts of the *voluntary* Chronic Argonaut to achieve time travel, the *drafted* Chronic Argonaut is brought to the future more or less unwillingly by the technologically advanced but somehow degenerate beings that live there. In any case, humans of the future are fundamentally *aliens,* and upon the precise character of that alienness the tale of an argonaut-draftee hangs. In A.E. van Vogt's "Recruiting Station" (2003), for example, a troubled young woman named Norma Matheson goes to work for the mysterious Dr. Lell, who is actually the agent of an embattled faction from the distant future that conscripts men from the past to fight for them after sapping their will through a depersonalizing technology. After her physics professor ex-boyfriend is shanghaied into the future (where his two-fisted

American gumption allows him to resist his programming and turn against his would-be masters) Norma eventually unlocks—with a little behind-the-scenes help from the opposing futuristic faction—her hitherto-untapped mental potential and uses her newfound powers to defeat Dr. Lell—the degenerate denizens of the future are no match for a couple of authentic red-blooded human beings in their prime.

Joe Haldeman's "Anniversary Project" (1975)—in which highly evolved telepathic human beings from the distant future snatch a couple of young American newly-weds from the twentieth-century beach where they are canoodling—is a somewhat sadder story. People from the future want to commemorate the anniversary of the (now obsolete) practice of reading, and so they have cast themselves through time to obtain authentic readers to observe during the festivities. The newlyweds will return to their own time in a few days, they are told, and they won't remember a thing. But because time casting is itself an old and little-practiced technology, when the woman returns to the moment from which she was taken—early in her marriage alone on the beach with her spouse—a slight error in the process causes her to subliminally experience her life and death as a mid-twentieth-century housewife with an alcoholic husband and troubled children. Back on the beach, and to her husband's great mystification, she bursts into tears, slaps him on the face, and runs back to their car. In Haldeman's story, the primitive "authenticity" of the twentieth-century humans is a limitation rather than a strength, and the evolution of human-ity will turn much that strikes us as quintessentially human—such as reading (and sex!)—into atavisms.

The Bootstrapper. The *Bootstrapper* is caught in the throes of time travel's para-doxes, like the hero of Robert A. Heinlein's "By His Bootstraps" (1941), who gives this type its name. Bob Wilson is alone in a locked room where he has been all day, working doggedly to complete his thesis, when a familiar-looking stranger arrives through a glowing circle he calls a "time gate." The stranger, who calls himself Joe, pours drinks and explains that a unique opportunity—helping "an old guy" run a country along with Joe—awaits Bob on the other side of the gate. A third man who closely resembles Joe arrives through the time gate; he wants Bob *not* to go through the gate. A physical altercation takes place, and Bob is knocked through the time gate. Bob wakes in the High Palace of Norkaal, thirty thousand years in the future, where a middle-aged man who calls himself Diktor wants Bob to go back and persuade the person on the other side of the gate to come through; Bob steps through, recognizes himself, and reexperiences the encounter with Joe, this time *as Joe.* Bob then follows his earlier self into the future, despite the protests of the third man whom Bob now recognizes as a later version of himself. He encounters Diktor once more, who shows him how to operate the time gate and gives him a list of books to acquire. But Bob grows suspicious of Diktor's motives and returns through the gate determined to put a stop to his earliest self's trip through the gate, but he fails (experiencing the same encounter in his room for the third time). When "Joe" returns through the time gate, Bob (alone once more in his room) tries to get back to work on his thesis, but he cannot resist another trip through the gate, the first of several decisions that result in Bob *becoming* Diktor and waiting for the day when his own earlier self arrives for the first time through the time gate to begin the process again. This extended summary only hints at the paradoxical recursiveness of this kind of time travel plot. Heinlein's story features many instances of circular causation, as when Bob copies a notebook, destroys the original, and realizes that his copy will be the one an earlier self finds in the High Palace of Norkaal, which raises the question of where the book came from in the first place. David Gerrold's *The Man Who Folded Himself* (1973) is a novel-length exercise in exactly the same sort of circular causation, and a classic of its kind.

Contexts and Issues. Time travel stories address persistent questions about the nature of causality and the character of experience, both at the level of individuals and at that of society or even the cosmos as a whole. At the micro or individual level, time travel stories explore logical puzzles of cause and effect, enabling the construction of paradoxical time loops wherein it is possible to go back in time and invest sufficient principal that its compounded interest will either fund the construction of the time machine, or give oneself a work of art that one then publishes under one's own name and becomes famous for, or even unwittingly impregnate one's mother with oneself (Lem 1974). In one of Heinlein's most famous stories, "All You Zombies" (1959), the hermaphroditic protagonist gives birth to herself after having been seduced by her transgendered later self who has been sent back in time by a still later version of himself (the narrator) for just such a purpose. "I know where I came from," he tells the reader at the end, "but where did all you zombies come from?"

But logical puzzles such as these, Lem argues, are embedded in a larger discourse about the ergodicity of history: to what extent are historical events necessary (i.e., largely determined by the operation of inexorable social forces) or contingent (i.e., largely the product of accidental confluences of circumstances)? Under the ergodic hypothesis, history possesses a kind of inertia that renders inconsequential any efforts to change the past (for example, a war averted will break out anyway for other reasons a little later and more fiercely, so that the net effect is the same). Under the anti-ergodic hypothesis, even seemingly minor changes can result in drastic alterations to the path of history (so that stepping on a butterfly in the Jurassic can mean that the traveler returns to a totalitarian nightmare rather than the democratic republic he left). So time travel stories speak to the consequentiality of human action: if history is ergodic, then our choices as individuals matter very little, because they will be swept away in the larger flow of events, perhaps even within our own biographies; if on the other hand it isn't, even the smallest of our decisions can take on highly fateful proportions.

Hellekson (2001) suggests that models of history can be categorized according to whether they are *genetic* (interested in processes of causation), *teleological* (driven by questions of intention or purpose), *eschatological* (focused on ultimate fates or destinies), or *entropic* (convinced of the randomness or at least purposelessness of events), and he argues that genetic models are most appropriate for alternate history stories, given their intense interest in how historical events come about. It may be that each of the other three models similarly corresponds to one of the types of time travel protagonist. The Connecticut Yankee story, the tale of an individual thrust backward in time, is fundamentally concerned with how the intentionality, beliefs, and knowledge of a single person can affect the course of events, and it is thus teleological at root. The Chronic Argonaut story is characterized by an eschatological perspective: the time traveler is permitted to see the end of the earth, humanity, the universe, or time itself and thereby gains an understanding of what it all means. And the Bootstrapper, embedded in time loops of uncaused effects and solipsistic acts of self-creation, embodies an entropic perspective. To the extent that mixed types of time travel stories are possible, however, this neat schema loses its force.

Reception. There have been numerous film adaptations of time travel stories. Movies seem to be a particularly apt medium for conveying the paradoxical qualities of time travel, perhaps because they themselves enable or even invite the reordering of events in sequence (as when the movie begins with its climax, and then moves back in time to show us the events that led up to that climax). *The Time Machine* itself has been remade twice, once by director George Pal (1908–1980) in 1960 and again in 2002. Ray Bradbury's short story "A Sound of Thunder" has been turned into the 2004 film of the same name (time-traveling dinosaur hunter messes up the future by stepping on a butterfly in the past).

A number of original time travel movies began to appear in the 1980s, notably *Back to the Future* (a high school student goes back in time and accidentally interferes with his parents' courtship; 1985) as well as Terry Gilliam's (1940–) *Time Bandits* (a little boy encounters a dwarfish band of criminals who have stolen God's map of the holes in the space-time continuum in order to indulge in an intertemporal crime spree; 1981), and *The Terminator* (a young woman is pursued by an android from the future to prevent her as-yet-not-conceived son from saving humanity from extermination in the twenty-first century; 1984). *Bill and Ted's Excellent Adventure* (a farcical cross-time scavenger hunt with two dudes from the Valley; 1989) and its sequels rely on time travel as well.

More recent time travel films have a darker edge. Terry Gilliam's *Twelve Monkeys* (1995) sends a man back in time, where he fails to prevent a terrorist attack that causes a massive human die-off. In *The Butterfly Effect* (2004), a young man—who can send his consciousness to earlier points in his own biography, where any changes in what he does can engender drastic alterations in hitherto established events—decides ultimately that he would be better off never being born, and commits suicide in his mother's womb. In the cult favorite *Donnie Darko* (2001), a teenager is visited by a bunny suit–wearing man from the future who gives him strange instructions, and the title character allows himself to die to save the universe from destruction. In *Primer* (2004), the co-owners of a garage-based start-up engineering company invent a time travel machine, use it for day-trading, and then the paradoxes start to catch up with them, leading to suspicion and betrayal.

Several American television series also rely on time travel. Irwin Allen's (1916–1991) *The Time Tunnel* (1966–1967) presented two scientists who, by going through the tunnel, tumbled each week into an adventure in a new era. In *Voyagers!* (1982–1983), a time traveler from the distant future ensures the proper unfolding of history with the aid of a boy from the 1980s. A similar but longer-lived series called *Quantum Leap* (1989–1993) involved a scientist who each week arrived in a new host body sometime during the twentieth century in order to solve a crisis facing that unwitting host. In *Time Trax* (1993–1994), a cop from the future arrives in the 1990s to track down escaped fugitives who had gone to ground in the past. *Early Edition* (1996–2000) was about a man who each morning mysteriously received the next day's paper and took it upon himself to prevent bad news from taking place. *Seven Days* (1998–2001) involved a "chrononaut" who was sent back in time one week in order to prevent disasters or tragedies that had occurred in the meantime.

Selected Authors. This section discusses six recent novels that exemplify the types of time travel stories laid out above. Each subsection summarizes the novels it considers and then highlights the important motifs or thematic considerations they address. In discussing these motifs, emphasis is given to how they treat or model the nature of history, and what normative judgments emerge from that modeling.

Connecticut Yankees. *Household Gods* (Tarr and Turtledove 1999) is a gloss on the classic Connecticut Yankee plot, and the product of a collaboration between Judith Tarr (1955–), an accomplished fantasist, and Harry Turtledove (1949–), the dean of alternate history. In the book, Nicole is the divorced mother of two and a Los Angeles lawyer who hits the ceiling at her firm when the partnership that she deserves is given to a male colleague instead. Furious and unhappy, she prays to live in Roman times, an era that she imagines as having less sexism than the late twentieth century. The gods Liber and Libera—present on her nightstand in the form of a souvenir plaque she had picked up in Italy on her honeymoon—hear her and grant her prayer. Nicole wakes in the body of Umma, a sixth-century widowed tavern keeper and a mother of two who happens to be Nicole's own distant ancestor, living in a Roman town near the frontier with barbaric Germanic lands.

Nicole is quickly disabused of her unrealistic notions about the egalitarian quality of the past, and her initial speculations about the possibility of getting rich by introducing modern conveniences (such as tampons and antibiotics!) give way equally quickly to the challenges of making a living and raising her children. Besides the culture shock that Nicole experiences trying to live as a Roman woman—the place stinks; everyone drinks; Christians are terrorists; violence is endemic—she must endure pestilence, barbarian occupation, and rape before she discovers how to reverse the wish that Liber and Libera have granted her. Despite having been in the past for many months, in the present only a week has passed, during which her "real" body was in a coma. The perspective that living in the past has given her allows her to become a better mother (she gives one of her kids a swat and he stops misbehaving), a tougher person (she goes after her ex-husband to make him pay the in-arrears child support he owes), and a partner in the law firm (given another assignment by her superiors, she performs ably and even goes to a male colleague for help in editing it, thus demonstrating maturity to be a team player).

The Life of the World to Come (Baker 2004) is part of Kage Baker's (1952–) ongoing Company series, which hinges upon the time-traveling enterprise of "the Company," also known as Dr. Zeus, Incorporated. Besides running Club Med–like resorts in the Mesozoic for the idle rich of the twenty-fifth century, the chief business of the Company is to send agents back in time to acquire valuable property that is about to go missing from the pages of history (e.g., the books of the Library of Alexandria) and secure it for the Company to keep and sell in the future. Its agents are themselves "acquired" in similar fashion: they are stolen out of time to avoid their deaths and pressed into service as immortal cyborgs.

This specific novel from the series centers on Alec Checkerfield, a twenty-fifth-century child of privilege who is unknowingly the product of a Company-sponsored genetic experiment to create a more tractable sort of agent. His strange abilities enable him as a young boy to subvert the programming of a sophisticated AI (artificial intelligence) playmate who adopts the persona of a pirate called the Captain and sets to work amassing a huge, secret, and highly profitable information database on Alec's behalf. Eventually, they learn of the Company, and Alec steals a time shuttle, fleeing backward in time to where the heroine of the series—a cyborg agent of the Company called Botanist Mendoza—is stranded Robinson Crusoe–like in the Mesozoic. Having met and fallen in love with two previous versions of Alec's genotype, she has been imprisoned there by order of a trio of effete and foppish

Company planners. An experiment by these planners produced a new version of Alec in order to prevent her from possibly meeting him again. Mendoza nurses Alec back to health, and he returns to the twenty-fifth century to complete a mission he's taken on, promising to return for her. The Company abducts her from her prison, however, and Alec raids the Company's headquarters to try to locate her. While inside the Company's headquarters, he downloads the stored and recorded personalities of the two previous genetic versions of himself. Cohabiting Alec's body, the three versions of himself (the first two and his present self) confront the three Company planners to find out what has been done to Mendoza. As the story ends, they set off in Alec's high-tech smuggling yacht (now modified for time travel) to find her.

In both *Household Gods* and *The Life of the World to Come,* the past is portrayed as somehow more authentic, but also crueler and more dangerous, than the present (whether that present is twentieth-century Los Angeles or twentieth-fifth-century London). Both novels mock over solicitous, politically correct social engineering that coddles rather than challenges. But they are also unsympathetic to an undiscriminating nostalgia that valorizes and glorifies the past. For example, Nicole is disabused of her fantasies about the past and comes to appreciate how modern legal services empower her as a single mother pursuing a deadbeat dad. And the foppish trio that created Alec and his predecessors play at re-creating obsolete experiences, making fools of themselves as they do it: imagining themselves to be emulating J.R.R. Tolkien and C.S. Lewis, they go for a walk in the English "countryside" (a strip of parkland in a crowded London) and unaccustomed to exertion fall prey to blisters, heat injury, and exhaustion. Their clownishness is a direct result of their blithe ignorance of the authentic past.

The central theme that emerges in both novels is a vindication of individual agency or intentionality: despite how one's circumstances constrain one, whether one is a woman in Roman times or the product of a genetic-engineering experiment gone awry, one is responsible for acknowledging those constraints and then striving anyway. At its core, the Connecticut Yankee story rejects the notion that people are unalterably shaped by their circumstances, because a sufficiently self-aware individual is capable of taking steps to resist and overcome them.

Chronic Argonauts. Dear Abbey (Bisson 2003) by Terry Bisson (1942–) is comic in tone but earnest in aspirations. It is the story of Lee and Cole, colleagues at a small community college in Connecticut. Lee, a Chinese physicist who speaks fractured English with a Texas accent, has a time machine in his personal digital assistant (PDA). Cole, an American studies professor with strong environmentalist leanings, has connections to the Green underground. The two men are recruited into an environmentalist scheme to acquire a formula from the future that will enable a genetically tailored virus to "severely inhibit the ability of humans to degrade the planet" by causing an infertility pandemic. On a Friday night, they travel to the future by using a kind of swinging metal couch stored in an underutilized room in the student center. As they rock back and forth on the couch, the calculations in the PDA send them in exponentially greater forward arcs in time. Their initial attempt to get the formula is thwarted, and as they swing further and further into the future, they learn of the course of future human history: people come to regret the waste and failure of the twentieth century, begin to restore the Earth, become able to live in more humane and sustainable ways, and finally fade away 2.4 billion years in the future.

Manifold: Time (Baxter 2000) is cosmic in tone and equally earnest. It is the first of three novels each of which is set in separate but parallel universes involving slightly different configurations of the same characters. In this novel, Reid Malenfant is an ex-astronaut turned space entrepreneur who has put together a venture to begin mining asteroids. An enigmatic mathematician named Cornelius Taine, who represents one of his major investors, persuades him to work on detecting signals from "downstream" (the future). These signals will help avoid the statistically inevitable "Carter catastrophe" that will cause the collapse of civilization and possible extinction of humanity 200 years in the future. The detected message identifies a solitary asteroid in a distant orbit around the Earth, and Malenfant blasts off for it with Emma Stoney (his ex-wife), Taine, and Michael—an autistic but brilliant child who is one of very many "blue children" being born with unusual abilities. Pursued by space troopers sent by the U.S. government to stop them, they find a mysterious circular portal that allows them to journey to future eras, where they see how intelligent life—human life!—carefully conserves the dissipating energies of the universe to the last moments, when matter itself begins to break down. Emma is shot, Michael disappears, and Taine sacrifices himself to stop a trooper who has followed them through the gate. Soon, only Malenfant remains, and he goes further still, into new "daughter" universes born of the collapse of previous ones. Reaching the end of the universe, he is given the chance to alter the past so that Emma doesn't come with him to the asteroid, and so lives. Meanwhile, however, the blue children, persecuted on Earth, flee to the moon, where they build a sort of doomsday device that destabilizes the vacuum of space itself. The resulting destruction of the universe is not an evil act, however, for the children are acting on behalf of the downstreamers, who see it as an act of *creation*: many daughter universes will result from the black hole–like singularities produced as the vacuum collapses.

These two novels thus offer complementary eschatological visions. In *Dear Abbey,* "Bisson's voyagers do not find a future in which mankind has conquered the galaxy. Instead, they find worlds in which our actions and inactions as regards the earth's environment have played out with consequences both somber and sobering" (Kleffel 2003), and they watch the world end with a whimper. To avoid a similar fate, the downstreamers of Baxter's novel send a message to the past that ends the world with a bang, obviating their own bleak existence and creating in the process new universes whose inhabitants "might be able to reconstruct what we were like, how we lived our lives" (p. 451). The Chronic Argonaut story is thus in direct contrast with the Connecticut Yankee; whereas the latter vindicates the individual, the former puts big-H History in the starring role, its forces driving the action to some ultimate end.

Bootstrappers. *The Time Traveler's Wife* (2003) by Audrey Niffenegger (1964–) is a romance, a mainstream novel that spent weeks on the best sellers lists despite the dismissive sniffs of some reviewers (e.g., Maas 2003). Clare and Henry meet, fall in love, get married, and try to settle down to a normal life. But Henry is afflicted with a strange genetic "chronodisplacement disorder" that occasionally sends him skirling naked across time for brief jaunts into his own past and future; so Clare meets Henry as a six-year-old girl, when he is 36; they marry when he is 31 and she is 23, finally having met in real (i.e., nondisplaced) time a few years earlier. As a love story, this novel focuses on what it means to be in love when each partner at any given time is drawing upon a different set of memories about their moments together: sometimes anticipating the joy the other has yet to feel, sometimes resentful of what for the other hasn't happened yet. As a time travel story, this novel is interesting for its treatment of the disorienting experiences attendant upon bootstrapping time travel, such as encountering others who know you but whom you haven't yet met.

Night Watch (Pratchett 2002) is part of the Discworld series by Terry Pratchett (1948–). This series comprises lighthearted comic fantasies set on a flat world supported on the back of a gigantic cosmic turtle. The earliest Discworld stories achieved their comic effect by poking fun at the conventions of genre fantasy, but later entries in the series downplay broad comedy for clever word- and idea-play and sympathetically drawn characters, the secret of whose appeal is that, at heart, they are just trying to do the best they can. In *Night Watch*, Commander Sam Vimes of the Ankh-Morpork City Watch is transported back in time twenty years while pursuing a murderer named Carcer through the grounds of the Unseen University, the city's school of magic (where experiments in high-energy thaumaturgy take place). The city of twenty years earlier is a grimmer, less hopeful place than it will be; it labors beneath a paranoid and despotic ruler known as the Patrician. Carcer's murder of the watch sergeant—who was Sam Vimes' first partner when he joined the force—changes the trajectory of history, and so Vimes (with the help of some time-controlling monks) must take the role of his old partner, teaching his younger self the ropes while trying to undo the damage that Carcer has done. All this happens as the city comes closer to the revolution that will bloodily unseat the Patrician—if Vimes' memory can be trusted.

Both of these stories—perhaps because they are located outside the genre of science fiction—avoid questions about the logical paradoxes of time travel—for example, having lived through an event once, what prevents one from doing something differently the second time around?—in favor of exploring what may be called its *experiential* paradoxes: what is it like to be unmoored in time? This is the essence of the Bootstrapper story.

Bibliography

Anderson, Poul. "The Man Who Came Early." *The Magazine of Fantasy & Science Fiction* 1956.

Ash, Brian. *The Visual Encyclopedia of Science Fiction: A Documented Pictorial Checklist of the Sci-Fi World*. New York: Harmony Books, 1977.

Asimov, Isaac. *The End of Eternity*. Greenwich, CT: Fawcett Publications, Inc., 1955.

Baker, Kage. *The Life of the World to Come*. New York: Tor, 2004.

Baxter, Stephen. *The Time Ships*. New York: HarperPrism, 1995.

———. *Manifold: Time*. New York: Del Rey, 2000.

Davies, P.C.W. *How to Build a Time Machine*. 1st American ed. New York: Viking, 2002.

De Camp, L. Sprague. *Lest Darkness Fall*. New York: H. Holt & Co., 1941.

———. "A Gun for Dinosaur." *Galaxy Science Fiction* Mar. 1956.

Dick, Philip K. *The Man in the High Castle*. Book Club ed. New York: Putnam, 1962.

Finney, Jack. *Time and Again*. New York: Simon and Schuster, 1970.

Foote, Bud. "The Connecticut Yankee in the Twentieth Century: Travel to the Past in Science Fiction." *Contributions to the Study of Science Fiction and Fantasy* no. 43. New York: Greenwood Press, 1991.

Frankowski, Leo A. *The Cross-Time Engineer*. New York: Ballantine/Del Rey, 1986.

Fraser, George MacDonald. *Flashman at the Charge*. 1st American ed. New York: Knopf, 1973 [distributed by Random House].

Gerrold, David. *The Man Who Folded Himself.* 1st ed. New York: Random House, 1973.

Groppi, Susan Marie. "Fiction Submission Guidelines: Stories We've Seen Too Often." 2006. http://www.strangehorizons.com/guidelines/fiction-common.shtml.

Haldeman, Joe. "Anniversary Project." *Analog* 1975.

Heinlein, Robert A. "By His Bootstraps." *Astounding* Oct. 1941.

———. "All you zombies." *The Magazine of Fantasy & Science Fiction* Mar. 1959.

———. *For Us, the Living: A Comedy of Customs.* New York: Scribner, 2004.

Hellekson, Karen. *The Alternate History: Refiguring Historical Time.* Kent, OH: Kent State University Press, 2001.

Kleffel, Rick. *Dear Abbey* [book review] 2003 [cited August 16 2006]. http://trashotron.com/agony/reviews/2003/bisson-dear_abbey.htm.

Lem, Stanislaw. "The Time-Travel Story and Related Matters of SF Structuring." *Science Fiction Studies* 1 (1974): 143–154.

Maas, Judith. "Book review: The Time Traveler's Wife by Audrey Niffenegger." *Boston Globe* Dec. 2003:B108.

McMullen, Sean. *The Centurion's Empire.* New York: Tor, 1998.

Moore, Ward. *Bring the Jubilee.* New York: Farrar, Straus, and Young, 1953.

Nahin, Paul J. *Time Machines: Time Travel in Physics, Metaphysics, and Science Fiction.* 2nd ed. New York: AIP Press/Springer, 1999.

Niffenegger, Audrey. *The Time Traveler's Wife: A Novel.* San Francisco, CA: MacAdam/Cage Pub, 2003.

Niven, Larry. *The Flight of the Horse.* New York: Ballantine Books, 1973.

———. *A World out of Time.* 1st ed. New York: Holt, Rinehart and Winston, 1976.

———. "Rotating Cylinders and the Possibility of Global Causality Violation." *Analog* Aug. 1977.

Pratchett, Terry. *Night Watch.* New York: HarperCollins, 2002.

Silverberg, Robert. *Up the Line.* New York: Ballantine, 1969.

Tarr, Judith, and Harry Turtledove. *Household Gods.* New York: Tor, 1999.

Tipler, F.J. "Rotating Cylinders and the Possibility of Global Causality Violation." *Physical Review D9* 8 (1974): 2203–2206.

Turtledove, Harry. *The Guns of the South: A Novel of the Civil War.* 1st ed. New York: Ballantine Books, 1992.

Twain, Mark. *A Connecticut Yankee in King Arthur's Court.* New York: C.L. Webster & Company, 1889.

van Vogt, A.E. "Recruiting Station." In *Transfinite: The Essential A.E. van Vogt.* J. Rico and R. Katze, eds. Framingham, MA: NESFA Press, 2003.

Wells, H.G. *The Time Machine: An Invention.* London: W. Heinemann, 1895.

Willis, Connie. "Fire Watch." *Isaac Asimov's Science Fiction Magazine* Feb. 1985.

———. *Doomsday Book.* New York: Bantam Books, 1992.

———. *To Say Nothing of the Dog, or How We the Bishop's Bird Stump at Last.* New York: Bantam Books, 1998.

Further Reading

Foote, Bud. *The Connecticut Yankee in the Twentieth Century: Travel to the Past in Science Fiction.* New York: Greenwood Press, 1991; Hellekson, Karen. *The Alternate History: Refiguring Historical Time.* Kent, OH: Kent State University Press, 2001; Malzberg, Barry N. *The Best Time Travel Stories of All Time.* New York: Pocket/ibooks, 2002; Nahin, Paul J. *Time Machines: Time Travel in Physics, Metaphysics, and Science Fiction.* 2nd ed. New York: AIP Press/Springer, 1999; Turtledove, H. and Martin H. Greenberg. *The Best Alternate History Stories of the 20th Century.* New York: Del Rey, 2001; Turtledove, H. and Martin H. Greenberg. *The Best Time Travel Stories of the 20th Century.* New York: Del Rey, 2005.

WILLIAM J. WHITE

TRANSREALIST FICTION

Definition. *Transrealism* is a term coined in 1983 by mathematician, computer scientist, and novelist Rudy Rucker (Rudolf von Bitter Rucker [1946–]) to describe *fantastic* fiction that draws much of its power and density from closely observed reality, especially the biographical experience of the writer. Equally, the term conveys an enlivening approach to *realistic* fiction that enhances the vividness of its characters and events by imbuing them with elements drawn from fantastical imagination. "The Transrealist," declared Rucker, "writes about immediate perception in a fantastic way." The specific goal was an enrichment of generic writing: "There will always be a place for the escape-literature of genre SF [science fiction or speculative fiction]. But there is no reason to let this severely limited and reactionary mode condition all our writing. Transrealism is the path to a truly artistic SF" (see online text of Rucker's "Transrealist Manifesto"). So a transrealist writes about the fantastic, the invented, the inverted, the dementedly shocking, via well-known literary techniques developed to capture and notate the world of immediate perception.

Transrealism in Literature. Transrealism is less a way of reading fiction, and more a recommendation to writers who intend to create fantastic worlds, or who wish to intensify narratives generally grounded in ordinary life. "The tools of fantasy and SF," notes Rudy Rucker, "offer a means to thicken and intensify realistic fiction." Yet "a valid work of art should deal with the world the way it actually is." In consequence, "Transrealism tries to treat not only immediate reality, but also the higher reality in which life is embedded" ("Manifesto"). The "trans-" part indicates aspects of the text that are transgressive, transformational, transmutational, and transcendental. Rucker coined the term "after seeing the phrase 'transcendental autobiography' in a blurb on the cover of Philip K. Dick's *A Scanner Darkly*" (*Transreal!* 1991, p. 529); Rucker's own fiction, both transreal and otherwise, is discussed at length in Broderick, 2000.

Parallel to transrealism, adjacent modes have emerged or been discerned and named: *slipstream* (Bruce Sterling [1954–]: "a contemporary kind of writing which has set its face against consensus reality . . . fantastic, surreal sometimes, speculative on occasion . . . simply makes you feel very strange . . . We could call this kind of fiction Novels of Postmodern Sensibility"), *interstitial* (Delia Sherman: "breaks the rules . . . lurk[s] near or on the borders of two, three, or more genres, owing allegiance to no single genre or set of conventions"), *postmodern SF* (texts with fluid reality boundaries, exemplified by William Gibson's cyberpunk *Neuromancer*, 1984), and the *New Weird* (China Miéville [1972–]: "Something is happening in the literature of the fantastic. A slippage. A freeing-up. The quality is astounding. Notions are sputtering and bleeding across internal and external boundaries"). All share a tendency to repudiate the restrictions and often the tropes—the standard symbols, icons, plots, shortcuts, etc.—of genre SF and fantasy, emphasizing instead more complex psychological development, stylistic sophistication, and what might be called social embeddedness, and sometimes political engagement of a distinctly personal coloration. Meanwhile, **magical realism** found its way out of Latin America, inserting impossible or fantastical elements into rich descriptions of life. All these methods share the interesting technical device of using metaphors and other figures of speech *mimetically*, that is, as if they referred directly to the real world. For example, if a child flies into the sky in company with a talking dog, this is to be taken literally; it is not a Freudian dream image, or a fanciful way of conveying the child's inward loneliness and aspiration. It might well do that also, and more, but the events are to be taken as part of the realistic record of imagined events.

History. The need for a transrealist approach to fantastic fiction arose from those frequently debased and stereotyped characters and plot events of consumer science fiction and fantasy, which comprises the bulk of the genre. Indeed, when the rotoscoped movie adapted from Dick's *A Scanner Darkly* was released in 2006, its director, Richard Linklater, commented, "What appealed to me about [the novel] is that it's not really about 'the future.' It's about Joe Everyman and his pals, worrying about money and sex and being frustrated. A lot of sci-fi deals with these amazing futuristic worlds where humans have suddenly lost all their humor and become emotionless automatons" (2006).

Is this charge justified? Dick was clearly unusual in this regard, compared to most science-fiction writers of the 1950s and 1960s, but it would be misleading to read the fictional characters of Isaac Asimov (1920–1992) and Sir Arthur C. Clarke (1917–) as emotionless automatons—except for Asimov's stoic robots. It is true that stories and characters of the period, and still today, tend to be driven by curiosity or wonder rather than, say, passionate romantic love or world-weary angst. James Blish's (1921–1975) characters, often regarded as "cold," seethe nevertheless with ferocious intellectual energy. Robert A. Heinlein's (1907–1988) fiction is full of emotion and humor, of a kind reminiscent of an updated Mark Twain (1835–1910), and the figures in Ursula K. Le Guin (1929–), Joanna Russ (1937–), and Samuel R. Delany (1942–) are very far from stereotyped or impassive.

On the other hand, SF critic Gary Westfahl (1951–) has suggested that the "geeky" cast of much SF and fantasy is due to its specialized appeal to writers and readers sharing some measure of Asperger's Syndrome: "a persistent failure to establish eye contact, visible discomfort in most social situations, obsessive interests in a few subjects, a tendency to fall into routines . . . and a tangible aura of emotional detachment, even in extreme situations." For an Asperger teenager in the 1930s (or even today), "a story about an astronaut encountering aliens on Mars might have had an air of comforting familiarity, in contrast to stories set in the bizarre, inexplicable, and thoroughly socialized worlds of Andy Hardy and the Bobbsey Twins" (Westfahl, 2006).

More generally, the tropes of fantastic fiction in the West were adopted or invented mainly by adventure storytellers writing hurriedly for the barely educated mass readership of inexpensive pulp magazines. Consequently, since much of today's fantastic fiction evolved from that pulp history, it often remains decidedly generic and formulaic in the ways it is constructed and read. The tired narrative conventions it frequently embodies, far from challenging us as "the extreme narrative of difference" (Broderick, 2004, 10), are designed as comforting, minimally-confronting mind candy. Stock characters and settings are templates put into creaking, predictable action. The craft of reliable genre writing is to disguise or superficially refresh this tired pattern of narrative action.

In part, this use of instantly recognizable stereotypes is understandable, since the figures and behavior of fantastical fiction are always, to some large extent, allegorical. Each represents or dramatizes only a handful of aspects of individual psychology or cultural dynamics. Genre characters are not intended as rounded portraits of humans in a richly known world. They tend toward the archetypal, the schematic, and the iconic. One way to defeat or surpass such generic temptations and limits is to draw upon the internalized understanding—the cognitive and emotional models within one's head and heart—of the endlessly surprising people one knows best:

In real life, the people you meet almost never say what you want or expect them to. From long and bruising contact, you carry simulations of your acquaintances around in your head. These simulations *are imposed on you from without;* they do not react to imagined situations as you might desire. By letting these simulations run your characters, you can avoid turning out mechanical wish-fulfilments. It is essential that the characters be in some sense out of control, as are real people—for what can anyone ever learn by reading about made-up people? ("Manifesto")

Trends and Themes. Because transrealism is not a school of writing (although Rucker's own acknowledged influences suggest that it can be seen as a very belated revival of Beat poetics), but rather a suggested method for enriching all kinds of imaginative writing, it is difficult to identify any particular trends, beyond the observation that the best fantastical fiction seems increasingly steeped in the experiences of the real world. For example, a thriller/mystery novel of telepathy, Spider Robinson's (1948–) *Very Bad Deaths* (2004), effectively reuses the author's own harrowing medical and other problems, which both restrict his narrator's capacity to act heroically and provide him with strengths of endurance that allow him a sort of muffled victory. Without this added texture, the book would have been slighter and less involving. By contrast, most bestsellers in the fantastical genres continue to recycle long-established idioms—starship captains, male or female, and their brave crews of loyal humans, aliens, and androids boldly going to very much the same places they have been for the last 40 years, sexy werewolves and vampires, mediaeval landscapes of magic and struggle against Dark Lords. The best of these traditional tales do enrich their time-honored plots and casts of characters with imaginative density—Lois McMaster Bujold's (1949–) Vorkosigan sequence and her more recent fantasies, for example—evincing a serious confrontation with the complexities of the real world. The commercial success of smooth familiarity, however, tends to ensure that any transrealist element, with its unexpected turns and potential for offensive shock, is minimal.

If there is any single theme recurring in transrealist writing, aside from the simple decision to throw much of the plot and representation of characters over to the machineries of the unconscious, it is an implicit interest in philosophical issues known technically as *epistemology* and *ontology*. The first asks how we know what we think we know about self, others, and world, while the second investigates the very nature of that world, that reality. During the twentieth century, it seemed increasingly obvious that our intuitive understanding of how things work is absurdly naive and often misleading. What we see as solid is more deeply a quantum haze of probabilities. The sky just overhead extends for billions of light years. The apparent unified mind looking at the deceptive world is itself an eerie composite, and its partitioned workings can be viewed in subtle brain scanners or modified by subtle pharmaceuticals. Questions of epistemology can tend, therefore, to whirl into gulfs and voids of ontological terror. To the extent that our knowledge of the world is constructed rather than simply given, do we have any certainty or security of that world's persistence, of its reliability, or indeed even of our own selves? These rather abstract concerns drove Dick's enjoyably crazy and sometimes incoherent plots, and they surface repeatedly in Rudy Rucker's work as well. Meanwhile, the same issues have been identified by the critic Fredric Jameson (1934–) as being the very hallmarks of postmodern textuality (see Jameson 1991, Broderick 1995), as well as the foundations for some of the best science fiction (Jameson 2005).

Contexts and Issues. Transrealism's approach to imaginative fiction might be mistaken for the banal advice "Write what you know." It also runs the risk of inviting the reader to commit the Intentional Fallacy, the error of supposing that the *meaning* of a text is identical to the author's *intention*. Rucker might tell us that he is basing his characters on himself and his friends, but we cannot be sure that this is so; transrealist fictions are not *romans à clef*. Nor should we really care which life experiences are infiltrated into the text. Still, some writers in and out of science fiction have fruitfully combined wild ideas with their own experience, creating a realistic thickening of the supposedly airy fantastic. "Geeky" writers soaking their culture's fantasies in the broth of their own idiosyncratic ways of construing the world will create work likely to unsettle and reward readers at large.

Here is a rudimentary example of how the process can work, from Rucker's extensive notes on his novel *Mathematicians in Love* (2006). Writing a scene, he was visualizing his characters as *The X-Files'* Fox Mulder and Dana Scully, but found the result "flat and dull. And I remembered the [transrealist] injunction that I've often given to beginning writers: 'Model your characters and situations on life, not on movies and TV shows!' . . . I thought of familiar human models for the agents, Michele G. . . . and my college friend Dick S. . . . and the agents got human and came alive" (Rucker, 2005). Unless we happen to be close friends of these particular people, it cannot help us to know this. But it does illuminate the process of an enriched, fantastical, transrealist creation.

Reception. Interpenetration of novelistic realism and the fantastical imagination has not been to everyone's taste. Thomas M. Disch's (1940–) novel *On Wings of Song* (1979) drew significantly upon his oppressive youth in mid-twentieth-century heartland America. Discussing the novel, Gerald Jonas noted that "except for an occasional *tour de force*, there is no room in science fiction and fantasy for the traditional novel of character. A science-fiction author may create characters to demonstrate how a change in technology or social organization alters the human condition; or he may invent entire exotic worlds to show how certain human traits—such as passion or greed—take different forms under different circumstances. But the focus is typically on the forces that shape character, rather than on the character development itself." It was precisely Disch's attention to character that dismayed Jonas: "Mr. Disch's primary interest is in delineating character. In a science-fiction context this is at first startling, but as a narrative strategy it is finally self-defeating." Perhaps, Jonas suggested, Disch chose the wrong model of realism. "Science fiction and fantasy have more in common with experimental fiction than with the novel of character" (1979).

It is certainly true that Rucker's transrealist work is very much closer to Beat experiment than to the traditional novel of manners. While only the last of Dick's books approach experimental fiction (*Valis* [1981] in particular), his blend of head-long delivery and down-to-earth characters, many of them blue-collar or frankly mad rather than bland starship admirals or galactic game players, was rare in the genre. Only one of Dick's mainstream novels of character was published during his life (*Confessions of a Crap-Artist,* 1975). Revealingly, his mainstream novels have seldom been deemed successful. It is interesting that while these novels seem even more directly based on the author's life and obsessions, it is the absence of the fantastical, the whimsical, and the terrifyingly ontological that reduces their value and impact. It is arguable that Dick's realist novels are insufficiently *trans*realist.

In Dick's non-SF novels—such as *Confessions, In Milton Lumpky Territory* (1985), and *The Broken Bubble* (1989)—all action springs from character, rather than from externalized menace (precognitive doom, robotic simulacra, slime molds from outer space, the crushing pressure of entropy itself). Yet that choice compromises the peculiar power of Dick's imagination, derived from his own odd relationship to reality. Perhaps this is why transrealism is not the narrative tool for all writers. A certain dislocation from consensus reality in the originating experience is needed, a detachment and even a somewhat delirious reworking that cannot be willed but needs to be known autonomously, from within.

There has been surprisingly limited formal discussion of transrealism to date. In 2005, Rucker and Broderick were guests of honor at the 26th Annual International Conference on the Fantastic in the Arts, Blurring the Boundaries: Transrealism and Other Movements.

Selected Authors. Since a considerable amount of "Golden Age" science fiction (roughly 1938–1950) was written by engineers or working scientists, often about characters solving engineering or scientific problems, it might seem that transrealism ought to have made an early appearance in such magazines as *Astounding Science Fiction*. Actually, the representation of such professions, concerns, and lifestyles in SF was significantly restricted by its adventure-story formats, or their comic parodies of life at the workbench under the tedious thumb of oppressive bureaucracies. In fact, it was not until Thomas Pynchon's (1937–) zany madcaps devastated these tropes that transrealist methods began to influence fictions written in the shadow of the technological age (*Gravity's Rainbow,* 1973), although there were predecessors such as G. C. Edmondson's (1922–1975) charming *F&SF* series in 1959–1964, which reported on the exploits of his "Mad Friend," employed at the Saucer Works (a version of Lockheed's "Skunk Works"). Subsequently, novels indebted to Pynchon, such as Robert Grossbach's *A Shortage of Engineers* (2001), brought the touch of transreal absurdity to the literary depiction of an absurd social order—in this case, a military-spec aerospace company on the order of Lockheed or Boeing. From an entirely different quarter, the supernatural fictions of Nobel laureate Isaac Bashevis Singer (1902–1991), written in Yiddish, were frequently drawn from his own life and circumstances. "The world is entirely an imaginary world," says his Gimpel the Fool (1957), "but it is only once removed from the true world." This somewhat transrealist perspective informs the more uncanny fiction of Marge Piercy (1936–), Joyce Carol Oates (1938–), Margaret Atwood (1939–), and many other non-genre writers.

There has always been an anarchic but somewhat autobiographical aspect to science fiction, portrayed as part of the background of *Rocket to the Morgue* (1942) by mystery and science-fiction writer Anthony Boucher (1911–1968), which features lightly disguised versions of Heinlein, Jack Williamson (1908–), L. Ron Hubbard (1911–1986), and other pulp writers, but this should not be mistaken for transrealism. In the 1950s, Wilson Tucker (1914–), a notable writer for science-fiction fanzines, used the names and physical descriptions of his friends and foes in such novels as *Wild Talent* (1954), a gambit now known as "tuckerization." More anarchic and genuinely transrealist, a quarter of a century later, was the Greenwich Village Trilogy (*The Butterfly Kid*, 1968, by Chester Anderson; *The Unicorn Girl,* 1969, by Michael Kurland, and *The Probability Pad,* 1970, by T. A. Waters), in which stoned hippies save the world from Blue Lobsters and other amusing aliens; the characters and their setting very faithfully represent the authors and their circle. It is a trope that Rucker would revive with a vengeance and a mathematical spin a further decade later in such books as *Spacetime Donuts* (1980) and *The Sex Sphere* (1983). The lyrical and snapping shaggy-dog surrealism of R. A. Lafferty (1914–2002) startled genre readers but is perhaps not quite transrealist; his drug of choice was alcohol.

The psychic and social upheavals of the 1950s and 1960s, often fueled by amphetamines and other mind- and mood-altering drugs, had their impact on Dick, especially in such books as *Time Out of Joint* (1960), *Martian Time-Slip* (1964), *Three Stigmata of Palmer Eldritch* (1964), *Now Wait for Last Year* (1968), *A Scanner Darkly* (1977), and especially *Valis* (1981), where he appears as Horselover Fat. Dick's central role in exemplifying and provoking the transrealist program (Rucker's "Transrealist Manifesto" was not published until a year after Dick's death in 1982) is explored in detail in Broderick, 2000. Highly intelligent and self-taught, Dick built an explanatory system from the philosophy of Immanuel Kant, Gnosticism, existential psychoanalysis, and a mix of acid-culture theories of mind and reality. These concerns predate the 1960s: *The Cosmic Puppets* (1953) stages a small-town conflict between embodied Zoroastrian divinities Ahriman and Ormazd, who transform daily reality into symbol. In *Eye in the Sky* (1955), a nuclear accident disrupts the local reality of eight characters whose shared world fluxes as they struggle for dominance. Alternatively, as a Dickian protagonist's personal construct of the world decays, the true essence of the world is revealed, often dreadfully. The transrealism in Dick's work reveals the fantastical transformations of his daily, if unusually eccentric, life-world. He was a writer drenched in SF imagery, where even in his bleakest and most intensely lyrical moments he found the perfect correlative to his inner states. His sometimes bleak, much-married life is echoed in the refrains of his life's work: doppelgangers, simulacra, apparent humans who turn out to be "electric ants," and programmed constructs. Arguably it was exactly his mastery of transreality that spared him the final banal temptation of guruhood. Our world, Dick assured himself, was already a collage, a superposition, of all possible worlds.

The feminist fiction of James Tiptree Jr. (Alice Sheldon, 1915–1987), beneath its male disguise, is often powerfully transreal, transforming the appalling confrontations of her life into unyielding science fiction. Sheldon was the daughter of widely traveled anthropologists, and worked in military intelligence. "Young Alice saw the genital mutilation of Kikuyu women, babies dying in the streets of Calcutta, a riot in Shanghai that was the start of the Chinese Revolution. She heard the screams of a man being killed for the cannibal pot. She even saw a crucifixion: 'The men had been stripped, tortured, tied to posts, and left to perish in the sun. . . . Auschwitz—My Lai—etc. . . . did not *surprise* me one bit, later on.'" (Scholz, 2006). Critic John Clute (1940–) notes: "Tiptree/Sheldon's life very deeply shaped what superficially might have looked like simply another competent set of iterations of familiar SF tropes. What was miraculous was how professionally she was able to fit her interior intensities and drives into the mold of those seeming conventional story types, ruthlessly infusing every great story she wrote with those extraordinary intensities, which cannot be copied." The same might be said of black novelist Octavia Butler (1947–2006), whose SF fables transduce the tragedies of poverty and slavery. That dislocation need not be uniquely strange, though. Russ achieved a quite terrifying intensity in *The Female Man* (1975), her important feminist utopia, by contrasting several invented alternative worlds to her own stifling middle-class experience growing up in the 1950s. Joe Haldeman's (1943–) own history, the bruising and morally conflicted experience of an American soldier badly wounded in Vietnam, made *The Forever War* (1974) stand out even in a period of striking technical advances by science-fiction writers such as Roger Zelazny (1937–1995) and Disch. On the other hand, two metafictional works that describe the anguished disintegration of science-fiction hack writers—Barry N. Malzberg's (1939–) *Gather in the Hall of the Planets* (as K. M. O'Donnell, 1971) and *Herovit's World* (1973)—are perhaps not transrealist so much as satirical or parodic, however revelatory.

Delany's early fiction from the 1960s—while less immediately identifiable as realistic, let alone autobiographical—is vividly coded with his experience as a black, gay man in America. In his early masterpiece, *Dhalgren* (1975), his genius flowered fully in a transrealist work set in a deconstructed cityscape where history is fallible, sun and moon(s) are unreliable, and the central figure is a possibly deranged amnesiac and dyslexic poet. Not until his non-science fictional *The Mad Man* (1996) would this confronting blend of scrupulously observed and somewhat biographical realism and highly disturbing perverse fantasy gel completely. Ray Davis notes: "In Delany's earlier porn, appalling acts are executed by dehumanized monsters. In *The Mad Man,* perversion, like other violations of taboo, is instead a profoundly humanizing act of courage" (in Sallis, 1996). So too is the candid, lacerating, and funny soul-baring of a failing writer in Jamil Nasir's *Distance Haze* (2000), in which the direct mystical experience of the divine is first simulated/stimulated and then obliterated by neurological engineering.

It might seem that transrealist work must be excessive to some degree—that since transgression is part of its definition, it must be offensive, even indecent, as well. By the standards of reigning power and convention, this might seem to be so. Jack Kerouac (1922–1969) and William Burroughs (1914–1997), whose work altered the course of mid-century U.S. fiction as radically as that of Ernest Hemingway (1899–1961) a generation earlier, spoke truth not so much to power as to the illusion of a safely domestic, self-simulating, shocking adventures from the comfort of an armchair. Yet the shocking devices of one period are the commonplaces of another. The endless road peeling away in front of Kerouac's windscreen was replicated in the scroll of paper nearly 35 meters long upon which he typed *On the Road* (1958); Rucker emulated that method a generation later when writing *All the Visions* (1991). Today, by contrast, almost all writers do just that, without any shock of release, on the infinite virtual page of the word processor screen. What was also unpeeled in this kind of radically autobiographical writing was the experiencing self, harried away from comfort by ruthless self-examination and crazy bursts of invention and lyricism. In a similar line of descent is Hunter S. Thompson (1937–2005), whose hysterical and bitingly insightful prose (notably *Fear and Loathing in Las Vegas,* 1971) is better understood as transreal rather than satirical or simply mannered, unlike the New Journalism of the 1960s and 1970s in general.

Thompson names himself explicitly as his protagonist, and this is one explicit marker of transrealism. J. G. Ballard's (1930–) *Crash* (1974) is narrated by James Ballard, and in *The Empire of the Sun* (1984) his child-self surrogate is Jim. Rucker sometimes calls his central character "Rudy Rucker," as in the recent *Saucer Wisdom* (1999), presenting itself mockingly as the true story of his mad friend Frank Shook, and Shook's adventures with saucer-borne multidimensional time travelers. In *Gaudeamus* (2004), prolific SF writer John Barnes (1957–), former assistant professor of theatre and communication in a small Colorado college, narrates very much in his own person a tale reported to him in a number of broken-off cliff-hanger segments by his mad friend Travis Bismark, another traveler in a flying saucer. But is this narrator, who has the same job and the same former wife as Barnes, a fully rounded representation of the author? Probably not, but it does not matter, because the weariness, the venom, the ambition, the bleak humor of the narrator are plainly motivated by reality, and speak to us for that reason more urgently than many of Barnes's more perfunctory entertainments.

Yet the transrealist prescription or diagnosis does not require excess. Justina Robson's (1968–) *Silver Screen* (2005) is packed with detail and naturalistic rendering of character that evades SF's expectations of melodrama and spectacular setting or event. For all their exotic idiosyncrasy and special gifts, Robson's super-smart characters are flattened into a sort of desperate ordinariness. A proponent of slipstream, she suggests that it "strives to duplicate the complexities of actual experiences by allowing experience to be paramount and letting everything else serve a purpose." The parallels with transrealism are clear. Her narrator seems at least in part transrealist, drawn to an unusual degree from the daily grind, irritations, opacities of her author's ordinary experience, fantasy enriched in its artful and persuasive rendering by the miseries and rewards of life here and now. Certainly this is true of the transrealist fiction of Jeffery Ford (1955–), one of the most talented current fantasy writers. In "Botch Town" (2006), for example, a coming-of-age novella blending autobiography and an uncanny mix of fantasy and horror, a facsimile town of plywood and clay in the narrator's basement echoes and then manipulates events in the already shadowy exterior suburban world. Thus, reality enriches and activates the fantastic imagination, *and vice versa,* of the transrealist artist.

Nor is transrealism necessarily marketed as genre. A best-selling romance, Audrey Niffenegger's (1963–) *The Time Traveler's Wife* (2003), is an elaborate time-twisting invention, a realist novel grounded in a fantastical Vonnegutian premise—that some people can come unstuck in time—a fantasy enriched by copious detail drawn from the real world of the author. What distinguishes *The Time Traveler's Wife* from, say, a traditional science-fiction entertainment like Poul Anderson's (1926–2001) *There Will Be Time* (1972), is its very ordinariness, its refusal, by and large, to use this paranormal irruption as an opportunity to showcase the time traveler's technical prowess, political *nous* or trans-historic destiny. Niffenegger has commented, "It's something that bugs me about actual science fiction, this effort to provide all the answers and make everything work out very neatly" (interview, 2003). But of course her novel *is* "actual science fiction," although more than *actual science fiction,* her novel is *actual transrealism.* The same can be said of Jonathan Lethem's (1964–) *The Fortress of Solitude* (2003), a supernaturally heightened autobiographical tale of growing up Jewish and white—with magic gifts of flight and invisibility—in a black part of Brooklyn in 1972. Philip Roth's (1933–) blend of autobiography, invention, and an alternative history of a near-Nazi America in the 1950s, *The Plot Against America* (2004), is a transreal transformation.

Paul Di Filippo (1954–), in a buoyant appreciation of Rucker, captured the key moves of transrealism: "as a unique individual, each of us must report back as faithfully as we can, sharing our insights in whatever artistic modes best suit us. . . ." Whenever he got stuck while writing, he "just 'twinked' Rudy (. . . a coinage . . . meaning 'to run a mental simulation of an individual on your personal wetware') and instantly all roadblocks vanished. I even tried to follow Rudy's scheme of 'transreally' incorporating bits and pieces of my autobiography into *Fuzzy Dice.* Transrealism being, in Rudy's memorable phrase, 'writing just like yourself, only more so.'"

Transrealist writing is founded, finally, in an insistence that empathy, or a suffering awareness of its absence, must suffuse the fantastic, supplanting rote blueprint or egotistic wish-fulfillment. It goes beyond stipulating cozy formulae about our world (traditional naturalist realism), or even asking how it is we know that world (the modernist, epistemological project). Situated in the complexity, the psychic and social density, of observed life, transrealism takes an extra step into systematic, exploratory doubt—the step intrinsic to postmodern science—and confronts the experiential varieties of all possible worlds: the liberating project of radically *ontological* fiction.

Bibliography

Broderick, Damien. *Reading by Starlight: Postmodern Science Fiction.* London: Routledge, 1995.

———. *X, Y, Z, T: Dimensions of Science Fiction,* Holicong, PA: Borgo Press, 2004.

Davis, Ray. "Delany's Dirt." 1996. http://www.pseudopodium.org/kokonino/dd4.html

Di Filippo, Paul. "Just Like Himself, Only More So." 2003. http://www.infinityplus.co.uk/nonfiction/pdif_rudy.htm

Jameson, Fredric. *Archaeologies of the Future: The Desire Called Utopia and Other Science Fictions.* New York: Verso, 2005.

———. *Postmodernism, or, The Cultural Logic of Late Capitalism.* Duke University Press, 1991.

Jonas, Gerald. "Science fiction." *New York Times.* 28 Oct. 1979: pp. 15–16.

Linklater, Richard. 2006. "Infintely Improbable." http://news.ansible.co.uk/a229.html.

Miéville, China. Qtd. in "Writer's Workshop." 2003. http://www.darkecho.com/darkecho/workshop/terms.html

Niffenegger, Audrey. *The Time Traveler's Wife.* New York: Harvest, 2004.

———, interview by Veronica Bond. "An Interview with Audrey Niffenegger," http://www.bookslut.com/features/2003_12_001158.php

Philip K. Dick online bibliography: http://www.philipkdick.com/works_novels.html

Sallis, James. ed. *Ash of Stars: On the Writings of Samuel R. Delany.* Jackson, MS: University Press of Mississippi, 1996.

Scholz, Carter. "Invisible man." Review of *James Tiptree, Jr.: The Double Life of Alice B. Sheldon,* by Julie Philips. New York: St. Martin's Press, 2006. http://www.bookforum.com/scholz.html

Sherman, Delia. "An Introduction to Interstitial Arts: Life on the Border." 2003. http://www.interstitialarts.org/what/intro_toIA.html

Sterling, Bruce. "Slipstream." 2005. http://www.eff.org/Misc/Publications/Bruce_Sterling/Catscan_columns/catscan.05

Thompson, Hunter S. *Fear and Loathing in Las Vegas: A Savage Journey to the Heart of the American Dream.* New York: Random House, 1971.

Westfahl, Gary. "Homo aspergerus: Evolution Stumbles Forward." March 6 2006. http://www.locusmag.com/2006/Features/Westfahl_HomoAspergerus.html

Further Reading

Rucker, Rudy. "A Transrealist Manifesto." *The Bulletin of the Science Fiction Writers of America* 82 (Winter 1983). Reprinted in *Transreal!* WCS Books, 1991, and *Seek!* Four Walls Eight Windows, 1999. Online with other essays on writing at: http://www.rudyrucker.com/writing/; Broderick, Damien. *Transrealist Fiction: Writing in the Slipstream of Science.* Connecticut: Greenwood Press, 2000.

DAMIEN BRODERICK

TRAVEL WRITING

Definition. Travel writing takes many forms, but the genre is generally associated with nonfiction narratives that recount, from a first-person perspective, the author's experience of a journey. Unlike a travel guidebook, which offers practical advice about sightseeing, dining, and lodging options, and which presupposes the reader's intent to visit the location described, a travel narrative is a literary form that reflects an author's personal perspective of a place. Attempts to define the genre more precisely are challenged by its hybrid qualities. For example, when describing the genre in an issue of *Granta* devoted to travel writing, editor Bill Buford observes that it is "the beggar of literary forms: it borrows from the memoir, reportage, and, most important, the novel. It is, however, a narrative told in the first person, authenticated by lived experience" (Buford 1984, 7). In addition to sharing traits with other genres, travel writing is remarkably varied in length, scope, style, tone, and subject matter. While some authors are also novelists or journalists, travel writers are as likely to be naturalists, historians, scientists, philosophers, or chefs, among other occupations. Inevitably, some writers make better traveling companions than others, but the diversity of travel writing has greatly contributed to the genre's enduring popularity.

History. Travel writing dates back to ancient times, when people first began recording stories of movement from one place to another. The genre emerged from heroic epics such as Homer's *Odyssey,* but accounts of exploration and pilgrimage throughout history also constitute early forms of travel writing. The genre developed significantly when improved modes of transportation allowed people to travel more frequently and widely, with less hardship and danger. In the eighteenth century, the British upper class flocked to the European Continent for educational Grand Tours via the coach, but the arrival of rail travel in the nineteenth century paved the way for mass tourism. In *The Norton Book of Travel,* Paul Fussell describes the nineteenth and early twentieth centuries as the "heyday of travel and travel writing": "It was the Bourgeois Age that defined the classic modern idea of travel as an excitement and a treat and that established the literary genre of the 'travel book'" (Fussell 1987, 271, 273). The period produced an outpouring of travel sketches, diaries, and guidebooks, as well as more artfully crafted narratives by authors since recognized as important literary figures. While the British are frequently credited with establishing travel writing as we know it today, American writers such as Mark Twain, Henry James, and Henry David Thoreau contributed significantly to the burgeoning genre in the nineteenth century. British explorers, however, must be acknowledged for popularizing a subgenre of travel writing that captured a reading audience around the world in the late nineteenth and early twentieth centuries. Polar exploration produced gripping accounts of treks to the ends of the earth, including Apsley Cherry-Garrard's masterpiece *The Worst Journey in the World,* which recounts British explorer Robert Falcon Scott's doomed quest for the South Pole as well as the author's calamitous experiences as a member of the expedition to Antarctica. Cherry-Garrard's memoir, published in 1922, remains a landmark of exploration literature from a period that evidenced heated international competition to reach and claim the most remote places on the planet. As a subgenre of travel writing, polar literature is marked by a consistent focus on endurance and survival. Those who lived to tell the tale of hauling sledges across the ice, falling into crevasses, and facing diminishing or non-existent food supplies, bequeathed narratives about heroic travel that no longer seems possible, aerospace achievements notwithstanding. In *Abroad: British Literary Traveling Between the Wars,* Fussell elegizes the 1920s and 1930s as travel writing's finest hour, characterizing the post-WWII world as unsuitable for worthwhile travel or travel writing: "The going was good for only twenty years, and after the war all that remained was jet tourism among the ruins, resulting in phenomena like the appalling pollution of the Mediterranean and the Aegean" (Fussell 1980, 226). Although Fussell's concerns about the effects of tourism on the environment are shared by many travel writers today, his implicit prediction of the demise of good travel writing has proven premature. After a lull of a few decades, the genre proved its endurance in the 1980s, a decade witnessing a resurgence of interest in travel writing. Random House began publishing its successful Vintage Departure series of travel narratives, while other publishers began reprinting classic travel books. New travel writing appeared with more frequency in bookstores as well as in magazines, including literary magazines such as *Granta,* which devoted three separate issues to the genre in the 1980s. Travel writing continues to flourish, its status aided by readers' increased interest in nonfiction in general, but the genre endures due to its ability to capture, reflect, and sometimes critique the complicated and diverse world in which we live.

Trends and Themes. Bookstore shelves now sag under the weight of new titles in the genre, many of which reveal how travel writers employ accounts of journeys in order to explore subjects or concerns that extend beyond the actual geographical context for such investigations. The flexible genre encompasses narratives focused on adventure, romantic relationships, disastrous trips, or dozens of other topics.

Publishers are perhaps most responsible for one distinct and recent trend in the genre—the numerous books on the market that recount an author's extended stay in another country, usually somewhere in Europe, often while he or she renovates an old house and acclimates to the surrounding culture. The success of Frances Mayes's *Under the Tuscan Sun* (1996), in which the narrator, a poet and gourmet cook, describes the pleasures of living in the Italian countryside, prompted a spate of similar books. Other writers lean toward what may be labeled *meta-* or *anti-travel writing*, narratives that explore traveling theoretically or philosophically and that conclude with implicit arguments for "armchair" travel or for simply staying at home. Such is the case with Alain de Botton's *The Art of Travel* (2002), in which the author suggests applying the receptivity of a "traveling mind-set" to our own locales, which then might become as interesting as "the high mountain passes and butterfly-filled jungles of Humboldt's South America" (Botton 2002, 242). Readers unfamiliar with the genre may reasonably expect travel writing to focus on travel—the actual movement from one place to another—but many contemporary writers suggest that the inner journey is as important as the outer one. To varying degrees, travel writers record the self-exploration that traveling often precipitates. As Casey Blanton observes, most contemporary travel writers see themselves as exiles: "A search for authenticity, wholeness, and meaning often drives their journeys as it did for travel writers in the past (Blanton 2002, xiv).

Travel writer Mary Morris argues that women writers are particularly likely to value the inner landscape, "the beholder as significant as the beheld" (Morris 1993, xvii), but many scholars take issue with such sweeping generalizations about gender. Kristi Siegel, for example, acknowledges that gender affects genre, but argues in regard to travel writing that "it is nearly impossible to construct a set of common-alities that would cut across lines of race and class" (Siegel 2004, 5). Morris's obser-vation, however, proffered in response to what she perceived as a neglect of attention to women's travel writing, is supported by the theme of self-discovery that emerges in a number of contemporary travel narratives by women, even though the internal landscape is by no means the exclusive province of female travel writers. In any case, women are producing travel narratives with increasing frequency in comparison to decades past. In 2005, Travelers' Tales published the inaugural edition of *The Best Women's Travel Writing,* but the press boasts seventeen collec-tions of women's travel writing since its first title on the subject appeared in 1995. Additionally, women now contribute to the subgenre of adventure travel writing, traditionally associated with male writers and generally characterized by risk-taking and physical challenge. Holly Morris, for example, recounts hunting for wild boar in Borneo and climbing the Matterhorn in *Adventure Divas: Searching the Globe for a New Kind of Heroine* (2005), describing her stories as "estro-charged globe-trotting" (Morris 2005, ix).

As contemporary travel writing is so richly varied, many publishers now offer anthologies or series focused on specific kinds of journeys, thereby creating addi-tional categories in the genre. The Crown Journeys Series, for example, includes titles by well-regarded novelists as well as by popular authors, each of whom describes a walk, or walks, in a particular city or circumscribed area. The nature of the series suggests the rewards of unhurried and grounded travel, in contrast to the global crisscrossing of adventure seekers. In one of the series' representative titles, *Time's Magpie: A Walk in Prague* (2004), Myla Goldberg describes wandering around the old European city, immersed in its history and attuned to the small pleas-ures that such leisurely travel affords. As the Crown Journeys Series indicates, an increasing number of novelists have become travel writers, perhaps because the flexibility of the genre and its familiar narrative form is so amenable to the devices and techniques of fiction.

Contexts and Issues. After many centuries of exploration, and in an era of increas-ing globalization and rapid development in electronic communication, the world today seems smaller and more familiar than it once appeared. Certainly, there are fewer and fewer places in the world that are unmapped or that have not already served as the subject of television shows or of previously published travel narratives. With the tourism industry thriving due to greater mobility in general, those seeking the unbeaten path are likely to be disappointed. Contemporary travel writers respond to such circumstances in varying ways: by choosing unusual forms of transportation to provide a new or distinct perspective of a place, by opting to remap or retrace the path of a predecessor, or by employing travel as a means of investigating particular social and cultural issues. Environmental concerns are consistently addressed in contemporary travel writing, particularly in narratives focused on places that were once considered exotic or remote. The inroads of tourism have been greatly responsible for damaging fragile ecological systems and have unavoidably altered ways of life in traditional cultures. While travel writers tend to distinguish their motivations and journeys from those of tourists, the distinction is problematic. As Patrick Holland and Graham Huggan observe, contemporary travel writers, "whatever their status or institutional affiliation, are continuing to provide sterling service to tourism—about to become the world's largest industry—even when they might imagine themselves to be its most strident adversaries" (Holland and Huggan 1998, 3). The seemingly vexed relationship between travel writers and tourism bears similarity to the relationship of the ethnographer and his or her subject in anthropological writing. Like ethnographers, travel writers describe people and their societies and cultures, and thus questions about the textual representation of "others" are frequently raised in regard to both forms of writing. As Holland and Huggan note, "Travel writers and anthropologists both occupy positions of power—granted largely by the economic differences between their societies and the societies they visit—that allow them to establish an often unwarranted authority over their subjects" (Holland and Huggan 1998, 12). Although travel writing and ethnography are forms of nonfiction, neither can make claim to absolute objectivity, for cultural description always reflects the writer's perspective. Accordingly, travel writers may strive for veracity in their narratives, but their field of vision is inevitably limited or affected by codes of class, race, gender, and culture. As a form of autobiography or memoir, travel writing is personal by definition. Practitioners in the genre must balance reader expectations for truthful reportage with the artistic demands of creative nonfiction. As Robert Root explains, "All literary genres essentially create representations of reality and require craft and design and discovery and process, but nonfiction is unique in that it alone is required by virtually unstated definition to apply those strategies and techniques to something that already exists" (Root 2003, 246).

Reception. Throughout its history, travel writing has had credibility problems, in part because historical exploration accounts were often notoriously unreliable, but also because the genre has traditionally been viewed as having less literary value than the "three genres" of fiction, poetry, and drama. Academics in the twentieth-century began to study historical travel literature as a viable subject for cultural studies, and the genre grew in significance with the rise of women's studies and theoretical spatial studies. Contemporary travel writing, however, received scant scholarly attention until the resurgence of the genre in the 1980s. Accordingly, initial studies argued for wider recognition of travel writing's merits. For example, in his introduction to *Temperamental Journeys: Essays on the Modern Literature of Travel,* Michael Kowalewski expressed frustration with "the venerable tradition of condescending to travel books as a second-rate literary form" (Kowalewski 1992, 2). *Temperamental Journeys,* presented as "the first collection to focus exclusively on twentieth-century travel writing," was soon followed by a number of scholarly studies devoted to contemporary examples in the genre, now a respected subject for academic study (Kowalewski 1992, 7).

Travel writing also continues to hold the interest of general reading audiences. Since 2000, Houghton Mifflin has published its annual anthology *The Best American Travel Writing,* each volume showcasing essay-length travel narratives previously published in well-regarded magazines such as *The New Yorker, The Atlantic Monthly, National Geographic Traveler,* and *Outside.* Series editor Jason Wilson explains why such literature deserves attention in his foreword to the first volume in the series:

> Travel writing is always about a specific moment in time. The writer imbues that moment with everything that he or she has experienced, observed, read, lived, bringing all of his or her talent to bear on it. When focused on that one moment, great travel writing can teach us something about the world that no other genre can. Perhaps travel writing's foremost lesson is this: we may never walk this way again, and even if we do, we may never be the same people as we are right now. Most important, the world we travel though will never be the same place again. This is why travel writing matters. (Wilson 200, xvi)

Selected Authors. Paul Theroux has published more than a dozen travel narratives since he began writing them in the 1970s, making him one of the best-known travel writers of the last four decades. For this author, the journey itself—the movement, the work, and the pleasures of going somewhere—is of greater value and interest than the destination reached. Thus train travel, especially, serves him as a means of vision, a particular way of seeing the world that makes him receptive to the insights afforded by constant movement. Theroux describes journeys by rail as "the purest form of travel"; "everything else—planes especially—is *transfer,* your journey beginning when you arrive" (*Sunrise with Seamonsters,* 126, 128). The four-month railroad odyssey to the Far East recounted in *The Great Railway Bazaar: By Train through Asia* (1975) exemplifies Theroux's philosophy of travel but also the manner in which his preferred mode of transportation serves the writer as well as the traveler: "Train travel animated my imagination and usually gave me solitude to order and write my thoughts: I traveled easily in two directions, along the level rails while Asia flashed changes at the window, and at the interior rim of a private world of memory and languages" (Theroux 1975, 166). Through such passages, *The Great Railway Bazaar* established the author's predilection for solitary travel and for personal reflection about the act and art of writing. His work often reminds readers that travel writing is a trip twice taken: the traveler moves through interior and exterior landscapes, recording images and observations that will later be transformed and shaped into a cohesive narrative. A self-proclaimed wanderer and a successful novelist, Theroux believes travel and writing are congruent enterprises:

> The nearest thing to writing a novel is traveling in a strange country. Travel is a creative act—not simply loafing and inviting your soul, but feeding the imagination, accounting for each fresh wonder, memorizing and moving on. The discoveries the traveler makes in broad daylight—the curious problems of the eye he solves—resemble those that thrill and sustain a novelist in his solitude. (Theroux 1985, 140)

Accordingly, *The Great Railway Bazaar* reminds readers that travel writing is more than mere documentation; rather, it is imaginative transformation, aided by memory and language, of lived experience into words on a page. Theroux is careful, though, to acknowledge that he is less free to invent in his travel writing than in his fiction; the nonfiction genre demands truthful eyewitness. In the narrative's conclusion, he states that he has learned that "the difference between travel writing and fiction is the difference between recording what the eye sees and discovering what the imagination knows" (Theroux 1975, 342). As Elton Glaser observes, Theroux's travel books, "like many of the twentieth century's most celebrated literary works, come with a built-in analysis of their own composition" (Glaser 1989, 193). Theroux's allegiance to accuracy and honesty is also underscored in the book's final sentences. After expressing pleasure at the prospect of rereading the notebooks kept during his trip, he cites the first words that appear in them, which also serve as the opening words of *The Great Railway Bazaar*. In addition to conveying the circular nature of travel—as one must usually return home—the ending implicitly promises readers a travel narrative created from carefully recorded observations.

In his study of the author, Samuel Coale states that Theroux is almost Puritan in "his precise faith in language, in the ability of words to conjure up a place, a people, a continent, and attach significant meaning to them, to make them ultimately signify" (Coale 1997). Focusing on Theroux's "Americanness," Coale views the author's travel writing as faithful to his heritage, particularly to romantic notions of the individual self: "The American myth shimmers with notions of self-renewal, rebirth, self-made men, . . . the lone self which confronts a wilderness or alien landscape and conquers it in terms of his own perceptions or his masterful technological skills" (Coale 1997). In *The Old Patagonian Express: By Train through the Americas* (1979), Theroux's second and perhaps most highly regarded travel narrative, he confesses that he is "taking a little-known route through Central America . . . made for lonely travel," but he also argues that "travel is at its best a solitary enterprise" (Theroux 1979, 121, 168). One of the ironies of the book surfaces in its stories of encounters with fellow passengers who are sometimes welcomed as company but who are just as often regarded as annoyances, even as the author presents himself as a solo traveler. Other people distract him from his writing and interfere with his perceptions. As Glaser notes, Theroux "takes great pains to convince us that he is a traveler in the grand tradition of philosopher observers, set far apart from the other characters who temporarily share his journey on the open road" (Glaser 1989, 197).

Theroux's persistent desire for solitude often makes his narrative persona appear self-absorbed. Throughout *The Old Patagonian Express,* he retreats from the imposition of his fellow travelers by seeking refuge in books. His reading material often reflects his mood or perspective, as is seen in his choice of Ambrose Bierce's *The Devil's Dictionary,* "a grimly humorous book of self-congratulatory cynicism," Twain's *Pudd'nhead Wilson,* in which Theroux inscribes "No privacy, no relief," and Poe's *Narrative of Arthur Gordon Pym,* which Theroux describes as "a nightmare journey," a phrase that also captures the author's perception of his passage through Costa Rica (Theroux 1979, 60, 79, 192). If writing and traveling are consonant occupations in their conduciveness to creativity, reading and traveling are similarly parallel in their unerring progress to a final destination. Poe's novel, a narrative that also recounts a journey south toward the Pole, features a hero who survives various catastrophes and terrors only to end up drifting by canoe in a blank nothingness of open water. Like Poe's suffering survivor, Theroux concludes his journey only to stare into the vast and empty space of Patagonian desert: "The nothingness itself, a beginning for some intrepid traveler, was an ending for me" (Theroux 1979, 404). Although he attempts to transform the experience into a paradoxical discovery of his existence, he concludes his narrative on a dark note, as if he has reached the limits of travel's rewards—and the limits of language itself—as much as he has reached the end of the actual road.

While Theroux has been praised as "one of America's most engaging travel writers" (Rose 2000, 17), he has also earned a reputation as a curmudgeon and cranky expatriate. In her review of Theroux's *Fresh Air Fiend: Travel Writings, 1985-2000* (2000), Lucretia Stewart observes that the author "demonstrates his mastery of the rapid scattergun approach to invective, devised, it would appear, specifically for the purpose of cramming in as many insults as possible into the shortest possible space" (Stewart 2000, 32). Theroux jokingly acknowledges his reputation as a "dyspeptic" in an interview with Dwight Garner, but he explains that critics misinterpret his irony as grumpiness:

> I think that, particularly in travel writing, we are used to sweetness and light. I decided very early on—more than 25 years ago when I published my first travel book, *The Great Railway Bazaar*—that a lot of travel writing was merely like a postcard saying: "Everything is fine. Wish you were here." But what I realized is that travel is a lot of misery and delay. (Garner 1996)

But many contemporary travel writers take a lighter approach to the travails of travel. Bill Bryson's witty, irreverent, and sometimes wiseacre observations about human foibles and cultural idiosyncrasies have made him one of America's most popular travel writers. Born in Des Moines, Iowa, he spent much of his adult life in England, where his first travel books, *The Lost Continent: Travels in Small-Town America* (1989) and *Neither Here Nor There: Travels in Europe* (1991), garnered a wide and enthusiastic readership. In *The Lost Continent,* he recounts a return to his native land, where he visits 38 states in his mother's aging Chevrolet and attempts to duplicate the family vacations of his youth. Divided into two parts, East and West, the book follows the author's trips to many backwater towns and tacky tourist traps, usually portrayed with a great deal of comedy. As one reviewer observes of another book, Bryson's writing provokes "body-racking, tear-inducing" laughter, through humor that falls "somewhere between the one-liner genius of Dave Barry and the narrative brilliance of David Sedaris" (Jennings 2006, 9). Such wit is evident in *The Lost Continent* when the author interweaves his narrative with memories of journeys led by his father, portrayed as a cranky task-master who forced the Bryson family to endure disastrous camping trips:

> And afterwards, in a silent car filled with bitterness and unquenched basic needs, we would mistakenly turn off the highway and end up in some no-hope hamlet with a name like Draino, Indiana, or Tapwater, Missouri, and get a room in the only hotel in town, the sort of run-down place where if you wanted to watch TV it meant you had to sit in a lobby and share a cracked leatherette sofa with an old man with big sweat circles under his arms. (Bryson 1989, 11)

Bryson writes with a dual-perspective in *The Lost Continent,* that of the insider and native son with unquestionable knowledge of his homeland's favorite pastimes, but also that of the expatriate who, aligned with his fellow Britons, is alternately amused and disturbed by the social practices, or intellectual shortcomings, of American life. While visiting Auburn University, for example, he complains about the absence of a single decent bookstore in a town with 20,000 students, but he balances his barbs with self-deprecating anecdotes: "In my day, the principal concerns of university students were sex, smoking dope, rioting and learning. Learning was something you did when the first three weren't available, but at least you did it." (Bryson 1989, 72). Bryson's humor makes *The Lost Continent* a very entertaining travelogue, but attentive readers will note that the author uses the occasion of his homecoming to proffer some sharp criticism of American life and practices. In describing a visit to the Great Smokey Mountains National Park in Tennessee, for example, he observes the squalor just beyond the park. Bryson is equally disturbed by American television newscasts (during which grisly murders are recounted casually), by the poverty and violence of so many cities, and by the vastness of the country that is so big "it just absorbs disasters" (Bryson 1989, 262). He reserves his harshest comments for Americans' sense of privilege, their all-consuming quest for material comforts, and their disregard for other cultures. "When you grow up in America," he observes, "you are inculcated from the earliest age with the belief—no, the *understanding*—that America is the richest and most powerful nation on earth because God likes us best" (Bryson 1989, 271). As the book progresses, *The Lost Continent* becomes tinged with melancholy, despite Bryson's efforts to offset the darker observations with adolescent memories of better times. One fully expects the author to conclude the account of his nationwide trek with a claim about not being able to go home again—the America of his past seems lost to him, as the title of the book suggests—but Bryson opts for a more positive ending, perhaps reluctant to betray his roots completely.

In *Neither Here Nor There,* Bryson captures the experience of the contemporary tourist through a narrative about journeys to more than a dozen countries in Europe. In casting a wider net than in *The Lost Continent,* he shifts from the narrative unity afforded by commentary on one country to a dizzying series of national portraits often marked by stereotypes. Bryson partly appeases potential charges of cultural reductionism by employing exaggerations that no one would be expected to take seriously. Thus, "Germans are flummoxed by humor, the Swiss have no concept of fun, the Spanish think there is nothing at all ridiculous about eating dinner at midnight, and the Italians should never, ever have been let in on the invention of the motorcar" (Bryson 1991, 35). The broad humor did not appeal to all critics, but some, such as Dervla Murphy, described it as distinctive, "depending on his cunning use of flamboyant exaggerations, grotesque but always successful metaphors and the deft juxtapositions of incongruous images—the whole presented in a style that boldly veers from laid-back colloquial American to formal clean-cut English" (28). In the decade following the publication of *Neither Here Nor There,* Bryson produced five more books that secured his reputation as a comic travel writer, although he has become equally known for books about the English language. As one critic observes, "What makes Bryson the most entertaining and interesting travel writer around is his singular facility to fashion a unique whole from historical facts, topographical observations, and geographical ramblings" (Maxwell 2000, 118). Bryson's consistently humorous approach to travel writing makes him a distinctive voice amidst his contemporaries working in the genre.

Like Bryson, Tony Horowitz, a Pulitzer Prize-winning journalist, aims to enter-tain readers in his travel books, but his most recent work exhibits more ambitious goals. In *Blue Latitudes: Boldly Going Where Captain Cook has Gone Before* (2002), he attempts to replicate Cook's epic voyages in a quest to understand the man who redrew the map of the world in the eighteenth century. Horowitz credits Cook with undertaking the first voyage of scientific discovery, with influencing the Western world's perception and understanding of unfamiliar and exotic cultures, and, for better and for worse, with opening up many new territories for subsequent explorers and empires. Inspired by Cook's journals, the author sets forth in the explorer's wake, initially serving as a volunteer aboard a replica of Cook's ship and subsequently resorting to more modern modes of travel, in a quest that takes him all over the South Seas and other parts of the globe. Part history, part travel narrative, *Blue Latitudes* underscores the limitations of modern travel:

> I'd gone where Cook went, but I couldn't share his experience. The problem wasn't simply that I traveled by jet, rather than by wooden ship, to lands that had changed utterly since Cook's day. It was also that I carried an image of every place I went before I got there. This was the curse of modern travel: it was like reading a book after you've already seen the movie adaptation. (Horowitz 2002, 222)

Horowitz's journeys to Tahiti, Alaska, Hawaii, and other locations visited by Cook, however, are recounted with humor as well as wistfulness, mostly due to the presence of his traveling companion Roger, an Australian who serves as comic foil to the author throughout much of the book. While Roger resorts to drinking at any trying leg of the trip, Horowitz becomes increasingly dismayed, and often irritated, by signs of Cook's tarnished reputation. He learns that the explorer is reviled in some countries, viewed as a wicked imperialist, and that his memory and legacy have been neglected even in England, Cook's native land. "In remembering the man," he writes, "the world had lost the balance and nuance I so admired in Cook's own writing about those he encountered" (Horowitz 2002, 296). *Blue Latitudes* seemingly seeks to restore the balance, moving between historical and contemporary perspectives of Cook in order to recalibrate the man's legacy. Without denying the fine line between exploration and exploitation, Horowitz pays tribute to Cook as one of the last great explorers: "In his wake, other discoverers filled in the few remaining blanks on the map. Eventually there wasn't anyplace left on earth where no man had gone before" (Horowitz 2002, 443).

Travel writers' recognition of exhausted space is often consonant with their obser-vations about exhausted planetary resources and other environmental concerns, issues that loom large in much contemporary travel literature and that reveal the genre's notable relationship to nature writing. Journeys through wilderness or natural settings frequently cause modern travelers to confront imperiled wildlife, altered ecosystems, and other distressing environmental conditions. Cultural losses often accompany such changes, particularly in regions of the world where people's traditions, beliefs, and means of survival are closely tied to the natural world. Nature-travel writers thus cross boundaries of genre as well as of geography, evident in books such as Peter Matthiessen's classic *The Snow Leopard* (1978), a critically-acclaimed account of the author's journey to remote parts of Nepal, where, accom-panied by a wildlife biologist, Matthiessen hopes to observe the elusive snow leopard. *The Snow Leopard* is also an intensely personal book, revealing the author attempting to cope with his wife's recent death and eventually coming to terms with her loss, as well as other losses, through Zen Buddhism. As Casey Blanton observes, Matthiessen's "grim awareness of late-twentieth-century ecology" and thematic exploration of humankind's destruction of the planet is ultimately balanced by his compelling spiritual inner journey (Blanton 2002, 74-75, 81).

A more recent example of nature-travel writing, Gretel Ehrlich's *This Cold Heaven: Seven Seasons in Greenland* (2003), is also focused on issues of loss. Ehrlich's narrative about her extended travels among the Inuit during the 1990s recounts dog sled adventures with subsistence hunters whose livelihood is threatened by global warming and the temptations of the modern world. Throughout the book, Ehrlich includes expedition notes from Knud Rasmussen, whose exploration of Greenland in the early twentieth century allowed him to document the culture of the Polar Eskimos, which had remained essentially unchanged for a thousand years. Ehrlich's book similarly records Inuit ways of life, but her narrative inevitably reveals change: people trying to preserve their traditions while they adapt to the realities of a new global economy. "Everyone is just trying to survive," one hunter tells her. "Before there were shops, we followed animals. Now it's started to be modern so with my children and grandchildren, I try to get them to travel around with me so they know the life. Before, there was hunting with your wife. Now, my wife has to work in town to pay the bills" (Ehrlich 2003, 174). While recording such losses, *This Cold Heaven* transcends cultural nostalgia by celebrating the beauty of the landscape and the resourcefulness of the people who live on it and with it: "The complexities of ice had taught the hunters to reconcile the imminence of famine and death with an irreverent joy at being alive. The landscape itself, with its shifting and melting ice, its mirages, glaciers, and drifting icebergs, is less a description of desolation than an ode to the beauty of impermanence" (Ehrlich 2003, xiii).

Rebecca Solnit's writing persistently pursues questions about place and humans' relationship to it. In her books, travel serves as a means to know a location deeply and intimately, but such a process also requires forays into the past and into the stories that give meaning to a particular place. As a cultural historian as well as art critic and social activist, Solnit focuses on various spatial practices—geographic, political, environmental—to illustrate that how we perceive a place affects how we treat it. In *Savage Dreams: A Journey into the Landscape Wars of the American West* (1994), she explores an unlikely pairing of locations, the Nevada Test Site and Yosemite National Park, in a two-part narrative about contested spaces. In addition to recounting her travel through these places, Solnit historicizes them through chronicles about the making of the atom bomb and the development of the American wilderness. Early in the book, she signals her thematic terrain by noting hikers' and explorers' obsession with virgin wilderness, with being "the first people ever to tread on a piece of land" (Solnit 1994, 24). Even if one were to step foot on ground never before touched by someone else, she explains, the place, however remote, is cultural territory, already covered and constructed by myth and imagination, by artists, writers, and history. Solnit illustrates this cultural construction of place in her account of a guided tour around Ground Zero, the Nevada Test Site, which remains one of the most bombed places on earth. Throughout her tour, she experiences the surreal sense of being in a movie or on a film set, ironically reinforced by the documentary film she watches during her visit: "The landscape of the Nevada Test Site was strangely innocent of its own history, even with all of its craters and ruins. It was the stories that brought it to life for me, the stories of . . . the atomic veterans, the local people. . . . [but] it was the journey that gave the landscape meaning for me, not this arrival" (Solnit 1994, 211). Solnit's turn to Yosemite in the second half of *Savage Dreams* initially appears as an odd narrative path to take after the seemingly conclusive end at Ground Zero, but the extension of her journey, and of the book, allows her to confront even more directly the relationship between actual and perceived place. Deciding to visit Yosemite on her way elsewhere, she stops at Lake Tenaya and quickly realizes that the national park, "the very crucible and touchstone for American landscape," would give her insight into "the peculiarities, blindnesses, ruptures, and problems that constitute the Euro-American experience of landscape" (Solnit 1994, 221). Thus, *Savage Dreams* traces and challenges historical depictions of the park by artists, photographers, explorers, and naturalists as uninhabited and virgin wilderness. Solnit also aligns such conceptions of the park with the landscape architect Frederick Law Olmsted's view of nature as art and with ecologist Bill McKibben's belief in the independence of nature. By interweaving her narrative with accounts of her own rambles through the park, she offers a countervision of nature, in which humans are not excluded. For Solnit, place is constructed and given meaning by people, by those who inhabit or interact with the location. She advises us to give up the story of virgin wilderness, which would allow us to "lay to rest some of the misanthropy of old-fashioned conservationists and recognize that culture does not necessarily destroy nature, and that the ravages of those in a hurry are not the only pattern in the book" (Solnit 1994, 308). Solnit's travel writing has been described as meta-travel writing, "Writing that speculates about the meaning of travel even as the trip goes on" (Cooper 1997). The description is particularly apt for her recent works, *Wanderlust: A History of Walking* (2000) and *A Field Guide to Getting Lost* (2005), both of which explore movement and mobility rather than a particular landscape or location. Henry David Thoreau, referred to in *Savage Dreams* and repeatedly referenced in the more recent books, serves as her touchstone for purposeful and meaningful travel. The nature writer and practitioner of civil disobedience informs her belief that walking, whether construed as crossing boundaries or trespassing into forbidden places, "can articulate political meaning" (Solnit 2000, 8). Inspired also by Thoreau's essay "Walking," *Wanderlust* follows the method of Solnit's previous books; that is to say, she uses her own experiences and travels to provide a framework for broader philosophical inquiry. Walking is thus a metaphor as well as an act: "It trespasses through everybody else's field—through anatomy, anthropology, architecture, gardening, geography, political and cultural history, literature, sexuality, religious studies—and doesn't stop in any of them on its long route" (Solnit 2000, 4). In tracing the evolution of walking, examining the literature of walking, and portraying everything else historically and culturally related to walking, Solnit wants readers of *Wanderlust* to recognize that the pace of walking, as opposed to other methods of movement or travel, fosters thinking and reflection. Walking keeps us grounded, literally, thereby engaging our minds and bodies with the world. While such philosophizing may appear to characterize Solnit's work as something other than travel writing, her book is ultimately an argument about how to travel in a postmodern era of standardized environments and disorienting speed. She also makes a case for conceiving travel as stories, and stories as travel, to underscore the connection between imagination and movement. She observes, "To read is to travel through that terrain with the author as guide—a guide one may not always agree with or trust, but who can at least be counted upon to take one somewhere" (Solnit 2000, 72).

GET LOST! A NONCONVENTIONAL GUIDE TO MOVING THROUGH THE WORLD

A celebration of dislocation and of travel as a state of mind, *A Field Guide to Getting Lost* is appropriately fragmented and non-linear. A nonconventional travel writer, Rebecca Solnit presents readers with an alternative to traditional journey narratives; she captures, in the form of her text, the sometimes disorienting experience of moving through and living in the modern world. At the same time, her innovative approach to writing about travel is not proffered as literary experiment for the sake of novelty but rather as a means of mapping the interior journeys that make the exterior ones matter. In pushing the boundaries of the genre, or perhaps dissolving them completely, she illustrates that new methods and forms of travel writing may best help us to navigate place and space in the postmodern era.

In *A Field Guide to Getting Lost,* she denies readers an actual "somewhere" by arguing for travel without destination. Solnit explains that people who literally get lost are not paying attention to the place around them and no longer attend to the natural signs that would help them to navigate their way. In contrast to being lost out of ignorance, Solnit proposes being lost as a state of mind because it leads to a life of discovery. A meditation on being lost and on various kinds of losses, the book acknowledges Thoreau as the best and truest travel guide. Solnit quotes *Walden:* "Not till we are lost, in other words, not till we have lost the world, do we begin to find ourselves, and realize where we are and the infinite extent of our relations" (Solnit 2005, 15).

Bibliography

Blanton, Casey. *Travel Writing: The Self and the World.* New York: Routledge, 2002.

Botton, Alain de. *The Art of Travel.* New York: Pantheon Books, 2002.

Bryson, Bill. *The Lost Continent: Travels in Small-Town America.* (1989) New York: HarperPerennial, 1990.

———. *Neither Here nor There: Travels in Europe.* (1991) New York: William Morrow, 1992.

Buford, Bill. "Editorial." *Granta* 10 (1984): 5-7.

Cherry-Garrard, Apsley. *The Worst Journey in the World.* London: Constable, 1922.

Coale, Samuel. *Paul Theroux.* In *Twayne United States Authors on CD-ROM.* New York: G.K. Hall and Co., 1997.

Cooper, Rand Richards. "Travel." Review of *A Book of Migrations: Some Passages in Ireland,* by Rebecca Solnit. *New York Times on the Web,* June 1, 1997. http://www.nytimes.com/books/97/06/01/reviews/970601.01travelt.html.

Fussell, Paul. *Abroad: British Literary Traveling Between the Wars.* New York: Oxford University Press, 1980.

———, ed. *The Norton Book of Travel.* New York: W. W. Norton and Co., 1987.

Garner, Dwight. "His Secret Life." Interview with Paul Theroux. *Salon,* September 2, 1996. http://www.salon.com/weekly/interview960902.html.

Goldberg, Myla. *Time's Magpie: A Walk in Prague.* New York: Crown Publishers, Crown Journeys, 2004.

Glaser, Elton. "The Self-Reflexive Traveler: Paul Theroux on the Art of Travel and Travel Writing." *The Centennial Review* 33 (1989): 193-206.

Holland, Patrick, and Graham Huggan. *Tourists with Typewriters: Critical Reflections on Contemporary Travel Writing.* Ann Arbor: University of Michigan Press, 1998.

Hooper, Glenn, and Tim Youngs, ed. *Perspectives on Travel Writing.* Aldershot: Ashgate, 2004.

Horowitz, Tony. *Blue Latitudes: Boldly Going Where Captain Cook has Gone Before.* New York: Henry Holt and Co., Picador, 2002.

Hulme, Peter, and Tim Youngs, ed. *The Cambridge Companion to Travel Writing.* Cambridge, MA: Cambridge University Press, 2002.

Jennings, Jay. "Happy Days." Review of *The Life and Times of the Thunderbolt Kid,* by Bill Bryson. *New York Times Book Review,* 15 October 2006: 9.

Kowalewski, Michael, ed. *Temperamental Journeys: Essays on the Modern Literature of Travel.* Athens, GA: University of Georgia Press, 1992.

Maxwell, Gloria. Review of *In a Sunburned Country,* by Bill Bryson. *Library Journal* (15 November 2000): 118.

Mayes, Frances. *Under the Tuscan Sun: At Home in Italy.* San Francisco: Chronicle Books, 1996.

Lucy McCauley, ed. *The Best Women's Travel Writing 2005: True Stories from around the World.* Palo Alto: Travelers' Tales, 2005.

Morris, Holly. *Adventure Divas: Searching the Globe for a New Kind of Heroine.* New York: Villard, 2005.

Morris, Mary. Introduction to *Maiden Voyages: Writings of Women Travelers.* Mary Morris with Larry O'Connor, eds. New York: Random House, Vintage Departures, 1993.

Murphy, Dervla. Review of *Neither Here Nor There,* by Bill Bryson. *Times Literary Supplement,* 25 September, 1991: 28.

Root, Jr., Robert L. "Naming Nonfiction (a Polyptych)." *College English* 65.3 (January 2003): 242-246.

Rose, Peter I. "Around the World in 15 Years." Review of *Fresh Air Fiend,* by Paul Theroux. *Christian Science Monitor,* 27 July 2000: 17.

Russell, Alison. *Crossing Boundaries: Postmodern Travel Literature.* New York: Palgrave, 2000.

Siegel, Kristi, ed. *Gender, Genre and Identity in Women's Travel Writing.* New York: Peter Lang, 2004.

———. *Issues in Travel Writing: Empire, Spectacle, and Displacement.* New York: Peter Lang, 2002.

Smith, Sidonie. *Moving Lives: Twentieth-Century Women's Travel Writing.* Minneapolis: University of Minnesota Press, 2001.

Solnit, Rebecca. *A Field Guide to Getting Lost.* (2005) New York: Penguin Books, 2006.

———. *Savage Dreams: A Journey into the Landscape Wars of the American West.* (1994) New York: Random House, Vintage Departures, 1995.

———. *Wanderlust: a History of Wandering.* New York: Viking Penguin, 2000.

Stewart, Lucretia. "On the Wrong Side of the Frontier." Review of *Fresh Air Fiend,* by Paul Theroux. *Times Literary Supplement,* no. 5098 (15 December 2000): 12.

Paul Theroux. *Fresh Air Fiend: Travel Writings, 1985-2000.* Boston: Houghton Mifflin Co., 2000.

———. *The Great Railway Bazaar: by Train through Asia.* Boston: Houghton Mifflin Co., 1975.

———. *The Old Patagonian Express: by Train through the Americas.* (1979) New York: Houghton Mifflin Co., Mariner, 1997.

———. *Sunrise with Seamonsters: Travels & Discoveries 1964–1984.* Boston: Houghton Mifflin Co., 1985.

Wilson, Jason, ser. ed. Foreword to *The Best American Travel Writing 2000.* Bill Bryson, ed. New York: Houghton Mifflin Co., 2000.

Further Reading

The International Society for Travel Writing, http://istw-travel.org; *Studies in Travel Writing,* http://www.studiesintravelwriting.com.

ALISON RUSSELL

TRUE CRIME LITERATURE

Definition. Although murder narratives and nonfiction crime writing have a history spanning centuries, modern American true crime literature made its earliest appearance in the pages of *True Detective Magazine* during the 1950s and 1960s, as a new way of narrating and understanding murder emerged—one more sensitive to context, more psychologically sophisticated, more willing to make conjectures about the unknown thoughts and motivations of killers. Modern American true crime texts tend to be formulaic and are characterized by a collection of technical and thematic conventions established during the 1970s and 1980s. Such conventions include a depiction of one crime or criminal, usually murder, and a preoccupation with certain kinds of crimes—domestic, sadistic, or sexual murders, serial killings, or the crimes of the rich and famous. The texts include a depiction of the social contexts and ordinary life details of both victims and killers, generally focusing on the personal history and psychology of the murderer, culminating in the skillful deployment of fiction masquerading as fact (most often seen in dialogue or the imagined thoughts of characters, known as "free indirect discourse"). They also rely on a writer/narrator who is positioned as an "insider" on the events, privy to special information about the case. The structure generally includes four event elements: background of the crime, pursuit, trial, and imprisonment/execution, although some texts narrate unsolved crimes, as well as a middle photographic section, which may include photographs of the killer, victims, crime scenes, weapons, and scenes from the trial. The text also balances simultaneous distancing from and identification with the killer, most often done by narrating the killer's thoughts and feelings, with the use of a rhetoric of evil and monstrosity to describe the actions and motivations of killers. True crime literature is dominated by murder narratives, although some texts focus on serial rapists, espionage, or criminal conspiracy.

History. Exemplary texts and writers of true crime include Truman Capote's *In Cold Blood* (1965–1966), Joseph Wambaugh's *The Onion Field* (1973), Vincent Bugliosi's *Helter Skelter* (1974), Norman Mailer's *The Executioner's Song* (1979), Ann Rule's *The Stranger Beside Me* (1980) and her many other books, and numerous titles by such writers as Harold Schechter, Jack Olsen, Carlton Stowers, Aphrodite Jones, and Mark Fuhrman. True crime has become a pop culture juggernaut in publishing, journalism, and television, as well as a cultural barometer registering shifting fears about crime and violence in America. From its inception and formation as a distinct genre, true crime has created a nonfiction American landscape of paranoia and danger, random violent crime and roaming serial killers, of mortal threats to women and children from sociopathic husbands and predatory child-killers. Paradoxically, the genre also assuages such fears, because most true crime narratives present cases that have been cleared or solved, thereby reordering the violently disrupted social world and reassuring readers that horrifying criminals do not escape punishment, although normal life is regularly and radically altered by acts of extreme violence.

Certain aspects of the genre's conventions first appeared in pulp detective magazines from the 1950s and 1960s (most notably *True Detective Magazine*, published from 1924 to 1995), and true crime techniques in nascent form are present in texts of that period, such as Joel Bartlow Martin's *Why Did They Kill?* (1952), Lucy Freeman's *Before I kill more . . .* (1955), Meyer Levin's *Compulsion* (1956), John Dean's *The Indiana Torture Slaying* (1966), and Gerold Frank's *The Boston Strangler* (1966). These early true crime offerings reflected the preoccupations of their times, with many texts focused on so-called "juvenile delinquent" killers, in response to the "teenaged threat" of the 1950s and 1960s. Murder narratives that focused on one contemporary murder became popular during this period, as writers began to move away from publishing collections of stories or new treatments of older, more sensational murders. Such story collections had been popular from the 1900s to the 1950s, but as true crime magazines became more numerous and readily available, with their journalistic and sensational treatments of national and local murders, readers came to expect and demand more up-to-the-minute stories from full-length texts.

Trends and Themes. The kinds of killers treated in true crime changed during the 1960s, largely due to the change in the most sensationally gruesome crimes being committed, and the growth of a large media-machinery that could hype and inflame fears about such crimes. Fears about the existence of "bushy-haired strangers" (the term used by Dr. Sam Shepard to describe the alleged killer of his wife in 1955), sex-murderers such as Albert DeSalvo (the Boston Strangler, 1962–1964) and Richard Speck (the Chicago nurse-killer, 1966), mass killers like Charles Whitman (the University of Texas tower sniper, 1966), and "cult killers" such as Charles Manson and his "family" (1969) were increased by heavy media coverage of these crimes and criminals. Each of these crimes generated many different textual and film true crime treatments, such as Gerold Frank's *The Boston Strangler* (1966) and its film version (*The Boston Strangler,* dir. Richard Fleischer, 1968).

At the same time, there was a growing fascination with the killer who had an inconspicuous and impeccably "normal" façade that obscured the homicidal maniac within. One of the most popular framing devices for killers in true crime is that of highlighting the seeming normalcy of the killer, and then trying to uncover and understand the monstrously aberrant personality lurking just beneath the surface. In this way, killers came to be framed as both monstrous violators of the boundaries of normal humanity, and yet still within those same boundaries. The terms *psychopath* and *sociopath* became part of the popular vernacular after 1941, with the publication of Hervey M. Cleckley's *The Mask of Sanity: An Attempt to Clarify Some Issues about the So-Called Psychopathic Personality,* which made the concepts and language of psychiatric criminal deviancy accessible to non-professional readers. The book was reprinted in 1950, 1955, and 1964. Another concept that entered popular consciousness during the 1950s was that of the *sex fiend,* or *sex psychopath,* the man who, because of some disorganization in his mind, was unable to control his sexual impulses and posed a significant threat to the perceived weakest part of American society, women and children.

During the 1970s, certain themes, types of killers, and modes of representation became most prominent within the emerging genre, with the serial and sex killer and feminized victims—women, children, and homosexuals—garnering the greatest interest. The genre was not dominated by any single author, but it was dominated by male writers. Typical examples include William A. Clark's *The Girl on the Volkswagen Floor* (1971), an unsolved-murder narrative largely concerned with psychics assisting the police, and John Gurwell's *Mass Murder in Houston* (1974), a small press publication about the Dean Corll homosexual killings of 27 teenaged boys in Houston. John Gilmore's *The Michigan Murders* (1976) is an early serial killer treatment that wonderfully evokes the culture of a late 1960s large university community (Ann Arbor/Ypsilanti). *Charlie Simpson's Apocalypse* (1974) is a berserk-Vietnam-vet tale with political and sociological undertones, a miniature

Helter Skelter. These texts present victims as objects, with details about the discovery of fatally wounded bodies, graphic accounts of violence, and means of death taking hideous precedence. Apprehension and description of the psychopathology of the perpetrator is of secondary concern, and in the 1971 text, the killer is never caught. Forensic science and descriptions of police work also gained prominence within the genre during this period, and the archetype of the strong male detective force battling other, deviant men to avenge female victims became commonplace.

True crime of the 1980s focused largely on serial killers, as that threat first appeared on the cultural horizon with the pursuit and apprehension of such killers as Ted Bundy, John Wayne Gacy, Henry Lee Lucas, Jeffrey Dahmer, and the "Green River Killer" (Gary Ridgway). Popular culture depictions introduced the figure of the "criminal profiler," as FBI programs such as VICAP (Violent Criminal Apprehension Program) and profiler training captured both federal funding and the popular imagination. Although the serial killer threat was never as widespread and lethal as was touted in the early 1980s, texts about serial killers proliferated during this decade. As the threat and hype around serial killers faded during the late 1990s, writers turned their attention to domestic murder, by far the most common and varied type of killing in America. Much modern true crime narrates the threats to both men and women of bad romantic choices, and the genre now reflects more anxiety about intimate relationships than the risks of being murdered by a serial killer. Husbands, wives, lovers, in-laws, children, and parents shoot, stab, poison, and incinerate each other with alarming frequency in true crime, and the genre is dominated by such perverse or reversed romance narratives.

There are also many more female writers working in the genre at present, the most popular being Ann Rule (b. 1935). Rule has shaped the modern genre and popularized the theme of deviant domesticity and exploration of gender expectations and roles, as well as placing greater narrative emphasis on victims' lives and foregrounding mundane details about the environments in which her killers and victims live. She has also enlivened the genre with stories about unforgettable female killers, and a more female-centered strand of true crime has emerged from her pioneering work.

Context and Issues. The way that real murder is narrated, and therefore understood in a given culture, changes over time and depends heavily on cultural context. Different stories, interpretations, emphases, and perspectives abound for any single murder case. In her book *Murder Most Foul: The Killer and the American Gothic Imagination,* cultural historian Karen Halttunen writes, "Any story of murder involves a fictive process, which reveals much about the mental and emotional strategies employed within a given historical culture for responding to serious transgression in its midst" (Halttunen 1998, 2). Because murder narratives are constructed and are always somewhat fictive, no matter the reality of the event being discussed, they reveal the underlying preoccupations and perspectives on "serious transgression" in ways that other texts do not. In the early formative true crime period (late 1960s through the 1970s), the murderer is often depicted as a stranger to his victims, a loner (or a pair of loners), a person from an abusive or violent background, alienated from most normal social ties such as friends and family, and most fundamentally, as a person lacking a conscience. Each of these features correlates to some element in the larger culture that caused anxiety or distress, and the killer in true crime literature became the expression for some of the fears, real or imagined, of 1960s America.

CRIME TRENDS OF THE 1960s AND 70s

Some cultural fears about crime are exploited and exaggerated in the pages of true crime books. One undeniably real trend in the last few decades in America was an escalating murder rate (the number of homicides committed per 100,000 citizens per year): in the 1960s, the murder rate underwent a dramatic upward surge, and in the decade between 1964 and 1974, the American murder rate doubled, from 5 to 10 homicides per 100,000 people per year. Stranger-killings—that is, homicide between two persons unknown to each other—became much more prevalent in the 1960s, and the clearance rate for murder, or the percentage of cases solved, was dropping. During this same period, the conventions of true crime were codified into a formula: murder narratives began to represent stranger-killings most frequently, and the structure of the true crime text settled into its ossified present form of crime–pursuit–trial–execution. The conflation of these three elements—a rising murder rate, an increase in the number of stranger-killings, and a corollary increase in the number of unsolved homicides—registered in true crime narratives as an emphasis on the unknown, and unknowable, killer.

Selected Authors. Most scholars and readers consider Truman Capote's *In Cold Blood* (1966) to be the first modern true crime text, for it brought together the themes and structures that would inform the genre for the next half-century, creating a template for the genre that persists to this day. By 1959, Capote (1924–1984) was a successful published author of such books as *Other Voices, Other Rooms, Tree of Night and Other Stories, The Grass Harp, The Muses Are Heard,* and *Breakfast at Tiffany's.* As told in two recent films about his life—*Capote* (dir. Bennett Miller, 2005) and *Infamous* (dir. Douglas McGrath, 2006)—Capote had been interested in writing nonfiction for many years, and in 1959 he found a suitable topic for a "nonfiction novel" in the rural Kansas shotgun murder of four members of the Clutter family in an apparent botched robbery. Richard Eugene Hickock and Perry Smith were arrested in Las Vegas on January 2, 1960, for the Clutter murders, and they were executed on April 14, 1965. For most of those five intervening years, Capote exchanged letters with the prisoners twice a week, and he lived in Garden City for extended periods of time, forming close relationships with not just the murderers, but also the detectives involved in the case. The result of all that work was published in *The New Yorker* in four installments between September and October 1965, and published in book form in January 1966. In 1967 the book was made into a film, also a spectacular success, starring the then-unknown Robert Blake as Perry Smith (*In Cold Blood*, dir. Richard Brooks, 1967).

In Cold Blood has been a best-seller since its publication, and in 1966 it received the Mystery Writers of America Edgar Allan Poe Award (the "Edgar") for Best Fact Crime Book of the Year. In his book, Capote solidified and perfected the nascent conventions of what would become true crime literature, and his basic formula, along with his research methods and techniques, have been copied ever since. Such techniques include the writer becoming an intimate insider in the case, the creation of a sense of simultaneous identification and distance between reader and killer, the shaping of real people into literary characters and the introduction of fiction-writing techniques into nonfiction writing, the crime-killer profile–trial–execution structure of the text, interweaving the actions of the killers and the victims by juxtaposing and "cross-cutting" scenes, the theme that random violence can easily destroy idyllic

American lives, and the representation of the normal-seeming killer or "sleeper" sociopath.

In his research for the book, Capote became an intimate of the killers, thereby gaining special access to their feelings and memories, and specific experiential knowledge of the judiciary procedures that would become a large part of true crime narratives. True crime writing of this period would spend more time narrating the aftermath of murder, not the crime itself, as trials became lengthier, debates about the legality and morality of the death penalty raged, and death-penalty appeals dragged out over years. (In 1967 the Supreme Court ruled that the death penalty was unconstitutional; in 1976, individual states began to reinstitute the practice, beginning with the Utah execution of Gary Gilmore.) Because Smith and Hickock were captured quickly, and because they were involved in appealing their sentences for nearly five years, Capote was put in the unique position of having to wait for them to die in order to finish his book, while growing closer to them personally during that time.

Capote's narrative treatment of his subject would draw the reader into an uneasy and unprecedented relationship with the killers. The reader experiences the disparity of closeness to the person and distance from the horror of the criminal's acts. Perry Smith's most famous statement about Herb Clutter, "I thought he was a very nice gentleman. Soft-spoken. I thought so right up to the moment I cut his throat," was emblematic of the organization of his entire personality (Capote 1966, 275). Capote crafted his narrative so that the reader shares his fascination with Smith, who was at once a devious and dangerous loner and a sensitive, wounded man. Capote's closeness to the subjects of his book would set the standard for a different degree of involvement between writer and subject, and would forever change the nature of murder narratives.

Another trope of true crime, the shaping of real people into literary characters and the introduction of fiction-writing techniques into nonfiction writing, is directly attributable to Capote's closeness to Smith and Hickock. Capote was able to use free indirect discourse, which interjects objectivity and intimacy with the subjects, because he gained unique access to the men's intimate thoughts and feelings. Another genre-setter was the familiar four-part structure of crime–pursuit–trial– execution, which gives true crime the shape of a classic detective tale; that is, the murder occurs in the first chapter, but we don't understand the killer's motives until the final chapters. One of the most striking aspects of *In Cold Blood,* and one that would become a major convention in true crime literature, is the way that Capote structured the sections of each chapter so that the actions of the killers and the victims are interwoven. Particularly in the first chapter, Capote cuts back and forth between scenes featuring either the Clutters or Smith and Hickock, in a technique borrowed from filmmaking. In fact, the book is strangely more filmic than the film version—there seems to be more juggling of scenes between the Clutters and their killers in the book, whereas the movie concentrates more heavily on Hickock and Smith.

The puzzle and threat of random violence is a significant true crime theme, and one that Capote beautifully explores in his book. The genre always sets innocence against evil, and this convention, combined with the filmic technique of interspersing scenes of victims and killers, portrays a strong sense of the inevitability of evil. The action seems fated, and murder seems destined to occur; the Clutters cannot escape their fate, and Smith and Hickock cannot resist forming their ill-conceived alliance that will ultimately lead them to their own deaths. In depicting that alliance, the book offers two competing views about what a killer is and what evil looks like. Richard Hickock is vulgar, ugly, brutal, and shallow; Perry Smith is sensitive, handsome, artistic, a dreamer. Hickock looks like a conventional murderer, whereas Smith does not fit the mold. Capote's innovation is that Hickock as killer is ultimately less disturbing and threatening—even though, ironically, he plans the crime—because it is clear from the outset that he is capable of violence. Smith, on the other hand, is a more fundamentally disturbing character because he *seems* like a good and harmless soul, even though he agrees to go along with Hickock and rob the Clutters. Capote reverses the reader's expectations by portraying his most deadly killer as the seemingly kind one, and the one who appears evil as essentially innocent. This new construction of the killer resonated with readers because it articulated an idea of evil as being hidden, insidious, and mysterious; the killer was becoming a literary character, a complex and masked figure, not the simply-conceived and emotionally separate monster of earlier depictions.

The early critical responses to the book were largely positive, as was the popular reception. *In Cold Blood* was an instant bestseller. The novel was published almost simultaneously with an interview in the *New York Times Book Review* in which Capote spoke about his creation of a new literary formula, the "nonfiction novel" (Plimpton 1997, 197). Capote's statement fuelled the critics, for in addition to the book earning wide acclaim and being worthy of thoughtful criticism, his grand statements about genre creation were taken as a ready-made challenge. Many critics focused in particular on Capote's claims to truthfulness or factuality. Such debates about strict factual accuracy swirled around early true crime, but have lost relevance in the contemporary genre. *In Cold Blood* has sold millions of copies and reappeared in 2005 on the *New York Times* paperback bestseller list.

Another outstanding true crime text is Joseph Wambaugh's (b. 1937) *The Onion Field*, published in 1973. *The Onion Field* showcases certain aspects of the maturing genre, including a more complex narrator/insider, with a different relationship to criminals and crime, and the inclusion of more complicated themes such as guilt, retribution, and exploration of the psychology of victims as well as killers. As a Los Angeles police officer, Wambaugh had a unique perspective on murder and undeniable credibility as a witness, a participant, and a commentator. *The Onion Field* further demonstrated that popular true crime could be subtle, sophisticated, and terrifically powerful, that the genre could support the exploration of serious themes, and that it is able to transcend displays of graphic violence and sensationalism.

The Onion Field is an account of the kidnapping of two LAPD patrolmen by two petty crooks in 1963. On a Saturday night in March of that year, officers Ian Campbell and Karl Hettinger, both relatively new to the job, were disarmed at gunpoint and driven to a remote California onion field by Gregory Powell and Jimmy Smith. Powell and Smith murdered Campbell, and Karl Hettinger narrowly escaped the same fate by running for his life through the field to safety. Hettinger returned to police work immediately, and suffered a nervous breakdown as a consequence of the murder of his colleague and the aftermath of the crime, which included the longest criminal trial in California history. An incredible series of appeals and retrials led to several juries overturning death penalty convictions for the murderers, largely as a result of changing laws and the institution of the Miranda Rights ruling in 1966. Wambaugh was an LAPD officer when the onion field crime took place, and his experiences working alongside cops and apprehending criminals shaped his narratives when he began to write.

The Onion Field both reinforced and further developed the conventions underway in murder narratives; because of his unique position as an "insider" in the world of policemen and criminals, Wambaugh brought an intensely intimate perspective to bear on true crime. Building on what Capote had started with the shifting position of the writer as an intimate of the killer, in both his police fiction and *The Onion Field,* Wambaugh furthered the notion that cops and murderers are separated by very thin fibers of moral structure, and that good and evil are almost inextricably interwoven concepts. Wambaugh's suggestion that cops and criminals are similarly human and driven by forces beyond their control leads the reader into both connection to and alienation from both groups. There are no unambiguous heroes in Wambaugh's writing, because his cops are gritty and flawed, his criminals twisted and damaged. His work is important to the growth of true crime because—like Capote—he invites the reader to experience a simultaneous attraction and repulsion to his "good" and "bad" characters equally. This duality underlines "evil" as a moral construct, which was in the 1970s crumbling under the mediation of social forces and new understandings of crime and criminality.

> *The Onion Field* is essentially a story about guilt, but not on the part of the murderers. One day after the kidnapping and murder of Ian Campbell, his partner, Karl Hettinger, who had himself almost been murdered, returned to the job; the LAPD offered Hettinger no psychological counseling, for at that time the Department did not recognize that suffering such a traumatic event could have severe psychological consequences.

Hettinger became so consumed by his unacknowledged, unconscious guilt that he began shoplifting; he then became so obsessed with guilt about stealing that he allowed himself to be caught and fired. The text focuses on Hettinger—it begins and ends with his internal monologue, and the narrative follows his psychological condition into and beyond his mental breakdown.

Wambaugh had published popular police fiction before writing *The Onion Field,* and he has continued to do so into the twenty-first century. He had a successful return to true crime in 2002 with *Fire Lover,* an arson narrative, which won an Edgar Award. *The Onion Field* won a Special Edgar Award in 1974, and Wambaugh has always been critically well regarded. William Marling reports that "Critics unanimously praised the book [*The Onion Field*], comparing it to Truman Capote's *In Cold Blood* and the author to Theodore Dreiser and James T. Farrell" (http://www.detnovel.com/Citation.html).

Perhaps the best-known true crime text of the 1970s is Vincent Bugliosi (b. 1934) and Curt Gentry's (b. 1931) *Helter Skelter* (1974), which narrates one of the most notorious mass-murders in American history. In August of 1969, followers of Charles Milles Manson slaughtered seven Los Angeles residents in their homes, including the actress Sharon Tate, as a means of bringing on what they called "Helter Skelter," Manson's vision of a futuristic, apocalyptic racial revolution. The Manson group also killed at least three other people, and speculations abound about other murders. Several members of the self-styled Manson "family," including Manson himself, are still serving life sentences in California for these crimes. Los Angeles District Attorney Vincent Bugliosi successfully prosecuted and convicted the

Manson family killers, and it is his narrative of the crimes in *Helter Skelter* that lives on in the American imagination.

The Manson slayings came to be viewed as the hideous—but not unanticipated—end of the joyful, hopeful, and innocent 1960s hippie counterculture. In the same way that Joseph Wambaugh folded anxiety about a growing culture of permissiveness into his true crime writing, noting the emergence of the psychopath as the logical endpoint of the perceived moral collapse of the 1960s and 70s, the Manson killings were seen as the logical outcome of communal living, loose sexual morals, and the wholesale rejection of modern society that characterized the values of the counterculture. *Helter Skelter* expressed the fears of the middle class about losing their children to cults, communes, and free love; the book also fascinated those same children, and has been one of the biggest-selling true crime texts in American history.

Bugliosi deploys and embellishes each of the conventions of murder narration that first appeared in *In Cold Blood,* and he introduces a new convention that would become standard in all true crime to date—the inclusion of photographs in the book. Bugliosi included a large number of photographs and a map in his text, and the entire section was labeled "A Chilling 64-page Photographic Record of the Victims, the Killers, the Evidence" (Bugliosi 1974, 346). Adding an extra dimension of titillation and veracity, nearly every mass-market true crime narrative since *Helter Skelter* includes a middle section of 6–10 photographs, usually consisting of before-and-after photos of the victim, snapshots of the crime scene, the murder weapons, the trial, and the killer. Sometimes, as in Joe McGinniss's 1983 *Fatal Vision,* there is even a photograph of the writer, reinforcing his or her status as a character in the narrative.

The Manson family crimes have inspired scores of true crime texts, written from late 1969 until the present. The first book about the murders was published in December 1969, shortly after the apprehension of Susan Atkins, whose dramatic confession during her incarceration for another offense led to the dismantling of the Manson family, and the latest was published in 2002. Each of the primary Manson family members has written an autobiography, usually with the help of a journalist or ghostwriter. As of this writing, there are approximately 25 books about the Manson events still in print, and several more that are out of print. There have been many film and television treatments of the subject, most notably the Robert Hendrickson documentary entitled *Manson* (1972), nominated for an Academy Award, and Jim Van Bebber's *The Manson Family* (2003). The Manson murders, often represented as a cultural milestone that signified the end of the hippie era and the beginning of the current period of media-created criminal sensations, have generated an enormous amount of popular and scholarly interest.

After the sensation of *Helter Skelter,* Bugliosi continued his writing career, penning several more true crime and nonfiction texts. Bugliosi's true crime was popular in the 1980s, although his writing is often thick with over-coverage of minute points of law and extended depictions of courtroom battles. As an attorney, he is preoccupied with the machinations of the criminal justice system, and many readers find his work compelling. Following the model set with *Helter Skelter,* Bugliosi continued to co-author true crime literature, working with Ken Hurwitz on *Till Death Do Us Part* (1978) and *Shadow of Cain* (1981), William Stadiem for *Lullaby and Goodnight* (1987), and Bruce B. Henderson for *And the Sea Will Tell* (1991), a murder narrative set on the tiny Pacific island of Palmyra. Although he began his career in the true crime trenches, Bugliosi has steadily moved out of that genre into straight nonfiction critiques of the American legal system by way of examining specific, sensational cases. Bugliosi's true crime is concerned primarily with jurisprudence, systemic failures of justice, and righting the social order. The inheritors of his tradition—writers such as Jack Olsen, Carlton Stowers, and Mark Fuhrman—are prominent within the genre today, and represent one strand of true crime writing that deals with deviant masculinity, jurisprudential issues, and depictions of sexual-sadistic gore.

During the 1970s, with skyrocketing American crime rates and the appearance of a frightening trend toward social chaos, true crime texts narrated and helped readers understand such seemingly senseless acts as the Manson killings and the apparent rise in sexually related murders of young women. The 1970s was also the formative decade of American feminism, and true crime registered the effects of that social movement, mostly as a deepening interest in the personhood of the murder victim. Many 1970s texts of this genre are cautionary tales for single young women, warnings against prosaic but new female activities such as hitchhiking and picking up strange men in bars. Judith Rossner's 1975 blockbuster, *Looking for Mr. Goodbar,* and Lacey Fosburgh's *Closing Time: The True Story of the "Goodbar" Murder* (1977) each cover the 1973 murder of Manhattan school teacher Katherine Cleary by a stranger she picked up in a singles bar. Rossner's novel was not true crime, strictly speaking; rather, she used the crime to depict in novel form the desperation of some newly-liberated single women's lives. Throughout the 1970s and 1980s, true crime that was authored primarily by men reflected an implicit fear of increased social, political, and sexual liberations for women. Not until the late 1980s and 1990s would true crime begin to contain female-centered themes such as warnings about bad romantic matches and greater empathy for the plight of female murder victims.

In the 1980s, true crime became a consumer-driven publishing industry category, garnering huge profits for mass-market paperback publishing houses as the larger ones (such as Random House and St. Martin's) created their own true crime imprints. The growth of the genre shows in a survey of titles in Ben Harrison's book *True Crime Narratives: An Annotated Bibliography,* published in 1997. In the 1960s, approximately 37 texts treated single cases of contemporary murder and/or the activities of single murderers. In the 1970s, there were 78 examples of the same; in the 1980s, there were 145, and in the 1990s, the number rose to 165 (Harrison 1997).

True crime as a literary genre has brought a tabloid sensibility into higher culture, and has illuminated the sordid with beams of truth: in its best exemplars, true crime questions its own motivations and reason for being. Since its inception as a genre, more "literary" authors or writers who normally work in other genres have produced stellar examples within the genre. One such text is Norman Mailer's (1923–2007) *The Executioner's Song,* co-authored with Lawrence Schiller (b. 1936) in 1979. This text represents a significant attempt to narrate and create meaning from murder, although in some ways it defies the definition of true crime. In 1976, longtime convict Gary Gilmore was sentenced to death for the murder of two men in Provo, Utah. At that time, there hadn't been an execution in the United States for ten years, since the 1967 Supreme Court ruling in *Furman v. Georgia* that the administration of the death penalty was unconstitutional. Gilmore forced the state of Utah to execute him by refusing to appeal, and his case caused a huge national and international sensation. Gilmore's high-profile truculence mushroomed into a media circus like that surrounding the Manson trial. Several months after Gilmore's execution, Mailer collaborated with Larry Schiller, the true crime media mogul who got his start with the Manson trial, and with whom Mailer had written his biography of Marilyn Monroe, to write *The Executioner's Song*. The book covers the nine months between Gilmore's parole in April 1976 until his execution in January 1977. It quickly became a bestseller and Mailer won the Pulitzer Prize in 1980 for fiction.

By 1979, true crime was defined by a group of narrative techniques and conventions, and Mailer uses most of them very effectively in *The Executioner's Song*. He skillfully blends fiction with nonfiction, calling his book a "true life novel." Mailer achieves his insider status through his chief researcher Larry Schiller, who was Gilmore's friend/confessor/publicist during the murderer's final days. Mailer expertly contextualizes the Gilmore crimes and ensuing media phenomenon within the late-1970s Western American social and cultural milieu, and very specifically within the Utah Mormon context. The book does not strictly follow the formulaic four-part narrative structure, for the narrative does not start with murder; still, *The Executioner's Song* is broken into chronological segments that treat first Gilmore's life and crimes, then his trial and execution. Mailer chose a murderer who fit the usual 1970s true crime criteria, for Gilmore's two murders are both random stranger-killings. Mailer creates a large and powerful sense of the inevitability of murder and the magnetic pull towards evil, as Gilmore is drawn, seemingly against his will, ever-closer to first his crimes, then to his own death. The book is a brilliant murder narrative, at once an insider's view into dysfunctional working-class 1970s American life and a sweeping portrayal of how that life both creates and sustains violence.

Unlike many books within the genre, *The Executioner's Song* is as much an exploration of the marketing of murder as it is of the act itself. The 1,056-page book is broken into two large sections, "Western Voices" and "Eastern Voices." The first section outlines Gilmore's life and crimes, and the second concentrates on a portrayal of the media frenzy surrounding his trial and execution. The concept of being able to sell one's criminal story was in 1976 as morally dubious as it is now, but the so-called "Son of Sam" laws, which prevent criminals from profiting from their crimes, were not enacted until 1978, so Gilmore was able to profit from marketing his story. Schiller, the prototypical murder journalist, is held up for scrutiny just as Gilmore, the prototypical murderer, is. And just as in his portrayal of Gilmore Mailer valorizes the psychopath, with his treatment of Schiller, Mailer legitimizes the vocation of murder journalist/shill by devoting such loving attention to the story. Schiller's sharp-witted professionalism as a murder-mogul lies in his ability to see the big picture, and to craft an audience as well as a consumable narrative for it from the bare bones of a sordid story. Mailer has said that the story of *The Executioner's Song* was like gold to him, that he could never have invented such a good tale, and that he wanted to just present the reality of the events as he found them reflected in court transcripts, documents, interviews, and Schiller's memories.

Beginning with her treatment of serial killer Ted Bundy, *The Stranger Beside Me* (1980), former policewoman Ann Rule, who had worked with Bundy, has become the premier American true crime writer, shaping and redefining the genre with her work, and building powerful and lucrative "name-brand" recognition for her product.

To date, she has published thirteen single-case texts, nine true crime collections, and one crime-based novel. Her most recent book, 2004's *Green River, Running Red* was about Gary Ridgway, the "Green River" serial killer, although she has generally avoided serial killers as a subject. Ann Rule has a Web site, www.annrules.com, an annual newsletter, and an enormous fan base; her books are regularly reviewed by publications such as *The New York Times* and *Publisher's Weekly*, she has received numerous Edgar Award nominations, and her books appear often on bestseller lists.

After a brief career as a Seattle policewoman, Rule began writing crime stories for pulp magazines such as *True Detective* in the 1960s, and continued that work throughout the 1970s and 1980s, with special jurisdiction over crime stories in the Northwestern states. Her first book, *The Stranger Beside Me,* was an exploration of deadly and sensational interpersonal betrayal, experienced on a very personal level. In 1971, Rule worked with Ted Bundy at a local suicide-prevention hotline, and during the next decade she and Bundy kept in touch and socialized intermittently. In 1976 Rule was assigned by *True Detective Magazine* to cover a series of abduction-murders of young women throughout the Northwest. Eventually, it became clear that her friend, Ted Bundy, was responsible for the serial murders, for which he was tried and convicted (and executed by the state of Florida in 1989). Ted Bundy would become infamous as one of the most prolific and heinous American serial killers (one detective who worked on the case estimates that he killed 100 women), and Rule had been handed the story of a lifetime. *The Stranger Beside Me* became a best-selling blockbuster, the first in a long line.

In addition to giving Rule her first subject, Bundy embodied a theory about the deviant human personality that would dominate true crime writing in the 1980s and 1990s—the notion of the sociopathic personality. The sociopath, anti-social personality, and the psychopath (the sociopath's crazier cousin) have become familiar figures in the popular media landscape of true crime and horror, and Bundy, as Rule says, has become the "poster boy for serial murder." (Rule 1980, 541) His ability to mimic human emotions, to appear psychologically "normal," to uphold a façade of ordinariness, has fascinated the public and professionals alike. Rule's knowledge about the sociopath has helped to legitimize her work, and she has become a widely-respected authority on serial killers. She is not viewed as a "pulp" writer, nor is her work seen as exploitative or sensational; rather, Rule is appreciated by her readers, reviewers, and by criminology professionals as an expert and a professional in her own right.

The Bundy case has shaped the trajectory of her career, and *Stranger* is her best-known and best-regarded book, largely because it transcends the simple story of a psychopath and his obscenely destructive acts. The most powerful and interesting storyline concerns Rule's own relationship to Bundy—her growing realization that he truly is a killer, the painful understanding of his betrayal of her, and the difficult decisions she must make to betray *him,* in a sense, by writing a book about him. After writing *Stranger,* she penned three quickie serial-killer texts—*The Want-Ad Killer* and *Lust Killer* in 1983 and *The I-5 Killer* in 1984—using her old pseudonym from magazine writing, "Andy Stack." *Small Sacrifices* (1987) is a story about Oregon child-killer Diane Downs, who shot her three young children in May 1983, killing one and seriously wounding the others. With this book, Rule finds one of the subjects that would occupy her career—deviant domesticity and sour relationships, in this book a case of mothering gone terribly wrong.

Rule's subsequent books concern perverse or obsessive domestic scenarios, and a survey of her titles shows a preoccupation with the ways in which romance can go wrong: *If You Really Loved Me* (1991), *Everything She Ever Wanted* (1992), *Dead by Sunset* (1995), *Possession* (1996), *Bitter Harvest* (1997), . . . *And Never Let Her Go* (1999), *Every Breath You Take* (2001), and *Heart Full of Lies* (2003). Rule narrated the emotional underside of the 1980s and 1990s, decades of soaring American divorce rates and huge economic losses and gains, of hidden unhappiness amid wealth and fortune. Perhaps in response to the fear-generating stranger-murders of earlier true crime in the 1960s and 1970s, Rule's texts offer a fearful return to the traditional site of domestic disturbance and violence, the home. Her subjects are more reflective of 1990s crime statistics, which showed a steady and sometimes dramatic decline in murder rates nationwide.

One interesting part of the true crime phenomenon is that as crime rates, and murder rates in particular, have fallen over the past decade, the genre still generates a climate and landscape of fear and paranoia about crime. Sociologist Barry Glassner says, "Between 1990 and 1998, when the nation's murder rate declined by 20 percent, the number of murder stories on network newscasts increased 600 percent (*not* counting stories about O.J. Simpson)" (Glassner 1999, xxi). The changing face of crime in America is one explanation for the increasing reliance on domestic or romantic murders within the genre, exemplified by Rule's writing.

Instead of proffering answers to the problem of evil, Rule's true crime is a minute examination of lives badly lived and horrifyingly ended, each offering a warning to men and women alike about the perils of loving the wrong person. For this reason, the conventional good vs. evil, detective vs. killer structure of her stories does not weaken the impact and importance of Rule's overarching objective of writing books for and about women. Her latest book is *Smoke, Mirrors, and Murder* (2007), twelfth in her Crime Files series. Her 2004 title, *Green River, Running Red*, examines the crimes of the so-called "Green River" serial killer, Gary Ridgway. Although the text is in many ways conventional, Rule focuses most of her narrative attention on the victims, instead of the killer, describing the sad lives and wretched deaths of many of Ridgway's 50 victims. In this way, she continues to challenge the stereotypes of the genre and expand the cultural work of the genre.

Carlton Stowers (b. 1942), a magazine and newspaper journalist well-known in his home state of Texas, is regarded as one of the finest contemporary writers of true crime. Material on his Web site states that "*The Houston Press* has called Stowers 'the dean of Texas true crime writers,' and famed novelist Jonathan Kellerman notes that 'when the dust clears, a handful of writers will be recognized as masters of the true crime book. And Carlton Stowers will be at the head of that class'" (http://www.truecrime.net/carltonstowers/). Among his works are a history of the Dallas Police Department (*Partners in Blue: The History of the Dallas Police Department,* 1983), a biography of Roy Rogers and Dale Evans, and numerous books on sports, notably the Dallas Cowboys football team. Stowers' true crime has garnered two Edgar Awards (*To the Last Breath* in 1999 and *Careless Whispers* in 1987) and a Pulitzer Prize nomination for 1990's *Innocence Lost*. Stowers receives high praise from critics and readers alike.

In his writing, Stowers typifies a conservative ideological strand in true crime, visible in his narrative bias towards law-enforcement and against the outsiders and misfits who populate the criminal class within the genre. His work also illustrates another of the generic conventions in his use of a simplified rhetoric of evil and monstrosity to describe the killers. *Innocence Lost* describes the murder of an undercover police detective by a group of high school students under investigation for drug activity. Stowers describes one of the convicted killers, 17 years old at the time, as having "piercing blue eyes [that] disturbed the officer more than the knife. They had a haunted, frightening quality he had never before seen" (Stowers 1990, 72). In true crime depictions, killers are routinely described with the language of gothic horror, as having a kind of quasi-occult power over others and a chilling effect on people. Another of the youthful murderers has a "coldness" in his eyes, and "appeared to have no feeling at all for his mother, father, or younger brother," all conventional descriptions of sociopathic killers (Stowers 1990, 135, 70).

The scene is set with similar overtones of gothic horror: in one description of the small town in the aftermath of the murder, Stowers writes that the townspeople's "comforting invisible barrier against outside evils had been ripped away. They pondered the town's newfound vulnerability while ministers prepared to deliver impassioned sermons on the strength and faith necessary to deal with the cataclysmic event that had visited their small corner of the world" (Stowers 1990, 237). The adults wonder, "How was it possible that some of their children had turned into such monsters?" (237). Such inflated language casts the story and its characters onto a heightened metaphysical plane, removed from the mundane meanness and moral ambiguity of real crime, and makes stark the competing notions of "innocence" and "evil" that for Stowers are at the heart of the true crime narrative.

One of Stowers's contributions to the genre is his narrative talent for an anthropological "thick description" of social contexts and the American scene that sometimes produces brutal criminal violence. Stowers shows that fine true crime writing is as much about contexts as it is about crime. Much of his books are given over to descriptions of the places where murder occurs, and the ways that the principal players in the story—law enforcement agents, killers, victims, and "ordinary" people—think and live. Through the descriptions of the characters' lives, Stowers (and many other contemporary writers) examines minute aspects of the broad categories of American life, including social class, race, romance and marriage, sexuality, friendship, education, religious beliefs, community goals and challenges, economic growth and stagnation, and a vast array of individual experiences. In some ways, true crime texts play the role that was formerly taken by the British "comedy of manners": they educate us about who we are and how we truly live. In true crime, however, the rich description of context is overshadowed by the impending horror, drawing the reader into surroundings that seem eerily like his own and creating narrative tension and suspense.

Mark Fuhrman (b. 1952) is best known as the former Los Angeles Police Department detective who found the infamous "bloody glove" at the site of the Nicole Brown Simpson/Ronald Goldman murder in 1994 for which O.J. Simpson was acquitted but found liable in civil court. Fuhrman's racist views, caught on an audiotape in 1985, and his resulting perjury conviction about his use of the word *nigger* sparked controversy during the Simpson trial and may have influenced its outcome. Fuhrman became a true crime writer after retiring from the LAPD in 1996, and his first true crime book was *Murder in Brentwood* (1997), about the Simpson case. In 1998 he published *Murder in Greenwich: Who Killed Martha Moxley?*, reviving the unsolved case of the 1975 murder of a 15-year-old girl in Greenwich, Connecticut. As a result of that book, one of Moxley's neighbors, Michael Skakel, was convicted of her murder in 2002, in a spectacular case of delayed justice. Other Fuhrman texts include *Murder in Spokane: Catching a Serial Killer* (2001), *Death and Justice: An Exposé of Oklahoma's Death Row Machine* (2003), *Silent Witness: The Untold Story of Terri Schiavo's Death* (2005), and *A Simple Act of Murder: November 22, 1963,* Fuhrman's contribution to the Kennedy assassination conspiracy theories, published in 2006.

Fuhrman's true crime is detail-laden and, as might be expected of a former detective, focused on trying to make a case. *Murder in Greenwich* reads like a primer in how not to conduct a homicide investigation; in fact, one of the chapters is titled "Homicide 101." As a special kind of insider, Fuhrman uses his knowledge of murder investigation techniques to explain what was done wrong and how the bungled investigation forestalled an arrest and conviction in the Moxley murder. Because of the topic—an unsolved case—the format of the book is not conventional, although it retains many of the standard true crime tropes, including opening the book with an account of the victim's last evening and discovery of her corpse the next day, disclosure near the end of the book of exactly how the murder occurred (surmised in this case), and the middle photographic section. The book is tightly organized by both chronology of events and themes or subjects: "Background," "Taking on the Case," "Examining the Evidence," "Profiling the Participants," and "Anatomy of a Murder Investigation." Perhaps still reeling from his devastating role in the Simpson case, Fuhrman takes on the Moxley case as a kind of crusade against the rich and powerful, writing in *Murder in Greenwich* that "Greenwich may be richer, prettier, and safer than most other places on earth, but it is not immune to evil. In fact, the massive state of denial under which the town seems to operate is a form of evil itself" (Fuhrman 1998, front matter).

Aphrodite Jones (b. 1960) is the author of seven true crime texts: *A Perfect Husband* (2004), *Red Zone: The Behind-the-Scenes Story of the San Francisco Dog Mauling* (2003), *The Embrace: A True Vampire Story* (1999), *Della's Web* (1998), *All She Wanted* (1996), *Cruel Sacrifice* (1994), and *The FBI Killer* (1992). *All She Wanted* is the Brandon Teena story, which became famous as the film *Boys Don't Cry* (dir. Kimberly Peirce, 1999). Jones presents herself to the media and her readers as a "crime profiler," and her Web site publicity materials focus on her desire to fight crime and help make the country safer, and to make Americans less afraid of violence. As quoted from her Web site, Jones says, "Every crime offers a lesson. In my books, I use a narrative technique, allowing insight into the minds of victims and sociopaths. I offer analysis of everything from media coverage to legal maneuvers. However, I tend to focus my attention on the larger social issues, with the hope that future crimes will be prevented" ("The Aphrodite Jones Home Page"). Jones writes about sensational murder events that also reflect some larger cultural significance, such as teenaged killers, cult killers, or homophobia, and her writing is simplistic, straightforward, and without stylistic embellishment. Sensationalistic and rife with clichés borrowed from the tabloids, Jones's work exemplifies some of the unsavory yet popular aspects of true crime literature.

In contrast, Harold Schechter (b. 1948) crafts scholarly and impeccably-researched historical true crime stories. A professor of English at New York City's Queens College, Schechter's expertise in research shows in his well-written accounts of older, less publicized killers. His specialty is nineteenth and early twentieth century American killers, and the title-formula he uses always describes the killer's unique attribute. His books include *Deranged: The Shocking True Story of America's Most Fiendish Killer* (1990), *Deviant: The Shocking True Story of Ed*

Gein, the Original "Psycho" (1991), *Depraved: The Shocking True Story of America's First Serial Killer* (1994), *Bestial: The Savage Trail of a True American Monster* (1998), *Fiend: The Shocking True Story of America's Youngest Serial Killer* (2000), and *Fatal: The Poisonous Life of a Female Serial Killer* (2003). Schechter has also published two murderer-compendiums: *The A–Z Encyclopedia of Serial Killers* (1996) with David Everitt, and *The Serial Killer Files: The Who, What, Where, How, and Why of the World's Most Terrifying Murderers* (2004).

Historical contextualization is a unique and leading facet of Schechter's true crime, an expansion of the convention that calls for true crime to explain the killer's world. Schechter opens *Bestial* (1998) with a detail-rich introduction to the history of serial killing that includes references to both known and unknown figures: Joseph Vacher (the "French Ripper"), Fritz Haarmann (the "vampire of Hanover"), author Edgar Allan Poe, criminologists Robert K. Ressler and Ron Holmes, and 1920s murder victims Reverend Edward Wheeler Hall and Mrs. Eleanor Mills (Schechter 1998, 1–4). The book intersperses meticulous reconstructions of murderer Earle Leonard Nelson's daily life and crimes with fantastically wide-ranging descriptions of daily life in 1920s America, such as this passage from Chapter 8:

> From the perspective of the present moment, the 1920s seem like a period full of quaint and curious customs, from the mah-jongg fad to the Charleston craze to the popularity of Dr. Emile Coué's surefire panacea (a twelve-word formula guaranteed to bring contentment if recited regularly: 'Day by day in every way I am getting better and better'). For all its wildness and sophistication, the Jazz Age seems like a time of sweet simplicity compared to the 1990s—the era of "My Blue Heaven" instead of "Murder Was the Case," *Son of the Sheik* instead of *Terminator II*, *Our Dancing Daughters* instead of *Teenage Bondage Sluts*. (Schechter 1998: 63)

A casual reader could be forgiven for mistaking Schechter's true crime for works of history, for his texts rely upon sophisticated and scholarly presentations of the social, political, and cultural contexts of the crimes they narrate. But Schechter can also sensationalize with the best of the true crime scribes, and each chapter ends with him ratcheting-up the fear, tension, and expectation of horrors to come.

Jack Olsen (1925–2002) is another well known and best-selling modern true crime author, with 12 true crime books published between 1974 and 2002, and three Edgar awards. A prolific writer and journalist, Olsen did not limit himself to true crime; he also published on sports, the environment, sociology, the game of bridge, race in America, and history, as well as penning award-winning magazine and newspaper journalism and fiction. As stated on his official Web site, "Olsen was described as 'the dean of true crime authors' by the *Washington Post* and the *New York Daily News* and 'the master of true crime' by the *Detroit Free Press* and *Newsday*. *Publishers Weekly* called him 'the best true crime writer around.' His studies of crime are required reading in university criminology courses and have been cited in the *New York Times* Notable Books of the Year. In a page-one review, the *Times* described his work as 'a genuine contribution to criminology and journalism alike'" ("The Jack Olsen Home Page"). His numerous true crime texts include *The Man with the Candy: The Story of the Houston Mass Murders* (1974), *Son* (1983), and *"I": The Creation of a Serial Killer* (2002).

Olsen's true crime is quirky and original, and his last book is an example of the innovations that the genre can foster. *"I": The Creation of a Serial Killer* (2002) narrates the life and crimes of Keith Hunter Jesperson, the so-called "Happy Face Killer," in a most unusual manner: first-person narration. First-person true crime is rare, largely because of the tangle of moral, ethical, and legal issues involved in allowing or encouraging murderers to have a strong voice. But Olsen's use of the first-person in this book illuminates Jesperson's thought process and brings a fresh perspective to the stale and overwrought depictions of the killer as a moral monster. Perhaps because the first-person chapters alternate with those written in the standard third-person authorial voice, the book largely stays within the convention-bound confines of the genre, conveying the sense of a strong moral center instead of implicitly sanctioning Jesperson's actions, as a first-person account could. In other respects, the book is in standard format, including narrative arc, focus on the killer's story and life, and the inclusion of mundane details and imagined dialogue. One significant difference is that Jesperson is not described in the language of evil and monstrosity; instead, the mystery of his personality stands, and Olsen frames him by using short quotations from criminologists about sociopathy and criminal psychology.

Olsen's book suggests that further innovations in true crime are possible; indeed, one of the nominations for an Edgar award in 2007 is Terri Jentz's first-person-victim true crime book, *Strange Piece of Paradise* (2006). Jentz and a friend were attacked by an axe-wielding stranger on a camping trip in 1975; both women survived, and the book is a meditation on the aftereffects of violent crime and Jentz's personal search for her near-killer, who was never apprehended. As the genre matures and evolves, various narrative possibilities and strategies appear and bear fruit, although the standard, formulaic true crime texts remain popular and lucrative for their writers.

Reception. Twenty-first-century true crime writing responds to murder with both irrational fear and compelling fascination; although laying strong claims to factuality, truthfulness, and realistic representation of actual events, the genre continues to be driven by and preoccupied with themes of an updated, contemporary gothic horror. American true crime both responds to and reflects its context and historical circumstance, showing changes and shifts in widespread philosophical and political understandings about crime, public policy debates, definitions of insanity, and shifting perspectives on the meaning and mystery of radical evil.

Bibliography

Bugliosi, Vincent, and Curt Gentry. *Helter Skelter.* 1974. New York: Bantam Books, 1995.

Capote, Truman. *In Cold Blood: A True Account of a Multiple Murder and Its Consequences.* New York: Random House, 1965.

Fosburgh, Lacey. *Closing Time: The True Story of the "Goodbar" Murder.* New York: Delacorte Press, 1975.

Freeman, Lucy. *"Before I kill more . . ."* New York: Crown Publishers, 1955.

Fuhrman, Mark. *Murder in Greenwich: Who Killed Martha Moxley?* New York: Avon, 1999.

Gilmore, John. *The Tucson Murders.* New York: The Dial Press, 1970.

———. *The Michigan Murders.* New York: Pocket, 1976.

Glassner, Barry. *The Culture of Fear: Why Americans Are Afraid of the Wrong Things.* New York: Basic Books/Perseus, 1999.

Halttunen, Karen. *Murder Most Foul: The Killer and the American Gothic Imagination.* Cambridge: Harvard University Press, 1998.

Harrison, Ben. *True Crime Narratives: An Annotated Bibliography.* Lanham, MD: The Scarecrow Press, Inc., 1997.

Jones, Aphrodite. *Cruel Sacrifice.* New York: Pinnacle Books, 1994.

The Aphrodite Jones Home Page. [January 2007]. <http://www.aphroditejones.com/>

Levin, Meyer. *Compulsion.* 1956. New York: Carroll and Graf, 1996.

Mailer, Norman. *The Executioner's Song.* Boston: Little, Brown Company, 1979.

Marling, William. "Joseph Wambaugh." 2007. <http://www.detnovel.com/Citation.html>

Martin, Joel Bartlow. *Why Did They Kill?* New York: Bantam Books, 1953.

The Mystery Writers of America Edgar Allan Poe Awards Best Fact Crime Winners and Nominees Webpage. [January 2007]. <http://mysterywriters.org/edgarsDB/edgarDB.php>

The Jack Olsen Home Page. [January 2007]. <http://www.jackolsen.com/>

Olsen, Jack. *"I"—The Creation of a Serial Killer.* New York: St. Martin's Press, 2002.

Plimpton, George. *Truman Capote: In Which Various Friends, Enemies, Acquaintances, and Detractors Recall His Turbulent Career.* New York: Anchor Books, 1997.

Rossner, Judith. *Looking for Mr. Goodbar.* New York: Simon & Schuster, 1975.

Rule, Ann. *The Stranger Beside Me.* 1980. New York: Signet/New American Library/Penguin Putnam, 2000.

———*Small Sacrifices.* New York: Signet/Penguin, 1987.

——— *Green River, Running Red.* New York: Free Press/Simon & Schuster, 2004.

Schechter, Harold. *Bestial.* New York: Pocket/Simon & Schuster, 1998.

Stowers, Carlton. Author Website. 2007. <http://www.truecrime.net/carltonstowers/>

——— *Innocence Lost.* New York: Pocket Books, 1990.

True Detective Magazine. 1924–1995.

Wambaugh, Joseph. *The Onion Field.* 1973. New York: Bantam/Doubleday/Dell, 1987.

Further Reading

Biressi, Anita. *Crime, Fear, and the Law in True Crime Stories (Crime Files).* New York: Palgrave-Macmillan, 2001; Black, Joel. *The Aesthetics of Murder: A Study in Romantic Literature and Contemporary Culture.* Baltimore: Johns Hopkins University Press, 1991; Borowitz, Albert. *Blood and Ink: An International Guide to Fact-Based Crime Literature.* Kent, Ohio: Kent State University Press, 2002; Browder, Laura. "Dystopian Romance: True Crime and the Female Reader." *The Journal of Popular Culture* 39 (2006): 928–953; James, Laura. *Clews: The Historic True Crime Journal.* [January 2007] http://laurajames.typepad.com/clews/; Jenkins, Philip. *Using Murder: The Social Construction of Serial Homicide.* New York: A. de Gruyter, 1994; Knox, Sara L. *Murder: A Tale of Modern American Life.* Durham, NC: Duke University Press, 1998; Lane, Roger. *Murder In America: A History.* Columbus: Ohio State University Press, 1997; Lesser, Wendy. *Pictures at an Execution: An Inquiry into the Subject of Murder.* Cambridge: Harvard University Press, 1993; Ressler, Robert K., and Tom Schachtman. *Whoever Fights Monsters.* New York: St. Martin's Press, 1992; Sanders, Ed. *The Family.* 1971. New York: Thunder's Mouth Press, 2002; Seltzer, Mark. *Serial Killers: Death and Life in America's Wound Culture.* New York: Routledge, 1998; Seltzer, Mark. *True Crime: Observations on Violence and Modernity.* New York: Routledge, 2006; Schmid, David. *Natural Born Celebrities: Serial Killers in American Culture.* Chicago: University of Chicago Press, 2005.

JEAN MURLEY

URBAN FICTION

Definition. Urban fiction, potentially so broad a term as to encompass any work set in a city, requires specific definition. One approach is to work from critical criteria of what makes a work's relationship to the city its definitive quality; another is empirical, observing that in the current publishing and retail markets, "urban" refers primarily to inner-city youth culture.

Critical definitions of urban fiction are necessarily inconclusive, and overlap extensively with other genres. Detective and crime novels, novels of immigrant experience, financial thrillers, and **chick lit** all remain popular fictional interpretations of city life. In an urbanized society few works, save perhaps those set in rural places, do not fall under the broadest definition of urban literature, and few works of urban literature cannot be placed in another genre. Settling on a useful definition requires shifting the focus from content to relationships between literary form and conceptions of urban life. Historically certain forms emerged when existing genres seemed incapable of representing newly urban ways of life: realism and the industrial city; neighborhood fiction and ethnic communalism; modernism and the cultural metropolis; postmodern fiction and the city as a figure for under-construction states of mind. Contemporary popular works that adapt these forms and essay new ones are often marketed as "literary" or general fiction. Identified as aspirants to an artistic canon, critics and publishers generally eschew genre labels such as "urban" as incommensurate with such works' capacity to interpret a cultural moment.

History. The history of urban fiction broadly defined is a history of relationships between social and literary structures, as suggested in the aforementioned list of forms, whereas the more specific trajectory that leads to the current publishing definition dwells in tales of particular urban subcultures, especially ethnic and racial, and in linguistic styles associated with them—types of content and narrative rhetoric that often formalize perceived social division. The following summary traces these latter elements as they arise in the broader development of the category.

URBAN LITERATURE AND HIP-HOP CULTURE

Turning to the empirical definition, the contemporary popular marketplace intensifies the division between the generic and the literary by narrowing the definition of urban literature to refer to works, by mainly black authors, that depict inner-city life, especially among its youth. This trend draws on the broader phenomenon in which the adjective "urban" has come, in the marketing of popular culture, to refer to hip-hop music, dance, fashion, and speech. Decades after the music and fashion industries capitalized on similar opportunities, publishers have seized on this mainspring of youth culture as a growth area, seeking to erect something approximating a prose wing of hip-hop culture. In this niche marketing strategy, publishers have responded to the success of black authors' self-published and self-distributed novels in the 1990s by creating "urban" imprints and series, while booksellers have established corresponding sections.

From the middle of the nineteenth century, popular representations of what was new, unique, and dangerous about the city dealt heavily in imagery of the low life, the urban underbelly that was, paradoxically, presented as both invisible to the middle class and implicitly playing an active role in its psyche and self-definition. Authors presented narrative personae that acted as both tour guides to these realms and moral guardians from its dangers. Titles such as *New York by Gaslight* (three different works from 1848 to 1881) were prominent in what critic David S. Reynolds (b. 1949) terms the "immoral" or "dark reform" mode, one of the most popular and controversial types of prose in the nineteenth century (59–84). Jacob Riis's (1849–1914) documentary project *How the Other Half Lives* (1890) marks the arrival of what twentieth-century readers would recognize as a legitimately reformist framing of voyeuristic material, the kind that still characterizes much of urban journalism and social science. Urban fiction in the early twentieth century drew on—even if in various ways it subverted or transcended--this voyeuristic and didactic realism. For example, Stephen Crane's (1871–1900) *Maggie, a Girl of the Streets* (1893), Theodore Dreiser's (1871–1945) *Sister Carrie* (1899), Paul Laurence Dunbar's (1872–1906) *The Sport of the Gods* (1902), and Upton Sinclair's (1878–1968) *The Jungle* (1906) are plotted around the controversial moral and material trajectories of the poor, the middle class, and the newly arriving black and immigrant populations in the city, respectively.

A subsequent generation of urban writers, many of whom were products of the urban working classes, adapted realism to forms more attentive to the communal structures of the city and the perspectives of its working-class inhabitants, in the neighborhood fiction of the 1920s and 1930s. Closely related to domestic ethnography and often presented as dramatized appeals to socialism, neighborhood novels are typically *bildungsromans* of assimilation, alienation, and/or political awakening, set in the ethnic quarters of the industrial city. Examples include Anzia Yezierska's (1881–1970) *Bread Givers* (1925), Claude McKay's (1889–1948) *Home to Harlem* (1928), Mike Gold's (1894–1967) *Jews without Money,* and James T. Farrell's (1904–1979) *Studs Lonigan* trilogy. Like much of the urban realism that preceded it, neighborhood fiction claimed access to a realm that was mysterious and problematic to a middle-class readership. Though mid-century critics characterized the first generations of neighborhood fiction as overly literal and didactic, much influential fiction of this latter period—by Richard Wright (1908–1960), Saul Bellow (1915–2005), Ralph Ellison (1913–1994), Bernard Malamud (1914–1986), Philip Roth (b. 1933), James Baldwin (1924–1987), and Paule Marshall (b. 1929), for example—is grounded in the neighborhood mode.

Much of **African American fiction** is drawn across the difference between the urban village and the anonymous metropolitan society. The Harlem Renaissance of the 1920s was predicated on the relationship to national culture of a single, identity-defined place, as the capital and embodiment of a racially defined community. This movement also birthed lyrical prose styles inspired by colloquial speech and the rhythms of blues and jazz. This musically centered culture is recognized as the source of the twentieth century phenomenon of cool style. Such style, the cultural expression of a particular community of identity and its shared experience, is associated with the broader notion of self-presentation as a feature of urban society, a phenomenon dramatized in the nineteenth century in the figure of the dandy or flaneur. The idea of detached, avant-garde individualism in the word "urbane" attached to a sense of the term "urban" that inflects its current marketing uses in the culture industries.

Variations on the cool style and jazz-influenced language were adopted by writers of the Beat Generation in New York and San Francisco, and in cultural commentary by self-consciously avant-garde writers including Norman Mailer. Ishmael Reed (b. 1938), in *Mumbo Jumbo* (1972), imagines a history of America through the origins and circulation of black music, to create an early entrant in the genre of postmodern metahistorical fiction. Reed's novel, like E.L. Doctorow's (b. 1931) *Ragtime* (1975), draws historical structure from a conception of New York as a multi-ethnic cauldron of American cultural exchange, a function embodied in the styles not only of characters but of the prose itself.

The tradition of Harlem writing as an epicenter of urban literary form continued beyond the 1920s, in not only the self-consciously literary novels of Ellison and Baldwin but also in a memorable detective series by Chester Himes (1909–1984). Himes's first novel, *If He Hollers Let Him Go* (1945), was a groundbreaking depiction of racial conditions in Los Angeles during World War II. Himes created two Harlem police detectives, Coffin Ed Johnson and Gravedigger Jones, in a series of ten novels from 1957–69, including *Cotton Comes to Harlem* (1965), which was adapted into an influential film in 1970. Himes's novels adopt conventions of the detective novel, but apply them in the social density of the neighborhood tradition, to explore racial issues freed from the obligations of earnest reform but not given over to the naïve notions of authenticity of the subsequent "street" genre.

The neighborhood mode proved a flexible vehicle for interpreting the dilemmas of urban crisis in the 1970s and 1980s. August Wilson (1945–2005), in his cycle of Pittsburgh plays (1982–2005), and John Edgar Wideman (b. 1941), in his *Homewood* trilogy (1985), structure broad explorations of the African American experience from the specific terms of contemporary black neighborhoods in Pittsburgh. Against the hardening notion that ghettos are permanently broken features of the urban landscape, these works find in black neighborhoods living evidence of high-functioning communalism inherited from both distant and recent pasts. While Wilson and Wideman emphasize the bonds of fatherhood and brotherhood, Gloria Naylor (b. 1950), in *The Women of Brewster Place* (1982), depicts the redemptive possibilities of matriarchal communalism on an isolated, near-broken tenement street. Naylor's popularity endures: Oprah Winfrey (b. 1954) produced and starred in a 1989 film adaptation of Naylor's novel, while a musical stage adaptation was scheduled to premiere in Washington, D.C. in 2007. The restored prestige of neighborhood genres owes in part to the rise of multiculturalism as an educational premise. For example, Sandra Cisneros's (b. 1954) *The House on Mango Street* (1985), a child's-eye-view Chicago neighborhood novel, remains among the most frequently assigned novels on middle and high school reading curricula.

The onset of the urban crisis period in the 1960s also factors into the current publishing trend toward sensational "street" fiction, beginning with a resurgence of the reform and protest modes in popular works of domestic anthropology, such as Elliot Liebow's (1925–1994) *Tally's Corner* (1966), in memoirs such as Claude Brown's (1937–2002) *Manchild in the Promised Land* (1965), and experimental novels such as *The System of Dante's Hell* (1965) by LeRoi Jones (now Amiri Baraka) (b. 1934). Brown's story of his life growing up on the streets of Harlem entered into elite conversations about race, poverty, reform, and writing. A spate of even more sensational memoirs in the following years partook of the late-1960s trend toward counter-cultural identities in pop culture. Titles such as *Pimp!* and *Dopefiend* led the street fiction that influenced the blaxploitation films of the 1970s. Although temperamentally associated with black revolutionary movements, no political role emerged; and this refusal or inability to seek a way out of the crisis—not even on the Afrocentric terms of the neighborhood novelists—suggests an acceptance of the mainstream sense that cities and the communities that called them home had been lost to history.

Leading figures in this movement were Robert Beck (a.k.a. Iceberg Slim) (1918–1992) and Donald Goines (1937–1974). Beck's 1967 memoir, *Pimp! The Story of My Life,* spawned a host of imitators. Beck followed it with a half-dozen novels in the 1970s that were said to draw mainly on this same stock of personal experience, blurring the line between fiction and nonfiction in a manner similar to the dark-tales mode of the nineteenth century. Goines was a heroin addict who, beginning in prison in 1971, wrote 16 melodramatic drug-crime novels before being shot to death in 1974. European reviewers, especially, praised the shocking content of Goines's work as the highest degree of authenticity, a notion that remains the central currency of street and hip-hop cultures. Beck and Goines helped to establish and continue to influence the street genres in which much of today's hip-hop film and fiction operates.

The gangsta rap of the late 1980s informed an aggressive, unrepentant tone in a resurgence of street fiction in the 1990s. This contemporary movement is more directly a product of the entrepreneurial efforts of a number of black writers who struggled to find outlets for sensational ghetto novels. The success of Sister Souljah's (Lisa Williamson, b. 1964) *The Coldest Winter Ever* (1999) helped open major publishing venues to the street and ghetto genres. Souljah was a prominent rapper whose militant rhetoric had become a conservative touchstone in the 1992 presidential campaign. Her novel, which juxtaposes a hedonistic young female product of the ghetto drug business with Souljah herself as a spiritually grounded Harlem activist, was hailed by mainstream reviewers for its social and linguistic realism.

Trends and Themes. Literary strands of popular urban fiction remain centered around efforts to construct historical narratives that make sense of the massive changes cities have undergone in the last century: to recall what cities were like in earlier eras, to understand how urban crisis happened, to imagine what might be recovered, and to develop forms that speak to what cities look like now. Prominent in these projects are inter-generational neighborhood novels, both retrospective and futuristic detective fiction, historical recreations of city life in the industrial era, and classic naïf-in-the-big-city *bildungsromans*.

Pete Hamill (b. 1935) is among the most popular authors of the historical novel; for example, *The Gift* (a 1973 novella re-released in 2005) and *North River* (2007) are stories of the 1950s and the 1930s in New York City that seek to recover in narrative the redemptive possibilities woven into the dense class and ethnic fabric of pre-crisis New York City. In the neighborhood genre, Diane McKinney-Whetstone's four Philadelphia novels, beginning with *Tumbling* in 1996, in a vein similar to Wilson and Wideman's Pittsburgh literature, depict black life in Philadelphia before the onset of urban crisis, both for clues as to what changed in recent decades and for sources of communal strength that are or could be the basis for regeneration.

Detective novelists remain active interpreters of city life. Walter Mosley's (b. 1952) Easy Rawlins (1990–2005) series about a black private eye in L.A., and his Fearless Jones novels (2001–2006), about an even more marginalized mystery-solver, dramatize social conflict in Los Angeles in the post-WWII period through the onset of urban crisis. In *Always Outnumbered, Always Outgunned* (1998), Mosley turns to a more explicitly neighborhood-oriented plot, surrounding the efforts of a convicted violent criminal to redeem himself and in the process begin to reform a Watts neighborhood devastated by the crisis period that culminated in the 1991 Rodney King riots. Similarly, Dennis Lehane's (b. 1966) Kenzie-Gennaro novels explore the effects of urban crisis and its aftermath on, primarily, white working-class Boston; like Mosley, when Lehane turned from the detective genre in *Mystic River* (2001), he moved in the direction of the neighborhood novel, dramatizing the fate of the working class in an era of gentrification.

The street genres that make ever louder claims on the category of "urban" have adopted the hip-hop sensibility and the trend in recent rap music toward sensational representations of ghetto life. This phenomenon appears not only in the content of the novels but in their packaging; framing material constructs an authorial persona as a street insider, a multifaceted entrepreneur, and a master of the genre. Long sets of acknowledgments, a melodramatic anthem about street life, an emotive dedication, testimony to having defied the "haters," and references to the author's apparent media empire together read like the first few minutes of a rap album, in which the artist establishes a persona and a social stance with shout-outs and exclamations descriptive of self and crew.

Rap-fiction crossover products are the latest development in this market. For example, in the fall of 2006 Vibe Street Lit, a publishing venture of *Vibe*, a magazine of "urban music and fashion"—urban meaning hip-hop—announced the publication of *Death Around the Corner*, the first novel by rapper C-Murder (Corey Miller, b. 1971). The announcement claims that the novel, about "family drama, school, jail, hustling, and the rap game," is the type of story that "mainstream publishing has long ignored or resisted." It emphasizes the fact that C-Murder began writing the novel while "facing a life sentence for second-degree murder" and that the novel features "a cameo appearance" by another rapper, Master P (Percy Miller, b. 1967) (*Vibe* press release). Similarly, MTV/Pocketbooks has partnered with 50 Cent (Curtis Jackson, b. 1975), the rap superstar whose authenticity is guaranteed by actual bullet wounds, and the G-Unit hip-hop brand to produce a series of street novels co-authored by 50 Cent with prominent writers in the genre, including Nikki

Turner. These novels are based on the kinds of personae used by the rappers in question. This trend takes the popular genre further in the direction of the adolescent melodrama, in a way that seems designed to replicate the extension of rap music and hip-hop fashion's primary consumer market from the city neighborhood to the middle-class suburb.

Some themes appear across multiple urban genres. For example, early entrants in the new ghetto novel, which remain among the most popular in the genre—Teri Woods's *True to the Game*, and Omar Tyree's *Flyy Girl*, for example—are similar to the novels of historical recreation. They present the 1980s as a unique and formative urban era of decadence, danger, and, especially for teenagers, previously undreamed of glamour and adventure. Additionally, they often echo the neighborhood novel in their attention to place, as in Shannon Holmes's Baltimore novel, *B-More Careful*.

Female heroines figure prominently in each of these genres. In the literary titles, this form often draws on Toni Morrison's (b. 1931) example of the black woman as the epicenter of historical trauma and the vehicle for potential regeneration. In the street genres it more often takes the form of a picaresque heroine, a resourceful survivor, typically a drug kingpin's moll, whose end comes in melodramatic punishment or sentimental triumph. In the less sensational modes, narratives typically work through the ordinary trials of female adolescence and young adulthood as they are structured and intensified by urban social problems.

Authenticity and realism have long been obsessions in popular urban literature, but in the new street genres the terms' import seems to overshadow all other considerations. Street authors and their readers often demand that the novels in every sense, not merely in representation, adhere to a code of the streets, remaining "true to the Game" regardless of narrative distance or moral messaging. The "Game," in general, stands not just for illegal hustling, but for materialism in general as a means of survival. Arguably the street genres' central dynamic is the effort to craft some edifying message out of extended celebrations of material acquisition and physical conquest.

Contexts and Issues. The primary context for the new street fiction is the business of pop culture, especially in terms of the profitability of hip-hop and the role of artist-entrepreneurs in that realm. Some of the leading authors of popular urban fiction established reputations while controlling the production and distribution of their works. Vickie Stringer, Relentless Aaron, and others self-published novels in the world of ghetto cultural promotion, selling their books and establishing their public identities in much the same ways that promoters flyer concerts and aspiring rappers circulate CDs (Johnson). Many have since been picked up by big publishers that reprint the most successful self-published novels (McCune). Tyree's *Flyy Girl*, for example, was published by a small press as early as 1993 but didn't find wide release until it was reprinted by Simon & Schuster in 2001 under its "Urban Classic" series. Others, though, have founded their own publishing companies and have continued to market at the street level. Woods's self-publishing enterprise began as an effort to publish and sell her novel *True to the Game*. After failing to find a publisher, in 1998, Woods began selling self-produced copies from the trunk of her car. In 1999 she launched her own publishing enterprise as a platform for the novel, subsequently mentoring Holmes, another of the most successful contemporary street novelists. *True to the Game* has since come to be seen as one of the founding entries in the contemporary genre, and was republished by Warner Books in 2007 in a "Special Collectors" edition.

Thus urban authors are subject to the dynamic that holds in most published fiction, by which publishers bestow legitimacy on writers and their works. But at the same time the street-oriented writers participate in the rhetoric and the reality of hip-hop business, in which personal control of production and distribution is a mark of authenticity, of having brought the supposed entrepreneurial mastery of the dealer and the pimp to the legitimate business world. The apotheosis of this business-model-as-artistic-content comes in the form of rap personae such as Sean "Diddy" Combs (b. 1969) and Jay-Z (Shawn Corey Carter, b. 1969). In fiction, the presentation of a similar role becomes part of the novel's packaging, speaking to the author's authenticity as a "Player in the Game." For example, Stringer, reputedly in prison for cocaine distribution in Columbus, Ohio, as late as 1998, co-founded Triple Crown Publications with Holmes in 2002 (Ghose). In the new crossover ventures by publishers and music companies, the rap star is named as an actual author.

The social context for urban fiction—the nature of the ghetto as it appears in pop culture—is still to a great extent defined by the difference between two social science models that have been touchstones in debates about urban crisis. Anthropologists in the 1960s found socioeconomic causes, centering around job loss and racism, for what were popularly perceived as historical after-effects or social and cultural failings in black neighborhoods. But Oscar Lewis's (1914–1970) work on the "culture of poverty" (1959–1969) argued that, for example, poor Puerto Ricans in San Juan and New York City shared with each other and handed down to their children a set of habits that not only expressed but also conserved their deprivation. This idea was taken up by the conservative movement and played a role in political debates over welfare in the 1980s.

William Julius Wilson (b. 1935), in sociological studies of ghetto poverty from the 1970s on, is among the social scientists who expressly counter Lewis's model with an economic one that views job availability as a determining factor in neighborhood status and, less directly, individual behavior. Wilson and others identify this approach as heir to W.E.B. Du Bois' (1868–1963) *The Philadelphia Negro* (1899) and St. Clair Drake (1911–1990) and Horace Cayton's (1859–1940) *Black Metropolis* (1945), works that bear close relationships to previous generations of urban fiction. Wilson, like his intellectual ancestors, found black neighborhoods to be structured by unusually proximate and easily traversable class differences, a dynamic identified initially by Du Bois as a product of racial segregation that is a source of both division and solidarity in the black community.

Broadly, the literary genres align with the economic argument while the street genres implicitly, and sometimes very explicitly, make the culture argument. Detective, historical, and neighborhood novels pay close attention to the kinds of jobs that are available to heads of household in a given era, and usually tie social stresses to the economic dynamics of the family and the surrounding community. They also tend to be very aware of the scale of class difference within a given neighborhood. The street genres, by contrast, insist that the hustling "Game" is an element of black culture that can and should survive material success, and that upwardly mobile individuals should "keep it real" by continuing to adhere to the code of the street. In this, despite their occasional flamboyant uses of civil rights and black power rhetoric, they come down clearly, if unintentionally, on the side of the culture argument.

But these popular genres also speak to Wilson and his forebears' description of class structure in black neighborhoods. Like rap music, recent urban fiction is influenced by the appeal, and the proximity, of street life to children of middle-class homes. Settings often encompass both high-functioning working-to-middle-class neighborhoods and the streets and projects of the impoverished ghetto. Drama arises from the conflicting appeals of each realm to a young protagonist in a stable family. This dynamic also appears in the lives of the genre's authors, including Goines and Stringer, who grew up in middle-class homes on the East Side of Detroit, but gravitated to street culture and drug sales (Cunningham). Here, too, the new popular genres often come down on the side of the culture argument. Conventional upward mobility is often available in these novels; it is not economic pressure but the allure of a morally defiant, physically adventurous version of ghetto life that often triumphs, if not over the main character then over the majority of her peers.

Reception. The reception of urban fiction speaks to the difficulty in defining it, a difficulty grounded in the divide in marketing and perception between literary and genre fiction. Works offered as literary—often in the genres of neighborhood, detective, and historical novels—are less often assessed in terms of how they imagine the city than in terms of how they imagine the mental and moral lives of their characters. A prominent reviewer praises Mosley's *Always Outnumbered, Always Outgunned,* because he "has not appliqued his morality; he has located its deep coiled root and tracked it up to the surface" (Birkerts). In a review of Pete Hamill's *North River*, New York City is a source of "detail and ambience" that "showcases" the novel's deeper truth, which is "the power of human goodness and . . . love" (Publishers Weekly).

While these novels are undoubtedly psychological, inattention to the ways they are informed by their conceptions of cities is another way in which, in popular culture, the "urban" field is ceded to genres that can be most directly associated with black youth culture. This latter category includes more than just street fiction; in a collection set in Harlem, award-winning young adult writer Walter Dean Myers (b. 1937) is said to achieve "an overall effect of sitting on the front stoop swapping stories of the neighborhood"; and to have successfully combined "the search for personal identity" with "the sense of place."

But it is the hardcore street novels that are understood to be most directly about urban life. The concept of authenticity colors heavily the reception of street fiction, as it does their content. The kinds of street fiction that come to the attention of book reviewers are often praised in the same terms ("straight from the streets") that fans bestow on the less polished variety ("keeping it real"). Mosley, for example, is quoted on the back cover of *The Coldest Winter Ever* calling Souljah "an Emile Zola of the hip-hop generation," and the novel "an unflinching eye at the truth."

Three factors contribute to producing this response: the works are packaged to maximize the perception of authentic realism; mainstream reviewers and readers often have no references by which to judge such claims; and young or otherwise unsophisticated consumers of culture, even those who live in the city, tend to be highly drawn to the framing of sensation and melodrama as reality. The stock defense of gangsta rap as documentary realism rings out from the record company boardroom to the lyric itself to the school playground, reframing even the most celebratory violence and misogyny as a form of protest; it is applied to street fiction as well. The appeal of this claim might be attributable to a dearth of other kinds of representations of the ghetto environment against which to compare the sensational. It is typically other modes of representation, not independent reality, by which qualities such as realism and authenticity are assessed.

Selected Authors. Among the best-selling authors of what publishers call urban fiction are Woods (*True to the Game*), Stringer (*Let that be the Reason*), Holmes (*B-More Careful*), Turner (*A Hustler's Wife*), Tyree (*Flyy Girl*), and K'Wan (*Hood Rat*). It is helpful, in understanding what "urban" means in these novels, to compare such visions of the city to those of popular authors whose work is published and sold independently of this new marketing imperative.

A comparison of two Philadelphia novels reveals what ground the literary and the street genres can share and where they tend to part ways. McKinney-Whetstone's *Leaving Cecil Street* was published in 2004 under HarperCollins's William Morrow imprint ("the highest quality fiction"). Tyree's *Flyy Girl,* originally self-published in 1993, was released by Simon & Schuster in its Urban Classic Novel series in 2000, the year after that publisher's success with Soujah's *The Coldest Winter Ever.* Tyree's novel is more "neighborhood" and less "street" than much of the new ghetto fiction, but it is an influential work in the genre and establishes a prototypical picaresque heroine. Both novels aim for broad, historically aware understandings of black city life, both in terms of its highest potentials and its worst degradations, by dramatizing the vulnerability of even the model neighborhood, as key opening passages reveal:

> Cecil Street was feeling some kind of way in 1969. Safely tucked away in the heart of West Philadelphia, this had always been a charmed block. A pleasure to walk through the way the trees lined the street from end to end and made arcs when they were in full leaf. The outsides of the houses stayed in good repair, with unchipped banister posts and porches mopped down daily because the people here sat out a lot, their soothing chatter jumping the banisters from end to end about how the numbers had come that day or what had happened on *Edge of Night.* And even though the block had long ago made the transition from white to colored to Negro to Black is Beautiful, the city still provided street cleaning twice a week in the summer when the children took to the outside and there was the familiar smack of the double-Dutch rope. (McKinney-Whetstone, 2004, 3)

> Dave was definitely a catch. His high income enabled them to move into a comfortable and scenic black neighborhood in Northwest Philadelphia. In Germantown, they had the luxury of private lawns, patios, driveways and lots of trees, which surrounded their three-bedroom twin house, things not affordable to the many Philadelphians who lived in crowded row-house areas. Patti worked at a nursing home as a dietitian, adding to their snug income. . . . . The seventies had been prosperous for blacks. (Tyree, 2000, 14–15, 21)

Thus each novel opens by explicitly connecting work, family, and neighborhood to the history of the city. In each, a neighborhood, which would seem to middle-class outsiders like a ghetto, is a model of prosperity and stability that has been aspired to and fought for. Both novels also begin with two-parent, lower-middle-class homes. The drama of each novel unfolds as the forces of instability are revealed to be close at hand and at every level, from sexual exploitation and drug sales to government apathy and hostility. These novels join the long tradition of urban literature, in which institutions from places of work, to modes of transportation, to living room decor, give structure to human needs and desires, providing vehicles for creativity, mastery, sexuality, and recovery from trauma, that are primarily healthy or destructive. In a sense, these novels about neighborhoods on the edge reveal the literal stakes of middle-class conventions that in other settings can seem petty: an authoritarian parental style or a broken teenage friendship comes, in these environments, to have potentially life-or-death consequences. But whereas the Philadelphia of *Leaving Cecil Street* provides for a communal solution, in *Flyy Girl* it is the tableau upon which a lone survivor adventures.

Leaving Cecil Street is set on one block in West Philadelphia in the summer of 1969. The ostensibly idyllic street is troubled by signs of impending crisis: the assassination of Martin Luther King Jr., the Vietnam War, heroin sales, sporadic violent crime, the deterioration of locally owned businesses, and hostility from previously supportive white authorities. Of greater concern to the narrative, though, are unresolved traumas and tensions in the lives of the central adult characters, and the effects on their adolescent children.

But the neighborhood structure that fails at first to recognize these fissures is also the source of their repair. The block is so "tight" as to have its own space-time, in which buildings are named after the day of the week their major activities occur. Homes are separated by thin walls permeable to emotion as well as sound. The block party is the apotheosis of this communal life, in which desires and identities interpenetrate in a striking example of the neighborhood novel's rebuke to orthodox individualism. The novel opens at one such party, in which the characters are so unsettled by their lifelong anxieties that they fail to notice a mysterious, frail woman, dying of alcohol-induced liver disease, crawling into a cellar, where she remains for much of the novel, not participating in but attuned to the psychological rhythms of the house and the neighborhood.

The narrative, playing back and forth between the neighborhood's present and the youths of its adults, reveals that this woman's quest to resolve her own trauma is bound to the events that are threatening the neighboring families. This narrative device, in which proximate urbanites, apparently thrown together randomly, are revealed to be embedded in a web of close relationships, is a staple of urban literature dating to Charles Dickens. The neighborhood is connected to the larger city by its residents' pasts, illustrated in one virtuosic chapter by another classic convention of urban literature: the el train acts as a narrative vehicle to limn the structure of the industrial city and the scope of the characters' lives. The novel culminates in another block party, in which again the signs of urban crisis appear in the form of black power rhetoric among the crowd and a hostile white police presence. But the expected violence never materializes, and instead the traumas afflicting the families are resolved in acts of purification and recombination. *Leaving Cecil Street* raises the expectation of calamity and disintegration, not only its internal narrative tensions, but also from the reader's knowledge of what happened to many such black neighborhoods in this era. But in its ending it rejects the historical logic of urban crisis in favor of a psychoanalytical logic of healing, the working-through being as much a communal process as an individual one.

Flyy Girl narrates one girl's childhood and adolescence in the Northwest Philadelphia neighborhood of Germantown in the 1980s, an era the novel identifies as uniquely expansive and dangerous for adolescents and black communities alike, an acceleration given color by frequent descriptions of fashion and music. Starting at age 13, the precocious Tracy Ellis plows through a series of partners, learning to manipulate boys as the only alternative, for a sexually adventurous girl, to being exploited. But even this position of power quickly becomes physically dangerous and spiritually destructive, as Tracy tries to conquer ever more willful and violent boyfriends. By contrast her next-door-neighbor Raheema is a bookworm who, bullied by her father, is afraid of boys and depressed. The novel does not apologize for Tracy's sexual adventuring and manipulative behavior, even as it suggests her parents' separation lies behind it; in fact Tyree's prose revels in her sexual pleasure, fashion sense, and mastery of the adolescent games of romance. The novel connects Tracy's personality to narrative art, rejecting the notion that the artist is a detached but imaginative observer. Tracy's charisma includes the ability to spin thrilling stories out of the everyday teen events in which she also plays the lead role, in contrast to Raheema, who can only look on, engage in unimaginative gossip, and wonder what it would be like to be a part of the drama. It is Tracy, not Raheema, who at the end of the novel becomes a poet in the self-dramatizing slam style.

As the 1980s proceed, rougher neighborhoods in North and South Philly exert a gravitational force on the adventurous youth of Germantown, especially as the drug trade becomes lucrative. Raheema's older sister Mercedes falls victim to crack, and in a period of reflection and sexual abstinence that follows, Tracy joins a group of college students who are interested in black culture and social issues. But Tracy returns to Victor, an ex-boyfriend from the street scene, who has been convicted of a violent crime related to his drug dealing. In prison, the intelligent but unschooled Victor joins the Nation of Islam and writes to Tracy asking her to wait for him and be his bride so that they can play their part rebuilding the black community. Victor's request is authoritarian, but his appeal to cultural regeneration, combined with the unwavering self-confidence, are too much for her to resist. The novel ends in a letter from Tracy at college to her father at home, telling him of her plans to wait for Victor.

Flyy Girl presents a girl caught up in the "Game" who learns lessons from hard, dangerous, experience. But though it probes the fatal boundaries of materialism and self-centeredness, its message is not that of the orthodox morality tale. A character like Tracy simply must have adventure and drama, the novel suggests, and young people reaching physical maturity will unavoidably experiment sexually. By contrast, *Leaving Cecil Street* looks to historical communal sources for the strength to withstand, and adapt to, the forces that threaten to pull apart individuals, families, and neighborhoods. *Flyy Girl,* while recognizing the importance of education, work, and parent-child relationships, emphasizes the strength of the individual survivor. This difference speaks generally for two distinct modes of popular urban fiction.

This distinction is reproduced in different visions of Harlem, by one of the most successful street novelists and by one of the leading authors of urban youth fiction. Woods's *True to the Game,* still among the best-selling works of the new ghetto fiction, is like a sexed-up, thug-life version of *Flyy Girl.* The main character, Gena, lives in Philadelphia, but she and her girlfriend Sahira travel among the cities of the East Coast, from Atlanta to New York, to party among young black men flush with the rewards of the late 1980s cocaine trade. The opening scene takes place in Harlem:

> 125th was a mini Greek playland in the middle of Harlem. Gena had no understanding. It wasn't like Philly. It was larger, and the niggas looked like Eric B and Rakim, with humongous gold chains and diamond medallions the size of bread plates. If it was meant to represent wealth, that shit did its job. And Gena liked it. She looked at the girls and could not help staring at them. They had no clothes on. They were sexy and

revealing, and Gena wanted to be amongst them, fucking with niggas, getting her life on. New York was the shit. There was no way she could live there, though. It was so fast, too fast. Fast niggas, fast cars, and fast lifestyles. The magnitude was large, as was the amount of men. Even the cars in New York looked different. Gena didn't know if it was the rims or the tires or what was going on. The dashboards were customized, leather MCM and Louis Vutton [sic] seats, not to mention the detailed piping and thousand-dollar sound systems. That shit turned her the fuck on. Everything about New York turned her on, especially the guys. (1–2)

This description of Harlem, though contemporary in its language, understands the city in one of its perennial modes: as a material Eden but a moral minefield, with a dazzling surface that snares the naive newcomer. In *True to the Game,* though, as in others of its kind, the celebration of excess is never contained by the moral of the story. As one might expect, Gena falls for a Harlem thug with a fast car, God-like looks, pitch-perfect style, and a heart devoted to only her; but, as one might also guess, the criminal life that funds all this perfection is more dangerous, and harder to get out of, than she could have imagined. Hard lessons are learned and lives are broken, but Gena survives intact and in possession of a baby blue Mercedes-Benz.

In the Harlem of Walter Dean Myers's *145th Street Short Stories,* a Mercedes-Benz is just an adolescent's fantasy:

I like a lot of things about Harlem, especially the block, which was how we talked about 145th Street. There were good people on the block, but what I wanted was to be more than what I saw on the block. Uncle Duke said I could be more, but if I put Harlem out of my heart I could end up being a lot less, too.

Yeah, well, I was ready to take my chances. What I wanted to do was to be a doctor and have a nice crib, and a Benz, the whole nine. Then the thing happened with Monkeyman. (74)

In "Monkeyman," a quiet youth risks his life standing up to a new gang; in hospital, he tells the narrator that after going to art school in Pittsburgh, he wants to return to Harlem and open a studio. The narrator, while not giving up his dream of a doctor's salary, wonders at the story's conclusion whether he might return to practice the healing arts in the old neighborhood.

Myers's Harlem is a multi-generational narrative where those who survive hardships gain in strength and wisdom, because the shared circumstances of the place bind them in familial relations. Like McKinney-Whetstone, Myers picks up the thread of black neighborhood fiction, in which community is more life-sustaining than repressive, and in which communal identity is a real part of each individual. Myers's narrative binds generations, not just among characters, but through the history of Harlem and black America. "A Christmas Story" opens, "It was rumored that Mother Fletcher was well over ninety years old. She had become a legend on 145th Street. If anybody wanted to know what the neighborhood looked like in the twenties, where Jack Johnson had lived, perhaps, or where James Baldwin's father had preached, Mother Fletcher could tell you" (105). This story examines a white police officer's perspective of the neighborhood, inhabiting his experiences sympathetically, something inconceivable in street fiction. Myers's collection is in control of its own narrative structure and its uses of colloquial language in ways the street novels are not; though the street novels trade in adolescent fantasy, it is *145th Street* that is published as a children's book.

Bibliography

Beck, Robert. *Pimp! The Story of My Life by Iceberg Slim.* Los Angeles: Holloway House, 1969.

Birkerts, Sven. "The Socratic Method." Review of Walter Mosley, *Always Outnumbered, Always Outgunned. New York Times.* 9 Nov. 1997.

Brown, Claude. *Manchild in the Promised Land.* New York: Macmillan, 1965.

Cisneros, Sandra. *The House on Mango Street.* New York: Random House, 1991.

C-Murder. *Death Around the Corner.* New York: Vibe Street Lit, 2007.

Concepcion, Mariel. "VIBE's Line of Urban Fiction Publishes Rapper C-Murder's First Novel." 1 Sept. 2006. *Vibe Books.* <http://www.vibe.com/news/news_headlines/2006/09/vibe_street_lit_publishes_cmurder_first_novel/>

Crane, Stephen. *Maggie, a Girl of the Streets and Other New York Writings.* New York: Random House, 2001.

Cunningham, Jonathan. "Romancing the Hood." *Detroit Metrotimes,* 22–28 June 2005.

Doctorow, E.L. *Ragtime.* New York: Random House, 1997.

Drake, St. Clair and Horace Cayton. *Black Metropolis: A Study of Negro Life in a Northern City.* New York: Harcourt, Brace, 1945.

Dreiser, Theodore. *Sister Carrie.* Boston: Houghton Mifflin, 1959.

Du Bois, W.E.B. *The Philadelphia Negro: A Social Study.* Philadelphia: University of Pennsylvania Press, 1996.

Dunbar, Paul Laurence. *The Sport of the Gods.* New York: Dodd, Mead, 1902.

Farrell, James T. *Young Lonigan.* New York: Penguin, 2001.

50 Cent and Nikki Turner. *Death Before Dishonor.* New York: G-Unit/Pocket Books, 1997.

Foster, George. *New York by Gaslight and Other Urban Sketches.* Berkeley: University of California Press, 1990.

Foye, K'Wan. *Hood Rat.* New York: St. Martin's Press, 2006.

Ghose, Dave. "Crime Does Pay." *Columbus Monthly,* Nov. 2004.

Goines, Donald. *Dopefiend.* Los Angeles: Holloway House, 2003.

———. *Never Die Alone.* Los Angeles: Holloway House, 2003.

Gold, Mike. *Jews without Money.* New York: H. Liveright, 1930.

Hamill, Pete. *The Gift.* New York: Random House, 1973.

———. *North River.* Boston: Little, Brown, 2007.

Himes, Chester. *If He Hollers Let Him Go.* Garden City, NY: Doubleday, 1945.

———. *Cotton Comes to Harlem.* Chatham, N.J.: Chatham, 1965.

Holmes, Shannon. *B-More Careful.* New York: Terri Woods, 2001.

Johnson, Lynne D. "Relentless Aaron—Urban Fiction's Don." *Vibe Book Talk,* 16 Sept. 2004. <http://www.vibe.com/news/online_exclusives/2004/09/book_talk_relentless_aaron_urban_fictions_don/>

Jones, LeRoi. *The System of Dante's Hell.* New York: Grove Press, 1965.

Lehane, Dennis. *Mystic River.* New York: William Morrow, 2001.

Lewis, Oscar. *La Vida: A Puerto Rican Family in the Culture of Poverty.* New York: Random House, 1966.

Liebow, Eliot. *Tally's Corner: A Study of Negro Streetcorner Men.* Boston: Little, Brown, 1967.

Mailer, Norman. "The White Negro: Superficial Reflections on the Hipster." *Dissent* IV (Spring 1957).

"Mama Black Widow." Dir. Darren Grant. Screenplay by Will De Los Santos, from novel by Robert Beck. Muse Productions, 2007 (in production). IMDb.com. <www.imdb.com/title/tt0301595/>

McCabe, James. *New York by Gaslight: A Work Descriptive of the Great American Metropolis.* New York: Crown, 1984.

McCune, Jenny. "The Rise of Urban Fiction." *PMA, the Independent Book Publishers Association.* Oct. 2005. <http://www.pma-online.org/scripts/shownews.cfm?id=1216>

McInerney, Jay. *Bright Lights, Big City.* New York: Vintage, 1984.

McKay, Claude. *Home to Harlem*. New York: Harper & Bros., 1928.

McKinney-Whetstone, Diane. *Leaving Cecil Street*. New York: HarperCollins, 2004.

———. *Tumbling*. New York: Simon & Schuster, 1996.

Mosley, Walter. *Always Outnumbered, Always Outgunned*. New York: Washington Square Press, 1998.

Myers, Walter Dean. *145th Street Short Stories*. New York: Random House, 2000.

Naylor, Gloria. *The Women of Brewster Place*. New York: Penguin, 1982.

Reed, Ishmael. *Mumbo Jumbo*. New York: Scribner, 1972.

Riis, Jacob. *How the Other Half Lives*. New York: Penguin, 1997.

Sinclair, Upton. *The Jungle*. New York: Norton, 2003.

Sister Souljah. *The Coldest Winter Ever*. New York: Simon & Schuster, 1999.

Stringer, Vickie. *Dirty Red*. New York: Simon & Schuster, 2006.

———. *Let That Be the Reason*. New York: A&B, 2002.

Turner, Nikki. *A Hustler's Wife*. Columbus, Ohio: Triple Crown, 2003.

Tyree, Omar. *Flyy Girl*. New York: Simon & Schuster, 2000.

Wideman, John Edgar. *The Homewood Books*. Pittsburgh, PA.: University of Pittsburgh Press, 1992.

Wilson, August. *Fences*. New York: New American Library, 1986.

Wilson, William Julius. *When Work Disappears: The World of the New Urban Poor*. New York: Knopf, 1996.

The Women of Brewster Place. Dir. Donna Deitch. Screenplay by Karen Hall, from novel by Gloria Naylor. Harpo Productions, 1989.

Woods, Teri. *True to the Game*. Haverton, PA: Meow Meow Productions, 1994.

Wright, Richard. *Native Son*. New York: Harper & Bros., 1940.

Yezierska, Anzia. *Bread Givers*. New York: Persea, 2003.

Further Reading

Auster, Paul. *New York Trilogy*. New York: Penguin, 1990; Bremer, Sidney. *Urban Intersections: Meetings of Life and Literature in United States Cities*. Urbana: University of Illinois Press, 1992; Calvino, Italo. *Invisible Cities*. Transl. William Weaver. New York: Harcourt Brace Jovanovich, 1974; Cappetti, Carla. *Writing Chicago: Modernism, Ethnography, and the Novel*. New York: Columbia University Press, 1993; Denning, Michael. *The Cultural Front: the Laboring of American Culture in the Twentieth Century*. New York: Verso, 1996; Dos Passos, John. *Manhattan Transfer*. Boston: Houghton Mifflin, 2000; Jurca, Catherine. *White Diaspora: the Suburb and the Twentieth-Century American Novel*. Princeton, NJ: Princeton University Press, 2001; Morrison, Toni. "City Limits, Village Values: Concepts of the Neighborhood in Black Fiction." In *Literature and the Urban Experience: Essays on the City and Literature*. Jaye, Michael C., and Ann C. Watts, eds. Piscataway, NJ: Rutgers University Press, 1981; Scruggs, Charles. *Sweet Home: Invisible Cities in the Afro-American Novel*. Baltimore, MD: Johns Hopkins University Press, 1993; Reynolds, David. *Beneath the American Renaissance: the Subversive Imagination in the Age of Emerson and Melville*. Cambridge, MA: Harvard University Press, 1988; Rotella, Carlo. *October Cities: the Redevelopment of Urban Literature*. Berkeley, CA: University of California Press, 1998; Williams, Raymond. *The Country and the City*. New York: Oxford University Press, 1973; Baker, Houston A. *Afro-American Poetics: Revisions of Harlem and the Black Aesthetic*. Madison, WI: University of Wisconsin Press, 1988.

EOIN CANNON

UTOPIAN LITERATURE

Definition. Utopian literature describes an imagined ideal society. The imagined society is usually marked by a universally fair political system and material abundance. Often, the inhabitants of these societies are required to follow schedules, share meals, live in communal housing, or otherwise limit their personal choices.

UTOPIA: NOT REALLY A PLACE AT ALL

Although the terms *utopia* and *utopian* are applied outside of literary studies, the concept itself was first named in a work of fiction. In his 1615 work of the same name, Thomas More created the word *utopia* by punning with two different Greek phrases: *eu topos*, the good or happy place, and *ou topos*, the place which is nowhere. Thus utopia is a happy place that has no true location.

One of the more common techniques used in creating a utopian tale is the travel narrative. In these stories, a visitor from the outside world stumbles upon a utopia and meets a guide who explains how his or her superior society works. Another common narrative frame is when someone who has traveled to a utopian society returns and shares tales of his visit to a perfect, or at least much better, society. Other fictional genres can also be employed to create utopian novels and stories. Authors generally produce this kind of literature in order to comment on their own society. An author may create a utopia to encourage her or his society to become better, or to criticize the failings of the society he lives in. *Utopian* can also be used as an adjective to describe elements of otherwise non-utopian texts that contain elements of an ideal political system or an ideal society. Science fiction, for example, typically contains utopian elements, even though most stories in that genre are not specifically written to envision ideal social relations. Furthermore, the term *utopian* is often employed dismissively when people are discussing real-world political ideas. This is partially because of the word's association with literary utopias, which are fictive and deliberately unrealizable. This entry will discuss works of fiction created either to showcase an ideal society or to question the ability of humanity to create an ideal society.

History. Western culture has been producing utopian literature for at least 2,500 years. The Greeks, who were experimenting with social reform as they developed participatory democracy, gave us two important early examples of utopian literature. These texts were created by near contemporaries, the playwright Aristophanes (ca. 448–388 B.C.E.) and the philosopher Plato (ca. 427–347 B.C.E.). Aristophanes's play *The Birds,* first performed in 414 B.C.E., exemplifies the creation of a humorous utopia to critique aspects of the author's society. Two Athenian citizens, Makedo and Goodhope, set out on a journey to find refuge from the various social ills of their city—militarism, crime, citizens addicted to lawsuits, and so forth. The travelers meet up with the Hoopoe, or king of the birds, and realize that these creatures live a carefree life. In order to permanently escape from the unpleasantness of Athens, Makedo and Goodhope help the birds create the floating city of Napheloccygia, which has been translated as cloud-cuckoo-land or cloud-cuckoo-town. Both the gods and the Greeks try to thwart this project, but ultimately Makedo is crowned king of cloud-cuckoo-land, where he's free to live out his days eating and procreating in a society patterned after avian life. Clearly Aristophanes was not suggesting cloud-cuckoo-land as a legitimate alternative to Athens, but he was creating an alternate version of society that championed ideals the playwright felt were better observed than the crass commercialism and militarism of the Greek city states.

Plato's *The Republic,* which was written between 387 and 360 B.C.E., does not present a fictional portrait of an ideal society, but instead describes the conditions under which an ideal society could be created. These conditions are often echoed in later utopian writing, so it is worthwhile to examine them here. Plato believed that only philosophers, who were ruled by reason, were fit to govern. These philosopher-kings would create societies that were entirely rational and therefore harmonious. Social problems, Plato argued, were caused by leaders who let their passions rule, resulting in passionate and disordered states. Plato's commitment to reason was so absolute that he proposed banning literature and art from his ideal state because they were generated by passion. Education would be strictly controlled, and people would be assigned to castes of workers, soldiers, and rulers. Plato's ideal society differs significantly from the floating pleasure palace of Aristophanes, but the tension between visions of the ideal society as a place of joy and as a place of order and reason persists into contemporary utopian writing.

Despite its ancient beginning, utopian literature languished for nearly 2,000 years before Thomas More published the book that would define the genre. There was little call for speculative representations of the perfect society during Europe's Middle Ages. In this period, the perfect political system was broadly conceived as a divinely appointed sovereign ruling over a docile populace with the help of the clergy. The Enlightenment, with its return to the Greek and Roman values and its emphasis on the ability of human reason to generate progress, encouraged a critical perspective of European societies. Evidence of this trend is revealed in Thomas More's *Utopia*, a rational society in the vein of the ideal government presented in Plato's *Republic*. Written in 1615, More's tale does not feature a lively plot, but rather a thorough description of the workings of Utopian society. The novel's informant is Raphael Hythloday, who has visited Utopia and greatly admires its relatively democratic social structure. Utopia is generally pleasant, though there is also much that would make a modern reader uncomfortable. The society is a republic governed by a prince, who typically rules for life but is chosen by the Philarchs, who are in turn chosen each year by the 30 families they preside over. Despite the ruler's noble title, this system was a far cry from the monarchies that dominated Europe during More's day; the Utopian method of selecting a ruler loosely resembles the structure of the modern American electoral college. Daily life in Utopia is designed to be both productive and rewarding; the six-hour work day provides enough material goods for the entire society. The Utopians devote the rest of their time to recreation and improving their minds.

There is much in Utopia, however, that threatens individualism and the disorder of creativity. The country is comprised of identical towns occupied by no more than 6,000 families, who live in identical houses. The inhabitants of these identical houses wear similar clothing and share communal meals with everyone who lives on their 30-house street. There is no private property, and housing assignments are rearranged every 10 years. Citizens cannot leave town without permission from the government, and the state can transfer families from one town to another to maintain desired population levels. Although the daily schedule may allow time for personal pleasure, that pleasure is often strictly regulated. For example, premarital sex is illegal and those caught violating this rule are forbidden to marry. The Utopians also view each other naked before marriage; and while this may at first seem titillating, its subordination of romance to reason, and its implied evaluation of one's betrothed as a farm animal on an auction block offends contemporary tastes. In More's Utopia, individual expression is often subordinated to the whole, and when individual taste is expressed, it must be rational and calculating, not impressionistic and spontaneous. This blend of freedom and suppression illustrates the central contradictions among utopias that have been taken up by contemporary authors.

America, established by those who hoped to create a superior political system, has a rich tradition of utopian writing. To understand the themes addressed in contemporary utopian writing, it will be helpful to examine two key utopian texts from America's literary tradition. Nathaniel Hawthorne's *Blithedale Romance,* published in 1852, shows us a failed utopia, critiquing the real-world applicability of utopian ideals. Edward Bellamy's 1888 novel *Looking Backwards* is an Americanized, technologically enhanced utopia in the tradition of More. Bellamy's text exemplifies the hope that technological advancement will create utopian conditions. While this hope is not unique to America, technology has always been a primary source of optimism about the future of American culture. These two novels represent contradictory views of utopia held in American literature: fear that utopia is unworkable and possibly dangerous, and hope that technological innovation will ultimately deliver what human nature has thus far prevented.

In the decades before the Civil War, America saw several utopian communities arise. Some of them were founded by small religious groups such as the Shakers, whose leader, Ann Lee, introduced this religion on American soil when she established a communal farm in Watervliet, New York, in 1774. Other groups were secular, influenced by the French social thinker Charles Fourier. In Fourier's utopia, people would be organized into a phalanx of 1,620 people, and live in a communal building called a phalanstery. There were several attempts to establish Fourierist communities in America, such as the North American Phalanx in Red Bank, New Jersey. This utopian experiment lasted from 1843 to 1856 and was endorsed by prominent people, including Horace Greely, the editor and publisher of the *New York Tribune.* Communities like the North American Phalanx were controversial because communal living did not blend easily with the wide-open capitalism of antebellum America. Furthermore, Fourier was notorious for his radical—even by today's standards—views on sexuality. In a phalanstery, at least in theory, people were free to have sexual relations with any other consenting adult. Unsurprisingly, even though "free love" was usually not a prominent feature of American utopian communities, the possibility that such unconventional behavior was occurring did not sit well with most Americans. These negative perceptions led most American Fourierists to refer to themselves as Associationists to avoid scaring away potential converts. But considering that the religious groups who founded utopian communities were also outside mainstream American thought, the failure of all of these alternative living experiments is understandable. The communities had trouble attracting both capital and capable people, and their eventual demise only confirmed the public's impression of the impracticality of their utopian schemes.

The popular cultural distrust of communal living is reflected in Hawthorne's thinly disguised account of his own time in a utopian community. For a few months in 1841, the author lived at Brook Farm, a secular utopian community in West Roxbury, Massachusetts, which was Fourierist before it closed in 1849 but not while Hawthorne was a resident. Through the poet-narrator Miles Coverdale, Hawthorne's tale questions the practicality of utopian communities. While the author found much to satirize in the idea of a poet working as a farmer, his fundamental critique of communal living highlights the inability of humans to treat one another fairly. The novel's dark conclusion centers on the love triangle involving the self-promoting Hollingsworth, who wants to transform Blithedale into a penal colony that he will run, the ardent feminist Zenobia, and her passive, feminine half-sister Priscilla. Hollingsworth's scheme depends in part on money the independently wealthy Zenobia would provide, and his decision to marry Priscilla leads the shamed Zenobia to drown herself. Of course, Zenobia's death signals the end of the community and leaves Hollingsworth and Priscilla spiritually broken. Hawthorne's tale suggests that the sharing of resources necessary for communal life is so counter to human nature that tragedy is bound to result. Zenobia's money and Hollingsworth's charisma both introduce ungovernable desires into the rationally planned utopia, whose fatal flaw was the assumption that people were capable of consistently setting aside personal desires in service of the greater good.

While the horrors of the Civil War called into question the faith in human progress that made experiments like Brook Farm, the North American Phalanx, and the Shaker communities possible, it also ushered in an age of rapid industrialization and technological progress that made a different type of utopia seem feasible. Many social thinkers began to believe that society was gradually evolving toward a mechanized paradise that would provide for everyone's material needs. This type of utopian thought was quite popular despite the daily experiences of people who worked in newly mechanized industry. Bellamy's novel *Looking Backwards* gives these utopian hopes literary form. In Bellamy's tale, wealthy Bostonian Julian West goes to sleep in 1887 and wakes up in 2000 to find society transformed by a bloodless revolution. After capitalists consolidated every industry into a single trust, the working class rose up and took over the mighty industrial machine that had been created. The plot of *Looking Backwards* is very similar to More's *Utopia* as primarily a description of an ideal society, though West does return to nineteenth century Boston and argues with his complacent friends and family. While More learns of Utopia from the traveler Hythloday, West is introduced to the new millennium's utopian America by his host Dr. Leete. West learns that society's technological prowess allows everyone to enjoy an extremely high standard of living. Dr. Leete explains that all citizens work in the industrial army until 45 and then retire to several decades of leisure. Prison is largely reserved for people who refuse to work. Although it features communal dining halls, Bellamy's society is best understood as a consumerist paradise where people use credit cards to shop in "sample stores" located in buildings resembling the twenty-first century's upscale malls. Products selected at the sample stores are then automatically delivered to the buyer's apartment. Contemporary readers may find Bellamy's vision both appealing and improbable, but *Looking Backwards* was regarded by many as a practical blueprint for the future. Readers formed Bellamy clubs, and the Populist Party incorporated Bellamy's ideas into their platform.

Trends and Themes. Twentieth-century utopian literature by American authors continued to reflect the contradictory tendencies revealed in the two nineteenth-century literary utopias discussed above. Some tales seem direct descendants of More's political or Bellamy's technological utopia, with ideal societies arising from the chaos of the contemporary world thanks to stunning technological breakthroughs. Kathleen Ann Goonan's nanotech series, with its depiction of this new technology radically transforming the world, is at least a spiritual descendant of *Looking Backwards*. Lincoln Child's novel *Utopia,* though primarily a straightforward techno-thriller, also argues for America's ability to protect its technological utopias from terrorists. One contemporary innovation in utopian literature, a variation on the positive utopias of More and Bellamy, can best be described as identity utopias. These are societies built by and for the members of a specific racial or ethnic group. Toure's *Soul City*, with its sometimes tongue-in-cheek depiction of an African American utopia built partially on the spiritual capital gained from the experiences of slavery and partly on African American popular culture, is a solid example of the identity utopia. The most common theme in contemporary American utopian fiction, however, is a critique of what can broadly be described as 1960s, or perhaps post-World War II, idealism. Susan Sontag's *In America*, Justin Tussig's *The Best People in the World*, and T. C. Boyle's *Drop City* all cast doubt on the possibility of the communal utopia, with Tussig and Boyle speaking directly to the experience of the late 1960s and early 1970s. In *The New City*, Stephen Amidon questions America's faith in the suburban ideal in general and in the utopian project of planned communities, and Richard Powers casts doubt on the ability of computer technology to create a durable utopia in *Plowing the Dark*.

Contexts and Issues. Contemporary utopian fiction continues to reflect tension between the hope that technology will soon deliver utopia and the fear that utopia is unworkable. This pairing is reflected in literature because the tension between optimism and distrust of utopia has been grounded in recent historical developments. Utopian thought in general has been called into question by both the genocidal utopias of Joseph Stalin and Adolf Hitler and the resurgence and perceived failure of utopian communities in the 1960s. On the other hand, the technological advances that have occurred during the last century, as well as the view that new media technologies have potential to dramatically change the world for the better, have suggested that utopia, or the material conditions for utopia, is still possible.

During the first half of the twentieth century, two totalitarian governments that claimed utopian trappings but caused widespread suffering and death emerged in Europe. Although the Russian Revolution claimed to be creating a worker's paradise, Stalin's forced collectivization of agriculture indirectly caused millions of deaths because of famine and made life miserable for the survivors. Furthermore, the dictator's purges of those he deemed disloyal generated a formidable body count. Nazi Germany, which presented itself as a utopian state for Aryans, also contributed a substantial degree of death and suffering with concentration camps designed to exterminate Jews, Gypsies, and homosexuals. Historian Russell Jacoby has argued that because the propaganda of these regimes had utopian overtones, in the years since the deaths of Stalin and Hitler there has been a strong tendency to equate political utopias with final solutions.

Another later-discredited utopian moment developed in the late 1960s and early 1970s. While the youth culture that flourished during that time was largely driven by hedonistic desires, it also sparked a legitimate political movement to stop the Vietnam War. This countercultural atmosphere of the late 1960s led some people to found communes. While these small-scale utopias were in many ways descendants of the Fourierist experiments of Hawthorne's day, in the popular imagination they were associated with the sex-drugs-and-rock 'n' roll atmosphere of the baby boomers' college years. When most of these communes failed and members were absorbed into middle and upper class communities, a widespread perception developed that these private utopias were primarily a place for white, middle-class adolescents to play, rather than serious attempts to create a social system based on principles of justice and a commitment to environmental sustainability.

While the twentieth century has produced both monstrous and lightweight political utopias, it has also generated its fair share of technologies that have genuinely changed the way people live. From the mass production of the automobile to the television to the Internet, each new technology has been marketed using utopian language. The easiest way to illustrate this perception of new technologies as harbingers of utopian change is to examine the way the Internet has been described by its promoters. Though originally developed by the Department of Defense so that researchers could share information with the military, the Internet is now widely touted as a means of breaking down barriers between people and creating a global society that is prosperous, well-informed, and diverse. This conceptualization of the Internet appeals to the widely held hope that technology can somehow lead to an ideal society.

Reception. It is difficult to accurately gauge the cultural impact of a work of fiction, particularly those that recently entered circulation. Four criteria can be used to gain a broad idea of how a book has been received: reviews give a good indication of the story's perceived literary value, film adaptations and sales figures demonstrate the popularity of a novel or story, and the historical popularity of a genre is a good way to gauge reception in relative terms. The novels and stories discussed below received favorable reviews in mainstream media outlets like *The New York Times*. It is still too soon for most of the contemporary utopian stories to garner the attention of significant academic criticism. There have been no plans by major studios to turn any of these works into films, and low sales suggest that current utopian stories have yet to capture the public's imagination. Utopian fiction has never truly commanded the popular imagination in America, and the relatively low cultural penetration of the texts under discussion should come as no surprise. The status of utopian fiction in American culture is borne out by the absence of significant or popular film adaptations of utopian stories and by the relatively low sales of Utopian tales.

Selected Authors. Unlike romance or mystery genres, most utopian literary works are unique creations, exploring themes that authors have addressed in other kinds of fiction by means of the utopia they create. The only common exceptions to this rule are found in science fiction, where writers occasionally produce an entire series of books about a utopia. The books discussed below were written by a range of authors—some prominent, some beginning their careers—and were distributed by major publishing houses.

Susan Sontag was one of the twentieth century's best know public intellectuals. A novelist, poet, and playwright, she was also made an honorary citizen of Sarajevo for the humanitarian work she did as a resident of that war-torn city in the 1990s. In intellectual circles she will most likely be remembered for her literary and social criticism's impact on discussions of popular culture. Her novel *In America* follows Hawthorne's *Blithedale Romance* and generates compelling historical fiction by revising past utopian experiments. In this novel, Sontag reimagines the story of Polish actress Helena Modrzejewska and her husband Count Karol Chlapowski, who immigrated to the United States in 1876 with a group of friends and briefly lived in a commune in Anaheim, California. Sontag renames Helena Maryna, calls Karol Bogdan, and portrays them as idealists dedicated to Fourier. As with most tales of failed utopia, the community they create cannot sustain itself and is torn apart by infighting amongst its members. Furthermore, Sontag compares Maryna's idealistic experiment in communal living to the city of Anaheim, a pseudo-utopia created and staffed by developers and wealthy landowners. The failure of these admirers of Fourier in the face of the quiet success of complacent capitalists leads Maryna to believe that all utopias "will not last." Consequently, utopia should be seen as "not a kind of place but a kind of time, those all-too-brief moments when one would not wish to be anywhere else" (175). This realization leads Maryna to return to the stage in America, and the final third of the novel becomes a chronicle of her gradual rise to superstardom. At the somewhat abrupt close of Sontag's narrative, the woman who had once been determined to live quietly on a grape farm is instead touring the United States in a private railcar. While Sontag's novel is grounded in the real story of Helena Modrzejewska, it also reflects the life trajectories of many individuals involved in utopian politics or communities in their youth who later rejected outward utopias and focused on their own career advancement.

Justin Tussig's first novel, based on a short story published in *The New Yorker,* is also an exploration of the failed utopian impulses of the late 1960s and early 1970s. *The Best People in the World* tells the story of Thomas Mahey, a Kentucky high school student facing a dull but secure future working in the same power plant that his father does. His sleepy life is disrupted when Tom begins an affair with Alice Lowe, one of his teachers, and sparks a tentative friendship with Shilo Tanager, a local ne'er-do-well. After Alice takes Shilo in when his home is destroyed in a flood, the three of them decide to leave town. They drive to Vermont, take over an abandoned house in the woods, and try to create a private utopia. Along the way, they meet Parker, an old friend of Shilo's who is now a drug dealer. Parker helps them get to Vermont, where they make contact with a commune run by Gregor. This false idealist, however, won't let Tom and his friends join unless they pay him several thousand dollars. Tussig sets his story in the mid-1970s, when 1960s utopian culture had run to seed, and there is a definite air of despair and futility in Parker's NYC drug lab/commune and Gregor's half-built rural compound.

These perverse utopias foreshadow the failure of Tom, Shilo, and Alice's experiment in communal living. Their garden dies from lack of attention, they deplete their money, they run out of firewood and are forced to burn parts of the house to stay warm, and the interpersonal dynamic between the housemates grows gradually worse as the group becomes more and more frustrated with their attempt to live together. The situation disintegrates further when Alice discovers that Shilo has been hiding the miraculously preserved corpse of his boyfriend in the basement. Parker arrives to remove the corpse, there is a scuffle, and Shilo knocks Parker down the stairway to the basement, killing him. The novel abruptly ends with the trio abandoning the house. There is no account of the fates of Shilo or Alice, and only minimal information about Tom.

The novel contains a parallel narrative concerning two unnamed investigators from the Holy See who investigate reports of miracles. The investigators make plans to see the body of Shilo's boyfriend because they hear reports that it has the ability to heal, but this never comes to fruition and the narrative strands do not otherwise cross. The investigators, who have uncovered many frauds and found only a few events that may evince the supernatural, are very jaded. Taken together, these two narratives suggest that the sixties commune movement was built—metaphorically— on the bodies of dead children and that there are no miracles in the world.

T. C. Boyle has written 19 books and numerous short stories, and has received many literary awards. Although the themes addressed in his novels range from *Budding Prospects*' depiction of marijuana cultivation to *Talk Talk*'s discussion of identity theft, Boyle's writing often focuses on eccentric figures in American history who were seen as radicals or utopians. *The Road to Wellville,* adapted for film in 1994, satirizes the utopia dedicated to healthy eating built by Dr. John Harvey Kellogg in

Battle Creek, Michigan. *The Inner Circle* depicts the lives of Alfred Kinsey's team of sex researchers.

In *Drop City,* Boyle turns to the post-utopian 1970s to explore the utopian impulses of both far-left and far-right America. The novel begins with a description of Drop City, a Northern California hippy commune founded by Norm, an aging flower child living off his dead parents' life insurance money. The commune is large and there are many members, but the story focuses on Paulette, a former elementary school teacher who goes by Star, and her boyfriend Marco, who is living in the commune to avoid the draft. Readers also meet Cecil, or Sess, and Pamela, newlyweds who have gone to live in the Alaskan bush. Sess is largely apolitical, but Pamela is a college graduate who has left a promising career to live in the wilderness because she thinks that American culture has become permanently corrupted. As Norm's commune slowly disintegrates under pressure from county officials and racial tensions within the group, he decides to create Drop City North on a large tract of land he has inherited in Alaska. Most of the commune boards a converted school bus and heads out for the last frontier. When the hippies arrive in Alaska, Sess discovers that they will be moving onto land that borders his.

Boyle does not present conflict between the hippie commune and the libertarian homestead, however. Sess and Pamela are kind to their new neighbors and the hippies are in awe of Sess's ability to survive in the wilderness. Instead, Boyle parallels the growth of Sess and Pamela's relationship with the demise of the commune. Unsurprisingly, the hippies simply cannot endure the Alaska winter and when Norman heads back to California, it looks like the end of Drop City. Star and Marco, however, have begun to learn survival techniques from Sess and Pamela. While there is never genuine political rapprochement between the two sides, Star ultimately realizes that Pamela was also "not buying into the plastic society" (Boyle 2003, 301). Boyle argues that the communalist critique of society offered in the 1960s was not inherently wrong, but also argues that creating a commune was not the answer. Rugged individualism, and not another Brook Farm, is the best way to reclaim something genuinely American.

Stephen Amidon's *The New City* takes up a more mainstream and understated strain of utopian thought that greatly influenced where and how Americans lived in the twentieth century: city planning and the flight to the suburbs. Amidon, whose mainstream fiction frequently centers on father-son relationships in novels such as *Splitting the Atom* and *Thirst,* is also a critic of suburban life, a theme picked up in *Human Capital,* published after *The New City.* Amidon's tale of failed utopia describes the demise of Newton, Maryland, an early 1970s planned community designed by a utopian architect named Barnaby Vine. As did most twentieth-century progressives, Vine believed that urban social problems resulted from economic and racial segregation. His solution was to design a bedroom community for Baltimore and Washington, D.C. that would eliminate physical barriers between races and classes. Vine recruits white lawyer Austin Swope and African American contractor Earl Wooten to build his community from the ground up. It has no fences and provides a great deal of public space where residents will ideally interact and build community. He has, in other words, built the kind of scaled-down utopia that planned communities perceive themselves to be.

Yet while Swope and Wooten become friends, Vine's city is plagued with problems from the beginning. The fish purchased to stock an artificial lake quickly die. Gas lamps used to light the city at night begin exploding. Japanese beetles descend and infest trees and shrubs. In addition to these physical problems, gangs from the government housing projects Vine constructed in Newton begin to terrorize the suburb's middle-and upper-class residents. Newton falls apart, however, when Wooten's son Joel and his white girlfriend Susan are caught in bed by her parents. Swope's son Teddy attempts to help Joel and Susan continue seeing each other, but when an exasperated Susan correctly diagnoses Teddy's homosexual attraction to Joel, Teddy kills her in a blind rage and then frames Joel for the murder. Ultimately, Susan's father mistakes Teddy for Joel and kills him before killing himself. As in any proper tragedy, the racial strife that Newton was designed to avoid became its undoing. The novel's end implies that this bloodbath will turn Newton into just another troubled development. Amidon, like Sontag, Tussig, and Boyle, forcefully argues that utopian social schemes are doomed because human nature and human jealousy will not allow them to succeed.

One concept that Thomas Moore likely did not foresee was the creation of virtual utopias, computer-generated ideal worlds tailored to the needs of individuals. If these digital realities serve only as a place of escape from a dreary analog one, then they are merely utopian. But when it becomes possible to completely and permanently escape into these artificial worlds, then we are dealing with utopia proper. This is the scenario Richard Powers explores in *Plowing the Dark*. Powers, an English professor with a background as a computer programmer, explored the interaction between the humanities and technology in *Galatea 2.2* and *Gold Bug Variations*. In *Plowing the Dark*, the author suggests that while creating a virtual utopia may be technically feasible, it may not be desirable. Most of Powers's novel focuses on the efforts of a team of artists, social scientists, and engineers, assembled by a Microsoft-like corporation, to create a virtual environment so powerful that the human mind cannot discern the difference between it and reality. Set in the late 1980s and early 1990s when virtual reality was first coming into public awareness, the story focuses on college friends Steve Spiegel, a poet-turned-computer-programmer, and Addie Klarpol, a gifted artist who has been wasting her talent on commercial illustration, as they and their colleagues work in a technological wonderland where it is "never anything o'clock" (Powers 2000, 3). At first, this cyber island really is a sort of scientific and artistic paradise, allowing them to create a visual and tactile paradise while they begin speculating about humanity's eventual move into a fully computerized existence.

Addie eventually abandons her work and her affair with Steve, however, when she realizes that most of the technology they were creating was used to help develop the smart bombs used by the United States Air Force in the first Gulf war. The author reminds us that the technology invested with utopian potential—the Internet, for example—often has roots in the military-industrial complex that will always cancel out any genuine utopian potential.

Author Lincoln Child taps into the utopian atmosphere of theme parks—artificial creations designed to produce pleasure—in *Utopia*, with an island of complete computerized control in the Nevada desert. Because of its advanced technology, Utopia attracts hundreds of thousands of guests who can escape into Victorian England or outer space for days at a time. Child's creation is even a quasi-political entity, with its own government and security forces that are only nominally responsible to the state of Nevada. Clearly, Child's choice of name for his theme park strongly suggests that he is creating a kind of technological cloud-cuckoo-land, the pleasure palace that Americans desire.

All is not well, however, as a gang of ruthless criminals infiltrate the metanet, the computer system that maintains the virtual worlds within Utopia. They begin killing guests and demanding that they be given the technology behind the metanet while simultaneously plotting to rob Utopia's casinos. Unfortunately for them, Andrew Warne, the inventor of the metanet, has been brought in to repair his creation, and the good professor uses his programming savvy to save the park—and his teenage daughter Georgia—from the criminals. This high-tech thriller is suitable for beach reading, no surprise considering Child's background as an editor of horror fiction anthologies and as co-author (with Douglas Preston) of a novel series about an FBI agent who solves unusual cases. But in his first solo novel, Child creates a technological utopia—an island of order in a chaotic world, but threatened by the same chaos it wants to avoid. Investing the inventor of the utopia with the power to save it from destruction suggests that the American technological utopia will survive in a world that is hostile to it.

If Child's *Utopia* represents a strain of contemporary utopian fiction similar to Aristophanes' *The Birds,* Kathleen Ann Goonan's New Orleans-based nanotech series brings readers an inevitable utopian revolution similar to that in Bellamy's *Looking Backwards.* Goonan is one of the few writers discussed here who has made her reputation largely on utopian fiction. The four books of the nanotech series, *Queen City Jazz* (1994), *Mississippi Blues* (1997), *Crescent City Rhapsody* (2000) and *Light Music* (2002), blend science fiction with international espionage as they describe an island city-state in the Caribbean produced by means of nanotechnology. Although the utopian climax is reached in *Light Music* as New Orleans/Crescent City is turned into a starship, *Crescent City Rhapsody* best establishes the broader utopian themes Goonan wants to explore.

Set in the near future, Goonan's novel illustrates the economic and social havoc that results when a regular series of electromagnetic pulses that apparently emanate from an alien intelligence disrupt electronic communications. While it becomes increasingly difficult to maintain social control by means of traditional technologies, nanotechnology allows cities and individuals to cheaply manufacture consumer goods for local markets. Prospects for a more libertarian and free market world are darkened, however, by international terrorists who want to use nanotechnology to produce viruses and super weapons. Hope for humanity is found in New Orleans, where Marie Laveau is gathering scientists and engineers to create Crescent City, an autonomous island city that will be beyond the reach of government taxation and will allow the brightest minds to work on a way for humanity to reach into space and contact the alien intelligences sending out the signals. Marie is best conceptualized as a heroine version of a James Bond villain: vastly wealthy, with a private espionage apparatus, and dedicated to using advanced technology to save rather than destroy the world. Marie is opposed both by the American and World governments and by various terrorist groups, but she and her operatives eventually triumph. In a now-ironic final scene, the citizens of New Orleans leave for Crescent City as a terrorist-infiltrated international army breeches the levees that protect the old city from Lake Ponchartrain during a powerful hurricane.

Goonan's novel ends with a vision of an unambiguous utopia. Crescent City is an island removed from a chaotic world, governed by reason rather than emotion. Its quirky admixture of pragmatic socialism and intellectual libertarianism both reflects a contemporary update of the American populism that informed Bellamy's utopia and represents a social order superior to those that had gone before it. Most importantly, however, Goonan's novel forcefully articulates the optimism that believes technology can save humanity from itself.

Among identity utopias, concerning the status of ethnic minorities, one of the most entertaining is *Soul City*. This novel was written by Toure, a correspondent for *Black Entertainment Television* and contributing editor for *Rolling Stone* whose work has also appeared in magazines like *Playboy* and *The New Yorker*. Toure begins his tale by quoting Oscar Wilde's assertion that "a map of the world that does not include Utopia is not even worth glancing at" and then goes on to describe an African American oasis that is "amazing, but not Utopia" (80). This clear invocation of utopia as political ideal is rare in light of contemporary questioning of the possibility of utopia, and rarer still is the bemused brio with which Toure describes Soul City. Founded by escaped slaves in 1821 and radiating outward from a 100-foot-tall statue of an afro pick topped by a black power fist, Soul City is literally the soul of the African American experience. Music pervades streets with names like Cool and Nappy Lane, courtesy of the mayor, whose primary responsibility is to act as DJ. All aspects of African American culture, from Fredrick Douglass to Tupak Shakur, are respectfully memorialized in Soul City.

Soul City is not merely a celebration of popular culture, however. Young people volunteer to spend a year in simulated slavery so that they can honor their ancestors. The slaves who founded the city are still alive, thanks to their ability to smell Death and evade his summons; one of them, Fulcrum Negro, regularly commutes to heaven to check in on Louis Armstrong and other African American luminaries. The main focus of the novel is describing the workings of Soul City, though there is an amusing subplot about race traitor John Jiggaboo's attempt to destroy Soul City by means of a shampoo that brainwashes even as it gives users perfect hair. Toure also occasionally checks in with Cadillac Johnson, a writer for the *Chocolate City* magazine—whose name is an unsubtle reference to a Parliament Funkadelic song about African American political hegemony—as he spends thirty three years trying to capture the essence of Soul City in a novel. Cadillac pursues Mahogany Sunflower, and their romance provides a diverting subplot. But as with most utopian writing, the primary function of the novel is to provide a vision of an alternative society.

Bibliography

Amidon, Stephen. *The New City*. New York: Doubleday, 2000.

Aristophanes. *The Birds and Other Plays*. Trans. David Barrett and Alan Sommerstein. New York: Pengiun, 2003.

Bellamy, Edward. *Looking Backward*. New York: Signet Classics, 2000.

Boyle, T. Coraghessan. *Drop City*. New York: Viking, 2003.

Child, Lincoln. *Utopia: A Novel*. New York: Doubleday, 2002.

Goonan, Kathleen Ann. *Crescent City Rhapsody*. New York: Avon Books, 2000.

Hawthorne, Nathaniel. *The Blithedale Romance*. New York: Penguin, 1983.

More, Thomas. *Utopia*. New York: Penguin, 2003.

Plato. *The Republic*. Trans. Desmond Lee. New York: Penguin, 2003.

Powers, Richard. *Plowing the Dark*. New York: Farrar, Straus, and Giroux, 2000.

Sontag, Susan. *In America: A Novel*. New York: Farrar, Straus, and Giroux, 2000.

Toure, *Soul City*. New York: Little, Brown, 2004.

Tussig, Justin. *The Best People in the World*. New York: HarperCollins, 2006.

Further Reading

Abbott, Phillip. "Utopians at Play." *Utopian Studies: Journal of the Society for Utopian Studies* 15.1 (2004): 44–62; DeKoven, Marianne. *Utopias Limited: The Sixties and the Emergence of Postmodernism.* Durham, NC: Duke University Press, 2004; Goonan, Kathleen Ann. *Queen City Jazz.* New York: TOR, 1994; Goonan, Kathleen Ann. *Mississippi Blues.* New York: TOR, 1997; Goonan, Kathleen Ann. *Light Music.* New York: EOS, 2003; Hatzenberger, Antoine. "Islands and Empire: Beyond the Shores of Utopia." *Angelaki: Journal of the Theoretical Humanities* 8.1 (2003): 119–128; Jacoby, Russell. *Picture Imperfect: Utopian Thought for an Anti-Utopian Age.* New York: Columbia University Press, 2005; Jameson, Fredric. *Archaeologies of the Future: The Desire Called Utopia and other Science Fictions.* New York: Verso, 2005; Weinberg, Steven. "Five and a Half Utopias." *Atlantic Monthly* 285.1 (Jan. 2000): 107–115.

MARK T. DECKER

V

VAMPIRE FICTION

Definition. Vampire fiction has been influenced by the conventions of Gothic literature, in that vampire stories are traditionally set in dark, mysterious castles, cathedrals, and mansions, or remote forests and mountains. In addition to the gloomy setting, vampire stories typically invoke fear and terror in the reader by unprovoked acts of cruelty, torture, and murder, thus anticipating and influencing modern horror literature. In the case of vampire fiction, the acts of cruelty are committed by vampires—animated corpses (the undead) who drink human blood by night and sleep during the day in underground crypts, avoiding the sun, which either reduces their powers or burns them to ashes. In addition to the vampires, who often do not appear until late in the story, the victims are stalked and bitten one or more times, eventually drained of their blood and turned into one of the undead, or simply left for dead. The vampire slayer, who has knowledge of vampires, then appears on the scene armed with religious relics and/or weaponry. The vampire slayer's goal is to hunt down the preternatural creature, which can be destroyed only by extreme measures: staking the heart, removing the head, snapping the spine, exposing the creature to the sun, or incinerating it with fire. The vampire novel *Carmilla* (1871), by Sheridan Le Fanu, probably provided Bram Stoker with the basic elements for the best-known vampire novel of all time—*Dracula* (1897):

> All of the rituals and set pieces common to the modern formula appear in *Carmilla*, beginning with its three-part formal design—attack, death-resuscitation, and hunt-destruction. Also included are the vampire's seduction of its victim, the telltale bite on the victim's neck, the slow physical deterioration of the victim, the confusion between dream and reality, the vain attempts to explain supernatural events in rational terms, and the folk recipes for recognizing, capturing, and killing vampires. (Campbell 1985, 228–229)

Although Campbell's succinct definition of the modern formula for vampire fiction is useful for understanding some nineteenth-century vampire stories, the formula does not work for most contemporary vampire fiction—for example, Anne Rice's Lestat and Chelsea Quinn Yarbro's Saint-Germain rarely attack humans or drink human blood, thus nullifying the "three-part formal design" identified by Campbell.

In *Our Vampires, Ourselves,* Nina Auerbach challenges the very notion that there is a fixed genre of vampire literature or a fixed definition of a vampire. She claims, "There is no such thing as 'The Vampire'; there are only vampires," and since vampires are "[e]ternally alive, they embody not fear of death, but fear of life: their power and their curse is their undying vitality. From Varney to Dracula . . . from Chelsea Quinn Yarbro's disenchanted idealist, Count Saint-Germain, to Lestat and his friends, vampires long to die, at least in certain moods, infecting readers with fears of their own interminable lives" (5). Genre distinctions have been blurred in the twentieth century, and genre boundaries are permeable and notoriously fluid, especially so with vampires, because the undead have lately been appearing in **Science Fiction, Romance Novels, Mystery Fiction, Spy Fiction, Fantasy Literature, Historical Fiction, Coming of Age Fiction, Graphic Novels,** horror novels, and **Young Adult Literature.**

History. Most scholars agree that John Polidori (1795–1821) wrote the first modern vampire story and published it in 1819 under Lord Byron's name. The idea for the story was originally Byron's, but Polidori—who took notes on stories told by Byron and the Shelleys in the summer of 1816 at Villa Diodati—eventually developed Byron's oral form into a written story about a dark, mysterious nobleman, Lord Ruthven, who suddenly appears in an elite social circle in England. Aubrey, a young English gentleman, decides to accompany Ruthven on a grand tour of Europe and finds, much to his regret, that Ruthven, though charming and articulate, leaves in his wake once-virtuous–now-ruined women. A disillusioned Aubrey leaves Ruthven's company, travels to Greece, and falls in love with a beautiful Greek peasant named Ianthe, who accompanies him to archaeological sites. Ianthe introduces Aubrey to stories of local vampires and warns Aubrey not to travel alone at night.

Aubrey, of course, is lost in the woods on a stormy night and, upon hearing a woman scream, rushes into a hut and attempts to neutralize the woman's assailant, who displays superhuman strength and escapes into the woods, but not before attempting to bite Aubrey. Aubrey begins to see apparitions of Ianthe, who has disappeared and been turned into a vampire. Now physically ill and psychologically distraught, Aubrey begins to realize that Ruthven has all the characteristics of a vampire. Nevertheless, he requests that Ruthven aid him in recovering his physical and emotional health. Ruthven nurses Aubrey back to health and elicits a promise that Aubrey will not speak about him for one year and one day. Aubrey agrees and returns to England only to find Ruthven courting his sister. On the midnight that the promise expires, Aubrey tells his sister's guardians about Ruthven and then dies. His sister's guardians attempt to intervene, but it is too late, as "Lord Ruthven ha[s] disappeared, and Aubrey's sister ha[s] glutted the thirst of a VAMPYRE!" (no page, Online Version).

Sheridan Le Fanu's *Carmilla* (1871), as noted above, provided Bram Stoker with the basic elements for *Dracula,* which was written twenty years later. Laura, the daughter of a wealthy widower, befriends Carmilla, a young woman who boards with her family while her mysterious mother is away for a few months. Laura begins to dream of being bitten in the chest by a feline monster as her health slowly declines. After medical examinations fail to explain her deteriorating health, Laura and her father encounter General Speiledorf, whose daughter had suffered a similar fate through the actions of a mysterious woman named Millarca. The General convinces Laura and her father that Carmilla and Millarca are actually one and the same person: a two-hundred-year-old vampire, formerly Countess Mircalla Karnstein. Carmilla is subsequently destroyed by the General and Laura's father. About Le Fanu, Campbell wrote:

> What Le Fanu added to the formula was a portrayal of a world turned upside down, a universe, as old General Spielsdorf complains, in which God tolerates vampiric lusts and all the malignity of hell. In such a world all values are reversed: dreams become reality, friends become enemies, death becomes life, love becomes hate, and rationality and science must turn to the irrational and the superstitious (folklore) to illuminate and to explain the forces of darkness. (Campbell 1985, 229)

Bram Stoker's *Dracula* (1897) is, of course, the most famous vampire story of all time, combining the Byronic hero of Polidori, the eroticism of Carmilla, and a dualistic Christian world and life view. Dracula is far and away the most popular and influential vampire novel of the nineteenth and twentieth (and perhaps twenty-first) centuries. "Despite its flaws, *Dracula* is a novel of monumental influence, one whose imitations and offshoots have become a veritable industry. Its title character has transcended his origin in a Victorian thriller to become an embodiment of an age-old myth and the incarnation of ultimate evil" (Daniels 375). Written as a series of letters and journal entries, *Dracula* tracks Count Dracula's movement from Transylvania to London, and back to Transylvania again. Beginning with Jonathan Harker, his first English victim in Transylvania, Dracula goes on to seduce Lucy Westenra—the best friend of Mina Harker and fiancé of Arthur Holmwood—and Mina Harker, in England. Dracula acts right under the noses of the ad hoc team hunting him, a team consisting of Jonathan Harker, Dr. John Seward (head of a psychiatric hospital), Arthur Holmwood (a wealthy aristocrat), Quincey Morris (a wealthy Texan), and Dr. Van Helsing, mentor of Dr. Seward and well versed in vampire lore. Holmwood, Morris, and Seward, though friends, have all fallen in love with Lucy Westenra, who finally chooses Arthur Holmwood, but the courtship is short lived as the Count has other plans for "poor Lucy."

The plot follows the "three-part formal design—attack, death-resuscitation, and hunt-destruction" pattern identified by Campbell. Harker, a solicitor, travels to Transylvania to meet Count Dracula and discuss the Count's recently purchased estate in England. Harker is held captive by Dracula and turned into his blood slave until the Count leaves for England after passing him along to the "three weird sisters," Dracula's brides. Once in England, Dracula turns Lucy Westenra into a vampire and then silently stalks Mina Harker. Van Helsing teaches Seward, Holmwood, and Morris what he knows about the undead, after they have been forced to stake and behead "poor Lucy." Word comes that Jonathan Harker is still alive but suffering from a "brain fever" at a hospital in Budapest. When Mina joins him, she learns that Jonathan has kept a journal while in Transylvania, which she promises never to read unless circumstances require unveiling the painful story. They both return to England and join Van Helsing, Seward, Morris, and the grieving Holmwood in their hunt for Dracula's lairs in London. These lairs each contain one or more of fifty boxes of sacred earth brought by the Count from the chapel at Castle Dracula. The vampire hunters are able to sterilize forty-nine of the boxes with the sacred host, thus driving Dracula out of England and back to Transylvania. The rest of the novel is an extended chase scene that describes the vampire hunters closing in on an elusive Dracula.

Count Dracula is at once a brooding Byronic hero whose seduction of his victims has strong erotic overtones, but he is also cursed by God for seeking immortality from the Evil one himself: Satan. On the one hand he is none other than the ruthless Vlad Dracul III, who valiantly fought the Turks in the late fifteenth century; on the other hand he is an evil, condemned monster who must feed on the blood of humans to flourish. Jonathan Harker initially describes him as "tall," "clean shaven," and "clad in black from head to foot" (Stoker, 25). He has a "strong face" and proves himself a good host, arranging Harker's meals and bedroom for him. In spite of doubts about the Count, Harker is impressed with his intelligence and knowledge of England. Later in the novel, Van Helsing informs his fellow vampire hunters that Dracula has the strength of twenty men, is skilled in necromancy, and can "direct the elements . . . and command . . . the rat, and the owl, and the bat— the moth, and the fox, and the wolf. He can grow and become small; and he can at times vanish and come unknown" (Stoker, 243). As a vampire, Dracula possesses even greater powers than he did as the ruthless and cunning king of Wallachia.

But the Count is evil, and we learn from Van Helsing that the horror of vampirism dates to ancient Greece, Rome, and the Orient. The Draculas ("dragons" in Slavic) "had dealings with the Evil One" and "learned the secrets" of immortality in the mountains by lake Hermanstadt (Stoker 246). Even though Dracula is evil, he has produced good and holy children through his "good women;" and "in soil barren of holy memories [Dracula] cannot rest" (Stoker, 247), which means that the Count has to haul boxes of sacred earth with him wherever he goes. He can only flourish on "the blood of the living" and "cannot die by mere passing of time." He does not cast a shadow or reflect in a mirror, yet he can see in the dark. Unlike many of his successors, Dracula can function in daylight, though his powers are dramatically reduced. In spite of all these evil powers, Van Helsing claims that "he is not free" (Stoker, 245). Dracula cannot enter a place uninvited, "he can only change himself [into another form] at noon or at exact sunrise or sunset" and must have with him his "earth home." In addition, he can be warded off with garlic, a consecrated host, or a crucifix; and a branch of wild rose placed on his coffin renders him helpless. A sacred bullet fired into his coffin can kill him, but to receive rest he must have a stake driven through his heart and his head removed (Stoker, 246).

Dracula is irresistible to women, and his attempt to turn Mina into one of the undead is presented by Stoker as a veiled sexual seduction. The men open the bedroom door to find the Count standing next to Mina: "With his left hand he held both Mrs. Harker's hands, keeping them away with her arms at full tension; his right hand gripped her by the back of the neck, forcing her face down on his bosom. Her white night dress was smeared with blood, and a thick stream trickled down his bare breast which was shown by his torn-open dress" (Stoker, 288). When Mina recounts the events of the seduction, she tells the men that Dracula told her that she was "flesh of [his] flesh, blood of [his] blood; kin of [his] kin . . . and shall be later on [his] companion and [his] helper" (293; cf. Genesis 2–3). The Count and Mina are now blood partners, though Mina feels tainted and unclean like a victim of rape. Earlier when the vampire hunters encounter Lucy at her grave, we see a profound sexual transformation: "The sweetness was turned to adamantine, heartless cruelty, and the purity to voluptuous wantonness." Her eyes are now "unclean and full of hell-fire, instead of the pure gentle orbs" (Stoker, 217). When Lucy recognizes Holmwood, she moves toward him seductively "with a languorous, voluptuous grace" and moans, "Come to me, Arthur . . . My arms are hungry for you. Come and we can rest together" (Stoker, 218).

Dracula is still read in many college English classes, and academic interest in Stoker's vampire novel continues, as evidenced by the publication of the Norton Critical Edition of *Dracula*—which celebrates 100 years since its first publication—a novel that "seemed commonplace in 1897" because it was simply one of "many fantastic adventure stories pitting manly Englishmen against foreign monsters" (ix). The 1880s and 1890s saw the publication of works by Kipling (*Jungle Book*), Stevenson (*Dr. Jekyll and Mr. Hyde*) and Wells (*The Island of Dr. Moreau*) that featured exotic places and strange encounters with a variety of monsters. Nina Auerbach and David Skal, editors of the Norton *Dracula,* argue that the greatest threats to the English at the time of the publication of *Dracula* were foreigners, women, and Oscar Wilde. The New Woman threatened the Englishman with her aspirations of independence, selfhood, and education, whereas a flood of strange immigrants from the far-flung corners of the British Empire threatened the racial purity of the Englishman. And because Bram Stoker knew Oscar Wilde well and may have had homosexual leanings himself, it is possible that "[t]he Wilde trials of 1895 . . . shocked Stoker into writing *Dracula* as we know it, for Wilde's two-year imprisonment for 'acts of gross indecency' gave Victorian England a new monster of its own clinical making: the homosexual" (xi). Literary critics analyzed *Dracula* from a variety of critical perspectives from the 1970s through the 1990s (see below), but scholarly interest in *Dracula* seems to have waned since the year 2000, in spite of the continued popularity of the Count and other vampires who appear in countless popular books, television series, movies, graphic novels, comic books, and Web sites.

Trends and Themes. In *Vampire Legends in Contemporary American Culture* (2002), William Patrick Day studies the figure of the vampire in the literature, film, and television of the United States from Bela Lugosi's Dracula (1933) through the popular Buffy TV series, which ended with its 100th episode in 2002. Day argues that there are three contemporary modes of the vampire story: (1) the liberated vampire who "is not a supernatural monster or Stoker's Antichrist but a post-Christian image of humanity ready to be set free from the restraints and limitations of an outmoded and repressive past"; (2) the "post human vampire" who is "self-alienated and without center, a mere creature of its needs"; and (3) the vampire slayer. Day points out that the slayer virtually disappears with the liberated vampire—after all, why kill a sensitive, aesthetic creature such as Rice's Louis or Yarbro's Saint Germain? Nevertheless, the slayer's services are once again needed with the appearance of the post human or rogue vampire (2002, 8–9). These three types of stories—the humane and human vampire, the monster vampire, and the slayer—account for a large number of vampire stories found in popular culture media.

For a history of vampires in film and television through 1999, see Day's *Vampire Legends* (2002) and Melton's *The Vampire Book* (1999). The figures of the humane vampire, the undead monster, and the slayer are evident in *Forever Knight* (1992–1995 TV series), *Bram Stoker's Dracula* (1992 movie), and *Buffy the Vampire Slayer* (1992 movie; 1997–2003 TV series). *Bram Stoker's Dracula* features Gary Oldham as the Count, and though faithful to Stoker's presentation of Dracula as a monster, it departs from Stoker's narrative by including a love story. *Forever Knight* tells the story of Nick Knight, a police officer who is also a vampire intent on keeping his dark secret while protecting humans from criminals. The movie version of *Buffy* (1992) was completely overshadowed by the popular 100-episode series starring Sarah Michelle Gellar as Buffy, the teenage vampire slayer from the Valley.

Interview with the Vampire (1994) brought Anne Rice's 1976 novel to the screen, starring Brad Pitt as Louis and Tom Cruise as Lestat. Rice's third novel was turned into a movie of the same name, *Queen of the Dead* (2002), which starred Aliah as Akasha, the Queen of vampires. *Underworld* (2003) featured Kate Beckensale as Celine, a millennium-old vampire who attempts to protect Michael Corvin from the Lycans (werewolves) only to see him morph into a new "vamplican" species. In *Underworld Evolution* (2006), the metamorphosis of Corvin is completed, and now the struggle is to protect humans from William (a lycan) and Marcus (a vampire), the twin sons of the original vampire Alexander Corvinus. *Salem's Lot* (2004) is a movie adaptation of the popular Stephen King novel about a New England town overrun by vampires. In *Van Helsing* (2004), we learn that Abraham Van Helsing has kept himself alive with blood from Dracula, who is entombed in a basement vault of the old slayer's antiquities business, and later awakened by foolish thieves. In the Blade movies (*Blade,* 1998; *Blade II,* 2002; and *Blade: Trinity,* 2004), Wesley Snipes stars as Blade, a vampire who can control his appetite for human blood and who fights against renegade vampires intent on turning the human race into dormant blood slaves. *Dracula 2000* is a rather weak attempt to retell the original Stoker tale in contemporary times; and *Dracula 3000* pushes the tale out into deep space, where the crew members of a salvage ship board a freighter filled with coffins, only to learn that they are the great-great-grandchildren of the original Stoker characters who have been lured by the Count into a final battle.

It is beyond the purview of this article to describe the ubiquity of the figure of the vampire in the variegated popular culture media. Melton identifies a revival of interest in comic book vampires, for example, with the issue of *Blood of the Innocent* by WarP Comics in 1986. This was followed by Apple Comics' *Blood of Dracula* (1987–1992), Marvel Comics' *Blood* (1987–1988), and Innovation's 12-issue adaptation of Anne Rice's *The Vampire Lestat* (1990). Melton notes, "The ten new vampire titles which appeared in 1990 became 23 titles in 1991. In 1992 no fewer than 34 titles were published, followed by a similar number in 1993" (Melton 1999, 137). Since then, Anne Rice's *Interview with a Vampire* and *Queen of the Dead* (Innovation) have been adapted as comic book series, as well as Le Fanu's *Carmilla* (Aircel) and Francis Ford Coppola's *Bram Stoker's Dracula* (Topps Comics).

The TV series *Buffy the Vampire Slayer* (1997–2003) spawned an industry all its own. *The Buffy Library* (www.cesnur.org/buffy_library.html) is an international annotated bibliography that includes only book-length studies of the series in a multiplicity of languages. *Slayage: The Online International Journal of Buffy Studies* was developed in 2001 and contains hundreds of journal, newspaper, and magazine articles (www.slayageonline.com) on the TV series. There are currently numerous online Buffy fanzines, and Darkhorse published a series of some sixty Buffyverse graphic novels, which are not based on actual TV episodes, being rather new adventures for Buffy and friends. Scholarly papers are presented every year on the series at the *Popular Culture Association* conference, and many of these papers are published in the *Journal of Popular Culture.* Jan Battis has analyzed family relationships, which are based on loyalty rather than heredity, in *Blood Relations: Chosen Families in Buffy the Vampire Slayer and Angel* (McFarland Press, 2005), and Open Court Press has published a volume of scholarly articles on Buffy from a number of philosophical perspectives entitled *Buffy the Vampire Slayer and Philosophy: Fear and Trembling in Sunnydale* (2003) in their Popular Culture and Philosophy series.

As far as fiction is concerned, the three modes identified by Melton—the humane vampire, the undead monster, and the slayer—have grown exponentially, especially in terms of book series. There are scores of vampire novel series currently in print in the United States, beginning with Anne Rice's *Vampire Chronicles* (1976–2003), featuring the vampire Lestat, and Chelsea Quinn Yarbro's Saint-Germain series (1978–2007), which continues with stories of Saint-Germain in historical hot spots. Lestat and Saint-Germain are the quintessential humane vampires who mourn the loss of their humanity and refuse to kill humans to feed themselves. Rice's and Yarbro's novels are written sympathetically from the perspective of the vampires whose loss and suffering are narrated at length. Laurel K. Hamilton's Master Vampire Jean-Claude and L.A. Banks's vampire Carlos continue this tradition of troubled, humane vampires deeply connected to and protective of humans.

Almost all of the popular vampire series include rogue vampires who feed on humans and destroy whatever harmony exists among vampires. Anne Rice's Santino, the Satanic cult leader, and Akasha, the Queen of the Dead, are renegade monsters. Laurel K. Hamilton's Anita Blake series has the vampire slayer Anita killing a multitude of rogue vampires in the earlier novels in the series and other more sophisticated undead in the latter part of the series to protect Jean-Claude's community of vampires. L.A. Banks's Damali (*Vampire Huntress Legends*) is joined by her community of guardians in protecting humans from vampires, shape-shifters, demons, and a plethora of other monsters. Elizabeth Kostova's retelling of the original Dracula story in *The Historian* revives the image of the arrogant, bloodthirsty monster Vlad Tepes III.

Though the figure of the slayer is also alive and well in contemporary vampire fiction, it is threatened with extinction as the vampires become increasingly human and humane. In Laurel K. Hamilton's 14-volume series (1993–2007), Anita Blake is a necromancer and vampire slayer who becomes increasingly involved in the world of both vampires and shape-shifters who now share legal status with human communities—but Anita still hunts and slays rogue shifters and vampires. In the eight novels in L.A. Banks's *Vampire Huntress Legends* (2003–2007), Damali is a Neteru who has power over vampires, but she attracts them too, because a vampire-neteru union can produce daywalkers—vampires unaffected by sunlight. Again, though Damali eventually marries Carlos, a human-turned-vampire-turned human, she slays vampires who are still connected to the Vampire Council, a group bent on the destruction of the human race. Charlaine Harris's Sookie Stackhouse, a telepath, hunts and slays both vampires and shape-shifters that threaten her rural Louisiana community.

Context and Issues. Vampires also appear in a variety of popular literary genres including historical fiction, romance, science fiction, fantasy, crime fiction, spy fiction, and—of course—comedy and satire. A favorite approach of contemporary vampire novelists is to place a vampire in a turbulent historical context with known historical figures or to show that a famous historical person was, in fact, a vampire. William Meickle sets his historical novel *The Coming of the King* (2003) in Wales, Scotland, and England in 1745. The vampire King is coming to claim the throne of England, and the group of slayers who have been watching for him have fallen into disarray. Mary Anne Mitchell's *In the Name of the Vampire* (2005), *The Vampire De Sade* (2004), *Tainted Blood* (2003), *Cathedral of Vampires* (2002), and *Sips of Blood* (1999) all tell the story of the Marquis de Sade, who was actually a vampire and continues his debauchery after his undeath. In *A Taste for Blood* (2003), Diana Lee narrates the story of Ryan, an 800-year-old vampire dating back to the Vikings.

Posing as a Scottish noble, Ryan turns a young Victorian woman into a vampire, and she must now learn the ropes of vampirism. In *Night of the Dragon's Blood* (1997), William Pridgen's mysterious heroine is none other than Eva Peron, who has been turned into a vampire by Adolph Hitler.

In *Mother Julian and the Gentle Vampire* (2000), the story of Lesbiana Boyd is told by Jack Pantaleo. Lesbiana is a 600-year-old Christian vampire whose bite and blood actually cause people to flourish and to become fully alive. Lesbiana, a contemporary of Julianna of Norwich, is pursued by the Five Pretties, vampire versions of the furies. Finally, Michael Schiefelbein's *Vampire Thrall* (2003) is about Victor Decimus, a 2,000-year-old vampire rejected by Jesus as lover who takes revenge on the church and monasteries over the course of two millennia.

Along similar historical lines are tales of revived revenants, vampires from nineteenth-century literature who never actually died. Kyle Martin's *Carmilla: The Return* (2000) updates Carmilla's story from the original Le Fanu novel with flashbacks to the nineteenth century. *The Book of Renfield: A Gospel of Dracula* (2005), by Tim Lucas, is set in Dracula's day and tells the story of Renfield, who has been in psychic contact with the Count all along. And Elizabeth Kostova revives the Count himself in *The Historian* (2005), and he is still bent on world domination (see below).

Vampires are apparently good lovers, given that many of the contemporary series present male and female vampires as capable of having great sex. Katie Macalister's *A Girl's Guide to Vampires* (2003), *Sex and the Single Vampire* (2004) and *Sex, Lies and Vampires* (2005) all tell stories of young women who fall in love with attractive men who turn out to be vampires. In *A Taste for Passion* (2003), Patrice Michelle's Rana Sterling falls in love with the perfect man, but he turns out to be a vampire who must assume leadership of an elite group on the condition that he have a wife. Rana is willing to take the vampire as her lover, but she is unwilling to be his wife. Finally, Nora Roberts's *Circle Trilogy* (2006) involves three young couples who fall in love while fighting an army of vampires intent on enslaving the human race (see below). Vampires also make good detectives and spies because of their night vision and stealth. Jon F. Merz's *The Syndicate: A Lawson Vampire Novel* tells the story of Lawson, a vampire cop working in contemporary New York City. Savannah Russe's *Beyond the Pale: The Darkening Chronicles* (2005) is about Daphne Urban, a vampire proficient in modern languages who has been pressed into service by the CIA to spy on arms dealers.

There are also comedies and parodies of the vampire genre. Lynsay Sands's *Single White Vampire* (2003), *Love Bites* (2004), *Tall, Dark and Hungry* (2004), and *A Quick Bite* (2005) tell the comedic and romantic stories of Lucern Argeneau and the vampires he has made, one of whom cannot stand the sight of blood. In *Carpe Jugulum: A Novel of Discworld,* Terry Pratchett satirizes vampires and the conventions of the genre. Charlaine Harris's Sookie Stackhouse (see below) is a mind reader who takes vampires and were-creatures as lovers and who works as a waitress at a local bar and shops at Wal-Mart. Christopher Moore's *You Suck: A Love Story* (2007) is the story of Thomas C. Flood, who wakes up as a vampire one morning after a date with a woman who turns out to be a vampire. Janet Maslin of the *New York Times* writes: "The title needs mentioning because the book will be too popular to be ignored. *You Suck* is funny enough to reanimate Mr. Moore's fans . . . It's sure to appeal to anyone who shares the author's ideas of a fun-loving vampire's priorities" (2).

Selected Authors. The vampire story has also taken a multicultural turn. What follows is a selective look at seven authors who have adapted the vampire tradition to a distinctive cultural context. This short discussion will hopefully give the reader a sense of the variety of cultural contexts explored by vampire literature. We will begin with Anne Rice's haute couture vampires Lestat and Louis, from the *Vampire Chronicles,* where the reader is introduced to an ancient, wealthy, and educated line of vampires. Next comes Chelsea Quinn Yarbro's Saint-Germain, a kinder, gentler vampire who loves human beings in spite of their folly. Then we move on to Laurel K. Hamilton's Anita Blake, a suburban huntress and necromancer by vocation who is regularly called by the police to carry out tasks involving vampires and shape-shifters. Then there is L.A. Banks's Damali, a hip-hop artist who together with the Guardians is attempting to forestall the Armageddon, the final battle between the forces of good and evil on planet Earth. From there we head to rural Louisiana to see Sookie Stackhouse, a simple country girl, lock horns with redneck shape-shifters and rural vampires. To end our discussion of contemporary vampire series, we turn to Nora Roberts's *Circle Trilogy* and her romantic vampires. Coming full circle, this review of American vampire literature ends with Elizabeth Kostova's *The Historian,* which is a return to the dark, gothic world of the old monster himself, Count Dracula. In addition to confirming Auerbach's thesis "that every age embraces the vampire it needs" (*Ourselves,* 145), this discussion should also make evident that every culture (and, perhaps, class) creates the vampire that it needs.

Anne Rice (1941–): Haute Couture Vampires and Lestat, their Prince. Anne Rice, far more than any other American author, has reshaped the vampire tradition and created a veritable vampire industry in the United States. Her 12-volume *Vampire Chronicles* (1976–2003) relate the stories of a number of ancient vampires—Marius, Pandora, and Armand, to name three—as well as the story of "those who must be kept," the ancient vampires Enkil and Akasha. But in the end, it is the figure of Lestat that dominates the *Chronicles.* The first of Anne Rice's vampire novels, *Interview with the Vampire* (1976), is narrated by Louis, an eighteenth- century French-American who owns plantations near New Orleans. Louis is a sensitive, humane vampire who is "turned" by Lestat, with whom he hunts New Orleans until he no longer can bear Lestat's cruelty and arrogance. During an interview to a reporter in the 1970s, he explains the difference between himself and Lestat: "I killed animals . . . Lestat killed humans all the time, sometimes two or three a night, sometimes more. He would drink from one just enough to satisfy a momentary thirst, and then go on to another. The better the human, as he would say in his vulgar way, the more he liked it" (41).

While hunting one night in New Orleans, Lestat takes Louis to a hospital filled with children dying of the fever. Lestat adopts one of the children by paying a priest, and he takes the young girl home with them. Louis feeds on Claudia, then Lestat allows her to feed from him, turning her into a vampire. Louis is horrified, but Lestat informs Claudia that he and Louis are now her parents. That first morning, at Lestat's insistence, Claudia sleeps with Louis in his casket. Although Lestat teaches Claudia how to refine her vampiric powers, she and Louis develop a deeper bond through exploration of the arts. Eventually, Louis and Claudia decide to murder Lestat and then travel to Europe in search of other, perhaps more humane, vampires. After disposing of Lestat's body, they head to Europe and travel extensively until they find a community of vampires at the Theatre des Vampires in Paris, France.

Armand, who will have a novel devoted exclusively to his life later in the Chronicles, is the head of the Theatre des Vampires, which produces surrealistic plays that invariably end with the sacrificial death of a woman. Louis and Claudia think they have found a home until they realize that Santiago, second in command at the Theatre des Vampires, is plotting to have them killed for Lestat's murder and Claudia's turning an older woman into her vampire mother. Armand helps Louis to escape, and the two travel together until Armand decides they must part. Sad and filled with pain, Louis heads back to New Orleans and discovers that Lestat has survived the murder attempt.

In *The Vampire Lestat* (1985), the second installment of the Vampire Chronicles, Lestat tells his own story retrospectively from the vantage point of 1984, when he is a rock superstar whose first album has sold over four million copies. Lestat opens with a flair, "I am the vampire Lestat. I'm immortal. More or less. The light of the sun, the sustained heat of an intense fire—these things might destroy me. But then again, they might not" (3). We learn that Lestat is six-feet tall, that he has thick, blond, curly hair and grey eyes, and that he was made a vampire in the 1780s, went underground in 1929 and was reawakened in 1984, when a rock band began to practice in a house near his, on Sixth Street in New Orleans.

The disenfranchised seventh son of a French aristocrat, Lestat runs away to Paris with his friend Nicki just prior to the French Revolution. They find work at Renaud's House of Thespians, Lestat acting and Nicki playing his violin. One winter night Lestat is abducted from his flat by Magnus, a very old vampire, and turned into a vampire at Magnus's tower just outside of Paris. The day after Lestat is given the Dark Trick, Magnus bequeaths his wealth and residence to Lestat then leaps into the roaring flames of a huge fire he has prepared inside the tower. Lestat, in despair, explores the tower and discovers Magnus's immense wealth as well as his sarcophagus, which has the faint outline of a cross on the lid. Lestat learns that neither the cross nor the writing "The Lord Jesus Christ" on the sarcophagus has any effect on himself. He also discovers that neither sacred images nor jewel-encrusted crucifixes affect him adversely and that he is able to see his image in a mirror. He thus concludes that God has no power over him. But he also learns that "vampires can love each other" (102), and that he had, indeed, loved Magnus, his maker.

And this love extends to humans as well—even the act of taking the life of a human contains "the perfect semblance of love" (142), at least for the vampire. Rice presents Lestat as a preternatural lover, making explicit what is only implied in Stoker's *Dracula*—that the blood feast is for vampires what sex is for humans: "I looked into her eyes and saw them glaze over. I felt the heat of her breasts swelling beneath her rags. Her soft, succulent body tumbled against me . . . I kissed her, feeding on her heat . . . There weren't any words for the rapture. But I'd had all the ecstasy that rape could give . . . The very blood seemed warmer with their innocence, richer with their goodness" (142). Lestat's new aesthetic vision of the world is that of the Savage Garden, and in this garden, governed by aesthetic principles and not natural theology, "these innocent ones belonged in the vampire's arms" (143).

And so the journey begins for Lestat, who quickly works the Dark Trick on his dying mother Gabrielle and his best friend, Nicki, who had been kidnapped by a superstitious coven of vampires trapped in the Christian worldview, seeing themselves as eternally damned. Lestat and Gabrielle travel throughout Europe in search of other vampires and find only ragged, superstitious vampires who believe themselves damned by the Christian god and condemned to dwell in cemeteries and catacombs. Gabrielle eventually goes off on her own in search of the beauties of nature, while Lestat continues his search for an ancient vampire named Marius, leaving messages for him everywhere he travels, but he eventually despairs of finding him and goes dormant in Cairo, Egypt. Lestat is awakened by Marius himself and taken to an island in the Mediterranean Sea, where Marius now tells his story, which is retold in greater detail in *Blood and Gold: The Story of Marius* (2001).

In the remainder of the novel, Lestat learns that vampires are much older and far more powerful than they are in the account given in Stoker's *Dracula*. In fact, Marius, himself the son of a Roman patrician, was given the Dark Trick in the time of Augustus Caesar. Most importantly, however, Lestat is introduced to "Those Who Must Be kept,"—the ancient, original vampire couple, Enkil and Akasha—who sit statuesquely on thrones, apparently in a dormant state, in a temple built by Marius. Lestat awakens Akasha by playing a violin, and Akasha draws him to herself in an exchange of blood. This "shimmering circuit" is broken by Enkil, who almost crushes Lestat, but Marius intervenes, threatening Enkil with the removal of Akasha, So Lestat is spared and flees immediately.

In addition to learning vampire history, Lestat also describes how he had fallen in love with Louis in the eighteenth century and how Louis, in *Interview with the Vampire*, had misrepresented him on a number of counts, especially in his claim that Lestat toyed with humans and then killed them, which becomes the justification for Louis and Claudia to murder Lestat. Lestat points out that Louis could not have understood that he "hunted almost exclusively among the gamblers, the thieves and the killers" being "faithful" to his "unspoken vow to kill the evildoer" (499). Lestat moves on to the nineteenth century and tells us that "vampires were 'discovered' by the literary writers of Europe." He then describes Polidori's and Le Fanu's vampires, ending with a description of Stoker's *Dracula*, "the big ape of vampires, the hirsute Slav Count Dracula" (500). Rice has both challenged and transformed the vampire tradition and created a novel mythology of vampire origins.

In *The Queen of the Damned* (1988), Akasha is awakened from her dormant state by Lestat's band, *The Vampire Lestat*. Akasha has drained Enkil of his blood and power and left Marius—the faithful warden of "Those Who Must Be kept"—buried under tons of ice and cement. Akasha summons Lestat, whom she now employs as her new consort and henchman to carry out her plan to create a new world order, in which the Queen herself—as the Goddess who will create a new Garden of Eden for women—rules. This, of course, will involve the destruction of all males, vampire and human, on planet Earth, and this she sets out to do with Lestat, unwilling yet subservient, at her side.

In this third installment of the Vampire Chronicles we learn more of the origins of vampirism, which stretch back 6,000 years and involve Maharet, Mekare, and a troublesome familiar spirit named Amel, who has been trying to impress Maharet and Mekare—powerful, redheaded twin witches who live with their ancient tribe in the caves of Mount Carmel, in Palestine. Akasha and Enkil, King and Queen of Egypt, learn of the telepathic abilities of the twins and send an army to slaughter the tribe and bring Maharet and Mekare to Egypt. Amel, who had been experimenting with passing through humans and tasting their blood, follows the twins to Egypt and raises havoc in the court to show off his power. The priests of Egypt are terrified by Amel's mischief, and fearing their own cult of the dead threatened, stab the royal couple to death one evening, telling the people that Amel had committed the crime. But a strange transformation occurs: "The Queen lay on the floor writhing as if in agony, the blood pouring from her wounds, and a great reddish cloud enveloped her; it was like a whirlpool surrounding her, or rather a wind sweeping up countless tiny drops of blood. And in the midst of the swirling wind or rain or whatever it could be called, the Queen twisted and turned, her eyes rolling up into her head" (386). Akasha has become the first vampire, and shortly after her revival, she heals the wounds of the king, who becomes the second vampire. She eventually turns Maharet, Mekare, and their trusted court advisor, Khayman, into vampires, and so the long story of vampirism begins. Now the ancient vampires must stop the renegade Akasha, but if they kill Akasha, they could all perish because Akasha possesses the core of what used to be Amel.

The Tale of the Body Thief (1992) is a side story involving Lestat's growing disillusionment with vampiric life. Indeed, Lestat desires to experience being human again, and he is approached by a man who claims to be able to trade bodies for a short time. Lestat immediately regrets the exchange, but it is too late: the body thief has disappeared and Lestat is left in an older, ailing body. In *Memnoch the Devil* (1995), Lestat meets the devil and learns that Memnoch is not the bad guy, but that God has blundered in so many ways that he was forced to send his son to die. Memnoch turns out to be an advocate for humans, and God a blundering, powerful creator who loses track of his creation and feels alienated from the crown of his creation—humans.

In the next five installments of the Chronicles, Rice tells the stories of five vampires. Armand (*The Vampire Armand* 1998) is given the Dark Trick by Marius and kidnapped by Santino, the head of the Satan-worshipping cult in Rome. In *Pandora* (1998), we are given the story of Marius's great love, Pandora, who disappeared for a millennium from Marius's sight. In *Vittorio the Vampire* (1999), Vittorio, a 500-year-old Italian vampire with a philosophical bent, tells the story of his search for meaning. *Merrick* (2000) is the story of Merrick Mayfair, one of the darkskinned Mayfair witches, who possesses an incredible power to call spirits and vampires to herself, which she does when she beckons David Talbot, Louis, and Lestat to her home in New Orleans. More than anything Merrick wants to become a vampire. Marius, in *Blood and Gold* (2001), tells his story of receiving the dark gift during the reign of Caesar Augustus, and he also narrates the long odyssey of caring for "Those Who Must Be Kept," as he moves their thrones and stiff bodies from Rome to Constantinople, then to Italy (just north of Venice) and finally to Dresden.

The final two novels in the Chronicles return to the continuing adventures of Lestat. In *Blackwood Farm* (2002), Rice brings her Mayfair witches and the vampire Lestat together at Blackwood Farm, the antebellum mansion of the Mayfair clan. Quinn Blackwood has been given the dark gift, but this turns his doppelgänger, Goblin, into a fierce opponent, which drives Quinn to seek out Lestat for help. Lestat's tale is brought to completion in *Blood Canticle* (2003), as he falls in love with Rowan Mayfair, the famous witch of the Mayfair Chronicles, who is married to Michael Curry. Lestat, fresh from his strange encounters in heaven and hell, now longs to be good and longs for redemption, and he achieves a redemption of sorts by refusing to turn Rowan Mayfair into a vampire. But he remains the tormented and arrogant vampire his fans have come to know and love: "I wanna be a saint, I wanna save souls by the millions, I wanna look like an angel . . . But you know me, and come sunset, maybe it will be time to hunt the back roads" (305–306). In an interview with *Book,* Anne Rice comments on the end of the series: "I had made the decision that I wanted to move away from the witches and vampires altogether.

I wanted to write something completely different. I no longer really wanted to write about people who were damned or who were condemned. . . . and I think [*Blood Canticle*] is about that—being the end of the road, the last of the chronicles" (Quoted in "Anne Rice," *Contemporary Authors*, NRS, 376).

With the Vampire Chronicles, Anne Rice has dramatically transformed the vampire tradition. Rice's central vampires—Lestat, Louis, Marius, and Pandora—see themselves as monsters, but they eventually stop preying on humans, unlike the monster Dracula. These vampires are beautiful, powerful, and devoted to the arts and learning. And, to the degree that it is possible for a vampire, they fall in love with humans and other vampires. Though vampires cannot have normal sexual relations, they have deep feelings and "sleep" together in heterosexual and homosexual arrangements. In addition, Rice removes the origin of vampirism from a Christian frame and places it into a world of spirits and demons where God, even if he does exist, matters very little. Finally, Rice is able to trace the history of vampirism through sequels and prequels involving Lestat and a host of other vampires from its origin 6,000 years ago to the present day.

The first two installments of Anne Rice's Vampire Chronicles met with critical acclaim as a fresh beginning for the vampire tradition, but in spite of continued popularity among fans, the last ten installments were not well received. The negative criticism begins with *Queen of the Damned*. For example, *New York Times* columnist Michiko Kakutani acknowledges that Rice has developed a fully coherent vampire mythology in *Queen,* but there are weaknesses: "By filtering staple mythic conventions—orphaned children, corrupt rulers, stark confrontations between good and evil—through her own Gothic sensibility, she is able to create an entertaining legend of her own. It's a campy, somewhat tongue-in-cheek legend, but like all successful legends it defines a coherent world that remains faithful to its own peculiar rules and logic" (15 October 1988, Online Version). In *Our Vampires, Ourselves* (1995) Nina Auerbach views Rice's Loius and Lestat as twentieth-century versions of Polidori and Byron, rekindling the pre-*Dracula* vampire tradition of intimacy and homoeroticism (152–154), but as the 1980s wear on she sees Lestat and the other vampires practicing an insular identity politics—withdrawn, depressed, and unconcerned about humans. Typical of the 1980s Reagan years, "Rice's vampires are beautifully devoid of social consciousness, another major attraction for disaffected readers" (154). In spite of negative criticism, a large number of sessions have been devoted to Rice's vampires at the *Popular Culture Association*'s annual conference for the last twenty years, and many of these papers appear in the *Journal of Popular Culture*. Unlike Stoker's *Dracula*, which continues to draw considerable scholarly attention, literary scholars have remained indifferent to Anne Rice's vampire novels.

Chelsea Quinn Yarbro (1942–): Saint-Germain: A Kinder, Gentler Vampire. Chelsea Quinn Yarbro opens her Saint-Germain series in 1978 with *Hotel Transylvania,* set in 1743 Paris and involving Madelaine de Montalia, a beautiful aristocrat in danger of being ruined by a group of Satanists. Saint-Germain has been a vampire for over four millennia, and he has learned painfully, through trial and error, how to live among humans. Yarbro subsequently sets all of her historical novels involving Saint-Germain in a politically turbulent time and place. Saint-Germain, the very antithesis of Lestat, has become wise and compassionate over the long millennia, adapting to the language and culture of a given place, adopting the clothing, the cuisine (for his servants), and the customs of the people he stealthily moves among. His longevity is his strength, and it tends to compensate for the vampiric weaknesses of needing native earth (to sleep and walk on) and blood (animal mostly and human when ethically possible), and experiencing vertigo when near running water.

The historical settings for Yarbro's novels vary widely and no doubt reflect Yarbro's historical interests. For example, in *The Palace* (1978) Saint-Germain is in Renaissance Florence during the rise of the intolerant Savonarola. In *Blood Games* (1979), Atta Olivia Clemens becomes his lover during the reign of Nero. Saint-Germain finds himself in China during the reign of Genghis Khan in *Path of the Eclipse* (1981). In *Tempting Fate* (1982), the Russian Revolution drives Saint-Germain to Germany, where the Nazi Party is on the rise. *Darker Jewels* (1993) places him in the court of Ivan the Terrible in Russia. Saint-Germain takes a sixteenth-century Inca Princess as lover and runs into trouble with the Spanish in *Mansions of Darkness* (1996). In *Writ in Blood* (1997), Saint-Germain is on a diplomatic mission, on behalf of Czar Nicholas from Russia, to England to attempt to stop the outbreak of World War I, and he takes as lover a young artist named Rowena Saxon. The plague strikes Provence in the fourteenth century, and Saint-Germain is forced to flee and take on the identity of a troubadour in *Blood Roses* (1999).

More recently, in *Come Twilight* (2000), Saint-Germain, now 3,500 years old, finds himself on the Iberian Peninsula, after he leaves Toletum for the Pyrenees in 620 C.E. He travels with his faithful servant (and ghoul) of 700 years, Rogerian. Yarbro divides this historical novel into four sections, each beginning respectively in 620, 720, 750, and 1117 C.E. and tracing Saint-Germain's and Rogerian's travels throughout Spain in pre-Moor, Moor, and post-Moor times. In addition to avoiding Muslim-Christian battlefields, Saint-Germain also attempts to avoid a vampire named Chimenae, whom he turned and who has created a community of vampires that preys on villagers and Muslim soldiers in and around the small village of Mt. Calcius. Yarbro has done her homework and is careful to show how Saint-Germain adapts his dress, language, and customs to the time and place. Saint-Germain is scarcely a vampire because he stopped drinking human blood centuries ago, subsisting on the blood of animals and on the erotic, heterosexual human touch.

Saint-Germain is a compassionate vampire who stops to help injured travelers with his medicaments and cares for his horses as if they were his children. Whereas Rice's Lestat is tortured by his memory and his boredom, Saint-Germain has become increasingly humane through the ages, and he values his experience: "Thought is always of value, and memory, no matter how painful, can illuminate life" (24). In *Come Twilight,* Saint-Germain is a slave, a beggar, a monk, and a courier. He is invariably misunderstood by the ignorant, greedy, and violent Christians and Muslims who seek to use his knowledge of history and languages to their own end. In addition, Saint-Germain attempts to teach Chimenae how to live as a vampire among humans. Over the 500 years that transpire in this novel we see Saint-Germain patiently calling on her to leave the cult of the blood that she has created in Mt. Calcius, and to stop making and destroying vampires as if they were toys to be played with then thrown away. Chimenae will not accept the long, historical vision of Saint-Germain, being rather like a child who lives for the immediate gratification of the next kill. Throughout the novel, Saint-Germain receives letters from Olivia, who is now in Rome and who stands in stark contrast to Chimenae. In her final letter to Saint-Germain, Olivia longs for ancient, pagan Rome as she reflects on the barbarism of the current Rome under the Holy Roman Emperor Lothair II, who must deal with two rival pretenders to the papal throne: Anacletus II in Rome and Innocent II in France.

In *States of Grace* (2005) Di Santo Germano is a Renaissance man—scientist (alchemist), historian, philosopher, musician, and overall humanist—who finds himself in Venice, Italy, in 1530, shortly after the commencement of the Spanish Inquisition (1522) by Charles I. Because he owns printing presses in Venice, Burges, Antwerp, and Amsterdam, Saint-Germain must travel through these cities in the Spanish Netherlands while Christians fight their internecine battles and Ottoman Corsairs raid merchant ships, including Saint-Germain's, on the Mediterranean. In Venice, Saint-Germain is the patron and lover of Pier Ariana Salier, composer and musician, whose music he publishes and whose welfare he has at heart. While traveling away from Venice to check on his publishing ventures, a plot is hatched by Venetian businessmen to steal Saint-Germain's property and appropriate his wealth, thus leaving Pier Ariana bereft of her benefaction.

Like all the later novels in this series, *States of Grace* is a carefully researched historical novel that attempts to be faithful to the late Renaissance culture of Western Europe under the Spanish Emperor Charles I (Carlos V). Yarbro skillfully depicts how a wise pagan might navigate the political and theological landmines of Catholic Italy and a growing Protestant movement in the Netherlands and Germany. Saint-Germain's claim to "follow no king and serve no known gods" (42) sets him up for serious trouble in a time and place where the state religion is determined by the theological leanings of the prince but can be overturned by the Pope or Holy Roman Emperor. The Peace of Westphalia (1648), the landmark treaty of religious toleration, is still 118 years in the future. In addition, Saint-Germain is publishing books on science, geography, music, and history—works that try to skirt but invariably assume a theological position at a time when printing presses in Catholic Europe are being censored and closed for publishing heretical tracts by Protestants. In this historical situation, the Catholic, Protestant, and Muslim zealot is each "purveying his own state of grace" (147–148) and the only thing that might unite them would be the discovery of a vampire in their midst. And, in fact, Saint-Germain is being watched closely by spies, because of his wealth and his publishing activities. If he is discovered to be a witch or a heretic, he will be burned at the stake.

Again, this is a historical novel about the ideal man, the true Renaissance humanist who is learned and compassionate and who agonizes over human folly. As a vampire, Saint-Germain lives largely on animal blood but needs human touch—the touch of a woman—more than he needs blood. Nevertheless, he takes small quantities of blood from his lovers while making love—generally limiting his encounters with his courtesans to five, because the sixth encounter turns the woman into a vampire. Unlike Lestat, Saint-Germain possesses limited strength, though he is a skillful warrior. Sunlight irritates him, and crossing water creates disorientation, which turns out to be a regular problem in Venice with its canals and harbors. He sleeps on boxes filled with his native earth and stuffs the same into the hollow soles of his boots. Apart from these irritations, Saint-Germain is Yarbro's ideal man—intelligent, selfless, and thoughtful. Through Saint-Germain, Yarbro implicitly critiques a modern world embroiled in ideological and religious wars.

Yarbro's Saint-Germain series has received positive reviews from *Library Journal*, *Science Fiction Chronicle*, and *Publishers Weekly* throughout the years and an occasional accolade from *The Washington Post* "Book World" critic, Brian Jacomb, who writes of the Saint-Germian series: "Among her works is a series of historical vampire tales featuring Count Saint-Germain, who is, in this reader's opinion, the most eloquent of all undead characters" (8 April 1999, Online Version). A year later

Jacomb reviewed *Come Twilight:* "Chelsea Quinn Yarbro has created a character who makes other vampires pale by comparison. This 3,500-year-old aristocrat has been keeping Yarbro's many fans home at night for two decades" (30 October 2000, Online Version). In *Our Vampires, Ourselves* (1995), Nina Auerbach claims that Saint-Germain "epitomizes the highly evolved vampire of the late 1970s, whose refinement is an implicit reproach to humanity. Like that of his nineteenth-century predecessor Carmilla, the vampirism of Yarbro's Count flows from a thirst for intimacy—the romantic intimacy Stoker's Dracula destroyed in his estranged rage for dominance" (147).

Laurel K. Hamilton (1963–): Anita Blake, Suburban Huntress. Anita Blake is a vampire hunter and necromancer, but in the St. Louis of the near future, vampires and other monsters are citizens, so Anita enters into romantic relationships with Jean-Claude, the master of the local vampires, and Richard, the Ulfric (leader) of the local were-wolf pack. By the sixth novel of the fourteen-novel series Anita, Jean-Claude, and Richard form a metaphysical—as well as physical-sexual—relationship that bestows special powers on each of them and enables them to work together to elim-inate human criminals, rogue vampires, zombies, and other monsters from the city of St. Louis, East St. Louis (Illinois) and Santa Fe (New Mexico). In addition to the killing of bad guys, there is a fair amount of explicit sex: Anita often has sexual intercourse with preternatural creatures in order to subdue and/or kill them. In this vampire world, even vampires can have sexual relations and produce offspring through other vampires or mortal humans, this in opposition to the standard tradi-tion that vampires lose the ability to have intercourse. In addition to being a vam-pire executioner, Anita is an animator, not the graphic design type, but a person with power to raise the dead and create zombies—a very handy ability because zombies are now legally permitted to give testimony in legal cases. As the series progresses, Anita finds that she has power over not just the dead but the undead as well—that is, she is able to call and control younger vampires, and she is able to resist the mind control and tricks of older, more powerful vampires.

The first eight novels of the series take place at local venues in St. Louis, where we get to see Anita Blake, vampire executioner and animator, work her magic in this wild world populated by humans, vampires, and were-creatures. In *Guilty Pleasures* (1993) Jean-Claude, the master vampire of the city of St. Louis, owns a strip club called Guilty Pleasures, and Anita works with him to find out who has been killing his vampires. *The Laughing Corpse* (1994) involves a case of a flesh-eating zombie at large in St. Louis, and here again Jean-Claude owns a comedy club called The Laughing Corpse. *The Circus of the Damned* (1995) is an after-dark amusement park, also owned by Jean-Claude, and in this novel we learn more about vampire politics and Jean-Claude's desire to have Anita as his human servant, a relationship that involves the reception of four marks given to the servant. This symbiotic rela-tionship provides both parties with enhanced powers, but the downside is, if the vampire dies, the servant inevitably dies as well. In addition to her relationship with Jean-Claude, Anita begins to date Richard, the Ulfric of the local werewolf pack. This triumvirate of Anita, Richard, and Jean-Claude develops and deepens through-out the *The Lunatic Café* (1996), *Bloody Bones* (1996), *The Killing Dance* (1997), *Burnt Offerings* (1998), and *Blue Moon* (1998).

In *Obsidian Butterfly* (2000), Anita escapes temporarily from her increasingly complex love life with Jean-Claude and Richard, and she joins Edward, a vampire executioner like herself, on a case in New Mexico. "Ted," Edward's local cover, is a bounty hunter whose help the police have sought because this case involves the disappearance or skinning-alive of local residents. Edward has two backups in addition to Anita on the case, Olaf and Bernardo. Olaf's specialty is mutilating women and Bernardo's specialty is killing. Edward has Anita on the case because he senses that there is a preternatural killer involved, and not just a human serial killer. *Obsidian Butterfly*, master vampire of the city of Santa Fe, provides Anita and Edward with the information needed to find the monster who has been committing the atrocities.

By *Incubus Dreams* (2004) Anita has grown into her role as Nimir Ra, the female warrior leader of the local were-leopard pack, and has actually formed an additional triumvirate that includes Micah, a were-leopard, and Damian, a vampire. As with her other triumvirate there is an upside and a downside. The upside is greater power for all three; the downside is that if Anita's power ebbs, so does the power of Micah and Damian. In fact, Damian almost dies when Anita fails to feed the *ardeur*, a strong sexual desire, inherited from Jean-Claude's line of vampires and going back to Belle-Morte, an old and sadistic vampire who made both Jean-Claude and Asher. Because of the *ardeur*, Jean-Claude is able to feed his blood lust with sex, but now Anita inherits from Jean-Claude a sexual drive that must be satisfied with some regularity, or she will go insane. This drive makes for quite a number of ménage-à-trois situations in *Narcissus in Chains* (2001), *Incubus Dreams* (2004), and *Micah* (2006).

The fourteenth novel of the series, *Danse Macabre* (2006), alludes to a ballet that is to be hosted by Jean-Claude and his St. Louis vampires to show humans that vampires are "more than monsters" (108) and to allow masters of the larger cities of the region to test Jean-Claude's power, as the Vampire Council in Europe is beginning to feel threatened by the growing power of Anita, Jean-Claude, and Richard. Much of the final novel is devoted to controlling and feeding the *ardeur* by way of a number of group sexual encounters that Anita has with Jean-Claude and Asher (vampires), Micah and Nathaniel (were-leopards), and Richard. In addition to defending their city against potential vampire takeovers, Anita begins to have dreams of Marnee Noir, the Mother of all Darkness, who is drawn to the interpersonal power shifts in Anita's relationships.

Anita Blake starts out in the series as a young, naïve virgin drawn ever more deeply into the vampire and were-politics of this futuristic universe because of her supernatural powers, marksmanship, and martial arts abilities. As Anita becomes less human, the series concentrates more on the supernatural sex she has with her vampire and were-partners than on hunting and executing rogue vampires and shape-shifters. Vampires have come a long way since Stoker's Dracula, who must hide his dreadful purpose, through the humanistic, but still undercover, Lestat and Saint-Germain. Though vampires must govern themselves in this new world or be executed, they have achieved legal and, for many, celebrity status. The vampire slayer is called to action only for rogue vampires, shape-shifters, and other renegade monsters.

Over the last fourteen years, Hamilton's Anita Blake novels have received positive reviews from *Library Journal, The Booklist,* and *Publishers Weekly. Obsidian Butterfly* (2000), published as an ACE hardback, was on the *New York Times* extended bestsellers list, and *Narcissus in Chains* (2001), the tenth book in the series, was on the *New York Times* bestsellers list for three weeks, rising to the fifth position. Following the publication of the eighth novel, Laurel Hamilton was able to secure a seven-figure deal with ACE publishing for the next three novels (Anonymous, *Chronicle,* October 2002, Online Version). There is no apparent interest in this series on the part of literary scholars.

L.A. Banks (1959–): Damali, the Hip Hop Huntress. In the first book of the Vampire Huntress Legend series, *Minion* (2003), we encounter Damali Richards, a hip hop artist for Warriors of Light Records. When not performing or recording, Damali and her team of Guardians hunt rogue vampires and other monsters. In this first installment of the series, Damali and her team track down a powerful vampire who not only drains his victims of their blood but mutilates their bodies as well. In *The Awakening* (2004), we learn that Damali is not just a run-of-the-mill vampire huntress; rather, she is the Millennial Neteru, a powerful being whom the topside master vampires want to kill but also desire for their own purposes. Damali's ex-lover Carlos enters the picture as a newly turned vampire whom Damali must trust to battle the vampires seeking her death.

In *The Hunted* (2004), the story continues for Damali and the Guardian forces who seek to protect humans from vampires, shape-shifters, and other demonic forces that surface from the nether regions below. In this installment of the series, Damali, who is a hip hop artist by day and a vampire hunter by night, becomes aware of a terrible disturbance in Brazil. She and her guardian force of seven (the mother-seer Marlene, Shabazz, Rider, Big Mike, J.L., Jose, and Dan) have just come off a tough mission and are in no shape to take on another deadly enemy. But innocent humans are being dismembered and slaughtered near the Amazon River in Brazil, and the team goes into action. In addition to the weariness caused by the recent mission, Damali believes that Carlos Rivera, her former mentor and lover turned vampire, died in quelling the recent vampire revolt. Her last memories of him are his carrying her up from Hell and protecting her from the onslaught of demons. Carlos, we learn, is a former LA drug dealer who took Damali in when she was orphaned as a child.

The Guardians are a worldwide group of 144,000 faithful Christians, Muslims, Buddhists, and members of other religious groups, and they are aware that a spiritual battle for planet Earth is raging and could soon culminate in Armageddon. The Guardians are ruled by the Covenant, a group of twelve council members whose ranks have included notables like the Knights Templar. In *The Bitten* (2005), Carlos and Damali are finally able to spend time together, but they are interrupted because a master vampire from the topside has stolen a key that is able to open the sixth seal of the *Revelation,* and, if used, could tip the balance of the final battle in the direction of evil. Damali is called before the Council of Neterus in *The Forbidden* (2006) to give an account about herself, and she learns that Lilith, the consort of the Unnamed One, has come up from level seven to level six to set things in order at the Vampire Council as all the master vampires topside had been killed.

In *The Damned* (2006), tortured souls (now flesh-eating ghouls) from level four escape up to the topside through portals that have been opened—unbeknownst to the Guardians—through Carlos's last trip to level six, during a previous battle. The five-member vampire council has been wiped out, but the Chairman, Dante, is at large somewhere in the world with the Book of Life and is attempting to find Eve—yes, the very Eve of Adam and Eve—but the Guardians are after him, and so are Lilith, his wife, and Dante's father, the Unnamed One. Armageddon is forestalled by the Guardians through a series of battles in the Himalayas, and the damned are returned to level four of the underworld. The portals to the topside are then closed. Because Carlos and Damali have been killing off high level vampires, Lilith and the Unnamed One seek revenge on the Guardians in *The Forsaken* (2007), by releasing a powerful monster able to defeat both Damali with her Neteru powers and Carlos with his post-vampiric powers. In *The Wicked* (2007), book eight of the series, Carlos and Damali are finally married, but Cain, the son of Eve, has become the new Chairman of the Vampire Council and, in attempting to consolidate his power, pushes the world to the doorstep of Armageddon.

In many ways the Vampire Huntress series is a return to traditional vampire lore: holy water, silver bullets (as well as silver laced C4, bazooka rounds, and earth rounds), and prayer can kill or at least keep vampires at bay. Also, after being killed, vampires need to be both beheaded and staked. Nevertheless, unlike Stoker's, Rice's, and Yarbro's vampires, and like Hamilton's and Charlaine Harris's vampires, these vampires are able to have sexual intercourse, and they do so quite often. Master vampires have lairs all over their territories and a bevy of female vampires at their beck and call. In fact, vampire on vampire sex is the best because two vampires can do a "double plunge," which is a mutual feeding at the moment of orgasm that greatly enhances the sexual experience. Blood-drinking is no longer a metaphor for sex; rather, it enhances sexual performance.

The Guardians are all African American, except for Jose and Carlos, who are Hispanic, and they all speak a combination of Ebonics and Spanglish. In *The Hunted* (2004), they join forces with a group of Brazilian warriors who speak Black English seasoned with Portuguese. For example, near the end of the book, Carlos brags about Damali's achievements as the Neteru and gives the following speech: "Say what you want, girlfriend is baad. Dusted a treasonous councilman . . . Did a drag race to protect my turf, rode shotgun with me . . .and kicked that bitch's ass up there, then served her a head trip like I ain't never seen. My boo is awesome" (481).

The cosmology of this series, cast in the contemporary world, is a curious mix of Christian and New Age ideas. The great divide among humans is between those who believe in some higher power and those who do not. In *The Damned,* Damali comments, "It doesn't matter which faith, as long as the foundation is about the Most High, the divine. If you believe and haven't been contaminated [by demons], you won't be possessed" (2006, 460). Hell is literally below, and Heaven is somewhere above; and the salvation of souls is a critical part of the balance between good and evil in this universe. In fact, Carlos's soul hangs in the balance, in purgatory, though he is a vampire whose soul should be completely lost. Vampires are ruled by a five-member Vampire Council from level six (below), and the topside vampire world (Earth) is carved up into large territories ruled by first-generation Master Vampires, such as Carlos. Even though Carlos is very young, he was turned by the Chair of the five-member Council, and he therefore has old blood in him and is very powerful. The first two levels of hell are populated with poltergeists and familiar spirits, levels three and four with ghosts and amanthras (large worm-like creatures); demons occupy level five, and vampires level six. As one would expect, in addition to going after humans, the evil beings on all these levels are jockeying for power among themselves to have ready access to the tasty humans topside. Level seven is occupied by the "Unnamed One" and the original fallen angels, though a comment made by the Chairman in *The Damned* suggests that he, a vampire, was also present when Lucifer himself and his angels fell from Heaven.

Since 2003, L.A. Banks's Vampire Huntress novels have received positive reviews from *Library Journal, The BookList,* and *Publishers Weekly*. Trina Love Abram of the *Tennessee Tribune* reviewed *The Damned* (2006) positively: "This magnificent urban epic is an amalgamation of mystical creativity, Christianity, masonry concepts, world history, and Biblical concepts. This explosive mixture of concepts is dangerously addictive, and Banks's solid writing style makes it all believable" (20

April 2006, Online Version). In an interview with *Femspec* magazine (30 June 2005, Online Version), L.A. Banks explains the purpose of writing about vampires after having written romance novels for so long: "This series was definitely designed to make several points. Vampirism in this series is the metaphor for being seduced by flesh, sex, money, the fast life that gives the illusion of immortality, only to find oneself the living dead—trapped in Hell and incarcerated by death, violence, and parasitic behavior. The compound that Damali lives in represents 'the village' where people of all ethnicities and religions come together as a world family to fight a common nemesis . . . it is a place that is safe, where the barriers of prayers and people watching each others' backs and children prevail."

Charlaine Harris (1951–): Sookie Stackhouse—Red Neck Vamps and a Hometown Telepath. Charlaine Harris's Southern Vampire mysteries feature Sookie Stackhouse, a seemingly simple country girl who reads minds and romance novels and lives in the small Louisiana town of Bon Temps. In addition, she dates vampires and werewolves, and she is deeply involved in local vampire and shape-shifter politics. Sookie lives for Wendy's hamburgers and regularly shops at Wal-Mart. To increase her vocabulary, she frequently uses her word of the day correctly when talking to other characters. Written in the first person, the reader has access to Sookie's thoughts as well as the thoughts of many others because Sookie is telepathic. Vampires have gone public in this quick-paced, humorous series, as in the Anita Blake series, and they are recognized as citizens, though shape-shifters remain illegal. Vampires are ruled by underground kings and queens who exercise absolute control over their minions' behavior. Eric, for example, is the king of a large area of rural Louisiana, and he rules from Shreveport, LA. New Orleans is the state's "vampire central."

In *Dead Until Dark* (2001), Sookie begins the story of how she started dating Bill, the vampire next door, who once drank human blood but now drinks a blood substitute, Trueblood, available in local bars, including Merlotte's, where Sookie waits on tables. *Living Dead in Dallas* (2002) opens with Sookie discovering the body of the cook at Merlotte's in the trunk of Bon Temps's Sheriff's car. Eric, Vampire Sheriff of Shreveport, asks that Bill and Sookie head down to Dallas, Texas, to help solve a case involving missing vampires. Eric figures that Sookie's telepathic abilities will help to crack the case. *Club Dead* (2003) is the name of a club in Jackson, Mississippi, where the local supernatural element hangs out and where Sookie hopes to find her boyfriend Bill, who has been kidnapped by a powerful vampire named Lorena. Eric—who also owns Fangtasia, a vampire club—requests that Sookie help rescue Bill with the aid of Alcide, a local werewolf. Sookie is attracted to Alcide, and Eric is attracted to Sookie, and all three are looking for Bill Compton. In *Dead to the World* (2004), Bill disappears again, and Sookie is left to deal with Eric, who has gotten a bad case of amnesia. Jason, Sookie's brother, goes missing as well, and a coven of blood-addicted witches moves into the area to harass the local vampire population.

A number of shape-shifters have been killed or injured in shootings in *Dead as a Doornail* (2005), including shape-shifter Sam, the proprietor of Merlotte's. Jason has just been turned into a were-panther, and other were-creatures now suspect that he carried out the shootings, because he seems a reluctant shape-shifter. Because Sam is largely incapacitated, he asks Sookie to go to Eric and request the loan of a vampire bartender. Eric complies and Charles, a one-eyed, former pirate of a vampire, steps in for Sam. While attempting to solve the series of crimes, Sookie herself is shot in the shoulder, ducking a split second before the assassin squeezes the trigger. Sookie had a love affair with Bill, who lives next door, and with Eric, the proprietor of Fangtasia who does not remember the affair because in the previous book he was under a witch's spell during the witch-were war. In addition to these relationships, Sookie is also being pursued by Alcide, a werewolf, and Calvin, the pack leader of the were-panthers in a nearby town.

In *Definitely Dead* (2006), the latest novel in the series, Sookie takes some time off to settle the accounts of Hadley, her twice-dead cousin in New Orleans, who died a vampiric death the night of the marriage between the Queen of New Orleans and the King of Arkansas. Hadley had been the vampire lover of the Queen and died mysteriously on the night of the wedding. With help from Hadley's landlady, a witch named Amelia, Sookie attempts to clean out Hadley's apartment only to discover a body in one of the closets, which puts Sookie in the middle of another mysterious murder. Sookie's new love interest, Quinn, the shape-shifting tiger, has been assigned by Eric to escort Sookie to New Orleans; and so Sookie has a new love interest to help her solve the crimes and keep her from getting killed.

This lighthearted vampire series places vampirism in a small, rural, Southern town with all its charm and secrets. In many ways the series reflects the world of Anita Blake—without the dark, Gothic elements. Sookie is a reluctant killer of vampires and shape-shifters, drawn into vampire and shifter politics because of her telepathic abilities. But again, vampire slayers are needed only for the occasional rogues, shifter or vampire. Sookie is far more interested in her appearance, her waitressing job, and her love life than she is in chasing after supernatural entities. Since the publication of *Dead Until Dark* (2001), Charlaine Harris's Sookie Stackhouse novels have received positive reviews from *Library Journal, The BookList,* and *Publishers Weekly.*

Nora Roberts (1950–): Romantic Vampires. In order to illustrate the popularity and pervasiveness of the vampire in the contemporary reading scene, we need go no further than the popular, prolific romance writer Nora Roberts, who has written a trilogy involving vampires. All three books came out in 2006 and, as of the writing of this article (January 2007), *Morrigan's Cross* and *Valley of Silence* were on the *New York Times* best-selling list for 14 and 8 weeks, respectively. The three books narrate vampire Lilith's attempt to take over the parallel worlds of Geall and Earth. They also narrate the stories of three men and three women who fall in love and eventually marry.

In *Morrigan's Cross* (2006), Hoyt Mac Cionaoith battles Lilith, the vampire who has turned Cian, his brother, into a vampire. To defeat her, the goddess Morrigan enables Hoyt to time-travel into the future to assemble a team comprised of a witch, a warrior, a scholar, a shape-shifter, and his now vampiric brother Cian. In contemporary New York, Hoyt recruits Cian, a red-haired witch named Glenna, and King, a friend of Cian's. These four are joined by Larkin and Moira, two warriors who have traveled from the world of Geall to aid them in the fight. The six are poised to fight Lilith, the vampire Queen, and the love focus of this first novel is on the relationship between Hoyt and Glenna. In *Dance of the Gods* (2006), the Circle of Six continues to prepare for the battle against Lilith, but the love focus is on the relationship between Larkin and Blair, who hail from different worlds—Earth and Geall, respectively—thus complicating their love life.

Roberts closes her vampire trilogy with *Valley of Silence* (2006), which completes the story of the three couples: Moira, now Queen of Geall and Cian, the 1,000-year-old vampire; Hoyt, a warrior, and Glenna, the witch; and Blair, a warrior, and Larkin, the shape-shifter. The Circle of Six gathers together on the planet Geall, whose civilization has reached the Middle Ages in Earth time, to fight the final battle in the Valley of Silence against Lilith, the 2,000-year-old vampire who would rule both Earth and Geall. The goddess Morrigan—who has great, though limited, powers—has blessed this circle of friends and lovers with special powers to stand against a much larger vampire army commanded by the cruel and sadistic Lilith.

Although this is a vampire novel with elements of science fiction (time and space travel through a worm hole), *Valley* continues the romance genre formula, focusing on the final couple-to-be: the tall, dark, handsome hunk of a man (Cian) who, at first, resists falling in love with the beautiful, intelligent, shapely Queen (Moira). They do fall in love, just before the great battle. The relationship is, of course, impossible. Cian is a wealthy New York vampire who is cynical about love and plans to return to Earth *if* he survives the battle of the Valley of Silence. He does, in fact, return to Earth after the battle only to descend into a booze-induced stupor, until Morrigan visits him and makes him an offer he cannot refuse: to be transformed back into a human and return to Geall to marry, reproduce, and live happily ever after. The novel ends with Cian and Moira, at the end of sixty years of marriage, walking "hands linked . . . in the softening sunlight . . . through the gates while the sound of children playing rang behind them" (318).

Elizabeth Kostova (1964–): The Historian—The Return of the Monster. After the humanizing tendencies of Rice, Yarbro, Hamilton, Banks, and Harris, and the romanticizing tendencies of Roberts, it is refreshing to revisit the vampire as an inhuman monster, bent only on its own survival and the enslavement and slaughter of humans. Elizabeth Kostova's *The Historian* (2005) opens in 1972 as the daughter of a historian opens up both an empty book with a dragon printed in the middle sheaves and a packet of yellowing papers in her father's study in Amsterdam. The first letter in the packet is addressed to the writer's "dear and unfortunate successor" (5), who turns out to be Paul, the narrator's father. Paul works for a foundation committed to world peace, and he is persuaded by his daughter to tell her the story of the papers and the book. What follows is a story about her father's and his mentor's research into the legends of Vlad the Impaler and Dracula.

The narrator and her father travel to Austria and then to Slovenia, where Paul begins the story of his research and travels in the 1950s and of Bartholomew Rossi's mysterious disappearance. As they travel, Paul discloses the contents of the yellowing letters. It turns out that Dracula is very much alive—and has been since the fifteenth century. In fact, in his first life he was Vlad III of Wallachia (1431–1476), the infamous Vlad the Impaler, who learned how to outwit "death by secret means" from a group of Latin monks in Gaul (675).

Professor Rossi's journal describes his first encounter with Dracula in one of his underground crypts. Rossi "felt almost as frightened" of his extraordinary clothing as he "did of his strange undead presence" (601). Shortly after, Paul "recoils" at the sight of a "stain of drying blood" on Dracula's lips and stares at him "in horrified paralysis" (601). Though as a historian he has grown curious about this creature who has lived five hundred years, his only thought is how to destroy the creature and escape. Dracula's "inhuman" gestures cause Rossi's stomach to "twist inside" (603). This is, indeed, a monster.

Dracula reveals his plan to Rossi, which involves Rossi's cataloging Dracula's library after being turned into a vampire. Rossi learns that Dracula has acquired a late fifteenth-century printing press and has nearly completed making 1,453 of his dragon books, which are then given to his servants throughout the world who do his bidding and gather books and information for him. The year 1453 is, of course, the year Constantinople, the Great City, fell at the hand of the Ottoman Turks, whom Dracula still despises. Dracula, it turns out, has become a historian, perhaps *the* historian, and has put together a library the likes of which the world has never seen, including many rare ancient books that have disappeared with the destruction of the great libraries in Alexandria, Rome, and Constantinople.

Though Kostova departs from the Stoker tradition by asserting the continuing existence of Dracula, *The Historian* reaffirms a number of traditional vampiric myths. Dracula has, in fact, angered God by seeking immortality apart from the Gospel, and he refuses to have a cross put on his sarcophagus. Not as powerful as Lestat or Louis, Dracula can be warded off with garlic and crucifixes, and killed with silver knives or bullets. In addition, one is turned into a vampire by being bitten three times, thus becoming infected with vampirism as with a disease. Kostova brings before the reader the obvious evil done by Dracula as a vampire, but she also describes the cruel and inhumane deeds of Vlad the Impaler, which are perhaps even more horrifying by comparison: the murdering and torturing not only of the hated Turks, but also of his own countrymen, women, and children. Thus, in life and in undeath, Vlad III is a monster who must be killed for past and present crimes against the human race.

Little, Brown & Co., has given Elizabeth Kostova a "two million dollar advance, a movie sale and the prospect of publication in at least 20 languages," in addition to a media blitz of 7,000 advance copies for book critics, according to Janet Maslin of *The New York Times* (13 June 2005, Online Version). Perhaps that is why the reviews of *The Historian* are so mixed. John Leonard of *Harpers* writes, "There is very little sex, quite a bit of torture, and I suppose we should be grateful for a narrative journey into medieval scholarship that's not about alchemy. Still, aren't vampires merely the alien abductors of an earlier system of superstitions? Even Anne Rice has given up on bloodsuckers in favor of Jesus" (July 2005, 86). Henry Alford of *The New York Times Book Review* laments Kostova's romanticizing of history and historians, but he praises her for "her interweaving of three sources of information— what the daughter tells us, what her father tells her and what the letters tell her and us" (10 July 2005, 16). Michael Gannon of *The Booklist* (15 May 2005, 16) gives the novel high praise: "Readers who think the legend of Dracula has become a trite staple of schlock fiction will find this atmospheric page-turner by first time author Kostova a bloodthirsty delight."

Reception. If literary critics exhibit a "comparatively dismissive attitude toward the Gothic in academic studies" in general (Riquelme, 588), then literary critics are particularly dismissive of the proliferation of vampire fiction and the appearance of its conventions in the popular culture genres discussed above. There are a few exceptions. Anne Rice's vampire novels, especially the first three, have been reviewed positively and discussed extensively in scholarly books and journals. Culture critics have shown a keen interest in what *Buffy the Vampire Slayer* tells us about late twentieth-century families and teens. And Nina Auerbach's *Our Vampires, Ourselves* (1995) argues that both the nineteenth-century vampire stories and the twentieth-century adaptations reflect the political (which encompasses race, gender, and creed) fears and desires of any given period in Britain and the United States.

For readers interested in contemporary academic interpretations of *Dracula,* the *Norton Critical Edition* of *Dracula* contains background essays on the legend of the vampire, early reviews of the novel, theatrical and dramatic adaptations, and contemporary essays. The collection of contemporary essays dates from the 1970s through the 1990s, demonstrating a renewal of interest in *Dracula* among academics. Nina Auerbach opens the essay collection with "Vampires in the Light," an excerpt from *Our Vampires, Ourselves* (1995). Auerbach reviews the Christopher Lee and Frank Langella film versions of *Dracula* and argues that these Draculas are "children of the light," unlike the earlier Lugosi and Karloff versions of the Count, who were monsters of the darkness. They are children of the light because they are killed by sunlight rather than by religious ritual. In this view, the modern Dracula, freed "from the old metaphysics" of a Christian worldview, is "allergic to sunlight—not repelled by its goodness" (391). Both the Lee and Langella Draculas are sensitive, thoughtful heroes interested in seducing women who realize that they don't need men. Auerbach notes that this change in the Count reflects the feminist interests of the 1960s and 1970s, and she concludes that "the rapidity with which our Draculas date tells us only that every age embraces the vampire it needs" (402).

Phyllis A. Roth's "Suddenly Sexual Women in Bram Stoker's Dracula" (originally published in *Literature and Psychology,* 1977) is a psychoanalytic read of the novel that argues that though there is clearly an Oedipal struggle on the part of the men to kill the Father (Dracula), there is an even deeper psychological struggle to first victimize then kill the mother(s) (Lucy and Mina): "Central to the structure and unconscious theme of *Dracula* is . . . primarily the desire to destroy the threatening mother, she who threatens by being desirable" (420). Carol Senf's "*Dracula*: The Unseen Face in the Mirror" (1979) approaches the novel from a biographical and cultural perspective and argues that *Dracula* addresses the threat of the primitive to nineteenth-century Victorians and that the novel is not so much a story of good triumphing over evil, rather of the similarity between good (the vampire hunters) and evil (Dracula). The unreliable narrators of the novel have attempted to kill off the evil part of themselves which is "masked" by social convention.

In "A Capital Dracula," (1988) Franco Moretti, taking a sociological approach to the novel, suggests that Dracula is a metaphor for monopolistic capital, a threat to the early capitalism of Great Britain. The count is also a threat to British cultural and linguistic values, and his defeat represents the triumph of English culture and capital over the foreigner. Finally, Moretti argues that sexuality, both desired and feared by the Victorians, is finally destroyed and sublimated with the deaths of Lucy and the Count, saving the English family. Christopher Craft also addresses the ambivalent attitude of Victorians toward sexuality in "'Kiss Me with Those Red Lips': Gender and Inversion in Bram Stoker's *Dracula*" (1984). Craft claims that the Victorian views of sexual difference are inverted in *Dracula* through Lucy's and Mina's transformations. Craft's new historical approach explores gender difference conventions set forth in Ruskin's essays and critiqued in Mill's essays.

Bram Dijkstra's "Dracula's Backlash" takes a feminist-cultural studies approach to the novel and argues that *Dracula* became the "commonplace book of antifeminine obsession" (460), with Dracula representing "effeminate sensuality" and Lucy and Mina representing the "two faces of Eve" (462). Steven D. Arata takes a cultural studies approach to the novel in "The Occidental Tourist: *Dracula* and the Anxiety of Reverse Colonization" (1990). Dracula, as an Occidental tourist in London, illustrates the possibility of England being overrun by the primitive, which is really the Irish who are despised by the English as savages. Two political equations are expressed in the novel: "not just, Dracula is to England as Ireland is to England, but, Dracula is to England as England is to Ireland" (469) in the sense that Dracula's "imperialism" is most like England's imperialistic domination of Ireland. Finally, Talia Schaffer's "'A Wild Desire Took Me': The Homoerotic History of Dracula" (1994) argues that the novel is Bram Stoker's *apologia* for Oscar Wilde's trial and imprisonment. Dracula, in this new historical-biographical read of the novel, is "Wilde as threat" (472) to Victorian sexual codes. Shaffer sees the first part of *Dracula* swinging "wildly between utter hatred of Wilde and utter sorrow for Wilde" (475) while the remainder of the book "enacts Wilde's story as a longing, lingering look at imprisonment" (477).

Bibliography

Anonymous, "Anne Rice." *Contemporary Authors: New Revision Series* 123 (2006): 369–376.

Auerbach, Nina. 1995. *Our Vampires, Ourselves*. Chicago, IL: University of Chicago Press, 1995.

Banks, L.A. *Minion*. New York: St. Martin's, 2003.

———. *The Awakening*. New York: St. Martin's, 2004.

———. *The Hunted*. New York: St. Martin's, 2004.

———. *The Bitten*. New York: St. Martin's, 2005.

———. *The Forbidden*. New York: St. Martin's, 2006.

———. *The Damned*. New York: St. Martin's, 2006.

———. *The Forsaken*. New York: St. Martin's, 2007.

———. *The Wicked*. New York: St. Martin's, 2007.

Bleiler, E.F., ed. *Supernatural Fiction Writers: Fantasy and Horror*. New York: Scribners, 1985.

Bleiler, Richard, ed. *Supernatural Fiction Writers: Fantasy and Horror*. 2nd ed. New York: Scribners, 2002.

Campbell Sr., J.L. "J.S. Le Fanu." In *Supernatural Fiction Writers: Fantasy and Horror*. E.F. Bleiler, ed. New York: Scribners, 1985, 219–231.

Daniels, L. "Bram Stoker." In *Supernatural Fiction Writers: Fantasy and Horror*. E.F. Bleiler, ed. New York: Scribners, 1985, 375–381.

Day, William P. *Vampire Legends in Contemporary American Culture*. Lexington, KY: The University Press of Kentucky, 2002.

Gordon, Melton J. *The Vampire Book: The Encyclopedia of the Undead*. Detroit, MI: Visible Ink, 1999.

Harris, Charlaine. 2001. *Dead Until Dark*. New York: Ace, 2001.

———. *Living Dead in Dallas*. New York: Ace, 2002.

———. *Club Dead*. New York: Ace, 2003.

———. *Dead to the World*. New York: Ace, 2004.

———. *Dead as a Doornail*. New York: Ace, 2005.

———. *Definitely Dead*. New York: Ace, 2006.

Kostova, Elizabeth. *The Historian*. New York: Little, Brown and Company, 2005.

Maslin, Janet. "The Vampire Wears Flannel, and He Cheats on His Tan." *New York Times Archives* 12 March 2007. Retrieved 12 March 2007 from www.newyorktimes.com.

Moretti, Franco. "A Capital Dracula." In *Dracula*. Nina Auerbach and David J. Skal, eds. New York: Norton, 1997, 431–444.

Polidori, J. *The Vampyre*. 1819. Retrieved 2 August 2006 from www.dagonbytes.com.

Rice, Anne. *Interview with the Vampire*. New York: Ballantine, 1976.

———. *The Vampire Lestat*. New York: Ballantine, 1985.

———. *The Queen of the Damned*. New York: Ballantine, 1988.

———. *The Tale of the Body Thief*. New York: Knopf, 1992.

———. *Memnoch the Devil*. New York: Knopf, 1995.

———. *The Vampire Armand*. New York: Knopf, 1998.

———. *Pandora: New Tales of the Vampires,* New York: Random House, 1998.

———. *Vittorio the Vampire*. New York: Knopf, 1999.

———. *Merrick*. New York: Knopf, 2000.

———. *Blood and Gold*. New York: Knopf, 2001.

———. *Blackwood Farm*. New York: Knopf, 2002.

———. *Blood Canticle*. New York: Knopf, 2003.

Riquelme, John Paul. "Toward a History of Gothic and Modernism: Dark Modernity from Bram Stoker to Samuel Beckett." *Modern Fiction Studies* 46.3(2000): 585–605.

Roberts, Nora. *Morrigan's Cross*. New York: Jove, 2006.

———. *Dance of the Gods,* New York: Jove, 2006.

———. *The Valley of Silence*. New York: Jove, 2006.

Roth, Phyllis A. "Suddenly Sexual Women in Bram Stoker's Dracula." *Literature and Psychology* 27 (1977): 113–121.

Stoker, Bram. *Dracula*. (1897) New York: Penguin, 1992 Reprint.

———. (1897) *Dracula*. In *Norton Critical Edition of Dracula*. Nina Auerbach and David J. Skal, eds. New York and London: Norton, 1997.

Yarbro, Chelsea Quinn. *Hotel Transylvania*. New York: St Martin's, 1978.

———. *The Palace*. New York: St Martin's, 1978.

———. *Blood Games*. New York: St Martin's, 1979.

———. *Path of the Eclipse*. New York, NY: St Martin's, 1981.

———. *Tempting Fate*. New York: St Martin's, 1982.

———. *The Saint-Germain Chronicle*. New York: Pocket, 1983.

———. *Better in the Dark*. New York, NY: Tor 1993.

———. *Darker Jewels*. New York: Tor, 1993.

———. *Mansions of Darkness*. New York: Tor, 1996.

———. *Writ in Blood*. New York: Tor, 1997.

———. *Blood Roses*. New York: Tor, 1999.

———. *Communion Blood*. New York: Tor, 2000.

———. *Come Twilight*. New York: Tor, 2001.

———. *A Feast in Exile*. New York: Tor, 2002.

———. *Night Blooming*. New York: Warner Books, 2003.

———. *Midnight Harvest*. New York: Warner Books, 2003.

———. *The Dark of the Sun*. New York: Tor, 2004.

———. *States of Grace*. New York: Tor, 2005.

———. *Roman Dusk*. New York: Tor, 2006.

———. *Borne in Blood*. New York: Tor, 2007.

Vampire Series. (These series either begin with the introduction of a vampire [or slayer] in the first novel, then subsequent installments either follow chronologically or highlight previous adventures of the vampire, if the vampire is particularly old.)

Butcher, Jim. *The Dresden Files* series:
Storm Front (2000)
Fool Moon (2000)
Grave Peril (2001)
Summer Knight (2002)
Death Masks (2003)
Blood Rites (2004)
Dead Beat (2005)
Proven Guilty (2006)
White Night (2007)

Collins, Nancy A.: *Sonja Blue* series:
Sunglasses after Dark (1989)
In the Blood (1992)
Paint It Black (1995)
Midnight Blue (1995)
A Dozen Black Roses (1996)
Darkest Heart (2000)
Dead Roses for a Blue Lady (2002)

Feehan, Christine. *Dark* series:
Dark Prince (1999)
Dark Desire (1999)
Dark Gold (2000)
Dark Magic (2000)
Dark Challenge (2000)
Dark Fire (2001)
After Twilight (2001)
Dark Legend (2001)
Dark Guardian (2002)
Dark Symphony (2003)
The Only One (2003)
Dark Melody (2003)
Dark Destiny (2004)
Hot Blooded (2004)
Dark Secret (2005)
Dark Demon (2006)
Dark Celebration (2006)

Huff, Tanya. *Blood* series:
Blood Price (1991)
Blood Trail (1992)
Blood Lines (1992)
Blood Pact (1993)
Blood Debt (1997)
Smoke and Shadows (2004)

Knight, E.E. *Vampire Earth* series:
Way of the Wolf (2001)
Choice of the Cat (2004)
Tale of the Thunderbolt (2005)
Valentine's Rising (2005)
Valentine's Exile (2006)

Koehler, Karen. *Slayer* series:
Slayer (2001)
Black Miracles (2002)
Stigmata (2003)

Lumley, Brian. *Necroscope* series:
Necroscope (1986)
Necroscope II (1988)
The Source: Necroscope III (1989)

Deadspeak: Necroscope IV (1990)
Deadspawn: Necroscope V (1991)
Necroscope: The Lost Years (1995)
Necroscope The Lost Years: Volume II (1996)
Invaders (1999)
Defilers: Necroscope (2000)
Avengers: Necroscope (2001)
Harry Keogh: Necroscope and Other Heroes (2003)
The Touch (2006)

Meyer, Stephenie. *Twilight* series:
Twilight (2005)
New Moon (2006)
Eclipse (2007)

Moore, Christopher. *A Love Story* series:
Bloodsucking Fiends: A Love Story (1995)
You Suck: A Love Story (2007)

Newman, Kim. *Anno Dracula* series:
Anno Dracula (1992)
The Bloody Red Baron (1995)
Judgment of Tears (1998)

Saberhagen, Fred. *Vlad Tepes* series:
The Dracula Tape (1975)
The Holmes-Dracula File (1978)
An Old Friend of the Family (1979)
Thorn (1980)
Dominion (1982)
A Matter of Taste (1990)
A Question of Time (1992)
Seance for a Vampire (1994)
A Sharpness on the Neck (1996)
The Vlad Tapes (2000)

Schreiber, Ellen. *Vampire Kisses* series:
Vampire Kisses (2003)
Kissing Coffins (2005)
Vampireville (2006)

Shayne, Maggie. *Wings in the Night* series:
Twilight Phantasie (1993)
Twilight Memories (1994)
Twilight Illusions (1995)
Beyond Twilight (1995)
Born in Twilight (1997)
Twilight Vows (1998)
Twilight Hunger (2002)
Embrace the Twilight (2003)
Run From Twilight (2003)
Edge of Twilight (2004)
Blue Twilight (2005)
Prince of Twilight (2006)

Strieber, Whitley. *Hunger* series:
The Hunger (1980)
The Last Vampire (2001)
Lilith's Dream: A Tale of the Vampire Life (2002)

Wolfe, Gene. Urth: *Book of the Short Sun* trilogy:
On Blue's Waters (1999)
In Green's Jungles (2000)
Return to the Whorl (2001)

Pike, Christopher. *The Last Vampire* series:
The Last Vampire
The Last Vampire 2: Black Blood
The Last Vampire 3: Red Dice
The Last Vampire 4: Phantom
The Last Vampire 5: Evil Thirst
The Last Vampire 6: Creatures of Forever.

Further Reading

Auerbach, Nina. *Our Vampires, Ourselves*. Chicago, IL: University of Chicago Press, 1995; Battis, Jes. *Blood Relations: Chosen Families in Buffy the Vampire Slayer and Angel*. Jefferson, NC: McFarland & Company, 2005; Day, William P. *Vampire Legends in Contemporary American Culture*. Lexington, KY: The University Press of Kentucky, 2002; Frayling, Christopher, ed. *Vampyres: Lord Byron to Count Dracula*. Oxford: Faber and Faber, 1992.

A.J. GRANT

VERSE NOVELS

Definition. The verse novel shares with the novel all the latter's traditional features except the medium of prose. In a present-day perspective the verse novel may seem an anomaly or a rudimentary form, since narrative fiction currently implies the use of prose. However, the verse format for the novel has never fallen quite out of use, although distinctly on the wane since the mid-nineteenth century, until a sudden upsurge was indicated towards the end of the twentieth century.

The closest relatives of the verse novel are, on the one side, prose fiction, and, on the other, narrative poetry. Just as the realist tradition is commonly considered the backbone of the novel in prose, the verse novel, building on formal conventions from the lyrical tradition, shows a tendency to veer toward the non-narrative moments of lyrical contemplation. The application of the term *verse novel* is consequently somewhat shifty, sometimes denoting fiction with the emphasis on the strong narrative plot dynamic characteristic of the realist mainstream novel, and sometimes, not infrequently nor without genre complications, denoting long poetry sequences held together by a common theme but otherwise characterized by the traditional priorities of the lyrical genre.

The verse mode (re-)adopted in some narrative fiction from the last decades of the twentieth century directs attention to the verbal work of art as existential statement, relying on elaborate structure and cultural resonance, of collective cultural experience amassed dynamically over time. The distinction between prose as the medium of narrative fiction, and verse, signalled by rhyme and rhythm, as the medium of poetry, is, however, a distinction valid only in a traditional genre context. In the broad perspective of contemporary culture, including popular and mass culture, versification with rhyme and rhythm is the resort of pop, rock, and jazz lyrics, rap and dub recitation/music, and of the ubiquitous jingles of advertising. Perhaps, then, in the wider context of the communication and artistic modes of present-day mass society, a novel written in verse does not seem so strange and disturbing as it may to a reading audience of a more traditionalist orientation.

History. In a long literary history, the use of prose for the epic or narrative genre is a relatively recent invention, coinciding with the rise of the novel in partial continuation of and reaction to the conventions of the verse epic. When in 1742 Henry Fielding prefaced his picaresque novel *Joseph Andrews* with the observation that he presented to the public a "comic epic poem in prose," his observation symptomatically reflected a contemporary need for the justification of his chosen prosaic medium of discourse. Fielding had to make proper space for his new species in an already existing order of literary texts originating in antiquity, among which the medium of prose for narrative fiction was not to be taken for granted. Whereas prose as the vehicle of fiction was coming into its own at the time of Fielding's apology, verse, however, lingered on for fictional narratives inclining towards medieval and Renaissance romance. They were tales of love and valour usually set in exotic places and medieval eras, and relying on varieties of quest for their plots. Romantic writers such as Percy Bysshe Shelley, Robert Southey, or Lord Byron cultivated verse romance either as a still productive format or as deliberate pastiche.

However, the verse medium for narrative fiction, even of the romance kind, was, by the mid-nineteenth century, indisputably turning into a sub-generic niche, overtaken by narrative fiction in prose. Tennyson was one of the last British poets to employ verse romance in his Arthurian tales. In American literature Henry W. Longfellow cultivated the verse-narrative format in *Hiawatha* (1855), an epic about Native Americans, as did Herman Melville in the convoluted story of a contemporary American's meditations and encounters in Palestine, *Clarel: A Poem and Pilgrimage in the Holy Land* (1876). In Britain Elizabeth Barrett Browning used the verse format for her female *bildungsroman Aurora Leigh* (1857), and in 1862 George Meredith published his narrative sonnet sequence *Modern Love*. Surely Browning's *tour de force The Ring and the Book* (1868-69) stands out as the last major achievement of narrative fiction in verse before the literary format made its reappearance toward the end of the twentieth century.

Trends and Themes. From the mid-1980s the verse novel seems to have become productive once again. The writers of the verse novels singled out for attention below do not seem to share any retrospective desires in the direction of re-establishing a grandiose modern epic, which would, anyway, have implications far beyond the verse mode. What they share, however, is a postmodern multi-media-conscious audience of a very heterogeneous nature. To that audience the novel as book is just one form among many in a very large information, entertainment, and infotainment market. The presentation of narrative of the mainstream realist novel is increasingly taken over by the screen media, and widely distributed poetry is a matter of lyrics for mass-marketed popular music.

Contexts and Issues. The long poems that came out of the modernist upheavals in literature tended to follow the experimentalist path of dedicatedly modernist writing rather than continued on the highways of realism or romance in verse. This modernist tendency has not necessarily been out of touch with the popular, as the success of proto-modernist Edgar Lee Masters's *Spoon River Anthology* (1915) in its day amply demonstrated. But long, modernism-related poems have,

A NEW NARRATIVE ART FORM

There is no denying that the mainstream realist novel still has considerable audience appeal, but competing with film and TV serials, features, and docudrama, it is no longer in almost sole dominance for fulfilling the craving for narrative. The rise of the verse novel should be seen in perspective of newly emerging narrative art forms, new combination modalities available among the media, and complex audience segmentations in constant flux. There are three "explanations" of the postmodern verse novel: generically as rudimentary epic, narratologically as metafictional experiment, or socially as aesthetic "re-grouping" in response to new synaesthetic formations. This last one has the advantage of being able to appeal directly to an audience not necessarily familiar with literary history, as required for the first two, but yet definitely highly aware of contemporary media forms. The verse novel, especially when performed, combines narrative drive with musical dynamics, a combination found in shorter measures of duration in pop-music ballads.

on the whole, been more successful with critics than with reading audiences. This applies to works like T. S. Eliot's *The Waste Land* (1922), Hart Crane's *The Bridge* (1930), David Jones's *In Parenthesis* (1937), Ezra Pound's *The Cantos* (published accumulatively since 1925 until the complete 117 cantos appeared in 1970), William Carlos Williams's *Paterson* (1946-1958), Charles Olson's Maximus cycle (1950-70), Edward Dorn's *Gunslinger* (1968-1975), and Louis Zukofsky's *A* (1967-1978). Alongside have appeared volumes of verse devoted to specific themes or topics in the manner of the lyrical sequence or cycle, but likewise lacking the narrative drive of the novel and tending towards the metaphorical. The British poet John Hartley Williams uses the expanding American West as the setting of his loosely connected poems in *Bright River Yonder* (1987). American author Marilyn Nelson Waniek's *The Homeplace* (1990), about her family history, and B. H. Fairchild's *The Art of the Lathe* (1998), about factory life, are likewise thematically and setting unified collections of poetry, based on the single poem as the constituent unit. Derek Walcott's *The Bounty* (1997), *Tiepolo's Hound* (2000), and *The Prodigal* (2004) are atmospheric poetry on the theme of cultural/ethnic difference strongly rooted in explorations of the poet's Caribbean background and his troubled sense of home. Fiona Sampson's and Carol Ann Duffy's respective volumes of love poems, *The Distance Between Us* and *Rapture* (both 2005) are poetry sequences rather than narratives.

If the verse novel faced a moratorium between the mid-nineteenth century and the late twentieth century, extended verse narrative of a non-fictional kind is found in the verse memoir. Among twentieth-century successors to the long, autobiographical poem of which William Wordsworth's *The Prelude* (1805) forms the epitome in English literature, are A.E. Housman's *A Shropshire Lad* (1896), John Edward Masefield's *The Everlasting Mercy* (1911), Louis MacNeice's *Autumn Journal* (1939), John Betjeman's *Summoned by Bells* (1960), and Jackie Kay's *The Adoption Papers* (1991).

Reception. The literary phenomenon of the verse novel has as yet no dedicated critical literature. There has been some critical interest in the long poem as a particular lyric phenomenon. In 1909 appeared W. M. Dixon and H. J. C. Grierson's *The English Parnassus: An Anthology Chiefly of Longer Poems*. The selected poems, by no means all of them long, were poems known to be popular and of varied "narrative, didactic, satirical, elegiac, eulogistic, and reflective" kinds, and "neither epical in scope nor yet wholly lyrical in quality" (Dixon 1909, vii). In 1986 Margaret Dickie published *On the Modernist Long Poem,* a study of American modernist long poems. According to Dickie there is a contradiction in the modernist privileging of the brief moment of lyric insight, focusing on the metaphor, and the cultivation, nonetheless, of long poems by such modernist poets as T. S. Eliot or Ezra Pound. She found that this very insight on the part of the poets "developed into satire, but satire without much laughter or mockery . . . . And in this mode, the movement from *The Waste Land* to *The Cantos* is toward an increasingly self-conscious, despairing, and conservative end" (Dickie 1986, 153). *The New Princeton Encyclopedia of Poetry and Poetics* from 1993 has "verse novel" under the heading "narrative poetry," using it as an example of "interpenetration of modes," a kind of narrative poem that "consciously exploit[s] a sort of hybridization" (*New Princeton Encyclopedia* 1993, 815). Referring to Elizabeth Barrett Browning's *Aurora Leigh* as the work that "first comes to mind," Leonard Nathan, the author of the encyclopedia article, quotes from R. Edmond's 1988 study of Browning, *Affairs of the Heart,* to the effect that the aim of the text is to give "that attention to everyday life which the novel manages so easily, without relinquishing the manner, power, and concentration of poetry" (815). In other words, the verse novel is seen not so much as a novel (re-)employing lyric means as the other way round, as narrative poetry availing itself of the (realist) novel's phenomenological range. Professor Nathan goes on to suggest Vladimir Nabokov's *Pale Fire* (1962) as a "more complex" example of the verse novel. In 2004 Brian McHale published *The Obligation toward the Difficult Whole: Postmodernist Long Poems.* As indicated in the title, the object of the study is the postmodernist-marked long poem subject to critical scrutiny within the framework of postmodernist discourse parameters, which in an earlier work he had been instrumental for instituting. In the same year appeared in *Orbis Litterarum: International Review of Literary Studies* Lars Ole Sauerberg's "Repositioning Narrative: The Late-Twentieth-Century Verse Novels of Vikram Seth, Derek Walcott, Craig Raine, Anthony Burgess, and Bernadine Evaristo," which attempted to account for the renaissance of the verse novel since about 1980 in contexts of genre and prosodic issues, and with a view to the intertextual implications of the verse novels in focus.

Selected Authors. Vikram Seth's *The Golden Gate* (1986) is a fictional narrative, paratextually signalled as a "novel written in verse" (back cover) and "The Great Californian Novel" (hype with reference to Gore Vidal, front cover). It is in thirteen chapters, of which the individual chapters consist of forty to sixty stanzas of fourteen lines of a somewhat irregular iambic-tetrameter prosodic pattern. The rhyme pattern in each stanza is *ababccddeffegg,* so we have sonnets of the English or Shakespearian variety with a final couplet, especially suited for a twist in the tail, a punch line or any other narrative effect relying on a conclusive thrust. Such a description is one that we expect in a perspective of literary history, and one on which the discussion of the choice of the four-foot rather than the traditional five-foot metre is discussed in his fifth chapter.

A comprehensive vista of literary history opens out, bearing not only on the history and typology of verse forms, but also on the cultural implications (satire, etc,) signalled by Seth's reference to "Hudibrastic tricks." But to the reader unacquainted with such detailed literary-historical detail there is hardly more to be got out of this stanza than that the breathlessness clearly conveyed by the rhythm is a matter of a need to hurry. (The literary historian would undoubtedly savor the oblique *carpe-diem* allusion to Andrew Marvell of "had I world and time" in addition to noting the Hudibrastic prosody). If the reader is offered an explanation, although of relative import depending on range of literary-historical knowledge, and as late as more than one-third into the narrative, this information relates to one part of the rationale for verse rather than prose in *The Golden Gate*.

Inspiration and source is Alexander Pushkin's *Eugene Onegin* from 1823-31, about the eponymous world-weary Russian officer and gentleman and his self-afflicted frustration in love. So the explanation of the choice of verse rather than prose for his Silicon Valley romance is double: there is the "have fun and try it" of 5.3.12, and there is the joy experienced by reading Pushkin, which is described as "spring of pleasure," "joy and inspiration," and then generally in the metaphor of source evoked by "spring:" "Sweet-watered, fluent, clear, light, blithe" (5.5.6-9). All in all a justification very much in terms of the Horatian *dulce*, inviting subsequently to reflection on the complementary *utile*.

Looking for origins in the Pushkin source pays off the literary historian and offers the reader appreciating metafictional maneuvrings ample material as well. But for the contemporary common reader, not necessarily aware of this point, there is a narrative which is surely to be contextualized in quite another and in its own ways as rigidly codified kind of narrative, the ubiquitous situation comedy of TV soap opera, whose conventions tend to format large areas of contemporary culture. Lay readers not initially scared off by the "strange" lay-out of the text will recognize both the world described (Californian rich and smart-set locale) and the anecdotal structure of the sitcom dialogue as a homology to the setting and the punch-line final-couplet structure of Seth's sonnets respectively.

The American poet, flautist, literary theorist, and ex-confederate soldier Sidney Lanier (1842-1881) is the focal point of Andrew Hudgins's verse novel (or novella) *After the Lost War: A Narrative* (1988). Hudgins's narrative appears as Lanier's autobiographical recordings, with the American Civil War as the great public and personal watershed. Hudgins has Lanier become increasingly preoccupied with what Wilfred Owen later called the "pity of war" and the need for a stoic frame of mind generally, as well as with the futility of the Confederate cause.

The plot of the narrative keeps pace with Lanier's life, with some deviations from the biographical progression in the form of musings and flashbacks. Lanier, who for the last years of his short life taught English literature at Johns Hopkins University in Baltimore, applied his interest and competence in music to develop rhythmical structures modelled on music and following the free flow of spoken language. Like British fellow poet Gerard Manley Hopkins, Lanier substituted for regular, accentual metre logaoedic variation between the number of unstressed syllables, using also the musical-beat principle as his inspiration. Hudgins, therefore, resorts to different stanza formats, but all of them unrhymed and in the logaoedic cadences of the subject of his verse novel. The voice of Lanier in Hudgins's verse novel only once lets on the kind of rhythmical dynamic aimed at. Shortly after the end of the war, Lanier seeks convalescence from his consumptive disease away from the humidity of his native Georgia. In the desert tracts of the west he sits down to comfort himself with his flute, but finds it difficult to get the rhythm right: "Because the flute's a woodland instrument,/I felt incongruous in the desert quiet./ But soon my playing built a decent forest"

(Hudgins, 51). And then suddenly there is an approximation of his playing to the sound and movement of nearby women washing clothes with stones at the riverside. Their dual rhythmic performances conclude:

> And all the while they held their rhythm:
> Slow primitive—slow, loud and certain.
> But as they worked and I played,
> I heard my thoughtless melody
> allure them slightly from the beat (51–52)

The organic naturalness of the rhythm, including the slight variations from the beat, is contrasted later with the fictitious Lanier's vehement reaction against the waste of the war: "I've come to hate/the lost cause and the cult of Beulah" (107). Before reading this conclusion he sees the maimed boy soldiers in terms of Latin verse. Boys who had been able to conjugate Latin verbs "now limp the streets of Beulah Land./The walk long-short, long-short, and mock/the Latin line, their bodies swaying to/the music of dead languages" (107).

Hudgins has modernized the mid- and late-nineteenth-century pomposity of Lanier's style that present-day readers find hard to swallow, but his account of the man's life made a point of communicating it in such prosodic terms as Lanier would surely have approved of.

By its title Derek Walcott's *Omeros* (1990) invites epic contextualization. On a reader ignorant of "world literature," a great many points and passages of the narrative will be lost: the Homeric plot parallels, the names of characters from Greek mythology, the references to Virgil's *Aeneid,* and to Dante's great Renaissance epic, whose terza-rima pattern is the one selected for Walcott's verse narrative. The erudite author also incorporates innumerable instances of intertextual dynamics drawing on a vast and encyclopaedic knowledge of literature and of (colonial and postcolonial) history generally.

References to the Homeric epics, both as structural underpinning throughout and as scattered elements, are quite overt, to the point of insistence even, so the literary historian may note that the narrator is extremely aware of his project as one in line with the epic tradition. The consistent metre and rhyme ensures a reading or listening experience akin to that of verse epic, supposedly, according to traditional epic poetics, lending dignity to the subject. Now, the low mimetic of the narrative on the whole provides an ironic angle to the notion of any *bona-fide* adoption of the epic format, so the literary historian might wish to draw a parallel to James Joyce's *Ulysses* (1922), likewise a low-mimetic application of the traditional epic, but in prose. Joyce himself suggested that in an age made unheroic by the pervasiveness of the common, the common man can be made to appear heroic given the right context, and thus Joyce applied a Homeric framework for Mr. Leopold Bloom. But Walcott goes a step further, a step that cancels out this line of interpretation, and by doing so shifts the validation of interpretation away from the literary historian and over to the reader, and by the same stroke obliterates the need for literary-historical guidance—a realisation summed up only a few pages further on when the narrator declares: "You were never in Troy, and, between two Helens, //yours is here and alive;" (p. 313, ch. LXII, ii) and underlined by the resumption of the sea image of the final verse: "When he left the beach the sea was still going on" (p. 325, ch. LXIV, iii).

Walcott's *Omeros* is, for all practical effects, a verse novel. Its ostentatious drawing on epic and its intertextual virtuosity turn out to be symbolic of a cultural memory which, eventually, is a matter of indifference to life here and now. By the same token, the common reader as implied reader is re-installed after having been put off by the host of learned implications, being virtually told to resist the onslaught of literary tradition.

Like Vikram Seth, Lyn Hejinian used Pushkin's *Eugene Onegin* as her inspiration and model for *Oxota: A Short Russian Novel* (1991). But unlike Seth Hejinian did not choose to follow in the immediate footsteps of the Russian poet by adopting the regular sonnet scheme as structural principle. Her sonnets—270 in all, divided epically into nine books, of which the last one is a coda —are unrhymed units of 14 lines (cp. "Even though we don't rhyme—ever/We achieve fidelity, we engage in gluing, sucking, seizing, and fusing/Adherence is difference" (ch.104, p. 118)). But the line lengths vary widely, all lines starting with a capital letter but all ending without any indication of partial completion in the form of full stop punctuation. The free verse imposes a certain order: "The rain fell, but even the irregularity of the drips couldn't obliterate the rhythm that attaches occasion to memory" (ch. 136, p. 151). Whereas Seth's Pushkin-derived narrative in its plot structure seems almost a pastiche of nineteenth-century melodrama, Hejinian offers a narrative much less adhering to narrative models, having her narrator observe, "But traditionally a novel integrates a person with the life it leads" (ch. 88, p. 100). The teleological implications of the novel are remarked upon in the final lines of chapter 109: "However there is a danger that life, being narrated, will turn into an 'adventure,' and every adventure moves inexorably towards resolution - but how can I say that I don't like adventure?/I think now of the truly startling antiquity of the sensation that *this is happening* "(p. 124). *Oxota* means *hunt* in Russian, and the entire narrative could be said to be a hunt for existential significance by a circle of Russian friends with whom the narrator spends time in Russia as the Soviet Union begins to decompose in the 1980s.

Lyn is named as the central consciousness of Lyn Hejinian's *Oxota* and offers sporadic comments on form, as when an opposition is suggested: "An elegy is continuous/It is slow and not alarmed/ . . . But this is a novel, in the literature of context" (ch. 23, p. 33). The difference between the prose and the poetry medium is noted but not elaborated on in the remark "Poetry is compressed according to one scale and prose according to another" (ch. 34, p. 44). Poetry is granted the edge somewhat further on: "Poetry is violent/the meanings of the words annihilate each other, Arkadii said/In this sense all the acts of the Marquis de Sade imitate writing" (ch. 43, p. 53). The author returns to the idea of compression once more: "There is a third principle, said Borya, and it's compression/Poetry anticipates a love of thinking/Yes, but also the mobility of experience/Untargeted experience" (ch. 45, p. 55). Hejinian's "short Russian novel" reads in the manner of the loosely structured episodic idea-cum-discussion novel familiar to readers of Wyndham Lewis, Henry Miller, William Burroughs, Charles Bukowski, or Don DeLillo.

According to the front-flap marketing blurb, Craig Raine's *History: The Home Movie* (1994) is "an epic history of Europe from 1905 to 1984," a designation recurring with a variation in the concluding commendatory remarks in the note: "Craig Raine's *History: The Home Movie* is a novel. It is an epic poem. It is the best film you'll ever read. There is nothing like it in literature." All these designations, however, have in common the indication of narrative, and Raine's text is a loosely composed narrative, a historical family novel, about members of two inter-married families, one

Russian and Jewish-bohemian artistic, one British and middle-class professional. As it also spans most of the twentieth century, it clearly earns the epithet of epic according to the broader and popular contemporary use of the concept and term.

Raine's media-consciously entitled *History: The Home Movie* consists of eighty-eight poems (including a quite brief prologue) of varying length but sharing the same pattern of unrhymed triplet and somewhat irregular trimeter stanzas. In addition there is a genealogical-tree preface, outlining the family patterns of the Pasternaks and the Raines, respectively. From a literary-historical point of view the narrative achieves its epic dimension by subjecting the fates of the two families to momentous forces outside the control of the individual, in the clash of competing civilizations. Here we have the trajectory of Soviet-Russian Communism and the rise and fall of Fascism/Nazism, pitted against the tradition of British pragmatism. As the condition of exile is the common lot of postcolonial mankind in Derek Walcott's *Omeros*, the genocide of European Jewry is the central pivot in Raine's narrative, tracing its causes and effects in a wide variety of attitudes, tendencies, and behaviour, both national and individual, from 1905 to 1984.

There is no intratextual evidence of reflections on the coming into being of Raine's text, on its "debt" to literary history. This is left completely to the flap-text designer(s). To the lay reader the contemporary sense of epic will prepare her or him for large-screen phenomena, the association to the cinema quite in keeping with the second part of the title of the work, history as "home movie." Just as Seth's narrative makes good sense to a reading audience familiar with TV situation comedy, there is, in the very title of Raine's narrative, an invitation to contextualize in terms of contemporary big-screen-media dynamics. Home movies being an alternative source of entertainment and information to potential book readers, providers of media material have long since introduced infotainment, with the fictionalization of the factual as a very popular and, hence, routine production recourse. Nothing works better for history to be made alive than to introduce the human element in terms of focused individualism, preferably with all kinds of detail, romantic, melodramatic, sordid, prurient, and so on. This is exactly what Raine does in his narrative. Each individual part (chapter or poem) is a kind of scene, a tableau of a certain year of the century in perspective of either branch of the family, lending dramatic power by novel-like particularization to whatever particular situation in the large-scale unfolding of history is at stake, also frequently drawing on the anecdotal for comic-relief purposes.

Anthony Burgess's *Byrne* (1995) offers ample intratextual evidence of generic context both adhered to and discarded. The narrator of the text, Tomlinson (Burgess 1995, 147), described as "an inferior pressman, salaried/To race for scandal round the spinning globe" (40) purports to have been commissioned by one Michael Byrne, born 1900, to write his biography, expressly in a form commensurate with his self-estimation. ("He thought he was a kind of living myth. . . .")

The narrator is well aware of generic traditions as manner of literary treatment relative to content. It is therefore very apt that what his taskmaster may have associated with Ariosto, and hence with a certain high-mindedness and dignity, was made a perfect medium of the mock-heroic in Byron's *Don Juan*. The narrator turns out to be a very deft handler of rhyme, enhancing the potential for humorous and witty effects in the concluding couplets of the *ottava rima*. For example, "He'd not been following the daily *Zeitung*./He heard the news with wide eyes and a dry tongue" (33), or even more atrocious ones like "His origin was Minsk or Pinsk or Moscow. Pe/Rusing Tim's chart he called for a bronchoscopy" (129).

The bathos is indeed part of the attitude to the subject matter, the kitschy music, painting and general life style of Michael Byrne, which is made clear when the narrator stops to explain further his use of verse on the man considered merely "good garbage for my garbage bin" (p. 40).

When the scene is shifted to the "occluded beauty/Of winter Venice," (83), the narrator finds occasion to change from one verse mode borrowed by Byron, and subsequently from Byron by Byrne's biographer, to the likewise borrowed and re-borrowed Spenserian stanza of *Childe Harold*. The narrative proceeds in a manner relative to the slower progress of Spenser's hexameter stanza and with less formal occasion for the word play invited by the couplets of the *ottava rima*. Changing back into the Ariosto/Byron verse format in part four, the narrator expresses relief and regret at the same time. *Ottava rima* holds out until the finale, when Byrne, considered dead long ago, returns to face his many bastard children in London. He has John Gielgud (!) read five sonnets that "sum up all our annals/In five disjunctive but connective panels" (140). These five sonnets purportedly written by Michael Byrne are flanked by two delicately lyrical poems, altogether producing a coda-like conclusion to the verse novel.

The narrator-persona of *Byrne: A Novel*, having sided implicitly with Wordsworth and Eliot in his distinction of "high-flying" poetry from merely "plodding" verse, makes no secret of his pragmatic attitudes and his disdain for what is out of his range, as when he assumes a rather populist stance on James Joyce "butchering English" (11). If the reading is to be wholly successful, it is indeed required that the reader know of Anthony Burgess's warm love for and outstanding expertise on the work of Joyce. The informed reader identifies a narrator detached from the author at an early point in the narrative, an observation with important consequences for the response to what follows, which will have to be refracted in a system of complex irony.

Byrne is, ultimately, a discussion of existential issues bearing on twentieth-century reality with all its cruelties and paradoxes ("Human pain meant/But little in the Gulf War's visual grammar, a/Big feast of death to feed the cinecamera" (54)) showcasing a father and three of his sons balancing precariously on the thin line dividing being from seeing. Split between complete anarchy on the one hand, when all being is reduced to seeming, and, on the other, strongly deterministic outlooks, parodied by Burgess in the treatment of the Rushdie fatwa transposed to a Muslim dislike of Dante as well as of the one twin brother's project of making a TV epic out of Calvin's life. There seems no way out of this, apart from what is suggested by Tim, the apostate priest, when musing on his doomed future. In combination with the final line of the narrative, "Blessing the filthy world./Somebody had to" (Burgess 1995, 150), there seems to be a concession to, even investment of hope in, form or craft as that which confers some modest degree of meaning on a "filthy" and meaningless world. Applied to the verse novel dismissed so peremptorily by the narrator, who would have preferred the prose novel, had he not been commissioned by Byrne senior, there remains the facts of prosodic impact and the tradition of literary history, both of which mark out the particular manner of this narrative from any prose version.

David Mason's *The Country I Remember* shares with Andrew Hudgins's *After the Lost War: A Narrative* (1988) the theme of the American Civil War. In terms of length tending toward the novella rather than the novel proper, its twin narrative strain combined with its temporal scope qualify it as novel rather than short story.

The two strains of the double narrative are sustained in the form of retrospective: Mrs. Maggie Gresham looks back on her life two years before her death in 1956. During a railway journey Maggie dreams of her childhood, when around 1880 she and her family moved from Illinois to Washington, ending up in a big house in Pomeroy in 1900. The years ensuing were for Maggie an attempt to discover her destiny. A certain restlessness combined with a vague artistic calling made her unable to settle down until she reached California in her mid-thirties. Her story is one of self-insight but also that of a family looking for new opportunities just before the closing of the frontier. Her story hints at her father's life. Lieutenant Mitchell was made an officer in the Union army on joining because of his fighting experiences in the West. Mitchell recalls his years as prospector, farmer, and soldier; his thoughts go back to the Civil War, the last part of which he spent as a POW, weakened by malnutrition.

Both narratives of recollection are conveyed in seven-line unrhymed stanzas, pulsating in a loose iambic measure that may, over stretches, be subject to scansion according to Andrew Hudgins's Sidney Lanier-inspired logaoedic metre. The pulse of the rhythm provides a discreet progressive insistence, from the opening lines' onomatopoeic anapaestic variation: "The rattle and way of the train as it clattered across/leagues of open grassland put me to sleep," (3) to the quiet pondering of "I had an idea I would write a book,/but I could never sit still long enough" (38).

Lieutenant Mitchell is allowed the last words, concluding that "America/is made by those who want to change themselves-" (50), and adding very practically, "I've told these tales before, but wanted someone/to set them properly on paper, now,/in case my mind in old age starts to drift" (55). What we have from Mitchell is the story of the atrocities of the American Civil War, in contrast to Hudgins, seen from the Union side, and the story of national expansion and settlement. Mitchell's senior view fades ultimately into Maggie's quasi-blessing on life in general: "and I was moved by everything that moved" (49).

Bernadine Evaristo's *Lara* (1997) only reveals its verse mode to the reader upon actually starting to read the text, or to the very circumspect reader who prefers to garner a thorough sense of the full textual lay-out before reading. To such a reader the last part of the text, the "index of first lines," 140 in all, will signal the conventions of poetry collections rather than those of prose fiction (Evaristo 1997, 145–147). Apart from this rather well-hidden signal, no paratextual information or hints of verse are offered to prepare less than circumspect readers, who, as argued above, have most likely learnt to associate fellow writer Mike Phillips's back-cover praise "A beautiful and exciting epic" with historical sweep and big-screen scope. The short biographical note prefacing Evaristo's text concludes "*Lara* is her first full-length work of fiction" without revealing the mode of discourse.

The narrative centers on the eponymous heroine, the fourth child of an Irish mother, Ellen, and Nigerian father, Taiwo, born in 1962, following her youth in London and her attempts to come to terms with her ethnicity, including visits to Lagos and Bahia as the epitome of the quest for roots. The narrative begins in 1844, setting the scene for the itineraries of Lara's father's ancestors from Nigeria to Bahia and back again before the father set out for London and better prospects in 1949.

The verse novel consists of 140 sections, none of them exceeding in length a printed page, several verse paragraphs filling not quite a whole page. Concession to formal traditions of the novel is made by division into 14 chapters bordered by prologue and epilogue. The individual chapters do not follow chronologically one after another, but, with the *Bildung* of Lara as the central issue, offer a timeline broken by frequent flash-backs to provide the causes in the past for present-day events. The verse may at first sight appear to scan somewhat irregularly, but as soon as the reader realizes the importance of spoken performance playing off against a somewhat hurried speech rhythm and begins to shape the dynamics of experiencing the text accordingly, the text unfolds its full rhythmical potential as narrative engine complementary to the narrative drive. In most verses five main stresses stands out clearly, creating a blank-verse drive, but there is an overall predilection for a falling trochaic cadence, with dactyls and spondees arresting and countering the rising iambic movement of the traditional blank verse.

The verse retains a pulse of five beats to a line, around which it builds its local effects by braking or speeding up, effects created by constant rearrangement of rhythmical patterning to suit the semantic import of the given moment. It is, though, quite in keeping with the paratextual reluctance of *Lara* to stand out from a tacit norm that the text, with one possible exception, refuses to discuss its own versification. The possible exception, which is when Lara's father confesses to a fondness for traditional verse, makes a very subtle point to do with rhythm: "he preferred a good rhyme really, /to chug a poem along" (80). Although offering no rhyme, the regularity of the three iambic stresses of "to chug a poem along" offsets with finely calculated effect the freedom provided by reading Walt Whitman, when the last part of the line is read with two stresses only, thus underlining the reaching out: "Still, this man took him places." (Emphases added to suggest stress/beat.)

Evaristo's choice of the verse mode lends substantiality to words in themselves. It is this attention to the verbal as the construction site for meaning rather than as its translucent filter which explains why the lyrical with its verbal play depending primarily on metaphor becomes such a natural part of Evaristo's enunciations, as in a passage describing the countryside where Lara's mother Ellen was sent for safety during the war. But there is more to it than just invitation to lyrical passages naturalized by the verse environment. A passage like the one just quoted, which reads like so much poetry of the idyllic Georgian school, may be what we expect from poetry, but it is singularly out of tune with the postcolonial theme sounded in *Lara*. In the context it indicates the kind of culture and the ways, here rendered by literature, in which this British culture is traditionally disseminated, how Britain is "sold" both at home and abroad. The verse mode with its rhythmical arrangement of sound is closer to the dynamics of the signification process than the prose employed by realist fiction, which implies pre- or extra-verbal signification. Evaristo's verse novel is written from the vantage point of verbal density, as it were, rendering any fixed meanings insecure as they dissolve into a wealth of interacting signifiers, with the five beats of the lines as the sole point of stable verbal orientation.

The full title of the Australian poet Les Murray's *Fredy Neptune: A Novel in Verse* (1999) makes plain its generic affiliation from the very start. Apart from the verse mode, made up of eight-line stanzas of highly irregular blank verse, the fictional narrative stands out from the mainstream realist format of the novel by its recourse to the device of magic realism. Suffering psycho-somatic trauma from having witnessed atrocious treatment of women in Turkey during the First World War and being prevented from coming to their rescue, Friedrich (Fredy) Boettcher loses his sense of touch. Fredy acts as a kind of everyman representing the necessary immunity to face the realities of a cruel twentieth century. His numbness only goes away when, at home in Australia for good, he realizes the need to forgive.

A passage reads like a turn of the screw on Coleridge's ancient mariner being required to bless the symbol of evil, the water snakes for the winds to move again and the albatross to fall from his neck. Fredy's final line, "But there's too much in life: you can't describe it" (255) is, contrary to the negation, an affirmation of life's crowdedness, and hence the need for pre-emptive forgiving.

Murray's verse novel does not present any external evidence in explanation of the author's choice of narrative mode. The title emphasizes its intended generic category as novel, whereas the publishers, Farrar, Straus and Giroux, categorize it as poetry, in both the bar-code data on the back of the book and the Library of Congress Cataloging-in-Publication Data entry. *Fredy Neptune* engages with traumatic twentieth-century world history. The body of its hero reacts to atrocities by calling attention to the non-working of the tactile sense. The reader, perhaps grown insensitive by an overkill of smooth-prose stories of suffering, is analogically forced to reconsider the very nature of the linguistic medium by its subjection of the word game of verse.

Bibliography

Burgess, Anthony. *Byrne*. London: Hutchinson, 1995.
Dickie, Margaret. *On the Modernist Long Poem*. Iowa City: University of Iowa Press, 1986.
Dixon, W. M. and H.J.C. Grierson, eds. *The English Parnassus: An Anthology Chiefly of Longer Poems*. Oxford: At the Clarendon Press, 1909.
Evaristo, Bernadine. *Lara*. Tunbridge Wells, Kent: Angela Royal Publishing, 1997.
Fielding, Henry. *Joseph Andrews*. 1742. London: Dent (Everyman's Library), 1962.
Hejinian, Lyn. *Oxota: A Short Russian Novel*. Barrington, MA: The Figures, 1991.
Hudgins, Andrew. *After the Lost War: A Narrative*. Boston: Houghton Mifflin Company, 1988.
McHale, Brian. *The Obligation toward the Difficult Whole: Postmodernist Long Poems*. Tuscaloosa and London: University of Alabama Press, 2004.
Mason, David. *The Country I Remember*. Brownsville, OK: Story Line Press, 1996.
Murray, Les. *Fredy Neptune* . New York: Farrar, Straus and Giroux, 1999.
Preminger, Arthur and T.V.F. Brogan, T.V.F., eds. *The New Princeton Encyclopedia of Poetry and Poetics*. Princeton: Princeton University Press, 1993.
Raine, Craig. *History: The Home Movie*. Harmondsworth: Penguin Books, 1994.
Sauerberg, Lars Ole. "Repositioning Narrative: The Late-Twentieth-Century Verse Novels of Vikram Seth, Derek Walcott, Craig Raine, Anthony Burgess, and Bernadine Evaristo." *Orbis Litterarum: International Review of Literary Studies* 59.6 (2004): 439–464.
Seth, Vikram. *The Golden Gate*. 1986. London: Faber and Faber, 1999.
Walcott, Derek. *Omeros*. London: Faber and Faber, 1990.

Further Reading

Dickie, Margaret. *On the Modernist Long Poem*. Iowa City: University of Iowa Press, 1986; Dixon, W. M., and H.J.C. Grierson, eds. *The English Parnassus: An Anthology Chiefly of Longer Poems*. Oxford: At the Clarendon Press, 1909; McHale, Brian. *The Obligation toward the Difficult Whole: Postmodernist Long Poems*. Tuscaloosa and London: University of Alabama Press, 2004.

LARS OLE SAUERBERG

WESTERN LITERATURE

Definition. While most people recognize a Western novel when they see one, defining the genre is another matter. Today's postmodern Western genre generally emphasizes a dominant male or female hero undergoing a series of dangerous ordeals or tasks in a lawless culture of unrestrained violence and sex in a place loosely called *the West* during the nineteenth century. But such a definition must be qualified by contrasting today's Westerns with those of the past. As with other action genres of twenty-first century popular fiction, Westerns have changed dramatically from older versions of the genre.

The geographic American West has always captured the imagination of Americans and Europeans alike as a place apart, and to a degree that remains true today. The region's vastness seems to allow one to feel closer to uncompromised nature. But human development of the West has significantly shaped our perception of it. It was once the frontier, representing a way of life that no longer is. Traditional or modernist Western novels, which include most Westerns up through the 1990s, celebrated something that was lost. New or postmodern Westerns, as a rule, no longer concern themselves with nostalgia. Historically the old West was a place just ahead of civilization, just ahead of the law. It was a place once inhabited by exotic native peoples. Great stories from this frontier romanticized the historic West: Lewis and Clark's expedition, the discovery of gold in California in 1849, the wagon trains traveling from St. Louis to Oregon, Indian battles such as Little Big Horn, Washita Creek, and Wounded Knee. And this historic West was inhabited by larger-than-life personalities: General Custer, Crazy Horse, Wyatt Earp, Jesse James, Billy the Kid, Geronimo, Calamity Jane. Above all else, it was a time and place of violence. Survival skills were a necessity in a dangerous, demanding environment. The old West tested one's character, producing a disproportionate number of heroic characters and ideals.

Modernist Westerns celebrate this imaginative construct of the West. Not all novels that are located geographically in the Western United States qualify as Westerns, and neither do all novels that are located historically in the frontier territories. Modernist approaches to the genre would say that in order for a story to be a Western, as opposed to merely a novel of the West, a story must partake of three elements: It must capture the Western Moment, the Western Myth, and the Western Place.

The Western Moment refers to a specific time in U.S. history, whether real, mythical, or nostalgic. Usually that moment is placed after the Civil War and before the turn of the twentieth century. However, frontier stories occurring before the Civil War are said to be Westerns because they look forward to the Western Moment, and some stories set in the early twentieth century can qualify as Westerns because they look back nostalgically to the Western Moment.

The Western Myth refers to the accumulated stories and traditions that through the decades have modified, often considerably, recollection of historic fact through oral tradition, customs, cinema, and popular fiction. Westerns do not reflect factual history. They reflect the myths that have accumulated through the years. What Billy the Kid was like as a real human being at a real moment in history is relevant to a Western story only as one element out of many in telling his story. For example, the myth gives us a handsome, devilish but likeable left-handed gunfighter, still a youth with a measure of puckish innocence. Above all else, the Western myth is based on individual prowess, and violence is simply a part of life. Westerns assume their readers are acquainted with the myths of the West.

The third element, Western Place, can generally be defined as a mythical place in a frontier American setting, usually, though not always, west of the Mississippi River. Early Westerns especially celebrated the Great Plains, but more recent Westerns have tended to celebrate the deserts and borderlands with Mexico. The chief requirement for Western Place is that it be open and endless. Thus, fenced off farms in Kansas and Montana cannot be part of the Western Place.

But this modernist understanding of the Western genre is rapidly losing ground in the twenty-first century. For postmodern readers of Westerns, the old stories of the West remain in the background, but they no longer capture the imagination. Postmodernism, by definition, repudiates the myths of the past, including the Western myths. For one thing, those myths tend to reflect a macho white male perspective. They encompass stories of white men conquering Native Americans and women and "winning" the West. Few postmodern readers can accept the values upon which modernist twentieth century Westerns were based. Thus creators of Westerns today, whether authors, editors, or corporate publishing enterprises, must search for new ways to overturn older paradigms of the Western story.

THE TWENTY-FIRST-CENTURY WESTERN

Twenty-first-century Westerns acknowledge only marginally the historical and geographical myths of the American West. Their West is a mythical place of open landscapes and huge panoramic vistas, but not specific landscapes. Even when named, most geography in twenty-first century Westerns is deliberately imaginative, or, as when a Ralph Compton novel is set on a real historic trail, such as the Whoop Up Trail, the emphasis is on the exaggerated exoticism of the place, not its true location in Montana. What ties a postmodern Western to the past is primarily the violence, unrestrained sex, lawlessness of society, and individual determination to survive.

History. The commonly known modernist Westerns trace their origins to Owen Wister's *The Virginian* (1902) a best-selling novel of the West that has always been recognized as an important literary work. The novel centers on the tension between the hero, the Virginian, and Trampas. The most famous line of any popular Western comes when Trampas makes the mistake of calling the hero "a son of a bitch." Quick as lightning the gun comes out and the Virginian says, "When you call me that, smile." At the end the two shoot it out. Nearly all the elements of the traditional modernist formula Western can be found in this prototype novel.

Subsequent early Westerns tended to look back toward a West that had only very recently closed and been won (for white people), a West that could be no more. Zane Grey became a best-selling Western writer with titles like *Riders of the Purple Sage* (1912) and *The Light of Western Stars* (1914), which, while full of sanitized violence and action, often read like travelogues celebrating the West as a place that retained its enchantment despite encroachments of civilization. Other early writers were B. M. Bower, a female Western writer who wrote a series about the Happy Family of the Flying U Ranch. Clarence Mulford wrote a series of Westerns from the World War I era through the late 1930s comprising tales of the Bar 20 Ranch and its leading hero, Hopalong Cassidy. All of these writers prided themselves on the historical and geographic authenticity of their Westerns, and from the beginning Western writers and readers have insisted that such authenticity was essential to the genre.

It didn't take long, though, for another trend to develop, a trend with more influence on postmodern Westerns than authenticity—the imagined Western. Beginning with the pulp magazines of the 1920s, a new kind of Western began to emerge, a Western that gloried not in the authentic but in the bizarre, in the purely imagined landscape and in purely mythic history. The greatest of all pulp writers, Max Brand, wrote 422 novels before his death on the battlefield during World War II. The typical Max Brand Western makes no effort to center its story in any identifiable location other than somewhere in the West. Town names, mountain ranges, rivers are nearly all imaginative. Historical events and real-life characters have virtually no presence in Brand's Westerns. Instead, his characters often are near superhuman and mythical in stature and presence, sometimes aided by near supernatural agents: dogs that can run faster than horses, horses larger than anything imaginable and endowed with unbelievable speed. For Brand, Westerns were not authentic anyway, so he need not bother to focus on authenticity or historical accuracy.

By the middle of the twentieth century, then, these two major trends—the authentic and the imaged—had been established. Hollywood reinforced the imagined Western with its B-grade Westerns of the 1930s and 1940s. Italian or "Spaghetti" Westerns of the 1960s continued the film trend away from authentic Westerns; this same period marked the shift of popular Western fiction away from authenticity as well.

Nevertheless, authentic Westerns dominated the paperback market. Writers of the 1940s and 1950s, such as Ernest Haycox and Luke Short, wrote about a real West. Louis L'Amour, arguably the most successful Western writer of all time, nearly monopolized the market from the 1950s until the 1980s. His reprinted novels continue to account for a large percentage of total Western sales in the twenty-first century despite being dated. For L'Amour, geographic authenticity mattered as much as any other element of a Western. Could a story really be a Western if its location could not be identified on a map? L'Amour fans have always claimed that if the L'Amour hero was crawling on his belly down a gully away from the sniper up on the ledge, you could count on it that Louis L'Amour himself once crawled down that same gully on his belly. Readers today, though, look back on L'Amour's Westerns and simply see a flawed modernist interpretation of the Western myths. His female characters and his marginalized minorities are unlike any that ever truly existed, and his views of human psychology are more superficial than insightful.

In the late twentieth century, L'Amour's Westerns were dominating the fiction bookracks. But other versions of Westerns were developing in influential European markets. *Lucky Luke* comic books were highly popular in France and French-speaking cultures. Lucky Luke was a wildly imaginative cowboy ever in pursuit of the Daltons. English *Black Horse* Westerns were also becoming popular. Late in the century Western-themed video games began to appear, based upon the imagined West of Spaghetti Westerns. In short, the public perception of the Western myth was changing rapidly as the twentieth century came to a close. As in other areas of American popular culture, the modernist paradigm was changing.

This transformation inevitably found its way into popular Western paperbacks as well. During the 1980s and 1990s, alongside all the Louis L'Amour Westerns, a new kind of Western began to appear, the adult Western. Playboy Press was one of the first publishers in this field. Large numbers of these very thin Westerns cropped up seemingly everywhere. Among the most popular were the Longarm series, the Trailsman series, and The Edge series. The Longarm series has been running since 1978 and still flourishes with over 300 novels in the series, written by numerous writers under the name Tabor Evans. The Edge series, actually written by a single author, George G. Gilman, begun in 1972, has been revived by Gilman since 2002 with a much older Edge character. These novels have two things in common: page after page of extraordinarily gruesome violence, and incredibly graphic, explicit sex. They are strictly imaginative Westerns, bearing almost no reference to historic authenticity. For many non-readers of Westerns, these novels have become the dominant image of what Westerns are all about. The traditional Western myths, for this audience, are dead. Publishers and authors, realizing this trend, had to change with the times as the new century dawned.

And thus the not-so-subtle change has occurred at the beginning of the twenty-first century from modernist Westerns to postmodern Westerns. Modernist Westerns saw the West as formative of masculine character. With white males at the center, all other characters—women, Native Americans, all non-white peoples—were marginalized. Modernist Western plots were based upon regenerative violence, violence that actually purified evil and brought about salvation. Authentic representation of history and geography validated the white male experience—after all, one could say, this was the way it really happened. The cultural codes of twentieth century modernism in general pervaded these Westerns as they based action and decisions by protagonists squarely upon the practical, the reasonable, and the thoroughly secular.

Postmodern Westerns written since 2000 rarely depict the West as formative of masculine character. In fact, the West might be said generally to corrupt character. Postmodern Westerns tend to be much more violent than modernist Westerns, yet the violence cannot be considered regenerative or redemptive. While many feminist critics might still see strong male domination in twenty-first century Westerns, comparatively speaking, these new Westerns are not strictly centered in a white male paradigm. At least the possibility of multiple paradigms is being considered. Stories centered on formerly marginalized peoples, as well as stories with women characters equally strong and consequential as men are common today. The nineteenth century's feminine ideal (that is, a woman whose primary duties were to support her husband and to tend to domestic affairs) is no longer validated in Western literature, nor considered normative. Instead, women in postmodern Westerns generally have a past or depth of character that allows them to assert themselves equal to men. Prostitutes often take the role of the typical woman of the West in an egalitarian way. Unrestrained and extensively described sex is typical but not necessary. Most sex is casual, commoditized, or the result of violent rape. But like the modernist Westerns, postmodern Westerns still are basically secular.

Trends and Themes. Many of the common trends and themes of Westerns written since 2000 were well in place by the late decades of the previous century. Because modernist Westerns seemed to have devolved into many versions of the same basic formulas, and because the market for the older Westerns was simply growing stale, recent writers have been forced to look for something new to write about and new ways of presenting their stories.

A far greater variety of subject matter appears in today's Western stories than in the past. For one thing, the Western Moment has been stretched backward as well as forward. No longer do we assume a Western will take place strictly after the Civil War or before 1900. For example, Mountain Men novels have become a popular subgenre of Westerns. William W. Johnstone made his reputation with his Mountain Man series and his First Mountain Man series. Larry McMurtry's Berrybender Narratives series take place in the 1830s and 1840s. Numerous Westerns have concentrated almost exclusively on Native Americans. Don Coldsmith's Westerns relate stories of Native Americans prior to European contact. Generally, the traditional formula stories, such as gunfighter narratives, are de-emphasized unless they can be told from an unusual perspective, through the eyes of a female character as in Jane Candia Coleman's *Doc Holiday's Woman*, for instance.

Contexts and Issues. A basic assumption among cultural critics when approaching any work of fiction is that the work truly reflects the era and culture in which it is written, rather than the culture of the fictional setting. A Western, for instance, is never about the old West. It is always about the culture of the time it was written. As we look back at Westerns of the twentieth century we can see how they responded to such historical events as the Great Depression, World War II, the Cold War, the Civil Rights Movement, the Vietnam War, and the Women's Movement. Westerns written during World War II might emphasize savage warfare with Native Americans, for instance, as a way of reflecting upon the savage combat with the Japanese.

So to what current developments do Westerns written since 2000 relate? The beginning of the twenty-first century saw the most aggressive direct attack on the United States in recent history with the September 11, 2001 attacks. A war with seemingly no end in sight with Iraq has occupied the U.S. military since 2002. Though these events have certainly impacted American culture, it is too early to determine how they will be reflected in Westerns. Other potential cultural trends that may appear in upcoming Westerns include stories about invasions from our neighbors to the south or the onslaught of alien peoples into a domesticated territory. We might see savage warfare stories again as well as stories with tyrannical powerful leaders. There is no doubt that Westerns will change in the twenty-first century, but exactly what trends will emerge is yet to be seen.

Reception. As with all popular media since 2000, the popular Western market depends heavily on Internet visibility. Virtually all writers have their own Web sites for their fans, and publishers devote web space to their Western products. Several writers such as William W. Johnstone have long-running discussion boards for their fans to chat about their novels. Writers such as Ed Gorman maintain continuous blogs for their fans to read, and the fans themselves blog regularly about their favorite writers and books. No longer can we consider the path of a Western as simply a chain of author/publisher/bookseller/consumer.

The main industry awards for Westerns and Western writers are the Spur Awards and the Western Heritage Awards. The Spur Awards are given each year by the Western Writers of America. The somewhat more prestigious Western Heritage Awards are awarded annually by the National Cowboy and Western Heritage Museum of Oklahoma City.

The commercial market for mass market traditional Westerns (as opposed to Westerns with contemporary settings) is serving *readers* of Westerns well in 2007. According to the Western Writers of America Web site, "Nielsen BookScan, which covers about 70% of U.S. book sales, says Western sales have increased by 9% in 2005 and 10% thus far in 2006. Books in Print says the number of Western titles produced has increased from 543 in 1995 to 901 in 2005."

AWARDS FOR WESTERN FICTION

The Spur Award, from the Western Writers of America

2007:	Best Western Long Novel: *The Night Journal* by Elizabeth Crook. Viking/Penguin.
2007:	Best Western Short Novel: *The Shape Shifter* by Tony Hillerman. HarperCollins.
2006:	Best Western Novel: Tie for Spur Winner: *Camp Ford: A Western Story* by Johnny D. Boggs, Five Star Publishing; and *The Undertaker's Wife* by Loren D. Estleman, Forge Books.
2005:	*Buy the Chief a Cadillac* by Rick Steber. Bonanza Publishing
2004:	*I Should Be Extremely Happy In Your Company* by Brian Hall. Viking.
2003:	*The Chili Queen* by Sandra Dallas. St. Martin's Press.
2002:	*The Way of the Coyote* by Elmer Kelton. Forge Books.
2001:	*Summer of Pearls* by Mike Blakely. Forge Books.
2000:	*Masterson* by Richard S. Wheeler. Forge Books.

Western Heritage Awards

2008:	*Harpsong* by Rilla Askew.
2007:	*Broken Trail* by Alan Geoffrion. Fulcrum Publishing.
2006:	*Buffalo Calf Road Woman, The Story of a Warrior of the Little Bighorn* by Rosemary Agonito and Joseph Agonito. The Globe Pequot Press/Two Dot Books.
2005:	*And Not to Yield,* by Randy Lee Eickhoff. Forge Books.
2004:	*Spark on the Prairie: The Trial of the Kiowa Chiefs* by Johnny Boggs. Signet.
2003:	*Moon of Bitter Cold* by Frederick J. Chiaventone. Forge Books.
2002:	*The Master Executioner* by Loren D. Estleman. Forge Books.
2001:	*Gates of the Alamo* by Stephen Harrigan. Alfred A. Knopf.
2000:	*The Contract Surgeon* by Dan O'Brien. The Lyons Press.

From Western Writers of America (http://www.westernwriters.org/spur_award_history.htm)
From National Cowboy and Western Heritage Museum (http://www.nationalcowboymuseum.org/default.aspx)

For *writers* of Westerns, the market news is not so promising, however. *Books in Print* lists include Print on Demand titles and vanity titles, and there are quite a few Westerns printed by vanity presses each year. But nowadays most publishers put all their non-catalog books into Print on Demand status. Thus, these books don't carry much reward for the authors. Worse yet, the entire Western paperback offerings are dominated by reprints of titles by Louis L'Amour, William W. Johnstone, and Ralph Compton. There are probably fewer than thirty working authors of mass market traditional Westerns in the U.S. market today. But again, readers can enjoy a variety of Westerns being placed on the shelves.

During the twentieth century Westerns were popular with movie makers, and several Westerns by Zane Grey, Max Brand, Louis L'Amour and others were adapted to film. However, since 2000 only a few Westerns each year have come out of Hollywood. Two of the most notable Western films based on Western novels since 2000 are *Open Range (2003)* based on Lauran Paine's novel of the same name in the same year, and *Broken Trail* (2006) based on Alan Geoffrion's 2006 novel of the same name.

Selected Authors. Obviously, plenty of writers who made their mark in the later decades of the last century are still active today and their work hasn't necessarily changed simply because we are in a new century. One such author still producing plenty of Westerns in the twenty-first century is Elmer Kelton, the Texas writer who published his first Western in 1955 and won the first of his seven Spur Awards in 1956. Besides the Spur Awards, Kelton has been voted all-time best Western author by the Western Writers of America and is a four time winner of Western Heritage Awards. Kelton's novels haven't changed noticeably over the several decades. *The Way of the Coyote* (2001) is set, typically, in Texas. It is the Reconstruction period and thus the story plays off conflicts between Reconstruction agents and defeated Confederate sympathizers. We are intended to read the novel with sympathy for the defeated Texans. Rusty Shannon, the main character, loses his farm due to legal shenanigans by the state authorities. In fact, all the Reconstruction agents and supporters are uniformly evil. No doubt Kelton counts on his readers sharing the views put forth in the novel. However, a more objective reading reveals attitudes incompatible with postmodern culture. Kelton, still the modernist, takes a racial realist view at every opportunity. In other words, he evidently sees his characters' race as inherent in their biological makeup rather than the more modern view that race is something constructed by culture. An African American character, former slave who is humbled by the Ku Klux Klan, supports his former oppressors and reviles the Reconstruction agents. One of the leaders of the Klan turns out to have a softer side. Perhaps most disturbing is a main character who was captured as a child and brought up in Comanche ways. He is "rescued" and, though he longs for his tribal ways, made to become "civilized." The title, *The Way of the Coyote,* comes from a major episode when he casts off his white ways and uses his tribal skills of tracking like a coyote in a long chase and pursuit scene. He saves another white boy captured by evil Comanche. At the end of the novel Andy symbolically cuts his hair and merges fully into his real people. No matter what his upbringing, his real racial identity is white Euro-American. The novel won a Spur Award in 2001.

Also making his reputation in the late twentieth century, Loren Estleman is that rare genre writer for whom character and style can transcend plot. Tending toward the Hemingway-esque, Estleman pares his prose close and delights in showing the humanness of the neglected and the stereotyped characters of the mythic West. A

Michigan native who wrote his first novel in 1976, he has remained consistently popular since 2000. According to his Web site, he has written 59 books along with numerous short works and he prides himself on writing exclusively on a manual typewriter. Estleman, like other Western authors, frequently crosses into other genres; he has received numerous awards for his mystery novels. His Westerns have earned him five Spur Awards and three Western Heritage Awards.

Estleman's *The Master Executioner* (2001) won a Western Heritage Award. A carpenter takes up the profession of hangman and, through an apprenticeship with a veteran hangman, learns the trade to become a master executioner. But Oscar Stone becomes so devoted to perfectionism in his trade that he loses everything in his dedication to what others see as abhorrent. Here, as in his other novels, Estleman de-emphasizes typical Western formula elements. In *The Undertaker's Wife* (2005), also a Spur Award winner, Estleman again chooses an unglamorous profession and develops a compelling story along with a shot of unexpected romance. Told through the point of view of his devoted wife, the undertaker is pressured to cover up a suicide on the corpse of a prominent financier in order to avert suspicion that economic times aren't what they seem. The novel features lots of inside the embalming room story material.

In *Black Powder, White Smoke* (2002) Estleman attempts to weave two parallel main plots with two subplots in a way not typical of older genre Westerns. Again he focuses on characters often ignored by classic Westerns: the African American owner of a brothel out to avenge the mutilation of one of his girls, and a lawless reveler who kills a Chinese immigrant running from an urban Chinese gang. *The Adventures of Johnny Vermillion* (2006) is a tale of an acting troupe out to gouge anybody and everybody, Wild West style. Shakespeare may be playing onstage but the bank's being robbed down the street.

Loren Estleman's most popular series is his Paige Murdock series. Murdock is a U.S. Deputy Marshal working for Federal Judge Harlan A. Blackstone. The main character frequently travels far afield in the pursuit of his duties. In *Port Hazard* (2004), Murdock travels to the Barbary Coast and in *White Desert* (2001) he pursues a ruthless band into the Canadian North Country.

Author Cotton Smith's motto, according to his Web site, is "Delivering a well-honed psychological edge to western history," and, indeed, his novels do emphasize characters' interior reactions to the various dilemmas they encounter. *Pray for Texas* (2000), for example, filters through the psyche of a crazed Confederate cavalryman who cannot accept defeat and thus joins an outlaw band. In his zeal to fight on, he confronts his childhood of abuse from his preacher father and confronts the demons of his past. The novel was nominated for the Western Heritage Award.

Peter Brandvold published his first Western in 1999. The back covers of all of his books boast, "Brandvold writes a lot like L'Amour." And, sure enough, Brandvold writes what at first might appear to be traditional, modernist Western fiction. His novels look like authentic Westerns. *The Romantics* (2001), for example, is based on a typical chase and pursuit after gold treasure deep into Mexico trailed by vile desperados, former Confederate followers of Bloody Bill Anderson. There is plenty of action and wonderfully portrayed regenerative violence. But Brandvold does recognize women, and it is through the presence of a female protagonist that *The Romantics* shifts slightly from modernist Westerns. One of the main characters is Maria, the gorgeous Mexican wife of the character with the treasure map. Maria's beauty proves a problem all along the journey as she faces numerous rape attempts. But she can ride and shoot and she proves as tough as anybody. At the end the gold is found and she survives along with the novel's hero, Jack Cameron. *The Romantics* is a twenty-first century Western with soft graphic language and merely suggestive sex, but graphic detailed violence and a portrayal of Native Americans as savages.

Although Westerns have traditionally been written by male authors from a male character's point of view, the genre has always included a handful of talented female writers such as B.M. Bower, and there are probably more women writing Westerns today than ever before. The Western Romance market, for example, is flourishing. A.H. Hope, Elizabeth Crook, and many others are actively marketing Westerns, both traditional and romantic.

Elizabeth Fackler, who made her reputation in the 1990s with Westerns with strong women protagonists, has devoted most of her efforts to crime fiction since 2000. However, she returned to Westerns in 2006 with *Bone Justice,* a story with horrific implications of a kindhearted outlaw on the road to reform suddenly faced with helping two women captives escape a destiny as Mexican prostitutes.

Probably, though, the dominant woman writer of Westerns today is Jane Candia Coleman, who has produced a wide variety of work beyond mass market Westerns. She has won two Spur Awards and one Western Heritage Award. For her popular Westerns she typically has taken historical women at the margins of the great Western narratives and retold the history from their points of view. Her 2005 novel *Doc Holliday's Woman* tells the story of the marginalized Big Nose Kate, a character in all the Wyatt Earp movies and stories but always at the edge of a scene, never the center of attention. An earlier novel, *Tombstone Travesty: Allie Earp Remembers* (2004), tells the old story from the perspective of Virgil Earp's wife. Coleman is a Western writer actively working to counter male-dominated interpretations of history and myth. She is also contributing to a trend that seems more prevalent in the last few years than in earlier popular Westerns: the novelization of great historical events and characters. While Hollywood has always been fascinated with history, paperback Westerns have generally kept the real characters and events of the West on the edges of the fiction. Max Brand probably never had a reference to a single historical character or event in any of his novels. But today we are revisiting history in popular fiction as well as on film and television.

Johnny D. Boggs's 2006 book *East of the Border* demonstrates this concept well. Like Loren Estleman, Boggs is drawn to nineteenth-century theatre. This is the story of Buffalo Bill Cody's first debut with show business. It primarily follows the 1873-1974 theatre season of the Buffalo Bill Connection as it tours the East. Boggs tells the story through distinct points of view, in alternating chapters, of Texas Jack, Wild Bill Hickok, and Buffalo Bill himself. Other than these features, the novel is episodic, as it follows the theatre troupe from one town to another. Jack is the educated one; he was once a school teacher in Florida and has read widely. He marries an Italian singer-actress on the road. Hickok drinks heavily and works the girls. Rough and rowdy, Cody is the real business mind behind the troupe. We see him coming to an awareness that his future is in show business. *East of the Border* is a novel about theatre, about performance—a very untraditional Western. There are a few good fights but overall surprisingly little violence. Sex in the novel is mainly suggestive. And it all takes place in the East. Boggs's more recent *Camp Ford,* a baseball story set in the Western Moment, won the 2006 Spur Award.

John D. Nesbitt, like Boggs, often disregards Western formulas in his fiction though he may borrow formulas from other popular genres. *Lonesome Range*

(2006) is a strange book. Everything about its packaging and marketing makes it look like a traditional popular Western, but there is little gunplay and few fistfights. An occasional scene of ranch work appears. The main character is a bookkeeper. Basically this Western is the story of an adulterous relationship carried out over several years from one town to the next. There is plenty of romance but not a typical romance plot. At the end the relationship is ended.

Like many Western authors, Ed Gorman writes primarily in other genres. Nevertheless, he is a Spur Award-winning writer. Perhaps as representative as any of his novels is *Cavalry Man* (2006). The Cavalry Man is Noah Ford, a federal agent. In Willow Bend to investigate the death of a fellow federal agent, Ford becomes involved in the hunt for a local bank robber, Mike Cheney, who just happens to be carrying on an affair with the bank president's wife. Cheney's sister interests Ford in the complicated case. Thereafter the novel is built around a lengthy chase and pursuit through rugged winter mountain terrain. Brutal sexual violence occurs along the way to a young mother in an isolated cabin and Ford must take the young child along who witnessed its mother's horrible death. Gorman has mastered suspense in a typical postmodern Western.

Although Ralph Cotton in interviews pays homage to Elmer Kelton, his own novels differ markedly from Kelton's modernist Westerns. In *Blood Lands* (2006) the protagonist is a woman with a past, who, after her natural father, a retired army colonel is killed, undergoes a brutal gang rape by a group of masked Southern sympathizers in the waning days of the Civil War. Discarded by the masked thugs, Julie Wilder desperately wants at first merely to escape town. But all she has in the world is the farmstead of her father's. Slowly she begins to identify the masked thugs one at a time. She experiences another sexual assault. Then she meets Baines Meredith, a professional bounty hunter. After a period of time away from town she returns, still a demure woman who just wants to be left alone—until she has her chance. Then with all the skills of a gun and a whip, learned from Meredith, she sets out to exact her revenge. The plot owes much to Max Brand's 1930s *Destry Rides Again*.

Elmer Kelton and Peter Brandvold, in the novels mentioned earlier, tend to portray Native Americans as unredeemed savages. Dan O'Brien, however, has a two-novel sequence based upon the Sioux "uprisings" of the 1880s in which he develops a slightly more progressive view of Native American history. The main character in the series is a true historical character named Valentine McGillicuddy, a reservation physician in one novel, *The Contract Surgeon* (the Spur Award winner for 2000), who is promoted to Indian Agent for the Pine Ridge Reservation in *The Indian Agent* (2004). The narrative of *The Indian Agent* follows closely the historical events of Red Cloud's various rebellions, the famous buffalo hunt with cattle substituting for buffalo, and even the Wounded Knee massacre. Throughout we follow McGillicuddy and his wife in his various political ventures in Washington as well as on the reservation. Although the character Red Cloud garners readers' sympathy, O'Brien seems to support the official efforts to merge Native Americans into mainstream Euro-American culture, while portraying characters who advocate preserving tribal heritage as foolish and comical.

One of the main differences between twenty-first century Westerns and those of the previous century has been the growing prominence of series Westerns. Several of the novels so far mentioned are parts of these series, and most of the prominent Western writers of today have multiple series in progress. Peter Brandvold, for example, has the Sheriff Ben Stillman series, the Rogue Lawman series, the .45-Caliber series, and the Bounty Hunter Lou Prophet series.

Larry McMurtry, perhaps the dominant Western writer of the 1990s with his Lonesome Dove series, has been developing a new series since 2000. The Berrybender Narratives is a four-novel series following a group of English settlers across the frontier in the 1830s and 1840s. The series, like the Lonesome Dove books, has a lengthy list of characters and multiple plot strands running throughout. Interestingly, when the characters we have been following for four novels finally reach Santa Fe, most have been killed off or died and there are no real happy endings. The series reads like a reality television show.

Richard S. Wheeler, the very prolific Montana writer, is the 2001 recipient of the Owen Wister Award for lifetime contributions to Western literature and a four-time Spur Award winner from Western Writers of America. While Wheeler's novels include only suggestive sex and light violence, his themes and style are postmodern. *The Bounty Trail* (2004), for example, follows three charming but despicable characters as they try to make their fortunes in a boom town situation. Pearlygates was a ghost town, owned by MayBelle Bertram, a beautiful woman recently divorced, whose legal claim to the town is the total of her worldly possessions. Through one situation after another, she is joined by Colonel C. P. Raines, a con artist, and Arnold "Safe" Cracker, an expert in all matters of explosives. Together they plot to start a gold rush on the town and make a fortune from all the fools they can find. Unfortunately for them they actually strike a real bonanza which is followed by a real gold rush and they lose the town, their mines, everything. The rest of the novel is devoted to their efforts to try other confidence schemes, with little success. Cracker blows up things, MayBelle turns private prostitute, and the Colonel blusters from one sucker to another promising riches untold. Everything the three set out to do is reprehensible, but the readers are meant to love these three anyway.

Wheeler has also been developing the Skye's West series since the 1980s and has written several volumes since 2000. *The Deliverance* (2003) continues the series with its English protagonist, Barnaby Skye, a former impressed British sailor who escaped on the West Coast in the 1830s and worked his way inland, becoming a famed mountain man, marrying a Crow maiden who he names Victoria and whose command of English involves a heavy dose of colorful cursing. In this novel he and Victoria head into Northern Mexico from the Republic of Texas to search for kidnapped children. They meet up with a colorful trader named Childers who has an ornate wagon of goods pulled by Clydesdale horses. He also has a trained monkey. They are waylaid by Utes, arrested by Mexican authorities as spies, and discover the horrors of the Mexican slave trade. Again, all the protagonists are of questionable character but all are thoroughly likeable. Wheeler keeps the pages turning.

James C. Work has been developing the Keystone Ranch series over the last few years. He grounds his novels in historical circumstance but also develops mythological connections. In *Ride West to Dawn* (2003) and *The Dead Ride Alone* (2006), for example, there is a link to Arthurian legends. *The Dead Ride Alone* is based on Tennyson's "The Lady of Shallot." *Ride West to Dawn* is one of the most complex, multi-layered Westerns written since 2000, although it contains all the classic elements of chase and pursuit, revenge, and shootout. Water mysteriously comes up missing north of the Keystone. An old man comes to the ranch for help. The foreman sends Will Jensen to investigate. But the cowboy comes face to face with The Guardian who strips him of his horse, his clothes, and his dignity. In fact, through the ordeal, Jensen nearly loses his sanity. When he returns to the ranch he deteriorates rapidly into alcoholism and dereliction. The water remains a problem so one-eyed Kyle Owen heads north to solve the mystery. He kills The Guardian. But the ghostly young girl, Luned, takes him by the hand and leads him to The Lady, whom Kyle marries and becomes the new Guardian overseeing a strange network of locks, canals, and watercourses that divert water to a large development of small ranches and farms unknown to the outside world. Characters experience profound change throughout the stories, and Work incorporates naturally occurring symbolism to good effect. Will is essentially a good cowboy, but his character is shattered by his ordeal and he never fully recovers. Kyle is also a good cowboy, but his character is corrupted profoundly when he becomes The Guardian. Yet the novel is left open-ended, awaiting its sequel for resolution.

While each of these writers is developing strong careers, two writers actually dominate the current market: William W. Johnstone and Ralph Compton. In fact, after Louis L'Amour, Compton and Johnstone books take up the majority of shelf space at mainline bookstores. Because large chain retailers concern themselves almost exclusively with titles that can be back inventoried in bulk, at least as far as mass market titles are concerned, there will usually be numerous titles by certain authors on the shelves and very little attention paid to isolated titles by non-prolific authors—which may partly explain the dominance of series Westerns and the dominance of Johnstone and Compton novels.

Ralph Compton began his career in 1992 and started several series in the 1990s. His longest running series is The Trail Drive series, beginning with the first title *The Goodnight Trail* (1992) and continuing to the most recent, *The Tenderfoot Trail* (2006). The Trail Drive series is unified by a basic premise rather than by a recurring set of characters. Each book centers around various problems encountered by a set of characters on a different historic trail. Beyond that basic premise each story is independent from the rest. *The Tenderfoot Trail* (2006) is probably as representative as any. A small-time rancher gets framed for a crime. His only hope for escaping jail and hanging comes from a well-heeled con man who breaks him out on condition that he escort a group of mail-order brides along the Whoop Up Trial in Montana to their awaiting husbands in Canada. It is a con game in more ways than one. The women turn out to be experienced prostitutes. Along the trail savage Indians attack only to be repulsed by some trappers who really just want to steal the women. The rancher falls in love with one of the girls who, of course, gulls him. He is left abandoned, barefoot, with no supplies, no water, in the most desolate part of the trail. A giant wolf befriends him, leads him to water, and rescues him on more than one occasion. Somehow he gets his ranch back, but the girl he believed in still turns out bad in the end. A similar series is Compton's The Sundown Riders series, premised around Teamsters traveling with goods-laden wagons over various legendary routes. The series began with such titles as *Across the Rio Colorado* (1997), *The Winchester Run,* (1997), *Devil's Canyon* (1998), *Whiskey River* (1999), *Skeleton Lode* (1999), and the like. This series remains active as of 2008.

Other Ralph Compton series, however, follow the lives and adventures of particular characters. The Danny Duggin series, begun in 1999, follows the career and fortunes of a cross-dressing gunfighter, Danielle Strange, who, out to avenge the murder of her father, takes up the persona of Danny Duggin. She rides her father's famous horse and carries her guns the same way he carried his. She strikes terror in the heart of her enemies who are mystified at this gunfighter's identity. By the third novel in the series she has claimed her revenge, but the series continues today as Danny Duggin finds other problems to solve. The last novel in the series is from 2003, but the Ralph Compton Web site promises more titles.

The William W. Johnstone industry has been busy since 1979 with simply an amazing output of novels. As with Compton novels, virtually all the Johnstone books are parts of various series. The original Johnstone series is The Mountain Man series, which follows the exploits of Smoke Jensen, mountain man, through more than thirty novels since 1979. A spinoff of The Mountain Man series is The First Mountain Man series, featuring a character called The Preacher. Both these series are still active.

But other William W. Johnstone series are more traditional. The Last Gunfighter series and the Blood Bond series continue the formulaic Western tradition proudly. Johnstone novels aren't quite as sexually graphic as Compton novels but they certainly do not hold back on graphic violence. *Slaughter Trail* (2006) of the Blood Bond series, for example, is premised on the idea that Matt Bodine and Sam Two Wolves have been blood brothers since childhood when Matt saved Sam's life. Matt is the son of a successful rancher and Sam is the son of a Cheyenne chief and educated woman of a wealthy Boston family. He has an Eastern education. The two brothers are so close that they can sense when the other is in trouble. In *Slaughter Trail* Sam has been arrested in Mexico and forced into hard labor at a slave camp run by an exceptionally cruel taskmaster. Matt is in Tombstone flirting with Wyatt Earp's fiancé when he senses Sam's trouble. The brutality of the slave camp is graphic and sustained.

Nearly every month, new Compton novels or new Johnstone novels appear on the market. But Ralph Compton died in 1999. His novels are now being written by a stable of writers who also write other novels under their own names. James A. West, for example, wrote *The Tenderfoot Trail*. He also writes a series of his own called Gunsmoke which uses all the old characters from the television series in new situations. The publishers do not hide the fact that Compton no longer writes.

The William W. Johnstone series are another matter. The books are printed with only Johnstone's name on the cover. Only inside on the copyright page is there a fine print disclaimer saying that a carefully selected writer has been chosen to continue the Johnstone legacy. Johnstone's death was carefully kept from his fans for three years and never acknowledged publicly. Only the fine print disclaimer admits the death of the author. Johnstone maintained his own Web site for years and maintained an active discussion forum for his novels, but one blogger, shocked at hearing of the author's death, claimed to have had email correspondence in 2004, 2005, and 2006 signed by Mr. Johnstone (who died, allegedly, in 2003). All Johnstone books are now written by Fred Austin who gets no printed credit for his work.

Unquestionably, popular Westerns at the beginning of the twenty-first century have changed considerably from the Westerns of the past. The essence of the Western, whether in movies or in popular novels, is a common theme of debate among readers and critics alike. Obviously Westerns no longer hold as large a share of the market as in the past, but the genre is flexible and adapting for a new generation of readers.

Bibliography

Boggs, Johnny D. *Camp Ford*. Farmington Hills, MI: Five Star, 2005.
———. *East of the Border*. New York: Leisure, 2004.
Coleman, Jane Candia. *Doc Holliday's Woman*. Tucson, AZ: Ravenhawk, 2005.

————.*Tombstone Travesty: Allie Earp Remembers*. Farmington Hills, MI: Five Star, 2004.

Compton, Ralph. *The Goodnight Trail*. New York: St. Martin's, 1992.

Cotton, Ralph. *Blood Lands*. New York: Signet, 2006.

Estleman, Loren. *Black Powder, White Smoke*. New York: Forge, 2002.

————. *Port Hazard*. New York: Forge, 2004.

————. *The Adventures of Johnny Vermillion*. New York: Forge, 2006.

————.*The Master Executioner*. New York: Forge, 2001.

————.*The Undertaker's Wife*. New York: Forge, 2005.

————.*White Desert*. New York: Forge, 2001.

Fackler, Elizabeth. *Bone Justice*. New York: Western Star, 2006.

Geoffrion, Alan. *Broken Trail*. New York: Fulcrum, 2006.

Gorman, Ed. *Cavalry Man*. New York: Harper Torch, 2006.

Johnstone, William W. *Slaughter Trail*. New York: Pinnacle, 2006.

Nesbitt, John D. *Lonesome Range*. New York: Leisure, 2006.

O'Brien, Dan. *The Contract Surgeon*. New York: Mariner, 2001.

————.*The Indian Agent*. New York: Harper Torch, 2005.

Paine, Lauran. *Open Range*. New York: Leisure, 2003.

Smith, Cotton. *Pray for Texas*. New York: Leisure, 2000.

West, James A. and Ralph Compton. *The Tenderfoot Trail: A Ralph Compton Novel*. New York: Signet, 2006.

Wheeler, Richard S. *The Bounty Trail*. New York: Pinnacle, 2004.

————.*The Deliverance*. New York: Doherty, 2003.

Work, James C. *Ride West to Dawn*. New York: Leisure, 2003.

————.*The Dead Ride Alone*. New York: Leisure. 2006.

Further Reading

Bold, Christine. *Selling the Wild West: Popular Western Fiction, 1800 to 1960*. Bloomington: University of Indiana Press, 1987; Calder, Jenni. *There Must Be A Lone Ranger*. London: Hamish, 1974; Cawelti, John G. *The Six-Gun Mystique Sequel*. Bowling Green, OH: Popular Press, 1999; Davis, Robert Murray. *Playing Cowboys: Low Culture and High Art in the Western*. Norman: University of Oklahoma Press, 1992; Hamilton, Cynthia. *Westerns and Hard-Boiled Detective Fiction in America: From High Noon to Midnight*. Iowa City: University of Iowa Press, 1982; Mitchell, Lee Clark. *Westerns: Making the Man in Fiction and Film*. Chicago: University of Chicago Press, 1996; Robinson, Forrest G. *Having It Both Ways: Self-Subversion in Western Popular Classics*. Albuquerque: University of New Mexico Press, 1997; Slotkin, Richard. *Gunfighter Nation: The Myth of the Frontier in Twentieth-Century America*. New York: Harper, 1992; Sonnichsen, C. L. *From Hopalong to Hud: The Unheroic Cowboy in Western Fiction: Thoughts on Western Fiction*. College Station: Texas A & M University Press, 1978; Tomkins, Jane. *West of Everything: The Inner Life of Westerns*. New York: Oxford University Press, 1992; Walle, Alf H. *The Cowboy Hero and Its Audience: Popular Culture as Market Derived Art*. Bowling Green, OH: Bowling Green University Press, 2000; Wright, Will. *Six Guns and Society: A Structural Study of the Western*. Berkeley: University of California Press, 1975; Wright, Will. *The Wild West: The Mythical Cowboy and Social Theory*. London: Sage, 2001.

Bibliography of Websites and Homepages

Boggs, Johnny D. http://www.johnnydboggs.com/

Brandvold, Peter. http://www.peterbrandvold.com/

Cotton, Ralph. http://www.ralphcotton.com/books.html

Dorchester Publishing. http://www.dorchesterpub.com/Dorch/Genre.cfm?L1=3&L2=9

Estleman, Loren. http://www.lorenestleman.com/

Fackler, Elizabeth. http://www.elizabethfackler.com/index.html

Johnstone, William W. http://www.williamjohnstone.net/
Kelton, Elmer. http://www.elmerkelton.net/
McMurtry, Larry. http://www.simonsays.com/content/destination.cfm?tab=2&pid=328664
Nesbitt, John D. http://www.johndnesbitt.com/
Smith, Cotton. http://www.cottonsmithbooks.com/
Spur Awards. http://www.westernwriters.org/spur_awards.htm
Western Heritage Awards. http://www.nationalcowboymuseum.org/e_awar_winn_wnovel.html
Western Writers of America. http://www.westernwriters.org/news.htm
Work, James C. http://www.jameswork.com/

PAUL VARNER

Y

YOUNG ADULT LITERATURE

Definition. Young adult literature is a fairly recent phenomenon in the sense that it has been recognized as a distinct category by publishers only since approximately the 1960s. Like its relative **children's literature**, young adult literature has become an increasingly autonomous genre, seeking to establish itself as a legitimate field in the eyes of both the academic and the popular communities. One major obstacle to realizing this goal is the difficulty in establishing what exactly constitutes young adult literature or, for that matter, a young adult. For some, this problem pertains to the semantics of the terminology. Across America, the terms *young adult, adolescent, teen, juvenile,* and *youth* are oftentimes used interchangeably. Similarly, universities offering classes in "children's literature" oftentimes use this as an umbrella term to refer to works written for the age groups from pre-kindergarten through to the end of high school.

A good definition is provided by writer Steven VanderStaay:

> Young-adult literature is literature wherein the protagonist is either a teenager or one who approaches problems from a teenage perspective. Such novels are generally of moderate length and told from the first person. Typically, they describe initiation into the adult world, or the surmounting of a contemporary problem forced upon the protagonist(s) by the adult world. Though generally written for a teenage reader, such novels—like all fine literature—address the entire spectrum of life. (VanderStaay 1992, 48)

Susan M. Landt reinforces this notion by saying, "Adolescence is a time of questioning and searching as young people strive to comprehend who they are and how they fit in the world" (Landt 2006, 692). Others have defined this genre as including any text that is written or published for young adults or that might be marketed to or purchased by young adults. Still others stringently say that Young Adult literature features issues of the teenage years, such as puberty, coming of age, and initiation and maturation into adulthood. It should also be noted here that Young Adult texts include fictional prose and poetry, nonfiction, and graphic novels.

History. Young adult literature as we know it differs greatly from texts written expressly for children in the early part of America's history. James Janeway's book *A Token for Children: Being an Exact Account of the Conversion, Holy and Exemplary Lives, and Joyful Deaths, of Several Young Children* (1676) demonstrates the desire by adults to write stories for children that would morally instruct while at the same time edifying their spirituality. With an extremely high infant mortality rate, and with families producing approximately seven or more children, it is no surprise that death was a constant reality and, therefore, a main topic of conversation for sermons and education curriculum. Supporting the Puritan doctrine of natural depravity—that humans are born with a sin nature—Janeway's book iterates that children are not too young to die and therefore reinforces the Puritan desire for children to be cognizant of their own salvation, and, by extension, personally literate to read the Bible.

While post-Revolutionary children's literature did not reflect the religious didactic nature of books like Janeway's did, texts written after this period still managed to teach. In the nineteenth century, literature for children was divided by gender: adventure stories for boys (e.g., Horatio Alger's *Ragged Dick,* 1868) and domestic stories for girls (e.g., Sarah Tuttle's *Female Influence, or The Temperance Girl,* 1834). By the twentieth century, American popular culture began to focus on the youth of the country. Scholars attribute this push to "youth culture" to many different reasons, but many consider the fact that teens began spending more time at school than at home an important factor, alongside the growth of media—film and television.

Scholars have noted several important authors who contributed to the young adult literature movement even before the genre became distinct. Throughout the past centuries, many youths read books that were originally intended for an adult audience. J.D. Salinger's *The Catcher in the Rye* (1951) became the most notable precursor to the young adult movement. The biographical article in *Contemporary Authors* notes,

> As the novel stands today, it represents perhaps the most sensitive portrait of coming-of-age in America in the years following World War II. Few other books have had as great an impact on a generation—so much so that Holden Caulfield [Salinger's protagonist] has entered the popular mythology of American culture alongside such figures as Jay Gatsby and Huck Finn. . . . It is little wonder that *The Catcher in the Rye* became a favorite among young people. It skillfully validates adolescent experience with its spirit of rebellion. ("J.D. Salinger" 2005)

It was not until the 1960s that the field of young adult literature started to find its independent niche with another groundbreaking novel, *The Outsiders.* As Cat Yampbell remarks, "In 1967, Penguin published S.E. Hinton's *The Outsiders* and began the market that would come to be recognized as Young Adult Literature (Yampbell 2005, 350). Kathy Latrobe and Trisha Hutcherson support this statement by saying,

> Unlike other publishing movements, young-adult literature in the United States became a phenomenon in almost a single year, 1967, when writers and publishers of materials

for teenagers reached beyond the simple plots and white, middle-class protagonists of the post-World War II era and presented the more culturally diverse and socially complex environment of the 1960s. (2002, 68)

The 1970s saw two more notable, influential novels, both by Judy Blume. *Are You There God? It's Me, Margaret* (1970) ushered in the subgenre so commonly associated with Young Adult literature—the "teen problem novel," which highlights a specific concern for the adolescent. Because these specific concerns mirrored contemporary society, oftentimes these novels faded out of the limelight once that specific problem became eclipsed by another issue. As a result, books dealing with drinking gave way to books concerning drug use, then those gave way to books on other issues, such as eating disorders and abuses of various kinds. Blume's next novel to cause quite a stir was *Forever* (1975), which concerns a young teen's first love and sexual experience. Blume was quite offended when her publisher advertised this text as a novel for adults when she clearly had intended it for young adults. Topics once considered taboo—including teenage sexuality—were gradually becoming discussed as primary topics in Young Adult novels. If we compare Nancy Garden's *Annie on My Mind* (1982), which was one of the earliest stories to feature homosexuality as a primary focus, to Beverly Cleary's *Fifteen* (1956), we can easily see how far Young Adult literature has come in terms of portraying the frankness and gritty realism of teens' lives.

The 1970s and 1980s also welcomed multicultural literature into the genre, with notable novels such as Mildred Taylor's *Roll of Thunder, Hear My Cry* (1976), which won the 1977 Newbery Award and further popularized the African American Logan family she had created in *Song of the Trees* (1975). *Roll of Thunder* was also adapted into a three-part miniseries for ABC in 1978. The Logan family became so popular that Taylor created a prequel to *Roll of Thunder* called *The Land* (2001).

During the mid-1990s, VanderStraay's ideas that Young Adult novel "assume[d] a particular kind of coming-of-age story and a particular kind of narrator who must live within strict ethical and narrative boundaries" (1992, 49) were quite relevant. For VanderStraay, the essential element to Young Adult is "autonomous thought," which oftentimes became the result of the culmination or climax of the Young Adult novel. But this did not remain the case as more and more postmodern novels challenged the boundaries. As an unidentified editor of Young Adult books mentions in an article in *Publishers Weekly,* "As more and more edgy fiction is being published, the books are dealing with issues that hadn't been dealt with before: oral sex, male rape, incest. There seem to be no boundaries any more" (Milliot et al. 2003, 39). Francesca Lia Block's Weetzie Bat series serves as a good example of this challenge of boundaries. As *Contemporary Authors* notes,

With the publication of *Weetzie Bat* [1989], she set the agenda for a new direction in young adult novels for the 1990s: stories of the Los Angeles subculture replete with sex, drugs, and rock 'n' roll—stories for adults and young adults alike. With a cast of characters ranging from Weetzie Bat, a punk princess in pink, to her lover, My Secret Agent Lover Man, and her best friend Dirk and his boyfriend, to their common offspring, Witch Baby and Cherokee, Block's novels create postmodernist fairy tales where love and art are the only cures in a world devoid of adult direction. ("Francesca Lia Block" 2005)

AWARDS FOR YOUNG ADULT LITERATURE

By the turn of the twentieth century, many different awards had been created to honor out-standing young adult literature, many of which are sponsored by the American Library Association. Among these awards is the Margaret A. Edwards Award, which is sponsored by the ALA's Young Adult Library Services Association and *School Library Journal,* which recognizes an author for his or her lifetime contribution to the field of popular young adult literature. Since 1988, the following authors (in chronological order) have received this award: S.E. Hinton, Richard Peck, Robert Cormier, Lois Duncan, M.E. Kerr, Walter Dean Myers, Cynthia Voigt, Judy Blume, Gary Paulsen, Madeline L'Engle, Anne McCaffrey, Chris Crutcher, Robert Lipsyte, Paul Zindel, Nancy Garden, Ursula K. Le Guin, Francesca Lia Block, Jacqueline Woodson, Lois Lowry, and Orson Scott Card ("Margaret A. Edwards Award" 2008).

The Michael L. Printz Award, annually given by the Young Adult Library Services Association in honor of a high school librarian, honors the best book of the year for young people. Recent winners have included the following:

2007	*American Born Chinese,* by Gene Luen Yang. First Second.
2006	*Looking for Alaska,* by John Green. Dutton.
2005	*how i live now,* by Meg Rosoff. Random House Children's Books.
2004	*The First Part Last,* by Angela Johnson. Simon & Schuster.
2003	*Postcards from No Man's Land,* by Aidan Chambers. Dutton/Penguin Putnam
2002	*A Step from Heaven,* by An Na. Front Street.
2001	*Kit's Wilderness,* by David Almond. Delacorte Press.
2000	*Monster,* by Walter Dean Myers. Harper Collins.

There are other awards given for young adult literature, including the National Book Awards. The 2008 award went to Sherman Alexie for *The Absolutely True Diary of a Part-Time Indian* (Little, Brown Readers, 2007). Previous winners have included, in 2007, *The Astonishing Life of Octavian Nothing, Traitor to the Nation, Vol. 1: The Pox Party* by M.T. Anderson (Candlewick, 2006) and, in 2005, *The Penderwicks: A Summer Tale of Four Sisters, Two Rabbits, and a Very Interesting Boy* by Jeanne Birdsall (Knopf Books for Young Readers, 2005).

Source: American Library Association, http://www.ala.org/ala/yalsa/booklistsawards, and The National Book Foundation, http://www.nationalbook.org

Trends and Themes. As mentioned previously, one of the growing trends in the Young Adult literature genre is the gritty realism allowing taboo topics to be primary foci of many recently published novels by high-profile authors. Yampbell does a great job of providing examples of controversial topics and instances where these topics can be found: for example, rape in Cynthia Voigt's *When She Hollers* (1994) and Laurie Halse Anderson's *Speak* (1999); abusive relationships in *Dreamland* (2000) by Sarah Dressen and *Breathing Underwater* (2001) by Alex Finn; self-disfigurement in Shelley Stoehr's *Crosses* (1991) and Alice Hoffman's *Green Angel* (2003); and teen fatherhood in Maragard Bechard's *Hanging on to Max* (2002) and Angela Johnson's *The First Part Last* (2003). But probably the book with the most controversial topics on Yampbell's list is Linda Glovach's *Beauty Queen* (1998), in which 19-year-old Samantha Strasbourg becomes a topless dancer and heroin addict (Yampbell 2005, 351).

As Judith Franzak and Elizabeth Noll remark, the ever-present violence that we see and hear on the news, in films, and on the Internet desensitizes us to a certain degree. Franzak and Noll report that the youth of today have "concerns [that] range from tomorrow's quiz to the kind of world that will be available to them in adulthood. The violence that infuses their world is eloquently captured in the genre of contemporary realism in young adult literature"; surprisingly, they note that "little critical attention has been paid to the role of violence in young adult literature" (2006, 662). They go on to say that "the study of textual representations of violence is an important and underdeveloped aspect of literary analysis" (663). Their article applies different theoretical perspectives to contemporary, realistic Young Adult literature that contains notable violence: *True Believer* (2001) by Virginia Euwer Wolff, *When Dad Killed Mom* (2001) by Julius Lester, *Monster* (1999) by Walter Dean Myers, *Big Mouth & Ugly Girl* (2002) by Joyce Carol Oates, *Speak* (1999) by Laurie Halse Anderson, and *Who Will Tell My Brother?* (2002) by Marlene Carvell.

Furthermore, it is not just the increasing acceptance of taboo topics that characterizes change in young adult literature. Contemporary technology (e.g., hypertext, Internet, Web sites) has contributed to how Young Adult literature is structured and conveyed to the twenty-first-century Young Adult reader. Jacqueline Glasgow describes this latest trend as reflecting what Eliza Dresang mentions in her book *Radical Change: Books for Youth in a Digital Age* (1999). The first phase of Dresang's Radical Theory involves changing the form or format; in describing this phase, Glasgow notes "the following characteristics: graphics in new forms and formats, words and pictures reaching new levels of synergy, nonlinear organization and format, [and] multiple layers of meaning" (2002, 43). Glasgow states, "As I examine young adult literature that reflects radical change, I find a departure from the traditional linear, sequential novels. These books are many-voiced, rhetorically diverse, and composed of many genres and perspectives within a single book" (42). As an example, Dresang discusses Avi's *Nothing but the Truth* (1991), which, according to Glasgow, "reveals how Avi and other young adult authors have moved away from linear systems to a digital age where 'bits' of information are nonsequential and rearrangeable, as exemplified by surfing the Internet" (42). Glasgow provides several other examples of nonlinear Young Adult texts, such as the graphic novel *Maus: A Survivor's Tale* (1986), Louis Sachar's *Holes* (1998), and Karen Hesse's *Out of the Dust* (1997).

Dresang's next type of change comes with the change in perspective. As Glasgow puts it, "Instantly available on the World Wide Web are the multiplicity of points of view on almost any topic. Young people can weave together an understanding of current events, people, and places by pointing and clicking on the topic" (Glasgow 2002, 44). All of this accessibility supports Dresang's ideas of a change in perspective to allow a new voice to be heard: the young adult's. Glasgow gives the example of Steven Chbosky's *The Perks of Being a Wallflower* (1999) to demonstrate the first-person narration technique used more in contemporary Young Adult literature.

Finally, Dresang's third type of change connects with what has already been mentioned by VanderStaay, dealing with changing boundaries: "subjects previously forbidden, settings previously overlooked, characters portrayed in new, complex ways, new types of communities, [and] unresolved endings" (Dresang 1999, 173). Reinforcing what Yampbell and Milliot have said, Glasgow reports,

> Radical change provides an opportunity for authors to push the boundaries as they explore actions, emotions, and life situations for youth. In doing so, the boundaries are

changing in dealing with subjects such as crime, personal abuse, and racial violence. In young adult literature, violence has become more central, bold, and graphic. While in the past incest may have been hinted at or threatened, in radical change literature the incest and abuse occur and must be dealt with by the protagonist. Authors like M.E. Kerr, Laurie Halse Anderson, Francesca Lia Block, Chris Crutcher, Cynthia Voigt, and Michael Cadnum have extended the scope of their characters' experience to explore prostitution, violence, suicide, incest, and rape. (2002, 49)

Context and Issues. In light of the growing acceptance and more common portrayal of homosexuality in American popular culture (e.g., TV shows *Queer as Folk,* 2000–2005; *The L Word,* 2004–?; *Will & Grace,* 1998–2006; and *Queer Eye for the Straight Guy,* 2003–? and Ellen DeGeneres's meteoric return to stardom in Disney's *Finding Nemo,* 2003, and her subsequent talk show, after outing herself on her TV sitcom *Ellen,* 1994–1998, and being ousted from popularity for a while), it is no surprise that sexual orientation is also a key issue addressed in Young Adult literature. Patti Capel Swartz says, "While the past twenty years have shown gains in including African American, Mexican, Latina/o, Chicana/o, Asian American, and Native American experience in curricula, the same is certainly not true for literature that includes experiences of [lesbian, gay, bisexual, transgendered, or intersexed] persons" (2003, 11). And while sexual orientation as an issue has only crept slowly into mainstream curricula, Swartz does provide examples of a few books that positively portray the issue of sexual orientation:

Books suitable for older children include Marion Dane Bauer's *Am I Blue? Coming Out of the Silence,* several of Chris Crutcher's sports/adventure novels, James Haskins's biography of Bayard Rustin, Gigi Kaeser's *Love Makes a Family,* Jacqueline Woodson's *From the Notebooks of Melanin Sun* and *The House You Pass on the Way,* both of which take on stereotypical constructions of race, gender, and sexuality. Kevin Jennings' *Becoming Visible: A Reader in Gay and Lesbian History for High School* is appropriate for middle school as well as high school children. (2003, 14–15)

Thomas W. Bean and Karen Moni point out that "adolescent readers view characters in young adult novels as living and wrestling with real problems close to their own life experiences as teens" (2003, 638). They go on to remark that one of the biggest problems adolescents face concerns identity and that "more recent postmodern conceptions of identity recognize its complex and multifaceted character" (639). This discussion of multifaceted identity segues nicely into this section's discussion of contextualizing Young Adult literature into contemporary American culture. As Pamela S. Carroll and L. Penny Rosenblum note, there still is a dearth of Young Adult novels portraying disabilities, specifically visual impairment:

For many adolescents with vision problems in the general education classroom, there is little opportunity to meet others who, like themselves, have difficulty seeing. Thus it is not uncommon to find an adolescent with a visual impairment who finds he has no one in his life who really understands the challenges he experiences. . . .

We were unable to find any recent empirical studies that examine the reading of young adult literature by students with visual impairments. We were also unable to locate studies that give specific emphasis to the portrayal of characters in Young Adult literature who have vision problems. This lack most likely stems, in large part, from the miniscule number of recent young adult books available, in which there is a main character with a visual impairment. (2000, 622, 623)

Three of the most recent Young Adult books that do discuss visual impairment as a primary element are Edward Bloor's *Tangerine* (1997), Sally Hobart Alexander's *On My Own: The Journey Continues* (1997), and Lynn E. McElfresh's *Can You Feel the Thunder?* (1999). Using A.B. Heim's theories, Carroll and Rosenblum provide five ways in which novels ought to portray characters with disabilities: (1) "accurate information must be used within the book, including the use of current terminology to describe the disability"; (2) "avoid stereotypes of the disabled; it should provide insight into the life of the person with disabilities"; (3) "like any other literary work[,] a book in which the character is disabled should be well written"; (4) "the book should confront the disability in a realistic manner, not overemphasizing the disability but providing evidence that the character faces challenges because of it"; (5) "avoid simply using a character who is disabled to promote the growth of a nondisabled character in the book" (2000, 624–26).

"What must it be like for readers to find only images representing those unlike them?" (Landt 2006, 694) is a question posed by Susan M. Landt that aptly identifies another issue that has been addressed by Young Adult literature in recent decades: multiculturalism. Landt says, "Children today have more options available. Increasingly, children's and young adult literature include selections by and about people of marginalized . . . parallel cultures" (694), and her article demonstrates the strides that Young Adult literature has taken to include voices from many different cultures, as is visible from the existence of several Young Adult literature awards sponsored by various associations to highlight different cultures: the Coretta Scott King Award (African American), the Pura Belpré Award (Latino/a), the Tomás Rivera Award (Mexican American), the Sydney Taylor Award (Jewish), and the Mildred L. Batchelder Award (foreign language translation). But an issue involving multiculturalism still remains at the front of controversy with contemporary scholars: insiders versus outsiders. Essentially, the question arises whether only authors from a specific culture are allowed to write about that culture. Landt answers this question by saying, "As a general rule, a book written by an author with an emic—insider—perspective is likely to be culturally authentic; a book written from an etic—outsider—perspective may or may not be culturally authentic" (696).

One issue that still remains to be completely addressed is the ambiguous nature of young adult literature itself. This refers to the awkwardness of adolescence as an in-between phase, just as young adult literature has become difficult to market. As Yampbell notes, "the Young Adult genre and market has been problematic since its inception. Defining and promoting the genre was, and continues to be, plagued by four major problems: audience, 'acceptable' subject matter, location in stores, and marketing and publicity" (2005, 350). Because of America's reliance on the Internet and technology to participate in popular American culture (e.g., voting electronically for TV's *American Idol*), publishers have found a way to combine commercialism with technology. For example, at www.teenreads.com, young adults can enter a contest regarding the book *Cathy's Book: If Found Call 650-266-8233* (2006), written by Sean Stewart and Jordan Weisman:

After the incredible success of our CATHY'S BOOK Comments and Clues Contest and the RAZR Giveaway, we just couldn't resist running ANOTHER contest! Now we're giving you the chance to win a 4GB 2nd Generation iPod Nano in the color of your choice (pink, silver, green, or blue). To enter, simply watch this ultra-cool CATHY'S BOOK trailer and answer this question—What is the name of the police officer who

Cathy is speaking to? Send your answer to the question, along with your name and mailing address to CathysBook@Teenreads.com. (Feature and Contest 2006)

This contest obviously instills a motivation beyond a simple love for reading by tantalizing the teenage (girl) with amazing technology prizes such as an iPod.

Reception. Young Adult literature is also not immune to scandal, as the 2006 Kaavya Viswanathan plagiarism case illustrates. In April 2006, Viswanathan's book *How Opal Mehta Got Kissed, Got Wild and Got a Life* was published. This book chronicles the misadventures of an Indian American teenager who has been rejected from Harvard for not being an "all American" representative. Shortly after the book was published, the *Harvard Crimson* reported that passages from *Mehta* seemed to surprisingly resemble two of Megan McCafferty's novels, *Sloppy Firsts* (2001) and *Second Helpings* (2003). At first, Viswanathan's publishers intended to republish the book in an edition without the "seeming similarities" because Viswanathan insists the passages were not plagiarism but simply "internalized" portions she somehow remembered from reading McCafferty's books. According to the *Harvard Crimson,* however, further allegations that Viswanathan also plagiarized portions of books by Salman Rushdie, Sophie Kinsella, and Meg Cabot supported Viswanathan's book publisher's decision to cancel any intended revised edition as well as the second book of her contract ("Opal Mehta" 2006).

Harold Foster's article in the *ALAN Review* discusses the relationship between the young adult novel and film. He lists many films that are literary adaptations and that were made approximately two decades ago or longer: *Huckleberry Finn, Lord of the Flies, A Separate Peace* (first in 1972 and recently remade in 2004), *From the Mixed-Up Files of Mrs. Basil E. Frankweiler* (which was made into two films, one in 1973 with Ingrid Bergman, and one in 1995 with Lauren Bacall), *I Am the Cheese, The Chocolate War, Tex, The Outsiders,* and *Rumble Fish.* The first line of Foster's article attests to the great reception of teen film adaptation: "Films are a powerful influence on most of our students. As much as teachers may not wish to face this fact, films compete with books as the primary mode of stories" (1994, 14). In other words, no other genre or form of entertainment represents the pulse of popular culture in America like the motion pictures of Hollywood. Though not expressly American-made or acted, the Harry Potter film series based on J.K. Rowling's books has been, and remains, a huge force to be reckoned with. The first four films alone rank among the top 40 grossing films of all time in the United States. With several more films in the franchise, Harry Potter will remain in American pop culture easily until the end of this decade and beyond.

Obviously, Young Adult texts are not the only texts to be turned into films, and like other genres of adult literature that have been adapted for the big screen or television, these Young Adult novels have for the most part suffered the same fate of being hit or miss. One example of a film adapted from a teen book that did not do well is *Hoot.* While Carl Hiassen's *Hoot* (2002) was a critically acclaimed book and a Newbery Honor winner for 2003 and was described by Edward T. Sullivan in *Book Links* as a story "full of offbeat humor and genuinely touching scenes of children enjoying the wildness of nature," (2004, 61), the film, released in 2006, unfortunately did not fare well at the box office. Averaging approximately a "C" rating and earning only 8 million in the box office (*Hoot* Overview, n.d.), *Hoot* was reviewed by *Chicago Tribune* reporter Michael Phillips, who said, "Kids are better off with a book than a middling movie adaptation of a book" (2006).

Examples of other "misses" in Young Adult film literature are Gail Carson Levine's *Ella Enchanted* (1997), turned into a film of the same name in 2004. Hoping to cash in on the popularity of actor Anne Hathaway's performance in another Young Adult literary adapted film, Miramax released a poor rendition of Levine's Newbery Honor winner. The film cost $35 million to make but only managed to make approximately $22 million at the box office (*Ella Enchanted* Overview, n.d.). *The Westing Game* (1978), by Ellen Gaskin, won the Newbery Medal in 1979, but the straight-to-DVD movie titled *The Westing Game* and sometimes *Get a Clue* (1997), was of very little literary quality. *Eragon* (2003), the highly successful beginning of a three-part epic, has attracted attention because of its being the brainchild best seller of a homeschooled teen prodigy from Montana. Written in a fantasy style reminiscent of Tolkien's *Lord of the Rings, Eragon* quickly turned into a movie, released in December 2006. Reviews were mixed, and to date, the domestic revenue of the first film of the trilogy has not matched its $100 million budget (*Eragon* Overview, n.d.).

Two other teen literary film "misses" are not reflected by a dismal box office return but rather by their performing a loose adaptation of a well-known **fantasy** series: Ursula K. Le Guin's Earthsea books. The first example comes from *A Wizard of Earthsea* (1968) and *The Tombs of Atuan* (1972), the first two books of an original trilogy, which has been expanded with other books in the Earthsea series by Le Guin in recent years. In 2004 the Sci-Fi television network produced *Earthsea,* which combines *Earthsea* and *Atuan* into one three-hour adaptation. Also in 2006, Le Guin's third book in the series, *The Farthest Shore* (1974), was adapted by the Japanese anime Studio Ghibli and directed by Gorō Miyazaki, son of the famous Hayao Miyazaki, who directed well-known anime films such as *Princess Mononoke* (1997), *Spirited Away* (2001), and *Howl's Moving Castle* (2004). The film was entitled *Tales from Earthsea* and was the number one movie at the Japanese box office when it was released in July.

However, both of these adaptations were seriously dismissed by Le Guin. On her Web site, regarding the Sci-Fi movie and its director's claims of remaining true to the spirit of the book, she says,

> I wonder if the people who made the film of *The Lord of the Rings* had ended it with Frodo putting on the Ring and ruling happily ever after, and then claimed that that was what Tolkien "intended . . ." would people think they'd been "very, very honest to the books"? (Le Guin 2004)

Her comments regarding Miyazaki were not much better:

Both the American and the Japanese film-makers treated these books as mines for names and a few concepts, taking bits and pieces out of context, and replacing the story/ies with an entirely different plot, lacking in coherence and consistency. I wonder at the disrespect shown not only to the books but to their readers.

I think the film's "messages" seem a bit heavy[-]handed because, although often quoted quite closely from the books, the statements about life and death, the balance, etc., don't follow from character and action as they do in the books. However well meant, they aren't implicit in the story and the characters. They have not been "earned." So they come out as preachy. There are some sententious bits in the first three *Earthsea* books, but I don't think they stand out quite this baldly. (Le Guin 2006)

Of course, there have been some moderate-to-huge successes at the American box office as well. *The Sisterhood of the Traveling Pants,* written by Ann Brashares in 2001, turned into a moderately successful motion picture in 2005, grossing over $41 million worldwide (*Sisterhood* Overview, n.d.). Another well-known story, recognized by critics and popular audiences alike, is Louis Sachar's *Holes,* which won the Newbery Medal in 1999. The 2003 film stars well-known Disney Channel actor Shia LeBeouf in the highly successful adaptation, which grossed over $70 million worldwide (*Holes* Overview, n.d.). With a production budget of $26 million and a worldwide gross of over $165 million, the film adaptation of *The Princess Diaries* (2001) is one of the biggest success stories of the teen lit film genre. Based on the 2000 novel by Meg Cabot, this film stars Julie Andrews and newcomer Anne Hathaway in a role that made her famous in American pop culture (*Princess Diaries* Overview, n.d.). Furthermore, *Princess Diaries 2: Royal Engagement* (2004), grossed more than $134 million worldwide, making it a hit as well (*Princess Diaries 2* Overview, n.d.). Competing with *The Princess Diaries* as one of the most successful teen lit film adaptations is *Lemony Snicket's A Series of Unfortunate Events* (2004). Though it did not make a profit until accruing over $208 million worldwide, it matches the popularity of *Princess* by showcasing Hollywood A-listers Jim Carrey, Meryl Streep, and Jude Law, in addition to winning an Academy Award for Best Makeup (*Lemony Snicket* Overview, n.d.). Starring Anna Sophia Robb, *Bridge to Terabithia* (2007) enjoyed more than $120 million in box-office receipts. Robb is no stranger to literary adaptations, having already starred in the adaptation of Kate DiCamillo's Newbery Honor recipient *Because of Winn Dixie* (2000) in 2005 and the latest adaptation of Dahl's *Charlie and the Chocolate Factory* in 2005.

Finally, one book that has not yet been adapted to film, but that likely could be in the next decade, is Walter Dean Myers's *Monster.* As Dean Schneider notes in *Book Links,* "This popular, ground-breaking novel is perfect for reader's theatre for older students, with its mature themes, innovative format, and large cast of characters in a courtroom drama" (2005, 57). No information about turning *Monster* into a motion picture has been released, but many readers would likely love to see that happen.

Selected Authors. Following are examples of authors who already were well established prior to 2000 and those who have extended strong publishing beyond the year 2000, as well as authors active just since the year 2000. While there are many other appropriate names to add to this list, there is not space here to discuss them all. One way to learn more about other notable names in young adult literature is to look at recipients of awards for young adult authors, such as those who have won the Margaret A. Edwards medal (see sidebar).

Julia Alvarez (1950–). Alvarez is well-known for several works, including *How the García Girls Lost Their Accents* (1991) and *In the Time of Butterflies* (1994). She has consistently produced books for all ages, including young adults, well into the twenty-first century. *Before We Were Free* (2002) was well-received by critics. Lauren Adams says that Alvarez's text is "a realistic and compelling account of a girl growing up too quickly while coming to terms with the cost of freedom" (2002, 565). For her contribution to the body of Latina literature, she received the Pura Belpré Award in 2004.

Laurie Halse Anderson (1961–). When Anderson's name is mentioned, many teens and Young Adult lit scholars immediately think of *Speak* (1999), Anderson's first and probably best-known novel. Anderson's portrayal of the protagonist's—Melinda's—

struggle to find peace after being raped and then socially ostracized from high school was praised by critics, and *Speak* was a National Book Award finalist. Dina Sherman of *School Library Journal* calls *Speak* "a compelling book, with sharp, crisp writing that draws the readers in, engulfing them in the story" (1999, 144). Anderson followed up with a historical novel about a 14-year-old girl during the time of the yellow fever epidemic in *Fever 1793* (2000). Kathleen Isaacs said, "Readers will be drawn in by the characters and will emerge with a sharp and graphic picture of another world" (2000, 177). *Catalyst* (2002), Anderson's next book, concerns 18-year-old Kate Malone, who discovers her desire to attend MIT is rejected, and in *Prom* (2005), 18-year-old Ashley finds interesting and amusing ways to help support her high school prom with fundraising.

Angela Johnson (1961–). Johnson began her publishing career in the early 1990s, writing for children of all ages. She has continued to write for young adults in the twenty-first century. *Running Back to Ludie* (2002), concerns a teen girl who confronts the mother who abandoned her, and Joanna Rudge Long comments that "Johnson's exploration of the process [of abandonment and resolution] is subtle and beautifully wrought" (2001, 766). Johnson's next book, *Looking for Red,* deals with guilt and death, as Red's sister Mike discovers the part she played in his death. Jean Gaffney says, "The strength of this story is the accurate portrayal of the surreal nature of grief laden with guilt" (2002, 120). Arguably, Johnson's best-known novel is *The First Part Last* (2003). What makes Johnson's story of teen parenthood unique is that this book's story is told from the teen father's perspective—Bobby from Johnson's earlier book *Heaven* (1998). It is not until the end of the book that we discover the reason for Nia's—the baby's mother's—absence: she's in a coma caused by eclampsia. This book won the Coretta Scott King Award and the Michael L. Printz Medal in 2004. Furthermore, it should be noted that Johnson was the recipient of the prestigious MacArthur Foundation "genius grant" in 2003.

Pam Muñoz Ryan (1951–). Winner of the 2004 Pura Belpré Award for her novel *Esperanza Rising* (2002) and the 2006 Pura Belpré Honor Award for her novel *Becoming Naomi León* (2004), Ryan has established herself as a preeminent Latina author for the twenty-first century. *Esperanza,* her best-known novel, describes the story of a young girl who experiences dramatic changes before her 13th birthday, fleeing from Mexico to the United States during the Great Depression and experiencing a demotion to a lower socioeconomic class. Francisca Goldsmith says that "this well-written novel belongs in all collections" (2000, 171).

Kate DiCamillo (1964–). Though she is better known for Newbery Honor recipient *Because of Winn-Dixie* (2000; also a popular film in 2005) and Newbery Medal winner *The Tale of Despereaux* (2004), DiCamillo also achieved success with her young adult novel *The Tiger Rising* (2001). A finalist for the National Book Award, *Tiger* takes place in a setting similar to *Winn-Dixie,* but as *Publishers Weekly* notes, "DiCamillo demonstrates her versatility by treating themes similar to those of her first novel with a completely different approach" (Review for *The Tiger Rising* 2001, 77). DiCamillo does this by revealing the protagonist Rob's feeling of constriction and grief through the metaphorical image of a tiger in a cage that Rob finds in the woods behind the motel where he lives.

Linda Sue Park (1960–). Linda Sue Park has become nationally known because of her Newbery Medal–winning book *A Single Shard* (2001). This story, which is set in twelfth-century Korea, follows the story of an orphan's apprenticeship. Her next book, *When My Name Was Keoko* (2002), is a stunning book that skillfully alternates narration between a brother and sister during the Japanese occupation of Korea in World War II. Following this novel, Park received the Chicago Tribune Prize for Young Adult Fiction for her novel *Project Mulberry* (2005). As *Publishers Weekly* states, "Besides celebrating intergenerational and interracial friendships, and presenting interesting details about the silkworm life cycle, the book introduces many issues relevant to budding adolescents" (Review for *Project Mulberry* 2005).

Francesca Lia Block (1962–). Known for her creative young adult novels, especially the Weetzie Bat series, Block received the Margaret A. Edwards Award in 2005 for her lifetime contribution to young adult literature. Collections of her Weetzie Bat books were reissued in 2004, *Beautiful Boys* (including *Missing Angel Juan* and *Baby Be-Bop*) and *Goat Girls* (including *Witch Baby* and *Cherokee Bat and the Goat Guys*). Since 2000, Block has consistently contributed literature that exemplifies magical realism and postmodern fairy tales. *Echo* (2001) is another story set in a Los Angeles neighborhood, and the protagonist seeks a place to belong among the bizarre inhabitants of an extraordinarily magic region. *Wasteland* (2003) received more mixed reviews because of its taboo subject: an incestuous relationship between Marina and her (unbeknownst to them) adopted brother Lex, who eventually commits suicide. As Catherine Ensley notes,

> While Block's prose is as poetic and lush as always, her narrative shifts may confuse less sophisticated readers. It's not immediately clear that the italicized portions are from Lex's journal, and chapters switch abruptly from Marina's voice to third person. Also, while parental flakes aren't unusual in Block's fiction, readers may have a difficult time buying into the mother's reason for not telling her children about the adoption. (2003, 158)

Ruby (2006) follows the story of a young woman who comes to Los Angeles from the Midwest and then seeks love in England. Though this book does not exhibit the punk style of Block's previous works, teens will definitely love the magical realism and experimental narration.

Walter Dean Myers (1937–). Myers received the Margaret A. Edwards Award in 1994 for his lifetime contribution to Young Adult literature. A seasoned veteran of writing, Myers's successful, popular book *Monster* (1999) marks a great segue into the turn-of-the-century look at Young Adult literature for the present century. Steve Harmon is Myers' 16-year-old protagonist who is on trial for murder. Harmon writes an account of his reactions to the court proceedings in an inventive and captivating way—through writing it as though it were a screenplay for his own personal movie. Attesting to the influential power of this book, Patty Campbell notes,

> Every decade or so a book comes along that both encapsulates a genre and sends it on a new course. In young adult literature, *Catcher in the Rye* is such a milestone book, as are *The Outsiders* and *The Chocolate War*. And now Walter Dean Myers's stunning new novel, *Monster,* joins these landmark books. Looking backward, *Monster* is the peak achievement of a career that has paralleled the growth of the genre; looking forward, it is a perfect example of the revolutionary new literary direction Eliza Dresang describes in her recent critical study, *Radical Change: Books for Youth in a Digital Age*. (1999, 769)

Monster received the inaugural Michael L. Printz Award and a Coretta Scott King Honor.

Myers's next work, *145th Street: Short Stories* (2000), is a collection of vignettes told from young adult and adult perspectives about the Harlem community in good and bad times. Myers also has a history of producing young adult nonfiction. He wrote a biography of Malcolm X in *Malcom X: A Fire Burning Brightly* (2000), followed up by *The Journal of Biddy Owens, the Negro Leagues* (2001). Myers's amazing writing career has not slowed down since the beginning of the twenty-first century. He has published seven young adult fiction novels since *Biddy Owens: Patrol* (2001), *Handbook for Boys* (2002), *Three Swords for Granada* (2002), *The Dream Bearer* (2003), *Shooter* (2004), *Autobiography of My Dead Brother* (2005), and *Street Love* (2006). In addition, he has been steadily adding more young adult nonfiction to his list of publications as well: *Bad Boy: A Memoir* (2001), *The Greatest: Muhammad Ali* (2001), *A Time to Love: Tales from the Old Testament* (2002), *I've Seen the Promised Land: The Life of Dr. Martin Luther King, Jr.* (2003), *Antarctica: Journeys to the South Pole* (2004), *USS Constellation* (2004), *The Harlem Hellfighters: When Pride Met Courage* (with William Miles, 2006), and *Jazz* (2006). Furthermore, Myers has been writing poetry in such collections as *Blues Journey* (2001), *Voices from Harlem* (2004), and *Here in Harlem: Poems in Many Voices* (2004).

Bibliography

Adams, Lauren. Review of *Before We Were Free*. *Horn Book Magazine* (Sept.—Oct. 2002): 563–565.

Alger, Horatio. *Ragged Dick*. New York: Penguin, 1990. Originally published 1868.

Anderson, Laurie Halse. *Speak*. New York: Farrar Straus Giroux, 1999.

Bean, Thomas W., and Karen Moni. "Developing Students' Critical Literacy: Exploring Identity Construction in Young Adult Fiction." *Journal of Adolescent and Adult Literacy* 46.8 (2003): 638–648.

Bechard, Maragard. *Hanging on to Max*. Brookfield, CT: Roaring Book, 2002.

Blume, Judy. *Are You There God? It's Me, Margaret*. Englewood Cliffs, NJ: Bradbury, 1970.

———. *Forever*. Scarsdale, NY: Bradbury, 1975.

Campbell, Patty. "The Sand in the Oyster Radical Monster." *Horn Book Magazine* (Nov. 1999): 769.

Carroll, Pamela S., and L. Penny Rosenblum. "Through Their Eyes: Are Characters with Visual Impairment Portrayed Realistically in Young Adult Literature?" *Journal of Adolescent and Adult Literacy* 43.7 (2000): 620–630.

Carvell, Marlene. *Who Will Tell My Brother?* New York: Hyperion Books for Children, 2002.

Chbosky, Steven. *The Perks of Being a Wallflower*. New York: Pocket Books, 1999.

Cleary, Beverly. *Fifteen*. New York: Morrow, 1956.

Dresang, Eliza T. *Radical Change: Books for Youth in a Digital Age*. New York: H.W. Wilson, 1999.

Dressen, Sarah. *Dreamland*. New York: Viking, 2000.

Ella Enchanted Overview. *Box Office Mojo*. Retrieved Jan. 26, 2007, from http://www.boxofficemojo.com/movies/?id=ellaenchanted.htm

Ensley, Catherine. Review of *Wasteland*. *School Library Journal* 49.10 (2003): 158.

Eragon Overview. *Box Office Mojo*. Retrieved Jan. 24, 2007, from http://www.boxofficemojo.com/movies/?id=eragon.htm

Feature and Contest. *Teenreads.com*. Jan. 23, 2007. Retrieved Jan. 24, 2007, from http://www.teenreads.com

Finn, Alex. *Breathing Underwater*. New York: HarperCollins, 2001.

Foster, Harold M. "Film and the Young Adult Novel." *The ALAN Review* 21.3 (1994): 14–17.

"Francesca Lia Block." *Contemporary Authors Online.* Sept. 28, 2005. Retrieved Jan. 19, 2007, from http://www.gale.com/servlet/ItemDetailServlet?region=9&imprint=000& titleCode=GAL2&cf=n&type=4&id=110195

Franzak, Judith, and Elizabeth Noll. "Monstrous Acts: Problematizing Violence in Young Adult Literature." *Journal of Adolescent and Adult Literacy* 49.8 (2006): 662–672.

Gaffney, Jean. Review of *Looking for Red. School Library Journal* (July 2002): 120.

Garden, Nancy. *Annie on My Mind.* New York: Farrar, Straus, Giroux, 1982.

Glasgow, Jaqueline. "Radical Change in Young Adult Literature Informs the Multigenre Paper." *English Journal* 92.2 (2002): 41–51.

Glovach, Linda. *Beauty Queen.* New York: HarperCollins, 1998.

Goldsmith, Francesca. Review of *Esperanza Rising. School Library Journal* (October 2000): 171.

Heim, A.B. "Beyond the Stereotypes: Characters with Mental Disabilities in Children's Books." *School Library Journal* 40.9 (1994): 139–142.

Hesse, Karen. *Out of the Dust.* New York: Scholastic, 1997.

Hinton, S.E. *The Outsiders.* New York: Viking, 1967.

Hoffman, Alice. *Green Angel.* New York: Scholastic, 2003.

Hoot Overview. *Yahoo! Movies.* Retrieved Jan. 25, 2007, from http://movies.yahoo.com/ movie/1808718642/info

Holes Overview. *Box Office Mojo.* Retrieved Jan. 24, 2007, from http://www.boxofficemojo. com/movies/?id=holes.htm

Isaacs, Kathleen. Review of *Fever 1792. School Library Journal* (Aug. 2000): 177.

"J.D. Salinger." *Contemporary Authors Online.* Sept. 28, 2005. Retrieved Jan. 20, 2007, from http://www.gale.com/servlet/ItemDetailServlet?region=9&imprint=000&titleCode=GA L2&cf=n&type=4&id=110195

Janeway, James. *A Token for Children: Being an Exact Account of the Conversion, Holy and Exemplary Lives, and Joyful Deaths, of Several Young Children.* New York: Garland, 1977. Originally published 1676.

Johnson, Angela. *The First Part Last.* New York: Simon and Schuster, 2003.

Landt, Susan M. "Multicultural Literature and Young Adolescents: A Kaleidoscope of Opportunity." *Journal of Adolescent & Adult Literacy* 49.8 (2006): 690–697.

Latrobe, Kathy, and Trisha Hutcherson. "An Introduction to Ten Outstanding Young-Adult Authors in the United States." *World Literature Today* 76.3–4 (2002): 68–75.

Le Guin, Ursula K. "Earthsea Miniseries: A Reply to Some Statements Made by the Film-Makers of the Earthsea Miniseries Before It Was Shown." Nov. 13, 2004. Retrieved Jan. 23, 2007, from http://www.ursulakleguin.com/Earthsea.html

———. "Gedo Senki, A First Response." Aug. 19, 2006. Retrieved Jan. 23, 2007, from http://www.ursulakleguin.com/GedoSenkiResponse.html

Lemony Snicket's A Series of Unfortunate Events Overview. *Box Office Mojo.* Retrieved Jan. 23, 2007, from http://www.boxofficemojo.com/movies/?id=lemonysnicket.htm

Lester, Julius. *When Dad Killed Mom.* San Diego: Silver Whistle, 2001.

Long, Joanna Rudge. Review of *Running Back to Ludie. Horn Book Magazine* (Sept.–Oct. 2001): 766.

Margaret A. Edwards Award. *Young Adult Library Services Association.* Retrieved Jan. 14, 2008, from http://www.ala.org/ala/yalsa/booklistsawards/margaretaedwards/ margaretedwards.htm

Milliot, Jim, John Mutter, John F. Baker, Diane Roback, and Edward Nawotka. "New Answers to Old Questions." *Publishers Weekly* 26 May 2003: 35–39.

Myers, Walter Dean. *Monster.* New York: HarperCollins, 1999.

Oates, Joyce Carol. *Big Mouth & Ugly Girl.* New York: HarperTempest, 2002.

"'Opal Mehta' Gone for Good; Contract Cancelled." *Harvard Crimson* 2 May 2006. Retrieved Jan. 25, 2007, http://www.thecrimson.com/article.aspx?ref=513231

Phillips, Michael. "Movie Review: *Hoot*." May 2006. Retrieved Jan. 20, 2007, from http://metromix.chicagotribune.com/movies/mmx-060505-movies-review-hoot,0, 6047899.story

Princess Diaries Overview. *Box Office Mojo*. Retrieved Jan. 25, 2007, from http://www. boxofficemojo.com/movies/?id=princessdiaries.htm

Princess Diaries 2 Overview. *Box Office Mojo*. Retrieved Jan. 26, 2007, from http://www. boxofficemojo.com/movies/?id=princessdiaries2.htm

Review of *The Tiger Rising*. *Publishers Weekly* 15 Jan. 2001: 77.

Review of *Project Mulberry*. *Publishers Weekly* 14 March 2005. Retrieved Jan. 25, 2007, from http://reviews.publishersweekly.com/bd.aspx?isbn=0618477861&pub=pw

"S.E. Hinton." *Contemporary Authors Online* 7 Jan. 2005. Retrieved Jan. 21, 2007, from http://www.gale.com/servlet/ItemDetailServlet?region=9&imprint=000&titleCode=G AL2&cf=n&type=4&id=110195

Sachar, Louis. *Holes*. New York: Farrar Straus Giroux, 1998.

Salinger, J.D. *The Catcher in the Rye*. Boston: Little, Brown, 1951.

Schneider, Dean. Review of *Monster*. *Book Links* March 2005: 57.

Sherman, Dina. Review of *Speak*. *School Library Journal* Oct. 1999: 144.

Sisterhood of the Traveling Pants Overview. *Box Office Mojo*. Retrieved Jan. 23, 2007, from http://www.boxofficemojo.com/movies/?id=travelingpants.htm

Sullivan, Edward T. "Review of *Hoot*." *Book Links* Nov. 2004: 61.

Swartz, Patti Capel. "Bridging Multicultural Education: Bringing Sexual Orientation into the Children's and Young Adult Literature Classrooms." *Radical Teacher* 66 (2003): 11–16.

Taylor, Mildred. *The Land*. New York: Phyllis Fogelman, 200.

———. *Roll of Thunder, Hear My Cry*. New York: Dial, 1976.

———. *Song of the Trees*. New York: Dial, 1975.

Tuttle, Sarah. *Female Influence, or The Temperance Girl*. Boston: Massachusetts Sabbath School Society, 1834.

VanderStaay, Steven. "Young-Adult Literature: A Writer Strikes the Genre." *English Journal* 8.14 (1992): 48–52.

Voigt, Cynthia. *When She Hollers*. New York: Scholastic, 1994.

Yampbell, Cat. "Judging a Book by Its Cover: Publishing Trends in Young Adult Literature." *Lion & the Unicorn* 29.3 (2005): 348–372.

Wolff, Virginia Euwer. *True Believer*. New York: Atheneum Books for Young Readers, 2001.

Further Reading

Barry, Arlene L. "Hispanic Representation in Literature for Children and Young Adults." *Journal of Adolescent & Adult Literacy* 41.8 (1998): 630–637; Cooley, Beth. "Jerry Spinelli's *Stargirl* as Contemporary Gospel: Good News for a World of Adolescent Conformity." In *From Colonialism to Contemporary: Intertextual Transformation in World Children's and Youth Literature*. Lance Weldy, ed. Newcastle, UK: Cambridge Scholars Press, 2006, 26–34; Crabtree, Sara. "Harry the Hero? The Quest for Self-Identity, Heroism, and Transformation in the *Goblet of Fire*." In *From Colonialism to Contemporary: Intertextual Transformation in World Children's and Youth Literature*. Lance Weldy, ed. Newcastle, UK: Cambridge Scholars Press, 2006, 61–75; Gebhard, Ann O. "The Emerging Self: Young-Adult and Classic Novels of the Black Experience." *English Journal* 82.5 (1993): 50–54; Hayn, Judith, and Deborah Sherrill. "Female Protagonists in Multicultural Young Adult Literature: Sources and Strategies" *The ALAN Review* 24.1 (Fall 1996): 43–46; Johannessen, Larry R. "Young-Adult Literature and the Vietnam War." *English Journal* 82.5 (Summer 1993): 43–49; McDiffet, Danton. "Prejudice and Pride: Japanese Americans in the Young Adult Novels of Yoshiko Uchida." *English Journal* 90.3 (Jan. 2001): 60–65; Tarbox, Gwen. *The Clubwomen's Daughters: Collectivist Impulses in Progressive-Era Girl's Fiction, 1890–1940*. New

York: Garland, 2000; Vandergrift, Kay E. "A Feminist Perspective on Multicultural Children's Literature in the Middle Years of the Twentieth Century." *Library Trends* 41.3 (Winter 1993): 354–377; Vandergrift, Kay. "Journey or Destination: Female Voices in Youth Literature." In *Mosaics of Meaning*. Kay E. Vandergrift, ed. Lanham, MD: Scarecrow Press, 1996, 17–46; Vandergrift, Kay E. "Literacies of Inclusion: Feminism, Multiculturalism, and Youth." *Journal of Professional Studies* 3.1 (Fall/Winter 1995): 39–47; Weldy, Lance. "Once Upon a Time in Idaho: Transforming Cinderella through A-temporality, Awkwardness, and Adolescence in Napoleon Dynamite." In *From Colonialism to Contemporary: Intertextual Transformation in World Children's and Youth Literature*. Lance Weldy, ed. Newcastle, UK: Cambridge Scholars Press, 2006: 46–60.

LANCE WELDY

Z

ZINES

Definition. Zines are independent, underground publications of noncommercial and personal nature produced by the most accessible and affordable technology available to the publisher, usually an individual or small group. The term *zine* rhymes with *seen* and derives from *fanzine*, a term **science fiction** fans use to differentiate their amateur publications from the commercial magazines that inspired them. Currently, the term *zine* is used primarily by members of the zine community—those who read and write zines—to refer to print zines only (the zine's electronic cousin is called an *ezine*). Accordingly, this entry focuses on print zines. However, whatever the ultimate medium they are published in, zines emerge in response to a perceived void in other media's coverage of a subject, which can range widely from a subcultural level (e.g., punk rock music) to an idiosyncratic level (e.g., the zine publisher's own life). A vigorous, if at times deliberately obscure, part of popular American literature, zines are published irregularly, according to the whim of the publisher, with most zines lasting only a few issues. Usually photocopied, zines can be found occasionally in bookstores, coffee shops, infoshops, libraries, newsstands, and record stores, among other places, but the most common means of distribution is through the postal system or otherwise directly from the publisher. Though some zines can reach print runs in the thousands, most zines have much smaller circulations. Nonetheless, the cumulative total audience for the thousands of zines published in the United States has been estimated to be in the millions (Gunderloy and Goldberg Janice 1992, 1). Furthermore, each copy of a zine often seems to be passed along from reader to reader, a tradition that eventually led to the creation of zine libraries in many cities. In addition, zines, being underground publications, have always had more influence on American popular culture than their ephemeral and limited print runs would suggest. For example, many significant figures have been involved in zines, often in their youth, including rock music critic Lester Bangs (1948–1982), science fiction author Ray Bradbury (1920–), film critic Roger Ebert (1942–), and Superman creators Jerome Siegel (1914–1996) and Joseph Shuster (1914–1992)

A POLITICAL ZINE

An example of a political zine is *Judas Goat Quarterly,* published by Grant Schreiber out of his apartment in Chicago, Illinois. He writes all the articles, lays out the artwork, uses a photocopier to print it, and distributes it using the postal system and by dropping off copies himself around Chicago. Schreiber publishes his zine to express his frustration at the current direction of American government and society. The only advertisements he runs in the zine are parodies he creates of political commercials and military recruiting posters. When one orders a copy of Schreiber's zine, one usually gets a personal note from Schreiber accompanying it. The zine is a mass medium, but paradoxically, it is one that keeps the individual nature of communication paramount, not very far removed from a letter from a friend. Indeed, if the print run of a zine ever rises above a certain level, it is no longer a zine, but a cottage industry.

(indeed, Superman's first appearance was in their zine *Science Fiction* as a villain). In recent years, the zine community has produced a number of writers who then entered other areas of literature, among them Aaron Cometbus (1968–), Jim Goad (1961–), Jeff Gomez (1970–), Pagan Kennedy (1962–), Joe Meno (1974–), and the writers of the Underground Literary Alliance (ULA). Furthermore, zines sometimes change and become professional magazines such as *Alternative Press* and *Bust,* both of which started as zines but to this day still carry some of the do-it-yourself (DIY) independent spirit of zines.

Although the term *zine* is applied liberally to many publications that really are not zines, the zine has certain defining characteristics that separate it from other publications. The first defining characteristic of a zine is that it is personal in nature and self-published by an individual or small group.

The next defining characteristic of the zine is that it is noncommercial in nature. It is produced for passion, not profit. At best, the miniscule funding the typical zine receives from a combination of sales and advertising merely subsidizes the zine publisher's hobby. For example, *Xerography Debt,* a zine that reviews other zines (a metazine if one will), is published by Davida Gypsy Breier (1972–) in Baltimore, Maryland, "with no financial incentive—just a dedication to small press."

The lack of focus on (and sometimes hostility toward) money in zines results in another defining characteristic of zines in that they are always produced by the most accessible and affordable technology available to the publisher, even if the resulting production quality would be considered crude in comparison with professional publishing standards. Throughout the history of zines, this "by any means necessary" approach to publishing has included letterpress printing, mimeographing, offset printing, and—the technology most identified with zines—photocopying. Indeed, it has been argued that the growth in the number of zines between the 1970s and 1990s was the direct result of the increasing availability of photocopiers (Gunderloy and Janice 1992, 1–3). Undoubtedly, the increasing accessibility and affordability of electronic publishing helps to explain why many people decide to publish online today. Fundamentally, however, the underlying sentiment remains the same: even if the production method is less than pristine, as long as the communicative urge is served, then the results are good enough.

In fact, some zine publishers relish the fact that their publications are not up to mainstream production standards. This is part of an overall opposition to mainstream culture, which is yet another defining characteristic of zines. From the DIY ethos that inspires zine publishers to attempt to become the media in the first place, to the readers of zines who are attracted to alternative publications, to subject matter that at times delves into areas that mainstream media avoids, such as the celebration of trespassing (or, as the zine *Infiltration* has called it, "urban exploration"), to the irregular publication schedule of zines, zines are immersed in nay-saying the larger culture that surrounds them, relishing their autonomy and independence.

Strangely enough, as much as the zine community heralds its self-reliance in the face of mainstream culture, the relationship within the zine community is one of interdependence and sociability. This is because zining is fundamentally a social activity. The zine publisher may create her or his zine alone, but the rest of the zine publishing process is interactive. Most zine publishers trade their zines with one another, through the mail or in person at zine conferences. Though zines often have a nominal price attached to them (anywhere from one to five dollars), the currency accepted most often is "the usual," a form of artistic bartering present from the earliest science fiction fanzines, in which the zine publisher accepts payment in the form of another zine, a piece of mail art, or a letter of comment, to name just a few of the more common items traded—for in the zine community, there is not much separating publishers from readers. Most participants in the zine community are publishers and readers and usually just called "zinesters." This sociability has led those involved with zines to network and hold local and national zine conferences. This self-consciousness of being in the zine community helps to explain why many publications that share some characteristics with zines (e.g., a photocopied church newsletter) are not zines. Psychologically, the underlying motive behind the creation of zines is a desire by the publishers to express themselves with no censorship, in an attempt to communicate with like-minded individuals, an urge present from the earliest science fiction fanzines.

History. Precursors of zines include self-published broadsheets and pamphlets by individual printers such as Benjamin Franklin (1706–1790); literary and cultural journals and magazines such as the American transcendentalist standard-bearer *The Dial*; dissident newspapers such as those produced by abolitionists and socialists; private writer compilations produced by writers such as Lewis Carroll (1832–1898), who "followed an old Victorian custom of compiling collections of his writings in manuscript form, arranged as if they were a printed magazine, and neatly bound" (Warner 1969, 2); Amateur Press Association publications (APAs) produced by hobbyist printers; the "little magazines" of literary modernism that published the early work of Ernest Hemingway (1899–1961) and Gertrude Stein (1874–1946), among others; the artist magazines produced by avant-garde movements such as Dada, which pioneered techniques that would become common in zines, including cut and paste collage and detournement (altering a text to subvert the original meaning, such as changing the words in a cartoon); mimeographed **Beat Poetry** chapbooks; the Mail Art network in which artists produced work to distribute directly to one another; the underground press of the 1960s fueled by the fast development of both radical politics and offset printing; and the subversive method of circulating manuscripts in the Soviet Union known as Samizdat. However, the direct lineage of the present-day zine begins with science fiction fanzines of the 1920s–1930s.

The first science fiction fanzines emerged out of the letter pages of pulp magazines such as *Amazing Stories*, which listed the addresses of the readers who wrote letters.

Because interest in science fiction was rarer then, a science fiction fan was often geographically isolated from anyone else who shared her or his interest. Thus, fans were eager to share their commentary, enthusiasm, and fiction by corresponding as pen pals. These correspondences soon evolved into creating their own publications. To distinguish the fan publications from the professional magazines such as *Amazing Stories* and the commercial newsstand publications of the time devoted to movie stars and pop singers called "fan magazines," fan Louis Russell Chauvenaut (1920–2003) coined the term *fanzine*; fans eventually shortened this to *zine*, which they used as a synonym for fanzine. These fanzines contained reviews, stories, and essays, all initially concerning science fiction and other fantastic literature, but the fanzines soon grew to encompass anything that interested those involved. Though other fan publications preceded it, the first fanzine is usually considered *The Comet*, published in May 1930, starting a tradition in science fiction fandom that continues to this day. Indeed, the science fiction fanzines would establish almost all of the characteristics associated with zines, such as use of the most accessible and affordable publishing technology (initially letterpress and then hectograph and mimeograph), noncommercial and personal ethos (i.e., preferring to trade for another fanzine or letter of comment instead of cash), self-publishing by an individual or small group, erratic and ephemeral publishing, and filling a need not met by other media.

As the idea of the fanzine caught on, fanzines devoted to subjects beyond science fiction began to appear. The first non–science fiction fanzines were devoted to related subjects, such as **comic books** and **fantasy literature**, and established such subgenres of zines as minicomics (comic book fans publishing their own comics, among them underground comics legend Robert Crumb, (1943–)). By the 1960s, fanzines had moved further afield, and fanzines devoted to rock and roll music, such as *Crawdaddy* by Paul Williams (1948–) and *Mojo Navigator Rock 'n' Roll News* by Greg Shaw (1949–2004), appeared. Both Shaw and Williams had published science fiction fanzines, and they now used the fanzine format to document their new interest. These early rock fanzines established the subgenre of music zines, which continue to flourish today. Music zines particularly flowered in the late 1970s when photocopying became more accessible and inexpensive, and when most mainstream music magazines were hostile to punk rock and new wave.

By the 1980s, zines were being published on just about every subject imaginable. Most of these publications would have likely remained of interest only to people in their particular subculture, with professional wrestling fans reading professional wrestling zines and anarchists reading anarchist zines. However, cross-pollination across subcultures was provided by Michael Gunderloy (1959–), who started publishing *Factsheet Five*, a zine that reviewed other zines. R. Seth Friedman (1963–), a later publisher of *Factsheet Five*, describes the zine's origin:

> In the early '80s, Mike Gunderloy spent a lot of time reading and writing for science fiction fanzines. After a while, he started noticing quite a few other types of zines, including punk rock fanzines, political newsletters, humorous pamphlets, and publications from fringe societies. Mike was an avid letter writer and wanted to tell all his friends about the unusual publications he'd come across. Instead of writing the same information over and over, he tried to simplify his life by producing a short mimeographed list, which he dubbed *Factsheet Five*. (Friedman 1997, 13)

Gunderloy's time-saving measure would eventually overrun his life, leading him to withdraw from the zine scene, but for the 17 years (1982–1998) or so that *Factsheet Five* lasted under Gunderloy and his successors, it served as the crossroads of zine culture, introducing all sorts of zine publishers from different subcultures to one another and creating the self-awareness of zinedom that continues today. Indeed, despite the existence of subsequent review zines such as *Xerography Debt* and *Zine World: A Reader's Guide to the Underground Press,* rumors that *Factsheet Five* will be resuming publication continue to circulate through the zine community.

In the 1990s, zines attracted attention from mainstream media such as *Time* magazine and the *Wall Street Journal.* Most of the coverage focused on the lurid and wacky aspects of zines and treated zine publishers as curiosity pieces, freak shows in the feature pages. However, zines gradually became acknowledged as the literary aspect of the emergence of underground culture into the mainstream, alongside alternative music and independent film. As a result, zines became prominent, even marketable, for a cultural moment, and several zine publishers had books published by mainstream publishers, culminating in a zine book boom in the late 1990s that included anthologies of zines in general, collections of individual titles, academic probes into the subculture, and how-to guides on publishing zines. As further proof of the penetration of zines into mainstream consciousness, the term *zine* even started appearing in dictionaries by the decade's end.

However, also at this time, electronic publishing had come of age and soon started attracting the media attention previously given to zines. Furthermore, electronic publishing started to represent the most accessible and affordable technology available for those who already owned a personal computer and had access to the Internet. Consequently, ezines, which had existed at least since the 1970s among computer hobbyists and users of electronic bulletin board systems (which were reviewed along with zines in the very first *Factsheet Five*), began to proliferate, whether being distributed through e-mail or the World Wide Web (webzines). In fact, the development of the Web made publishing online easier than ever with the emergence of Weblogs, or blogs, negating the need to learn any computer code in order to publish online. The growth of online publishing led many people, including such zine stalwarts as John Marr (1961–) of *Murder Can Be Fun,* a zine devoted to horrific if humorous true crime stories, to suggest that the zine as a form was outdated. However, currently there appear to be as many print zines published as ever (including *Murder Can Be Fun*), and clearly the form remains viable, if no longer the default form for personal publishing (which now seems to be the blog, particularly for newcomers).

Trends and Themes. In the twenty-first century, zines have continued to evolve. Some of that evolution has included zine publishers leaving print behind in favor of electronic publishing, but despite the seeming rivalry between the zine and electronic publishing forms such as the blog, zinesters have made extensive use of the Internet. Uses have included *alt.zines* and other discussion boards for things zine related; archiving out-of-print issues of a zine online; publishing issues of a zine in both electronic and print format; using the Internet as a distribution medium for zines published as Adobe Portable Document Format files (PDFs) or other electronic publishing formats that can be printed out by the end user, saving the publisher both postage and printing expenses; electronic mailing lists and Web sites devoted to publicizing zines (given the eccentric publishing schedule for most zines, useful for letting readers know about the release of a new issue); online catalogs for zine distros (operations that distribute and sell a variety of zines); ezines such as *Zinethug.Com* that only review print zines; and, in an odd twist, collecting the best of a blog or Web site in a printed zine. Fundamentally, the relationship between electronic and print publishing is more complex than a simplistic either-or dichotomy, and a major trend in zine publishing is making use of some aspect of electronic publishing in order to complement print publishing.

Of course, for every action, there is a reaction, and another trend in zines has been neo-Luddism, in which zine publishers reject electronic publishing altogether and further embrace print publishing. Such zinesters utilize letterpresses, screenprints, woodcuts, and other labor-intensive production methods to produce publications that double as stunning works of art. In this approach, they challenge the typical zine ethos of using the most accessible and affordable technology. Most zinesters who take this approach are suspicious of electronic publishing and argue that a zine cannot be considered underground when it is published online and theoretically accessible to anyone on the Internet. Instead of being awash in information overload online, these zinesters delight in print as a medium, making zines that call as much attention to their form as to their content.

Of course, most of the neo-Luddites are longtime zinesters who have honed their craft over a number of years. Other zinesters who have developed considerable expertise have taken different approaches. One such approach is the megazine, the zine that has become so much an institution that it resembles a magazine and typically needs the volunteer equivalent of a magazine staff to be produced. Most of these zines, such as *Maximumrocknroll,* which weathered the death of its founder Tim Yohannan (1945–1998), have print runs in the thousands but continue to hold to a zine characteristic of some sort (often noncommerciality or reviewing other zines) that keeps them in the zine subculture. Other megazines include *Punk Planet* and *Razorcake.*

Another phenomenon among experienced zine publishers is that they often realize for all the effort they expend on publishing a zine, they might as well publish a book. Consequently, numerous zinesters have started publishing books, their own books as well as others', founding small presses such as Gorsky Press and Microcosm Publishing. Furthermore, many of the publishers share information with other zinesters on how to publish on this larger scale. For example, Jim Munroe (1973–) of No Media Kings has organized a touring circuit for zine publishers and other DIY media types called the Perpetual Motion Roadshow. However, book publication has brought zine publishers into contact with larger literary publishing circles in a manner more confrontational than when many zine publishers scored contracts during the zine book boom of the late 1990s. Indeed, the ULA, a group of zine publishers, routinely sparks controversy by critiquing the practices of mainstream literature and contrasting its products with those of the zine underground.

One key difference between mainstream and underground literature practices is the focus on cooperation rather than competition in the underground press. After all, zine publishing is a noncommercial and social activity. This cooperation can be demonstrated in the numerous local, regional, and national zine conferences and fairs, where publishers meet to trade zines and knowledge. Most larger cities have a zine fair, such as the Boston Zine Fair (formerly known as Beantown Zinetown) in Boston, Massachusetts, and some of the events attract zinesters from around the country, such as the Portland Zine Symposium (which includes a "Zinester Prom") in Portland, Oregon, and the Allied Media Conference in Detroit, Michigan.

The Allied Media Conference (which began in 1999 as "The Zine Conference" in Bowling Green, Ohio) is also indicative of another trend in zines: convergence with other media. Zine publishers have found companions in pirate radio enthusiasts, independent filmmakers, radical DIY Web publishers such as the numerous participants in the Independent Media Center movement, indie rock record labels, and other noncorporate media-makers. Such cross-fertilization has resulted in records to accompany zines (such as the 7" vinyl record *Music to Wash Dishes By* inspired by the zine *Dishwasher*), "DVDzines" of short films (such as *Novel Amusements*), and zines that publish different versions online and in print (such as *The 2nd Hand*).

Of course, keeping track of all this zine-related activity can be difficult, so various mechanisms arose to keep zinesters apprised of zine news. For a few years running, Brent Ritzel (1968–) published *Zine Guide,* a huge directory of zines, and Jen Angel (1975–) and Jason Kucsma (1974–) published *The Zine Yearbook,* a book collecting selections from the year's best zines. In addition, *Zine World* and its Canadian counterpart, *Broken Pencil,* cover zine news and list zine events, supplemented by such online ventures as *Zinewiki.Com,* an open-source zine encyclopedia launched in response to *Wikipedia*'s lack of consistent coverage of zines and zine culture.

Another trend has been the growth of zine libraries and regular libraries' inclusion of zines in their collections. Zine libraries are specifically devoted to archiving and circulating zines. They are sometimes attached to radical infoshops, community centers for progressive and even anarchist political activists, but often exist on their own. For example, the Independent Publishing Resource Center in Portland (which seems to have replaced San Francisco, California, as the geographic center of zines, based on the number of titles published from there) has a large collection of zines and other materials available for circulation and reference use. The center also offers expertise and workspace to self-publishers, even hosting an annual "Zine Camp" for children. In addition to the volunteer-driven zine libraries, a number of zine publishers have become professional librarians in recent years, with the result that a number of public libraries such as the Salt Lake City Public Library in Salt Lake City, Utah, have started collections of zines. In fact, Julie Bartel, founder of the Salt Lake zine collection, authored *From A to Zine: Building a Winning Zine Collection in Your Library,* published by the American Library Association and aimed at assisting librarians in building zine collections. Furthermore, several academic libraries host zine collections for scholarship purposes, among them the Ray and Pat Browne Library for Popular Culture Studies at Bowling Green State University and New York State Library in Albany, New York, home of the original *Factsheet Five* zine collection (a donation from Gunderloy when he finished his tenure at *Factsheet Five*). Libraries, of course, mesh well with the noncommerciality of zines, but there are also a number of zine-centered and zine-friendly stores, including Quimby's Books in Chicago, Atomic Books in Baltimore, and Reading Frenzy in Portland.

Context and Issues. Though zines can at times seem to belong to another world, they are nonetheless firmly linked to this one, with the zine subculture drawing much energy from the larger culture that surrounds it. Consequently, zines react to events and ideas in mainstream culture and society just as other media do. However, because zines usually represent a minority viewpoint (often a minority of one), the take on current events and ideas in a zine is typically very different from that offered in other media. While mainstream journalism prides itself on objectivity, zines delight in subjectivity, usually of an irreverent and subversive, if not profane, variety. Minus commercial pressure from advertisers or editorial gatekeepers of taste, zines provide total autonomy for the writers and artists creating the content, who of course are also typically the publishers themselves. Readers enamored of zines find much of the medium's attraction to be rooted in just this raw, unfiltered sensibility. In fact, zines, like their electronic progeny blogs, represent a thirst for autonomous personal participation in mass culture. Unlike ultimately controlled outlets for expression, such as electronic bulletin board postings, talk radio, and letters to the editor, the zine publisher is not subject to editorial restraint. For better or worse, a zine is an exercise in passion that often puts the personality of the zine publisher on parade.

However, such radical exercises in freedom of expression have become the target of censorship. Most attempts to censor zines occur in schools, where the young zine publisher is suspended or expelled, or at the very least banned from distributing the zine on campus. Every issue of *Zine World* comes complete with a news section documenting the latest censorship attempts. None of the attempts at censorship are pleasant for the publishers involved, no doubt, but some experience even more severe results than expulsion from an educational institution. The most notorious case of censoring a zine occurred in the 1990s in Largo, Florida, where zine publisher Michael Diana (1969–), a cartoonist whose *Boiled Angel* zine featured graphic illustrations of sex and violence, found himself charged with three state obscenity violations, after initially being considered a murder suspect essentially based on the content of his cartoons. Found guilty of all three charges, Diana spent a few days in jail awaiting his sentence of three years probation, a $3,000 fine, 1,300 hours of community service, compulsory enrollment in a journalism ethics course, a psychiatric evaluation at his own expense, a restraining order banning him from being closer than 10 feet to anyone under 18, and most chilling, a ban on drawing anything that could be considered obscene, which was enforced by officers given a warrant to search Diana's home at any time without prior notice. Upon appeal, one of the convictions was dropped, but ultimately Diana served out his sentence, finishing it up in New York doing volunteer work for the Comic Book Legal Defense Fund, which had defended him, for his final community service hours. Arguably, Diana is the first American artist to be convicted of obscenity. Ironically, the case attracted attention to his artwork, bringing him a larger audience than he had ever had for his self-published zine.

Even if one finds Diana's conviction more shocking than his comics, his conviction is a testimony to the power of zines. In a society in which a handful of media corporations become larger and larger with each subsequent buyout or merger, and the concentration of media power has become a political concern, the zine remains an open, democratic medium, accessible to almost all. Because zines are so available, grassroots efforts of all sorts use them to propagate ideas. Thus, zines often serve as a distant radar system for ideas long before they enter the consciousness of mainstream society. For example, to a mainstream media reader, the social justice and democracy protests against corporate power seemed to come out of nowhere into prominence during the Seattle, Washington, World Trade Organization meetings in 1999. But to a reader of zines, one could see this movement building throughout the 1990s. By the end of the decade, the movement had already moved from ideas in various zines to spawning its own magazine in *Clamor* (run by a couple former zine publishers to boot). Beyond political ideas, zines can serve as early tip sheets for all sorts of things, from food products (vegan zinesters wrote rants praising soymilk long before it started showing up regularly in supermarkets) to rock bands (in many punk zines, Green Day was bitterly accused of selling out when they signed with a major label, long before their albums went multiplatinum and won awards).

Indeed, zinesters sometimes make news themselves. One such example is Russ Kick (1969–), a former *Factsheet Five* writer who now edits the Disinformation series of books. In April 2004, Kick succeeded in a Freedom of Information Act (FOIA) request to obtain photographs of flag-draped coffins carrying remains of soldiers from the Iraq war to Dover Air Force Base. In 2003, just as the war had started, the military had banned such media coverage of fallen soldiers on military bases, so when Kick posted the photographs at his Web site, *thememoryhole.org,* it was the, first time the American public had seen such images from that war. Predictably, many American newspapers followed Kick's lead and published the photographs on their front pages. Just as predictably, though, none of them apparently had thought to file a FOIA request for such photographs themselves. Not every zine-spawned news scoop makes the mainstream media headlines, but because zines often focus on areas that the mainstream media are not covering adequately, they properly serve as a supplement to the conventional wisdom in matters such as the September 11, 2001, terrorist attacks or presidential election fraud (as the reader might guess, most zines take more seriously what might be labeled as "conspiracy theories" by mainstream media).

Furthermore, zines take seriously A.J. Liebling's (1904–1963) assertion that "Freedom of the press is guaranteed only to those who own one" (1975, 32) and can be seen as part of a growing movement of independent, noncorporate, nongovernmental media. This movement has grown in response to critiques of mass media such as *The New Media Monopoly* (2004) by Ben Bagdikian (1920–) that argue that the concentration of media into fewer hands is a danger to democracy. In addition, this concentration of media ownership has also resulted in less local media, such as news coverage of community concerns. Bagdikian points out, "Five global-dimension firms, operating with many of the characteristics of a cartel, own most of the newspapers, magazines, book publishers, motion picture studios, and radio and television stations in the United States. Each medium they own, whether magazines or broadcast stations, covers the entire country, and the owners prefer stories and programs that can be used everywhere and anywhere. Their media products reflect this" (2004, 3). In their small way, zines serve to counteract this media trend by focusing attention on matters that would otherwise be overshadowed in the quest for profits and synergy by media conglomerates and the stockholders they serve. In fact, zine publishers often consciously attempt to complement, supplement, or even oppose more established media. Thus, the publishing collective behind *The Zine Yearbook* was pointedly called "Become the Media."

Reception. Zines have not become the media, however, just a medium among many others. In fact, though such an encounter is rarer than in the past, it is still possible to meet people who have never heard of zines or who pronounce the word so that it rhymes with "sign." Nonetheless, zines have become more recognized by scholars, in various areas of popular culture and in society generally. In certain subcultures such as science fiction fandom and punk, zines have even become a tradition. For example, the Hugo Awards, one of science fiction's most well-known honors, have a fanzine category. Furthermore, some zines have become collectibles because of their rarity and been offered for auction on eBay, among other places.

In the academy, scholarship devoted to zines has been occasional but enlightening. Along with various research and scholarly libraries preserving the primary sources of zines themselves (the importance of which cannot be overestimated given the ephemeral nature and low print run of the typical zine, an activity also engaged in outside the academy by those Web sites archiving fanzines and zines online such as Fanac.org), the documentation of zine culture by assorted scholars over the years has been and will continue to be crucial to any coherent understanding of the genre, particularly because so many of those inside the zine scene, even at the heart of it, such as the various publishers of *Factsheet Five* or Doug Holland (1957–), who started *Zine World,* have a propensity to leave the scene entirely eventually (an exception to this trend toward burnout is Chip Rowe [1968–], editor of the anthology *The Book of Zines* and its accompanying website, www.zinebook.com, an indispensable resource for keeping tabs on zines and one continually updated for a decade now).

Strangely enough, the earliest book-length scholarship on fanzines came from one of the most unlikely sources: Dr. Fredric Wertham (1895–1981). Wertham, a psychiatrist, is most famous for his 1954 book *The Seduction of the Innocent,* a polemic against the comic book industry for corrupting the nation's youth that led to U.S. Senate hearings on the matter, the establishment of the Comics Code Authority (a self-policing exercise by comic book publishers), and much upheaval in the comic book industry. Fortunately for fanzine publishers, Wertham found fanzines more benign and praised them as a human scale form of mass communication in his 1973 book *The World of Fanzines: A Special Form of Communication.*

Subsequent scholarship on zines has for the most part continued to be infatuated with the subject matter. It also has followed zines as they have branched out beyond science fiction, fantasy fiction, and comic books fandom, from providing a history of rock fanzines (Ginsberg 1979) to describing how zines about work provide another outlet for disgruntled employees (McQuarrie 1994). Other notable scholarship on zines includes work by Stephen Perkins, Roger Sabin (1961–), Amy Spencer (1979–), and Teal Triggs. An exception to the general praise of zines by critics is *Notes from Underground: Zines and the Politics of Alternative Culture* (1997) by Stephen Duncombe, which argues that the revolutionary potential of zines is too idiosyncratic in its very nature to ever amount to a genuine political force.

Zines have also been brought into the classroom for study, usually in the function of encouraging students to create their own zines. Indeed, entire courses have been organized around zines, such as Zines and Do-It-Yourself Democracy, taught by Doug Blandy (1952–) at the University of Oregon in Eugene, Oregon, and articles written about the usefulness of zines in the curriculum. Though zines appear to be accepted in the academy today, that was not always the case. An exhibit of zines at Boise State University in Boise, Idaho, in 1992 met with such a controversial response that the curator, Tom Trusky, published not only an exhibition catalog but also a facsimile of the guestbook from the exhibit.

Participants in the zine community have also critiqued and documented zine culture. *Beneath the Underground* (1994) by Bob Black (1951–) provides an interesting insider's look at the zine scene of the 1980s, while *Zines!* (1996, 1997), the two volumes of interviews with zine publishers compiled by V. Vale (1948–), does the same for the 1990s. Other such books by zine publishers include how-to guides (e.g., *Make a Zine!* 1997, by Bill Brent), anthologies (e.g., *The Factsheet Five Zine Reader: The Best Writing from the Underground World of Zines,* 1997, edited by Friedman), and cultural criticism (*We Want Some Too: Underground Desire and the Reinvention of Mass Culture* 2000, by Hal Niedzviecki [1971–]). Beyond print, zines have also been the focus of documentary films and videos, such as *A Hundred Dollars and a T-shirt: A Documentary about Zines in the Northwest U.S.* (2004).

Beyond the zine community, zines have attracted attention in various areas of popular culture. Books such as *Zine Scene: The Do It Yourself Guide to Zines* (1998) by Francesca Lia Block (1962–) and Hilary Carlip introduced neophytes to zines in the 1990s, while twenty-first-century youth learn about zines from *Whatcha Mean, What's a Zine?* (2006) by Mark Todd (1970–) and Esther Pearl Watson. In fiction, various authors have included characters who publish zines, most notably Ellen Wittlinger (1948–) in *Hard Love* (1999), a young adult novel about a teenage zine publisher who falls in love with another teenage zinester. Similarly, comic strips such as *Underworld* by Kaz Prapuolenis (1959–) and comic books such as *Hate* by Peter Bagge (1957–) have featured zine-publishing characters. Likewise, animated cartoons (e.g., *Rocket Power*), films (e.g., *Conspiracy Theory*), and television shows (e.g., *Our Hero*) feature zine-publishing characters. Furthermore, zine publishers have also been featured in films (e.g., Friedman in the documentary *Capturing the Friedmans*), and zines have made appearances on television shows (e.g., the music zine *The Big Takeover* in *Gilmore Girls*). Zine publishers have been guests on television and radio talk shows such as *The Late Show with David Letterman* (e.g., where in 1995 Dishwasher Pete Jordan [1966–] sent a friend to impersonate him, and the friend memorably—and based on David Letterman's reaction, somewhat disturbingly—set his hand on fire in the spirit of a Letterman "Stupid Human Trick") and *This American Life* (e.g., where in 1997 Jordan told the story of his prank on *The Late Show*). In addition, given the vast number of music zines, it is not surprising that musicians have returned the favor by writing songs mentioning zines (e.g., "Flagpole Sitta" by Harvey Danger) or having zines as the topic of the song (e.g., "Fanzine" by Holly and the Italians, "Letter to a Fanzine" by Great Plains, and "Fear of Zine Failure (Ode to Self-Publishing)" by The Hidden Cameras).

Some zines even more so than others seem to attract attention in popular culture. For example, David Greenberger's (1954–) *The Duplex Planet,* a zine featuring reflections on life from elderly nursing home residents, has spawned numerous offspring in other media. In addition to the zine, CDs, books, comics, stage performances, lectures, art exhibits, films, and even a card set have spun the concept off into other areas of popular culture, with the individual residents of the nursing home, such as late-blooming poet Ernest Noyes Brookings (1898–1987), becoming quasi-celebrities in their own right.

Furthermore, zines have become a vehicle for the launching of subsequent careers in more established media. Political commentator Thomas Frank (1965–), media commentator James Romenesko (1953–), and fiction writers Gomez and Kennedy, among others, all got their professional starts arguably in the zine scene. All published in zines that led to career opportunities (i.e., Frank's *The Baffler,* Romenesko's *Obscure,* Gomez's *Our Noise,* and Kennedy's *Pagan's Head*).

Selected Authors. Although some authors may regard their zine writing as juvenilia or a self-guided apprenticeship before they went on to other pursuits, many authors remain attached to the medium. For example, Frank continues to publish *The Baffler,* though it has evolved quite a bit since 1988. Consequently, zine writing can be said to constitute its own genre of literature. Despite the egalitarian ethos of zines, some authors tend to stand out from others, granting them a staying power at odds with the ephemeral nature of most zines. In many cases, the author's work is collected into book form, making it more accessible to readers beyond the zine community and to readers within the zine community who have difficulty getting a copy of the original zine publications.

Arguably the author most identified with zines is Aaron Cometbus (surname Elliot), who has published the zine *Cometbus* since 1983. Originally a punk zine covering bands in the San Francisco Bay area, the zine soon shifted to a focus on Cometbus's own life, becoming the quintessential perzine (a contraction of "personal zine"). Charmingly written by utilizing Cometbus's block letter handwriting, Cometbus's zine documents in a heartfelt way the gutter-punk lifestyle of dumpster diving, squatting in abandoned houses, going to music shows, and drinking too much coffee. His often humorous descriptions of this life and his reflections on it have endeared him to numerous readers, with issues of the zine reaching print runs in the thousands for each new issue. His work has also been collected into book form with *Despite Everything: A Cometbus Omnibus,* a collection of issues of the zine, and the novels *Double Duce,* based on an issue of the zine, and *I Wish There Was Something That I Could Quit.* Although Cometbus has seemed to focus on longer works such as the novels in recent years (he even gave up publishing the zine for a short time in order to concentrate on books), his work excels in the short-short story form, such as "My Secret Life as a Student," where his prose achieves a poetic quality. Unfortunately, Cometbus's work, like that of most zine authors, has received scant critical attention, presumably because it flies, as the title of Sabin and Triggs's (2002) book on zines suggests, below critical radar. Rather than follow the normal channels of literary culture in society, Cometbus sticks close to the zine world, still pricing new issues of his zine inexpensively at two dollars; consequently, his distribution is accordingly limited. When critical commentary of his work has appeared, it has taken place typically in a work exploring zines as a subculture. Given the stature some of the zine writers such as Cometbus are starting to attain, however, it is likely that critical attention will move to focus on the individual authors in the future. Despite the lack of critical attention, Cometbus's work has been tremendously influential in the zine community, with reviewers of zines sometimes even disparaging zines too openly derivative of the Cometbus style.

Though often compared to Cometbus, Cindy Gretchen Ovenrack Crabb (1970–) manages to maintain her individuality. Best known for her long-running zine *Doris,* Crabb's writing, like Cometbus's, draws much of its charm and power from its personal nature. However, for every lighthearted reflection on coffee drinking or road tripping, Crabb offers an exploration of deeper resonance such as politics or her own experience having an abortion. Crabb's work is representative of a large number of zines written by women, fueled by the riot grrrl movement of the early 1990s in which young women confronted sexism in society and in the punk subculture specifically. The diversity of this vital genre of zines can be found in the 1997 anthology *A Girl's Guide To Taking Over the World: Writings from the Girl Zine Revolution* (Green and Taormino 1997), but it also continues today. Indeed, strains of riot grrrl feminism can be found in many contemporary zine writers, such as Moe Bowstern (1968–), who documents life as an Alaskan fisherwoman in her zine *Xtra Tuf,* and Jessica Disobedience (surname Wilber) (1982–), a writer whose evolution in style is often accompanied by a shift in persona (e.g., Edna Million, Rose Red the Ghost Heart Girl, etc.).

However, feminism in zines goes beyond riot grrrls with another burgeoning genre of zines being "mamazines," wherein older female zine publishers explore issues related to motherhood, but also other matters of concern, whether tradition-ally identified with women or not. Prominent writers in this genre include Ariel Gore (1970–) and Ayun Halliday (1965–). Gore, best known for her zine-turned-magazine *Hip Mama,* has edited and written several books, including *Atlas of the Human Heart,* 2003, a memoir of her teenage years when she traveled alone through Europe and Asia. Her work often critiques societal attitudes toward and government policies affecting women, including welfare (she once even debated conservative politician Newt Gingrich about welfare reform on television). Less political than Gore, Halliday has also published several books, including *The Big Rumpus: A Mother's Tale from the Trenches,* 2002, based upon her zine *The East Village Inky,* which humorously documents her experiences raising two children in New York City.

For a less wholesome take on motherhood, among many other topics, readers can turn to the writing of Lisa Crystal Carver (also known as Lisa Suckdog) (1968–), publisher of the zine *Rollerderby.* Also the author of several books, Carver has been a controversial and fascinating figure in the literary underground for years, explor-ing extreme sexuality and other taboo subjects. Similarly, Jim (1961–) and Debbie Goad (1954–2000), who published *ANSWER Me!,* represent the more confronta-tional and extreme wing of zines. Author of books such as *Shit Magnet* 2002 and *The Redneck Manifesto* 1998, Jim Goad seems to delight in taking positions con-trary to those of most on matters ranging from racism to rape.

Although most of the zine writers mentioned thus far focus on nonfiction work, particularly **autobiography and memoirs**, a considerable number of zine writers write fiction or **poetry**. Since the 1980s at least, "the mimeograph revolution" of small press poets (documented well in the book *A Secret Location on the Lower East Side;* Clay and Phillips, 1998), the Mail Art movement, and zines have often converged where poetry was concerned. Even writers as celebrated as Charles Bukowski (1920–1994) were published in literary zines (or *litzines* as they are called) such as *Impetus,* edited by poet Cheryl Townsend (1957–). Among fiction writers, in addition to Gomez and Kennedy, a number of other novelists have emerged from the zine community, including Sean Carswell (1969–), author of *Drinks for the Little Guy* (1999); Joe Meno (1974–), author of *Hairstyles of the Damned* (2004); and Jeff Somers (1971–), author of *Lifers* (2001). In addition, the literary zine writers of the ULA have joined together to promote underground literature and protest corruption in the mainstream literary culture.

Zines are a lively literary culture, and the authors mentioned here represent only a few of the thousands of writers who have published or contributed to zines over the years. However, because the zine community operates in an interconnected manner, reading any of these authors or any zine will usually serve to introduce a reader to other zines and zine authors. And working on a photocopier somewhere right now undoubtedly is a new author making copies of her or his first zine.

Bibliography

A Hundred Dollars and a T-shirt: A Documentary about Zines in the Northwest U.S. DVD, directed by Basil Shadid et al., 1 hr. 11 min. (Microcosm, 2004).

Bagdikian, Ben H. *The New Media Monopoly.* Boston: Beacon Press, 2004.

Black, Bob. *Beneath the Underground.* Portland, OR: Feral House, 1994.

Block, Francesca Lia, and Hilary Carlip. *Zine Scene: The Do It Yourself Guide to Zines.* Los Angeles: Girl Press, 1998.

Clay, Steven, and Rodney Phillips. *A Secret Location on the Lower East Side: Adventures in Writing, 1960–1980.* New York: New York Public Library/Granary Books, 1998.

Cometbus, Aaron. *Despite Everything: A Cometbus Omnibus.* San Francisco: Last Gasp, 2002.

Crabb, Cindy Gretchen Ovenrack. *Doris: An Anthology 1991–2001.* Portland, OR: Microcosm, 2005.

Duncombe, Stephen. *Notes from Underground: Zines and the Politics of Alternative Culture.* New York: Verso, 1997.

Friedman, R. Seth, ed. *The Factsheet Five Zine Reader: The Best Writing from the Underground World of Zines.* New York: Three Rivers Press, 1997.

Ginsberg, David D. "Rock Is a Way of Life: The World of Rock 'N' Roll Fanzines and Fandom." *Serials Review* (Jan./Mar. 1979): 29–46.

Green, Karen, and Tristan Taormino, eds. *A Girl's Guide to Taking Over the World: Writings from the Girl Zine Revolution.* New York: St Martin's Griffin, 1997.

Gunderloy, Mike, and Cari Goldberg Janice. *The World of Zines.* New York: Penguin Books, 1992.

Liebling, A.J. *The Press.* 2nd ed. New York: Ballantine, 1975.

McQuarrie, Fiona. "New Reactions to Dissatisfaction: Exit, Voice, and Loyalty in Zines." *Organizational Behavior* 15.5 (1994): 142–51.

Perkins, Stephen. *Approaching the '80s Zine Scene: A Background Survey and Selected Annotated Bibliography.* Iowa City, IA: Plagiarist Press, 1992.

Rowe, Chip. *Zines, E-Zines, Fanzines: The Book of Zines Directory.* Retrieved August 2006 from http://www.zinebook.com

Sabin, Roger, and Teal Triggs, eds. *Below Critical Radar: Fanzines and Alternative Comics from 1976 to the Present Day.* Hove, UK: Slab-O-Concrete, 2002.

Spencer, Amy. *DIY: The Rise of Lo-Fi Culture.* New York: Marion Boyars, 2005.

Todd, Mark, and Esther Pearl Watson. *Whatcha Mean, What's a Zine?: The Art of Making Zines and Mini-Comics.* Boston: Graphia, 2006.

Trusky, Tom, ed. *Some Zines: American Alternative and Underground Magazines, Newsletters and APAs.* Boise, ID: Cold-Drill, 1992.

Vale, V., ed. *Zines! Vol. I.* San Francisco: V/Search, 1996.

Vale, V., ed. *Zines! Vol. II.* San Francisco: V/Search, 1997.

Warner, Harry, Jr. *All Our Yesterdays: An Informal History of Science Fiction Fandom in the Forties.* Chicago: Advent, 1969.

Wertham, Fredric. *The World of Fanzines: A Special Form of Communication.* Carbondale: Southern Illinois University Press, 1973.

Wittlinger, Ellen. *Hard Love.* New York: Simon & Schuster, 1999.

Wright, Frederick. *From Zines to Ezines: Electronic Publishing and the Literary Underground.* PhD dissertation, Kent State University, 2001.

FREDERICK WRIGHT

Contemporary Authors by Genre

The following lists contemporary authors who are or were recently active in their respective literary genres.

ACADEMIC FICTION:

Martin Amis
A.S. Byatt
Amanda Cross
Clare Chambers
Brett Easton Ellis
D.J.H. Jones
David Lodge
Estelle Monbrun
Marion Rosen
Jane Smiley
Alexander Theroux

ADVENTURE FICTION:

Tim Cahill
Peter Mathiessen
Jon Krakauer
Bill Bryson
Paul Theroux

AFRICAN AMERICAN LITERATURE:

Maya Angelou
Amiri Baraka (LeRoi Jones)
David Bradley
Trey Ellis
Albert French
Ernest J. Gaines
Edward P. Jones
Andrea Lee
James McBride
Terry McMillan
Toni Morrison
Ishmael Reed
Colson Whitehead
John Wideman

ARAB AMERICAN LITERATURE:

Diana Abu-Jaber
Rabih Alameddine

Hayan Charara
Suheir Hammad
Nathalie Handel
Mohja Kahf
Laila Lalami
Naomi Shihab Nye

ARTHURIAN LITERATURE:

T.A. Barron
Dan Brown
Meg Cabot
Robert Doherty
Kathleen Cunningham Guler
J. Robert King
Aaron Latham
Sara Maitland
Nancy McKenzie
Mark J. Mitchell
Mary Pope Osborne
Judith Tarr
Jack Whyte
James C. Work
Sarah Zettel

ASIAN AMERICAN LITERATURE:

Jeffrey Paul Chan
Frank Chin
Chitra Devakaruni
Jessica Hagedorn
Le Ly Hayslip
David Henry Hwang
Lawson Fusao Inada
Gish Jen
Maxine Hong Kingston
Chang-rae Lee
Bharati Mukherjee
Amy Tan
Shawn Wong

AUTOBIOGRAPHY AND MEMOIR:

Maya Angelou
Sven Birkerts
Amiri Baraka
Augusten Burroughs
Mary Carr
Joan Didion

Pete Hamill
bell hooks
Maxine Hong Kingston
Carolyn Knapp
Kien Nguyen
Tim O'Brien
Dave Pelzer
Gore Vidal

BEAT POETRY:

Amiri Baraka
Gregory Corso
Lawrence Ferlinghetti
Joanne Kyger
Michael McClure
Gary Snyder
Anne Waldman

BIOGRAPHY:

Christopher Andersen
Debby Applegate
Carl Bernstein
Jeremy Bernstein
Sarah Bradford
Chester Brown
Tina Brown
Frank Bruni
Allan Bullock
Paul Burrell
Arthur H. Cash
Joyce E. Chaplin
Laura Claridge
Jennet Conant
Alexis De Veaux
Thomas DiLorenzo
Steve Dougherty
Joseph Ellis
Daniel Mark Epstein
Suzanne Finstad
Antonia Fraser
Jon Goodman
Gregg Herken
Walter Isaacson
David Kaufman
Kitty Kelley
Pamela Killian
Gavin Lambert

Robert Lamberton
Barbara Leaming
Roger Lewis
Janet Malcolm
George M. Marsden
David McCollough
Bill Minutaglio
Elizabeth Mitchell
Vicky Moon
Jay Mulvaney
Jerome Murphy-O'Connor
Sylvia Nasar
David Nasaw
Nigel Nicholson
Abraham Pais
Robert Parry
Kevin Phillips
Stacy Schiff
Joshua Shenk
Sally Bedell Smith
Edward Steers, Jr.
David Talbot
Sherrill Tippins
C.A. Tripp
Tom Tucker
Nick Webb
Sasha Su-Ling Welland
Barry Werth
Andrew Wilson
Gordon S. Wood

"CHICK LIT":

Melissa Bank
Candace Bushnell
Helen Fielding
Nicola Krause
Emma McLaughlin
Terry McMillan
Elissa Schappell
Plum Sykes
Jennifer Weiner
Rebecca Wells

CHILDREN'S LITERATURE:

Herm Auch
Mary Jane Auch
Ann Howard Creel

Carmela D'Amico
Steven D'Amico
Mark Dartford
Jennifer Fandel
Nikki Giovanni
Daniel Handler
Brendan January
Antoinette Portis
Peter Parnell
Justin Richardson
Laura Amy Schlitz
Jane Shuter
Sonia Sones
Carole Weatherford
Melanie Wentz
Leah Wilcox
Jane Yolen

CHRISTIAN FICTION:

Ted Dekker
Jerry B. Jenkins
Karen Kingsbury
Tim LeHaye
Stephen R. Lawhead
Janette Oke
Frank Peretti
Francine Rivers

COMEDIC THEATRE:

Eric Bogosian
Christopher Durang
David Lindsay-Abaire
Craig Lucas
Steve Martin
Theresa Rebeck
Neil Simon
Wendy Wasserstein

COMIC BOOKS:

Jessica Abel
Brian Michael Bendis
Warren Ellis
Neil Gaiman
Devin Grayson
Todd McFarlane
Mark Millar

Frank Miller
Gail Simone
Chris Ware

COMING OF AGE FICTION:

Steve Almond
Melissa Bank
Mark Barrowcliffe
Thomas Beller
Marshall Boswell
Ann Brashare
Ian Caldwell and Dustin Thomason
Mark Childress
Sandra Cisneros
Junot Díaz
Don DeGrazia
Dave Eggers
Tristan Egolf
Leif Enger
Jonathan Safran Foer
Kaye Gibbons
Rebecca Godfrey
Mark Haddon
Kim Wong Keltner
Watt Key
Dave King
Gordon Korman
Jhumpa Lahiri
Jonathan Lethem
Jim Lynch
Claire Messud
Nick McDonnell
Scott Mebus
Joe Meno
Michael Morris
Lauren Myracle
Joyce Carol Oates
Ann Packer
Marisha Pessl
Delores Phillips
DBC Pierre
Jodi Picoult
Dan Pope
Francine Prose
Mark A. Rempel
Jack Riggs
Paul Ruditis

David Schickler
Alice Sebold
Jim Shepard
Lionel Shriver
George Singleton
Curtis Sittenfeld
Kyle Smith
Todd Strasser
Kali VanBaale
C.G. Watson
Debra Weinstein
Brad Whittington
Christopher Wilson
Tom Wolfe
Tobias Wolff

CONTEMPORARY FICTION:

Julia Alvarez
Russell Banks
Saul Bellow
T.C. Boyle
Michael Chabon
Don DeLillo
E.L. Doctorow
Dave Eggers
Bret Easton Ellis
Lousie Erdrich
Jeffrey Eugenides
Richard Ford
Jonathan Franzen
Mary Gaitskill
Gail Godwin
Rolando Hinojosa
John Irving
Gish Jen
Barbara Kingsolver
Jhumpa Lahiri
Betty Ann Mason
Cormac McCarthy
Toni Morrison
Joyce Carol Oates
Tim O'Brien
Cynthia Ozick
Annie Proulx
Thomas Pynchon
Philip Roth
Richard Russo

Jane Smiley
Amy Tan
Anne Tyler
John Updike
David Foster Wallace

CYBERPUNK:

Kathy Acker
Pat Cadigan
William Gibson
Rudy Rucker
Lewis Shiner
John Shirley
Neal Stephenson
Bruce Sterling
Vernor Vinge

DRAMATIC THEATRE:

David Auburn
Nilo Cruz
Tom Donaghy
Eve Ensler
Horton Foote
Richard Greenberg
John Guare
Stephen Adly Guirgis
A.R. Gurney
Tony Kushner
Neil LaBute
Warren Leight
Tracy Letts
Romulus Linney
Kenneth Lonergan
David Mamet
Donald Marguiles
Terrence McNally
Anne Nelson
Lynn Nottage
Dael Orlandersmith
Suzan-Lori Parks
John Patrick Shanley
Sam Shepard
Anna Deveare Smith
Diana Son
Paula Vogel
Doug Wright
Mary Zimmerman

DYSTOPIAN LITERATURE:

Margaret Atwood
Cheryl Bernard
T.C. Boyle
Pat Califa
David Allen Cates
Robert Coover
Cory Doctorow
Ignatius Donnelly
Lisa Learner
Sinclair Lewis
Philip Roth
Kurt Vonnegut

ECOPOETRY:

A.R. Ammons
Jonathan Bate
W.S. Merwin
Mary Oliver
Gary Snyder

EROTIC LITERATURE:

Pat Califia
Mary Gaitskill
Chris Packard
Carol Queen
Cherysse Welcher-Calhoun

FANTASY LITERATURE:

Poul Anderson
James Blaylock
Dan Brown
Susannna Clarke
Charles de Lint
Stephen R. Donaldson
Neil Gaiman
David Gemmell
Karen Hancock
Robin Hobb
Elizabeth Kostova
Ursula K. Le Guin
Michael Moorcock
Tim Powers
J.K. Rowling

Charles R. Sanders
Darrell Schweitzer
Art Spiegelman
Richard L. Tierney

FILM ADAPTATIONS OF BOOKS:

Shari Springer Berlman
Stephen Daldry
Jonathan Safran Foer
David Frankel
Josh Friedman
David Hare
Ron Howard
Christine Jeffs
Spike Jonze
Charlie Kaufman
David Koepp
Ang Lee
Richard Linklater
Aline Brosh McKenna
Garry Marshall
Frank Miller
Susan Orlean
Harvey Pekar
Robert Pulcini
Robert Rodriguez
Eric Schlosser
Julian Schnabel
Liv Schreiber
Steven Spielberg
Julie Taymor
Lauren Weisberger
Terry Zwigoff

FLASH FICTION:

Gail Galloway Adams
Kim Addonizio
Steve Almond
Michael Arnzen
Aimee Bender
Elizabeth Berg
Mark Budman
Robert Olen Butler
Ron Carlson
Brian Clements
Lydia Davis
Denise Duhamel

Stuart Dybek
Dave Eggers
Utahna Faith
Sherrie Flick
Ian Frazier
Barry Gifford
Molly Giles
Ursula Hegi
Robin Hemley
Amy Hempel
Jim Heynen
William Heyen
Barbara Jacksha
Harold Jaffe
Jesse Lee Kercheval
Peter Markus
Josip Novakovich
Lon Otto
Pamela Painter
Ethan Paquin
Bruce Holland Rogers
Daryl Scroggins
Don Shea
Virgil Suarez
James Tate
Anthony Tognazzini
Jessica Treat
Mark Tursi
Deb Unferth
G. C. Waldrep
Ron Wallace
Katherine Weber
Derek White
Tobias Wolff
Allen Woodman

GLBT LITERATURE:

Michael Cunningham
David Ebershoff
Allan Gurganus
Annie Proulx
Sarah Waters
Edmund White

GRAPHIC NOVELS:

Jessica Abel
Brian Michael Bendis

Warren Ellis
Neil Gaiman
Devin Grayson
Todd McFarlane
Mark Millar
Frank Miller
Gail Simone
Chris Ware

HISTORICAL FANTASY:

Shana Abé
Alex Archer
Orson Scott Card
Suzanna Clarke
Neil Gaiman
Stephen Grundy
Stephen King
Alisa Kwitney
Karen Marie Moning
Phillip Pullman
Anne Rice
Judith Tarr

HISTORICAL FICTION:

T.C. Boyle
Geraldine Brooks
Michael Cunningham
Don DeLillo
E.L. Doctorow
David Anthony Durham
Charles Frazier
Charles Johnson
Thomas Mallon
Thomas Pynchon
Philip Roth
William Safire

HISTORICAL MYSTERIES:

Rennie Airth
Boris Akunin
Caleb Carr
P.F. Chisholm
Max Allan Collins
Paul Doherty
David Fulmer
Matthew Pearl

Lynda S. Robinson
Andrew Taylor

HISTORICAL WRITING:

Thomas Cahill
Felipe Fernandez-Armesto
Erik Larson
Thomas Friedman

HOLOCAUST LITERATURE:

Melvin Jules Bukiet
Michael Chabon
Don DeLillo
Jonathan Safran Foer
Thane Rosenbaum
Philip Roth

HUMOR:

Thomas Berger
Bill Bryson
Christopher Buckley
George Carlin
Pat Conroy
Don DeLillo
Al Franken
John Irving
Michael Kun
Benjamin Kunkel
Bill Maher
Frank McCourt
Christopher Moore
P.J. O'Rourke
Philip Roth
Christina Schwarz
David Sedaris
Jane Smiley
Jon Stewart
Colson Whitehead

INSPIRATIONAL LITERATURE (NONFICTION):

Vicki Caruana
Oswald Chambers
John Eldredge
Edward Grinnin
Annie Graham Lotz

Max Lucado
Joel Osteen
Rick Warren
Phillip Yancey

JEWISH AMERICAN LITERATURE:

Pearl Abraham
Shalom Auslander
Paul Auster
Saul Bellow
David Bezmozgis
Abraham Cahan
Michael Chabon
E.L. Doctorow
Nathan Englander
Jonathan Safran Foer
Michael Gold
Rebecca Goldstein
Allegra Goodman
Sana Krasikov
Norman Mailer
Bernard Malamud
Tova Mirvis
Cynthia Ozick
Chaim Potok
Tova Reich
Henry Roth
Philip Roth
Gary Shteyngart
Isaac Bashevis Singer
Art Spiegelman
Steve Stern
Anya Ulinich
Lara Vapnyar
Nathaniel West
Anzia Yezierska

LANGUAGE POETRY:

Rae Armantrout
Charles Bernstein
Lucie Brock-Broido
Lyn Hejinian
Fanny Howe
Myung Mi Kim
Harryette Mullen
Michael Palmer

Ron Silliman
Juliana Spahr

LATINO AMERICAN LITERATURE:

Miguel Algarin
Isabel Allende
Julia Alvarez
Rudolfo Anaya
Gloria Anzaldua
Raymond Barrio
Arturo Campa
Ana Castillo
Angel Castro
Denise Chavez
Fray Angelico Chavez
Sandra Cisneros
Judith Ortiz Cofer
Jesús Colón
Lucha Corpi
Junot Diaz
Stella Pope Duarte
Aurelio Espinoza
Roberta Fernandez
Roberto G. Fernández
Gustavo Perez Firmat
Cristina Garcia
Beatriz de la Garza
Francisco Goldman
Oscar Hijuelos
Rolando Hinojosa
Enrique Laguerre
Graciela Limón
Aurora Lucero
Jaime Manriquez
Demetria Martinez
Pablo Medina
Nicolasa Mohr
Cherrie Moraga
Alejandro Morales
Elías Miguel Muñoz
López Nieves
Achy Obejas
Philip D. Ortego
Nina Otero
Ernesto Quiñones
Tomás Rivera
Abraham Rodriguez
Octavio Romano

Piri Thomas
Alisa Valdes-Rodriguez
Richard Vasquez
Jose Antonio Villarreal
Helena Maria Viramontes
Jose Yglesias

LEGAL THRILLERS:

Dudley W. Buffa
Michael Crichton
Christopher Darden
John Grisham
Phillip Margolin
Brad Meltzer
Scott Turow

LITERARY JOURNALISM:

Richard Ben Cramer
Jon Krakauer
Jane Kramer
William Langewiesche
Adrian Nicole LeBlanc
Michael Lewis
Sonia Nazario
Susan Orlean
Lawrence Wright

MAGICAL REALISM:

Maria Arana
Jonathan Safran Foer
Abby Frucht
Joe Hill
Steven Millhauser

MANGA AND ANIME:

Kazuo Koike
Hayao Miyazaki
Takeshi Obata

MILITARY LITERATURE:

David Alexander
Mark Bowden
Rick Bragg
Tom Clancy

David Drake
Sabina Murrary
Jeff Shaara
Anthony Swofford
James and Melanie Thomas
Harry Turtledove
Buzz Williams

MUSICAL THEATRE:

Jason Robert Brown
William Finn
Stephen Flaherty
Ricky Ian Gordon
Adam Guettel
Mark Hollman
Stephen Schwartz
Jeanine Tesori
David Yazbeck

MYSTERY FICTION:

Claudia Bishop
Dan Brown
Caleb Carr
Mary Higgins Clark
Susan Conant
Michael Connelly
Amanda Cross
Jeffrey Deaver
Andrew Greeley
Thomas Harris
Walter Mosley
Bill Pronzini

NATIVE AMERICAN LITERATURE:

Sherman Alexie
A.A. Carr
Louise Erdrich
Linda Hogan
Thomas King
Leslie Marmon Silko
James Welch

NEW AGE LITERATURE:

Echo Bodine
Dan Brown

Sylvia Browne
James Redfield
Eckhart Tolle
Doreen Virtue

OCCULT AND SUPERNATURAL FICTION:

Stephen King
Dean Koontz
Peter Straub

PARAPSYCHOLOGY:

Sylvia Browne
Rhonda Byrne
John Edward
Uri Geller
Charles Honorton
Harry Houdini
Robert Jahn
J.Z. Knight
Stanley Krippner
Dean Radin
James Randi
J.B. Rhine
Helmut Schmidt
Rupert Sheldrake
Upton Sinclair
Montague Ullman
James Van Praagh

PHILOLOGICAL THRILLERS:

Steve Berry
Dan Brown
Sam Bourne
Ian Caldwell
Umberto Eco
John Fasman
Robert Harris
Raymond Khoury
Elizabeth Kostova
Kathleen McGowan
Kate Mosse
Matthew Pearl
Iain Pears
Arthur Phillips
Dustin Thomason

POETRY:

Sherman Alexie
Miguel Algarin
Jimmy Santiago Baca
Amiri Baraka
Billy Collins
Robert Creeley
Rita Dove
Louise Glück
Jorie Graham
Donald Hall
Lyn Heyjinian
Sarah Jones
Linton Kwesi Johnson
Yusef Komunyaka
Stanley Kunitz
Adrienne Rich
Charles Simic
Derek Walcott
Anne Waldman

REGIONAL FICTION:

Russell Banks
Michael Collins
Jonathan Franzen
Ernest Herbert
Bobbie Ann Mason
Annie Proulx
Richard Russo
Whitney Terrell

ROAD FICTION:

Amiri Baraka
Joyce Johnson
Hettie Jones
Hunter S. Thompson
Tom Wolfe

ROMANCE NOVELS:

Loretta Chase
Diana Gabaldon
Kristin Gabriel
Dorothy Garlock
Julie Garwood
Barbara Hannay

Linda Howard
Sabrina Jeffries
Lisa Kleypas
Stephanie Laurens
Marion Lennox
Debbie Macomber
Judith McNaught
Sandra Steffen

SCIENCE FICTION:

Michael Crichton
Joe Haldeman
Elizabeth Moon
Richard Powers
Kim Stanley Robinson
Dan Simmons
Vernor Vinge
Connie Willis
Robert Charles Wilson

SCIENCE WRITING (NONFICTION):

Richard Dawkins
Timothy Ferris
Stephan Jay Gould
Brian Greene
Carl Sagan
Dava Sobel

SEA LITERATURE:

John Barth
Nathaniel Philbrick
Caryl Phillips
Dava Sobel
Kurt Vonnegut

SELF-HELP LITERATURE:

David Allen
John Amodeo
Sherry Argov
Peter Block
Peter Boxall
Harriet B. Braiker
Jill Conner Browne
Kelly Bryson

Rhonda Byrne
Julia Cameron
Marla Cilley
Winn Claybaugh
Will Clower
Diane Conway
Paul Coughlin
Stephen R. Covey
Maggie Craddock
Neil Crofts
Leanne Ely
Michael J. Gelb
Mireille Guiliano
Robert T. Kiyosaki
Phil McGraw
Dave Ramsey
Rhonda Rich
Laura Schlessinger
Patricia Schultz
Judith Wright

SERIES FICTION:

Jean Auel
Patricia Cornwell
Jeffery Deaver
Terry Goodkind
Sue Grafton
Daniel Handler
Tony Hillerman
Jerry B. Jenkins
Tim LeHaye
Walter Mosley
Elizabeth Peters
Anne Rice

SPACE OPERA:

Kevin J. Anderson
Catherine Asaro
David Brin
Louis McMaster Bujold
Orson Scott Card
Edward Carmien
Tony Daniel
Elizabeth Moon
John Ringo
Dan Simmons
Scott Westerfield
John C. Wright

SPECULATIVE FICTION:

Octavia Butler
Michael Chabon
Kathryn Davis
Tananarive Due
Elizabeth Kostova
Cormac McCarthy
Scott Smith
Donna Tartt

SPORTS LITERATURE:

Buzz Bissinger
Lucy Jane Bledsoe
Don DeLillo
David Halberstam
Don Haskins and Dan Wetzel
Karol Ann Hoeffner
John Updike
John Edgar Wideman

SPY FICTION:

Alex Berenson
Frederick Forsyth
Raelynn Hillhouse
Janette Turner Hospital
Joseph Kanon
John le Carré
Francine Matthews
Henry Porter
Daniel Silva
John Updike

SUSPENSE FICTION:

Dale Brown
Mary Higgins Clark
Michael Connelly
Robin Cook
Patricia Cornwell
Catherine Coulter
Michael Crichton
Jeffrey Deaver
Vince Flynn
Stephen Frey
Terris Gerristsen
John Grisham

Tami Hoag
Iris Johansen
Jonathan Kellerman
Steve Martini
Michael Palmer
James Patterson
Richard North Patterson
Kathy Reichs
Nora Roberts
Karin Slaughter
Scott Turow

SWORD AND SORCERY FICTION:

Leigh Brackett
Robert E. Howard
Harold Lamb
Fritz Leiber
Michael Moorcock
Karl Edward Wagner

TERRORISM FICTION:

Lorraine Adams
Nicholson Baker
Clifford Chase
Don DeLillo
Kinky Friedman
Art Spigelman
John Updike

TIME TRAVEL FICTION:

Kage Baker
Stephen Baxter
Robert A. Heinlin
Audrey Niffnegger
Terry Pratchett
Judith Tarr
Harry Turtledove

TRANSREALIST:

John Barnes
Paul di Filippo
Jeffrey Ford
China Miéville
Audrey Niffnegger

TRAVEL WRITING:

Bill Bryson
Gretel Ehrlich
Tony Horowitz
Peter Mathiessen
Rebecca Solnit
Paul Theroux

TRUE CRIME LITERATURE:

Mark Fuhrman
Aphrodite Jones
Ann Rul
Harold Schechter
Carlton Stowers

URBAN FICTION:

Paul Auster
James T. Farrell
K'wan Foye
Donald Goines
Pete Hamill
Shannon Holmes
Dennis Lehane
Dianne McKinney-Whetstone
Walter Dean Myers
Vickie Stringer
Omar Tyree
Anzia Yezierska

UTOPIAN LITERATURE:

Stephen Amidon
T.C. Boyle
Lincoln Child
Kathleen Ann Goonan
Richard Powers
Susan Sontag
Justin Tussig

VAMPIRE FICTION:

L.A. Banks
Laurel K. Hamilton
Charlaine Harris
Elizabeth Kostova
Anne Rice
Nora Roberts
Chelsea Quinn Yarbro

VERSE NOVELS:

Anthony Burgess
Bernadine Evaristo
Brian McHale
Les Murray
Vikram Seth
Derek Walcott

WESTERN LITERATURE:

Johnny D. Boggs
Jane Candia Coleman
Ralph Cotton
Loren Estleman
Elizabeth Fackler
Alan Geoffrion
Ed Gorman
William W. Johnstone
John D. Nesbitt
Dan O'Brien
Lauran Paine
Cotton Smith
Richard S. Wheeler
James C. Work

YOUNG ADULT LITERATURE:

Julia Alvarez
Laurie Halse Anderson
Francesca Lia Block
Kate DiCamillo
Angela Johnson
Walter Dean Myers
Linda Sue Park
Pam Muñoz Ryan

ZINES:

Sean Carswell
Lisa Crystal Carver
Aaron Cometbus
Cindy Gretchen Ovenrack Crabb
Jessica Disobedience
Jim and Debbie Goad
Ariel Gore
Ayun Halliday
Joe Meno
Jeff Summers

Suggestions for Further Reading

Anderson, Patrick. *The Triumph of the Thriller: How Cops, Crooks, and Cannibals Captured Popular Fiction*. New York: Random House, 2007.

Annesley, James. *Blank Fictions: Consumerism, Culture, and the Contemporary American Novel*. London: Pluto, 1998.

Aragay, Mireia, ed. *Books in Motion: Adaptation, Intertextuality, Authorship*. Amsterdam: Rodopi, 2006.

Backscheider, Paula R. *Reflections on Biography*. New York: Oxford University Press, 1999.

Bandy, Susan J., and Anne S. Darden. *Crossing Boundaries: An International Anthology of Women's Experiences in Sport*. Champaign: Human Kinetics, 1999.

Bell, Bernard W. *The Contemporary African American Novel: Its Folk Roots and Modern Literary Branches*. Amherst: University of Massachusetts Press, 2004.

Biressi, Anita. *Crime, Fear, and the Law in True Crime Stories (Crime Files)*. New York: Palgrave, 2001.

Blanton, Casey. *Travel Writing: The Self and the World*. New York: Routledge, 2002.

Block, Geoffrey. *Enchanted Evenings: The Broadway Musical from Show Boat to Sondheim*. Oxford: Oxford University Press, 2003.

Borowitz, Albert. *Blood and Ink: An International Guide to Fact-Based Crime Literature*. Kent: Kent State University Press, 2002.

Britton, Wesley. *Beyond Bond: Spies in Fiction and Film*. Westport: Praeger, 2005.

Broderick, Damien. *Transrealist Fiction: Writing in the Slipstream of Science*. Westport: Greenwood Press, 2000.

Browne, Ray Broadus, and Lawrence A. Kreiser, eds. *The Detective as Historian: History and Art in Historical Crime Fiction*. Bowling Green: Bowling Green State University Popular Press, 2001.

Carnes, Mark C., ed. *Novel History*. New York: Simon & Schuster, 2001.

Casto, Pamelyn. "Flashes on the Meridian: Dazzled by Flash Ficton." *Writing World*. <www.writing-world.com/fiction/casto.shtml>.

Cavallaro, Dani. *Cyberpunk and Cyberculture*. London: Athlone Press, 2000.

Charters, Ann, ed. *Beat Down to Your Soul: What Was the Beat Generation?* New York: Penguin, 2001.

"Chick Lit Books: Hip, Smart Fiction for Women." <http://www.chicklitbooks.com>.

Clements, Jonathan, and Helen McCarthy. *The Anime Encyclopedia: Revised and Expanded Edition.* Berkeley: Stone Bridge Press, 2006.

Conway, Jill Ker. *When Memory Speaks: Reflections on Autobiography.* New York: Knopf, 1998.

Crow, Charles L., ed. *A Companion to the Regional Literatures of America.* Malden: Blackwell, 2003.

Desmond, John, and Peter Hawkes. *Adaptation: Studying Film and Literature.* Columbus: McGraw-Hill, 2005.

Durix, Jean-Pierre. *Mimesis, Genres and Post-Colonial Discourse: Deconstructing Magic Realism.* New York: St. Martin's Press, 1998.

Eaglestone, Robert. *The Holocaust and the Postmodern.* Oxford: Oxford University Press, 2004.

Edward James, and Farah Mendlesohn, eds. *The Cambridge Companion to Science Fiction.* Cambridge: Cambridge University Press, 2003.

Fitzpatrick, Kathleen. *The Anxiety of Obsolescence: The American Novel in the Age of Television.* Nashville: Vanderbilt University Press, 2006.

Fonseca, Anthony J., and June Michelle Pulliam. *Hooked on Horror: A Guide to Reading Interests in Horror Fiction, New Edition.* Westport: Libraries Unlimited, 2003.

Gaetan Brulotte, and John Phillips, eds. *Encyclopedia or Erotic Literature.* New York: Routledge, 2006.

Gary Westfahl, ed. *The Greenwood Encyclopedia of Science Fiction and Fantasy: Themes, Works, and Wonders.* Westport: Greenwood Press, 2005.

Gay, Lesbian, Bisexual, Transgender, and Queer Culture website <www.GLBTQ.com/social-sciences/domestic_partnerships.html>.

Gidmark, Jill B., ed. *Encyclopedia of American Literature of the Sea and Great Lakes.* Westport: Greenwood Press, 2001.

Gordon, Melton J. *The Vampire Book: The Encyclopedia of the Undead.* Detroit: Visible Ink, 1999.

Gottlieb, Erika. *Dystopian Fiction East and West: Universe of Terror and Trial.* Montreal: McGill-Queens University Press, 2001.

Griswold, Jerry. *Feeling Like a Kid: Childhood and Children's Literature.* Baltimore: Johns Hopkins University Press, 2006.

Hartsock, John C. *A History of American Literary Journalism: The Emergence of a Modern Narrative Form.* Amherst: University of Massachusetts Press, 2000.

Herbert, Rosemary. *Whodunit? A Who's Who in Crime and Mystery Writing.* New York: Oxford University Press, 2003.

Heuser, Sabine. *Virtual Geographies: Cyberpunk at the Intersection of the Postmodern and Science Fiction.* Amsterdam: Rodopi, 2003.

Hintz, Carrie, and Ostrey, Elaine. *Utopian and Dystopian Writing for Children and Young Adults.* New York: Routledge, 2003.

Hischak, T.S. *American Theatre: A Chronicle of Comedy and Drama, 1969–2000.* Oxford: Oxford University Press, 2001.

Houen, Alex. *Terrorism and Modern Literature: From Joseph Conrad to Ciaran Carson.* Oxford: Oxford University Press, 2002.

Jameson, Fredric. *Archaeologies of the Future: The Desire Called Utopia and Other Science Fictions.* New York: Verso, 2005.

Johnsen, Rosemary Erickson. *Contemporary Feminist Historical Crime Fiction.* New York: Palgrave, 2006.

Johnson, Sarah L. *Historical Fiction: A Guide to the Genre.* Westport, CT: Libraries Unlimited, 2005.

Joshi, S. T., and Stefan Dziemianowicz. *Supernatural Literature of the World.* Westport: Greenwood Press, 2005.

Jurca, Catherine. *White Diaspora: the Suburb and the Twentieth-Century American Novel.* Princeton: Princeton University Press, 2001.

Kelley, Donald R. *Frontiers of History: Historical Inquiry in the Twentieth Century.* New Haven: Yale University Press, 2006.

Klock, Geoff. *How to Read Superhero Comics and Why.* New York: Continuum, 2002.

Kramer, Michael P., and Hana Wirth-Nesher, eds. *The Cambridge Companion to Jewish American Literature.* Cambridge: Cambridge University Press, 2003.

Lundquest, Suzanne Eversten. *Native American Literatures: An Introduction.* New York: Continuum, 2004.

Lupack, Alan, ed. *New Directions in Arthurian Studies.* Cambridge: Brewer, 2002.

Lutz, Tom. *Cosmopolitan Vistas: American Regionalism and Literary Value.* Ithaca: Cornell University Press, 2004.

Mattawa, Khaled, and Munir Akash, eds. *Post-Gibran: An Anthology of New Arab American Writing.* Syracuse: Syracuse University Press, 1999.

McCloud, Scott. *Reinventing Comics: How Imagination and Technology are Revolutionizing an Art Form.* New York: Perennial, 2000.

McHale, Brian. *The Obligation toward the Difficult Whole: Postmodernist Long Poems.* Tuscaloosa: University of Alabama Press, 2004.

Moorcock, Michael. *Wizardry and Wild Romance: A Study of Epic Fantasy.* Austin: Monkeybrain, 2004.

Murphy, Bruce F. *The Encyclopedia of Murder and Mystery.* New York: Palgrave, 1999.

Nahin, Paul J. *Time Machines: Time Travel in Physics, Metaphysics, and Science Fiction.* 2nd ed. New York: AIP Press, 1999.

Native American Authors Project (Internet Public Library). <www.ipl.org/div/natam/>.

Patten, Fred. *Watching Anime Reading Manga.* Berkeley: Stone Bridge Press, 2004.

Primeau, Ronald. *Romance of the Road: The Literature of the American Highway.* Bowling Green: Bowling Green State University Popular Press, 1996.

Quetchenbach, Bernard W. *Back from the Far Field: American Nature Poetry in the Late Twentieth Century.* Charlottesville: University Press of Virginia, 2000.

Rasula, Jed. *Syncopations: The Stress of Innovation in Contemporary American Poetry.* Tuscaloosa: University of Alabama Press, 2004.

Rasula, Jed. *This Compost: Ecological Imperatives in American Poetry.* Athens: University of Georgia Press, 2002.

Regis, Pamela. *A Natural History of the Romance Novel.* Philadelphia: University of Pennsylvania, 2003.

Roberts, Neil, ed. *A Companion to Twentieth-Century Poetry.* Oxford: Blackwell, 2001.

Robinson, Forrest G. *Having It Both Ways: Self-Subversion in Western Popular Classics.* Albuquerque: University of New Mexico Press, 1997.

Rojek, Chris, ed. *Touring Cultures: Transformations of Travel and Theory.* New York: Routledge, 1997.

Russell, Alison. *Crossing Boundaries: Postmodern Travel Literature.* New York: Palgrave, 2000.

Sabin, Roger, and Teal Triggs, eds. *Below Critical Radar: Fanzines and Alternative Comics from 1976 to the Present Day.* Hove: Slab-O-Concrete, 2002.

Scanlan, Margaret. *Plotting Terror: Novelists and Terrorists in Contemporary Fiction.* Charlottesville: University Press of Virginia, 2001.

Schwartz, Richard B. *Nice and Noir: Contemporary American Crime Fiction.* Columbia: University of Missouri Press, 2002.

Siegel, Kristi, ed. *Gender, Genre and Identity in Women's Travel Writing.* New York: Peter Lang, 2004.

Singh, Amritjit, Joseph Skerrett, and Robert E. Hogan, eds. *Memory and Cultural Politics: New Approaches to American Ethnic Literatures.* Boston: Northeastern University Press, 1996.

Sloane, David E. E., ed. *New Directions in American Humor.* Tuscaloosa: University of Alabama Press, 1998.

Spencer, Amy. *DIY: The Rise of Lo-Fi Culture*. New York: Marion Boyars, 2005.

Springer, Haskell, ed. *America and the Sea: A Literary History*. Athens: University of Georgia Press, 1995.

Stableford, Brian. *Historical Dictionary of Fantasy Literature*. New York: Scarecrow, 2005.

Thomas, Rebecca L., and Catherine Barr. *Popular Series Fiction for K-6 Readers*. Westport: Libraries Unlimited, 2004.

Thomas, Rebecca L., and Catherine Barr. *Popular Series Fiction for Middle School and Teen Readers*. Westport: Libraries Unlimited, 2005.

Thomsen, Brian M., ed. *The American Fantasy Tradition*. New York: Tor Books, 2002.

Vernon, Alex. *Arms and the Self: War, the Military, and Autobiographical Writing*. Kent: Kent State University Press, 2005.

Watten, Barrett. *The Constructivist Moment: From Material Text to Cultural Poetics*. Middletown: Wesleyan University Press, 2003.

Weldy, Lance, ed. *From Colonialism to Contemporary: Intertextual Transformation in World Children's and Youth Literature*. Newcastle: Cambridge Scholars Press, 2006.

Williams, John. *Back to the Badlands: Crime Writing in the USA*. London: Serpent's Tail, 2007.

Womack, Mari. *Sport as Symbol: Images of the Athlete in Art, Literature and Song*. Jefferson: McFarland, 2003.

Woods, Gregory. *A History of Gay Literature: The Male Tradition*. New Haven: Yale University Press, 1998.

Wright, Bradford. *Comic Book Nation: The Transformation of Youth Culture in America*. Baltimore: Johns Hopkins University Press, 2001.

Yuknavitch, Lidia. *Allegories of Violence: Tracing the Writing of War in Twentieth-Century Fiction*. New York: Routledge, 2001.

About the Editor and Contributors

ABOUT THE EDITOR

KENNETH WOMACK is Professor of English and Head of the Division of Arts and Humanities at Penn State University's Altoona College. Womack has published widely on twentieth-century literary and popular culture. He serves as editor of *Interdisciplinary Literary Studies: A Journal of Criticism and Theory* and as coeditor (with William Baker) of Oxford University Press's celebrated *Year's Work in English Studies*. His most recent book publication is *Long and Winding Roads: The Evolving Artistry of the Beatles*.

ABOUT THE CONTRIBUTORS

MEGAN ALRUTZ is an assistant professor of theatre at the University of Central Florida where her creative and scholarly interests focus on directing theatre and digital storytelling to explore voice and identity, facilitating drama across the curriculum, and investigating drama-based pedagogy for the university classroom. Her articles have been published in *Stage of the Art, Teaching Artist Journal,* and *TYA Today*.

JASON ARTHUR is a doctoral candidate at the University of Missouri. His dissertation, *Thinking Locally: Provincial Affiliations and Cosmopolitan Affect in American Literature since the Great Depression,* examines the major developments in localizing narrative techniques since 1939. Jason is particularly interested in analyzing how recent innovations in regional orthodoxies expose the politics of thinking territorially. He recently won a research fellowship from the Harry Ransom Research Center in Austin, Texas.

MIKE ASHLEY has written and compiled over 80 books including the award-winning *The Mammoth Encyclopedia of Modern Crime Fiction* (Robinson 2002) and the biography of Algernon Blackwood, *Starlight Man* (Constable 2001). He is a retired Local Government Officer and is now a full-time writer and researcher, living in Kent, England.

ANNE BAHRINGER is the author of numerous nonfiction essays and fictional literature. She works in library science and research in the Milwaukee, Wisconsin, area.

KLAUS BENESCH is Professor of English and American Studies at the University of Munich (Germany). He was a 2004 Mellon Fellow at the Harry Ransom Humanities Research Center of the University of Texas (Austin), and has taught at the University of Massachusetts (Amherst) and Weber State University (Utah). Recent publications include: *The Power and Politics of the Aesthetic in American Culture* (editor/2007); *African Diasporas in the New and Old Worlds: Consciousness and Imagination* (editor/second edition 2006); *Space in America: Theory, History, Culture* (editor/2005); *The Sea and the American Imagination* (editor/2004); and *Romantic Cyborgs: Authorship and Technology in the American Renaissance* (2002).

JOHN BIRD is the founding editor of *The Mark Twain Annual* and the author of *Mark Twain and Metaphor* (University of Missouri Press, 2007). He is Professor of English at Winthrop University.

RUSSELL BLACKFORD is a freelance writer, critic, and editor, based in Melbourne, Australia. He teaches part-time in the School of Philosophy and Bioethics at Monash University, and is editor-in-chief of the *Journal of Evolution and Technology*. His academic interests include philosophical bioethics, legal and political philosophy, and the history and current state of the science fiction genre. He is an editorial consultant to *Science Fiction Studies,* and his many publications include *Strange Constellations: A History of Australian Science Fiction* (Greenwood Press, 1999), coauthored with Van Ikin and Sean McMullen.

PATRICIA BOSTIAN teaches at Central Piedmont Community College, Charlotte, North Carolina.

DAMIEN BRODERICK is an Australian science fiction writer and critical theorist, and a Senior Fellow in the Department of English and Cultural Studies at the University of Melbourne, Australia. His books include *The Architecture of Babel* (1994), *Reading by Starlight* (1995), *Transrealist Fiction* (2000), and *x, y, z, t: Dimensions of Science Fiction* (2004). In 2005, he received the Distinguished Scholarship Award of the International Association for the Fantastic in the Arts.

LESLIE BUSSERT is the Ethics and Humanities Reference and Instruction Librarian at the Campus Library serving the University of Washington–Bothell and Cascadia Community College in Bothell, Washington. She has published articles on comic book resources aimed at public and academic librarians, and is interested in how comic books can be used in higher education in art, design, literature, composition, and cultural studies curricula.

EOIN CANNON is an instructor in History and Literature at Harvard University. He has written essays and given talks on urban literary and cultural topics from

Henry James and Jack London to boxing and immigration. His research interests also include religion in American culture.

JOHN CARLBERG teaches English at the University of Wisconsin-Whitewater and distinctly recalls being the first person in the galaxy to go see *Star Wars*.

PAMELYN CASTO teaches online flash fiction courses through flashquake. Her poetry and fiction have appeared in several publications, most recently in *Mslexia Magazine, Wild Strawberries,* and *Mindprints*. She has been a Pushcart Award nominee and she has co-written feature-length articles on flash fiction for *Writer's Digest* and their other publications. She has a BA in philosophy through the University of Texas at Arlington and has earned approximately 60 hours toward her PhD.

MICHAEL COCCHIARALE is coeditor of *Upon Further Review: Sports in American Literature* (Praeger, 2004). He is Associate Professor of English at Widener University, where he teaches American literature, creative writing, and composition courses. He holds a PhD in American literature from Purdue University.

DAVID COCKLEY is a PhD candidate in English at Texas A&M University where he teaches contemporary literature and critical theory. His recent publications focus on aesthetic production in the age of terrorism and neoliberalism.

LUIS A. CORDÓN is a professor of psychology at Eastern Connecticut State University in Willimantic, Connecticut. His research has focused on the role of motivation in school performance, strategies used by parents in teaching children, and belief in paranormal phenomena among college students. He is the author of *Popular Psychology: An Encyclopedia* and is currently working on a reference book about Sigmund Freud and his world.

KIRK CURNUTT is the author of nine volumes of fiction and literary criticism, including, most recently, *Breathing Out the Ghost*, the *Foreword Magazine* December 2007 Book Club Selection. He also published two additional works in 2007: *The Cambridge Introduction to F. Scott Fitzgerald* and a fictional dialogue with Ernest Hemingway entitled *Coffee with Hemingway* (with a preface by John Updike). Among his other efforts is the short-story collection *Baby, Let's Make a Baby, Plus Ten More Stories*.

JAMES M. DECKER is Associate Professor of English at Illinois Central College. He is the author of *Ideology* (Palgrave, 2003) and *Henry Miller and Narrative Form: Constructing the Self, Rejecting Modernity* (Routledge, 2005).

MARK T. DECKER is Assistant Professor of English at Bloomsburg University in Bloomsburg, Pennsylvania. He has published articles on Charles Brockden Brown, William Faulkner, Richard Wright, and Thomas Pynchon.

JENNIFER M. DE COSTE is a dual PhD candidate in Women's Studies and Curriculum & Instruction at Penn State University. She is also the Associate Vice President for Institutional Diversity Initiatives at Clarkson University. Her dissertation focuses on GLBTQ [Gay, Lesbian, Bisexual, Transgender, and Queer] issues in sex education.

MICHELLE DEROSE is an Associate Professor of English at Aquinas College in Grand Rapids, Michigan, where she teaches African American and world literature and directs the honors program. She is an active poetic scholar, publishing both her own poetry and scholarship on Caribbean poets, and enjoys leading poetry workshops for the young.

PEGGY LIN DUTHIE is a writer. She graduated with honors from the University of Chicago and received her MA from the University of Michigan. She has contributed entries to the *Oxford Encyclopedia of Children's Literature,* the *African American National Biography,* and the *Dictionary of Unitarian and Universalist Biography.*

SCOTT D. EMMERT is coeditor of *Upon Further Review: Sports in American Literature* (Praeger, 2004). He is Associate Professor of English at the University of Wisconsin–Fox Valley. In addition to sport literature, his research interests include American realism and naturalism, the short story, and the fiction and film of the American West. He earned his PhD in American literature from Purdue University.

HAZEL ARNETT ERVIN is an associate professor of English and Director of the General Education Program at Morehouse College. At the college, she teaches sections of interdisciplinary world literature and senior-level African American literature courses. A Fulbright Scholar and recipient of NEH and UNCF/Mellon fellowships, Ervin is also the editor of *African American Literary Criticism, 1773 to 2000; The Handbook of African American Literature; The Critical Response to Ann Petry; Ann Petry: A Bio-Bibliography;* and (with Hilary Holladay) *Ann Petry's Short Fiction: Critical Essays.*

A.J. GRANT is an Associate Professor of Communications at Robert Morris University in Pittsburgh, Pennsylvania. He currently teaches undergraduate and graduate courses in communications, rhetoric, literature, and philosophy, and has offered a variety of professional workshops on writing and professional communication in corporate settings. Grant's research interests include writing in the academic disciplines and professions, literature, the history of communications, and popular culture topics. He has published articles on these topics in scholarly journals, including the *Journal of American Culture* and *Rhetoric Society Quarterly.*

JOHN C. HARTSOCK, PhD, is the author of *A History of American Literary Journalism: The Emergence of a Modern Narrative Form* (University of Massachusetts Press, 2000), as well as numerous articles on the subject of literary journalism. He teaches at the State University of New York at Cortland.

SABINE HEUSER is the author of *Virtual Geographies: Cyberpunk at the Intersection of the Postmodern and Science Fiction* (Rodopi, 2003). Since 2002 she has been teaching American, British, and Canadian cultural studies as well as English at Philipps University, Marburg, Germany.

CHAD R. HOWELL is currently the Director of Development at Andrew College. He has previously taught English at Abraham Baldwin Agricultural College and Andrew College.

TRICIA JENKINS is an assistant professor of media studies and digital culture at Sacred Heart University, where she teaches a course in spy film and television.

HOWARD ANDREW JONES is managing editor of *Black Gate* and www.swordandsorcery.org and helmed the e-zine *Flashing Swords* for its first six issues. Jones is the foremost authority on Harold Lamb's historical fiction and has assembled and edited four volumes of Lamb's Cossack stories for the University of Nebraska Press. A freelance writer and editor, Jones's own sword and sorcery had been published in many venues and received an honorable mention in the 18th *Year's Best Fantasy and Horror* anthology. He earned a Masters degree in Liberal Studies from the University of Southern Indiana in 2008.

CAROLYN KYLER is Professor of English at Washington & Jefferson College where she also directs the Gender and Women's Studies Program. She teaches courses in American literature, African American literature, and American women writers. Her scholarly interests include African American literature, historical fiction, American women writers, and gay and lesbian studies.

PETER LAWSON is the author of *Anglo-Jewish Poetry from Isaac Rosenberg to Elaine Feinstein* (Vallentine Mitchell, 2005) and has edited an award-winning anthology of verse, *Passionate Renewal: Jewish Poetry in Britain since 1945* (Five Leaves, 2001). He teaches English and Jewish literature at the University of Tampere, Finland.

JULIA LISTENGARTEN is Associate Professor of Theatre at the University of Central Florida. Her translation of the Russian absurdist play *Christmas at the Ivanovs'* premiered on Off-Broadway at Classic Stage Company and was included in the anthology *Theater of the Avant-Garde, 1890–1950*. She is the author of *Russian Tragifarce* (2000), and her recent articles include "Translating Politics and Performing Absurdity" and "Jewish Comedy and the Art of Affirmation." She is currently working on the collection *Theater of the Avant-Garde: 1950–2000*.

RACHEL LISTER currently teaches American fiction at the University of Durham, England. She has published articles on a number of twentieth-century American women writers, including Grace Paley, Eudora Welty, and Joyce Carol Oates. Forthcoming publications include essays on Louise Erdrich, A.S. Byatt's *Matisse Stories,* and the short fiction of Katherine Anne Porter.

LI ZENG has published books and articles on Asian American literature and comparative Chinese literature, among which are *Studies of Asian and Asian American Literature* (edited, a special issue of *Language and Literature* XXVIII, 2003) and *Tradition and Creation: Essays in Comparative Literature* (Guizhou People's Press, 2005). He is an assistant professor, teaching Chinese literature and East Asian cultures at the University of Louisville in Kentucky.

MARK C. LONG is Associate Professor of English and American Studies at Keene State College, where he teaches courses in American literature, with an emphasis in poetry and poetics, literature-and-environment studies, and expository writing.

CHAD MCLANE is a graduate student at Marquette University, studying nineteenth- and twentieth-century American literature. His interests include discussing how literature is used in multiple contexts outside of literary circles, as well issues of popular use of literature, especially in issues of appropriation.

AMY MALLORY-KANI serves as an editorial associate for the journal *The Year's Work in English Studies* and an editorial assistant for *Interdisciplinary Literary Studies: A Journal of Criticism and Theory.* Her research interests include postcolonial theory, modernism, and technology.

TAMMY MIELKE is an assistant professor of children's and adolescent literature at the University of North Carolina, Charlotte. She has chaired a panel on Graphic Novels as Adolescent Literature and is interested in how the graphic novel has emerged from its comic roots to the present cultural views in both graphic and textual ways.

GEORGE B. MOORE'S works include Gertrude Stein's *The Making of Americans: Repetition and the Emergence of Modernism* (Peter Lang, 1998), *Headhunting: Poems* (Edwin Mellen, 2002), *The Petroglyphs at Wedding Rocks: Poems* (Edwin Mellen, 1997), and *All Night Card Game in the Backroom of Time* (Pulpbits Books, 2006). He is a Senior Instructor in English with the University of Colorado, Boulder.

KENNETH R. MOREFIELD is an assistant professor of English at Campbell University in Buies Creek, North Carolina. His work has appeared in the journals *Persuasions, Style, Midwest Quarterly,* and the anthology *Perceptions of Religious Faith in the Work of Graham Greene.* He has published film reviews for *The Cary News, The Matthews House Project, Looking Closer,* and *Christian Spotlight on Entertainment.*

JEAN MURLEY is an assistant professor of English at Queensborough Community College (CUNY) in Queens, New York. Her research interests include true-crime writing, mystery and detective fiction, and hip-hop. She is currently writing a book about true-crime in popular culture, *The Rise of True Crime: 20th Century Murder and American Popular Culture.*

FELIPE DE ORTEGO Y GASCA is Scholar in Residence at Western New Mexico University–Silver City. He is considered the founder of Chicano literary history with his pioneering work *Backgrounds of Mexican American Literature,* the first study in the field (University of New Mexico, 1971). Among other awards he has received, Dr. Ortego y Gasca is the 2007 recipient of the *Letras de Aztlan Award* from the National Association of Chicana and Chicano Studies (Tejas Foco), and was the 2005 recipient of the *Patricia and Rudolfo Anaya Critica Nueva Award* from the University of New Mexico.

MONICA OSBORNE is a PhD candidate in Modern and Contemporary Jewish Literature and Thought at Purdue University and will be a Mellon Postdoctoral

Scholar in Jewish American Literature at UCLA. She focuses on midrashic theory, Jewish American and Holocaust literature, and the work of Emmanuel Levinas. She has taught classes in American literature, the Hebrew bible, and film. Her work appears in *Tikkun, Studies in American Jewish Literature*, and *Shofar*. She is also a regular contributor to Jewcy.com, where she writes about everything from literature and the Holocaust, to religion and pop culture.

GILLES POITRAS is a librarian in the San Francisco Bay Area. He is the author of *The Anime Companion, Anime Essentials*, and the *Anime Companion 2*, sits on the senior board of *Mechademia*, writes a monthly column for the magazine *Newtype USA*, and is a frequent speaker on anime and manga.

CATHERINE RAINWATER'S essays on Native literature appear in many books and journals. She won the Foerster Prize in 1990 for an article on Erdrich. Her recent books are *Dreams of Fiery Stars: The Transformations of Native American Fiction* (1999), and *Figuring Animals: Essays on Animal Images in Art, Literature, Philosophy, and Popular Culture* (2005), co-edited with Mary S. Pollock.

ROBIN REESE, Assistant Professor, Theatre Arts at Penn State Altoona, is a professional actor, director and playwright. She holds her masters of fine arts degree from the Actors Studio Drama School/New School University where she was the Teaching Fellow and received voice and acting scholarships. She is a recipient of new theatre and performance grants from the DIA Center for the Arts, the Pennsylvania Council on the Arts and the Bread and Roses Community Fund. In December 2007, Robin's one-act play, *The Inquisition*, was produced at The Looking Glass Theatre in New York.

DOUG RESIDE is the assistant director of the Maryland Institute of Technology in the Humanities at the University of Maryland in College Park and the founder of the website "Musical Theatre Studies" (http://www.musicaltheatretstudies.org). He is currently working on an electronic edition of *The Black Crook* as well as a book on the technologies used to compose and preserve musical theatre.

ROBERT RHODES is an attorney, book reviewer, and writer. His fiction has been accepted by several markets, including *Black Gate Magazine* and Flashing Swords Press. He is also affiliated with the Shared Worlds creative writing program at Wofford College. His Web site is <http://rrhodes-writer.blogspot.com/>.

DARCIE D. RIVES is Assistant Professor of English at Augustana College in Sioux Falls, South Dakota. Her research focuses on gender, race, and sexuality in popular writing, and in particular speculative fiction. She has published "Haunted by Violence: Edith Wharton's *The Decoration of Houses* and Her Gothic Fiction" in *The Edith Wharton Review*, and she is currently at work on a book-length study of women writers of speculative fiction at the turn of the twentieth century.

DONIKA ROSS is a fellow in the James A. Michener Center for Writers at the University of Texas at Austin. A long-time avid reader of erotica, her scholarly areas of interest also include contemporary world literature, poetry, and studies of race and gender.

ALISON RUSSELL is the author of *Crossing Boundaries: Postmodern Travel Literature* (Palgrave, 2000) and of articles on fiction, travel writing, and pedagogy. She teaches creative nonfiction, rhetoric, and American literature at Xavier University, Cincinnati, Ohio.

LARS OLE SAUERBERG is Professor of Literature in English at the University of Southern Denmark. He is the author of *Secret Agents in Fiction: Ian Fleming, John le Carré and Len Deighton.* (1984), *Fact into Fiction: Documentary Realism in the Contemporary Novel.* (1991), *Versions of the Past—Visions of the Future: the Canonical in the Criticism of T. S. Eliot, F. R. Leavis, Northrop Frye and Harold Bloom* (1997), and *Intercultural Voices in Contemporary British Literature: The Implosion of Empire* (2001). He is General Editor of *Orbis Litterarum: International Review of Literary Studies,* and a book reviewer in the largest-circulation Danish national newspaper.

SHANNIN SCHROEDER is an associate professor in the Department of English and Foreign Languages at Southern Arkansas University, where she also directs the university's writing center. The author of *Rediscovering Magical Realism in the Americas,* her scholarly interests also include contemporary world literature in translation and popular culture. She serves on the editorial board for the *Philological Review,* has been a reviewer for *Comparative Literature Studies* and *The Writing Lab Newsletter,* and is Secretary/Treasurer for Sigma Tau Delta, the international English honor society.

ANDREA SHALAL-ESA is a correspondent for Reuters news agency and an independent scholar of Arab American literature. Her work has appeared in Reuters, *Al Jadid: A Record and Review of Arab Culture and Arts* and numerous newspapers. Her interview with Diana Abu-Jaber is included in the paperback version of Abu-Jaber's novel *Crescent,* and her paper on Arab American women writers will be included in the forthcoming book, *Etching our Own Image: Voices from the Arab American Art Movement,* edited by Holly Arida and Anan Ameri (2006).

BENJAMIN SZUMSKYJ is a high school teacher. He has written several essays and articles, edited and co-edited books such as *Two-Gun Bob: A Centennial Study of Robert E. Howard* and *Fritz Leiber: Critical Essays,* and is the general editor of *Studies in Fantasy Literature.*

RAYMOND H. THOMPSON, Professor Emeritus of English at Acadia University in Canada, is the author of *The Return from Avalon* (1985), an associate editor of *The New Arthurian Encyclopedia* (1991), and coeditor of its supplements, the *Merlin Casebook* (2003) and the *Gawain Casebook* (2006). He has also conducted a series of interviews, *Taliesin's Successors: Interviews with Authors of Modern Arthurian Literature* <http:www.lib.rochester.edu/camelot/intrvws/contents.htm>.

DEBBIE K. TRANTOW's poems have appeared in several literary magazines and journals. Her chapbook, *Hearing Turtle's Words,* was published by Spoon River Poetry Press in 2004. She received a 2001 Gesell Summer Writing Fellowship, and has taught English courses in the University of Wisconsin system and at the University of Minnesota.

PAUL VARNER is Professor of Language and Literature at Oklahoma Christian University. He has published on Max Brand for the *Dictionary of Literary Biography* and has two books forthcoming on cinema Westerns and Westerns in film and fiction.

JOSEPH S. WALKER received his doctorate in contemporary American fiction from Purdue University. He has published a number of essays on contemporary fiction and film, and has a special interest in representations of crime and violence. He lives in Indiana, where he works as a freelance writer and scholar.

LANCE WELDY is an Assistant Professor at Francis Marion University. His chapter, "Dreams, Imaginations, and Shattered Illusions: Overlooked Realism in Carol Wiseman's Film Adaptation of Burnett's *A Little Princess*," was recently published in *In the Garden: Essays in Honor of Frances Hodgson Burnett*.

WILLIAM J. WHITE is an associate professor of communication arts and sciences at Penn State Altoona. He has reviewed science fiction for the young adult librarian professional magazine *Voice of Youth Advocates,* and his research interests include the intersection of science and popular culture.

JAMES WHITLARK is Professor and Associate Chairperson of English at Texas Tech University; he is the author of two books (*Illuminated Fantasy,* 1988; *Behind the Great Wall,* 1991) and the coauthor of 16 others.

FREDERICK WRIGHT has studied zines since his master's thesis. He also participates in the zine community under the name "Wred Fright," and is a member of the Underground Literary Alliance. In addition to publishing zines, he is the author of the rock and roll novel *The Pornographic Flabbergasted Emus* (2006).

Index

Note: Page numbers in **bold font** refer to the main articles on the topic. If a title does not appear in the index, check author entries.